DATE DUE

GAYLORD   PRINTED IN U.S.A.

Returning to Tradition

Returning to Tradition

THE CONTEMPORARY REVIVAL OF ORTHODOX JUDAISM

M. Herbert Danzger

Yale University Press
New Haven & London

Published with assistance from the Kingsley Trust Association Publication Fund established by the Scroll and Key Society of Yale College.

Set in Sabon type by The Composing Room of Michigan, Inc. Printed in the United States of America by Vail-Ballou Press, Binghamton, New York.

Library of Congress Cataloging-in-Publication Data

Danzger, Murray Herbert.
   Returning to Tradition : the contemporary revival in
America and Israel / M. Herbert Danzger.
     p. cm.
   Bibliography: p.
   Includes index.
   ISBN 0-300-03947-6
    1. Orthodox Judaism—United States—History—20th century.
   2. Orthodox Judaism—Israel—History—20th century. 3. Jews—Return
to Orthodox Judaism. I. Title.
   BM205.D27 1989   88-27735
  296.8'32'095694—dc19   CIP

10   9   8   7   6   5   4   3   2   1

"The human soul is God's light"
    —Proverbs 20:27

Dedicated to the memory of
    Josef Leib Kirschenbaum—Zaydie
    Hinde Beyle Kirschenbaum—Bubie
    Ida Danzger—Mom
Whose lights guide us

Contents

Acknowledgments   ix
Introduction   1

I. Origins of Return
1   The Roots of Return   13
2   Portals of Return: Home and Synagogue   27
3   Portals of Return: Yeshivot   44
4   The 1960s and the Emergence of the Ba'al T'shuva   71

II. Institutions and Values
5   The Ba'al T'shuva Yeshiva   99
6   The New Curriculum   117
7   Value Conflicts   142
8   The Hidden Conflict: The Basis of Religious Authority   164

III. The Returnees
9   Recruitment   193
10   Why They Return   222
11   Wrestling with Judaism: Community Boundaries   251
12   Wrestling with Judaism: Practices and Beliefs   273
13   Striking Roots   298

IV. Conclusions
Conclusions   327
Appendix: Tables on the Newly Orthodox in the
   Greater New York Metropolitan Area   342
Glossary   346
References   356
Index   367

Acknowledgments

S upport for this research came from several sources. I received a Fulbright fellowship for the 1975–1976 academic year, during which time I served as professor of sociology and American studies at the Hebrew University in Jerusalem. At the same time, Herbert H. Lehman College of the City University of New York provided a sabbatical leave and the additional financial support necessary for that year. Funds for the transcription of interviews, which were conducted under the auspices of the Institute for the Study of Contemporary World Jewry, were provided by The Hebrew University. The Research Foundation of the City University of New York supplied two grants, one in 1980 for the transcription and analysis of data and a second in 1982 for a return trip to Israel. A grant was also awarded by the George N. Shuster Fund of Lehman College. The support provided by all of the above is hereby gratefully acknowledged.

I also gratefully acknowledge the help and encouragement I received from a number of individuals. Murray Hausknecht and Sidney Aronson read the manuscript in its earliest stage and made invaluable suggestions on sociological and stylistic matters. Rabbi Marvin Speigelman and I spent hours together discussing the first few chapters, and he offered useful comments on modern Orthodoxy and Jewish education. Abbot Katz and Chaim Waxman made detailed comments on the entire manuscript. Sections were also read by and discussed with Larry Grossman, Charles Leibman, Gerald Handel, and Glen Nygreen. The many people, students, deans, rabbis, the newly Orthodox, and the Orthodox from birth who have provided information and insights into Orthodox Judaism and this movement of return are too numerous to mention. Thanks are also due to Paula Danowitz for her careful typing of the manuscript and to Stacey Mandelbaum for her fine work as manuscript editor. I take this opportunity to express my gratitude to each of them.

Gladys Topkis, Senior Editor at Yale University Press, deserves special recognition for her share in shaping this work. She provided advice on the structure of the book, raised pointed questions, read and offered detailed comments on several versions of this work, and was enormously helpful in turning a manuscript into a book.

My greatest debt is to my wife, Mimi, with whom I discussed this project at every stage. She shared this intellectual struggle fully, read and commented on many versions of this work. Her sparkling wit, humor, and insights bolstered me in this venture.

Introduction

In recent years the mass media have featured stories of young Jews reared in nonreligious families who are seeking out Judaism and becoming practicing Orthodox Jews. In the face of statistics indicating an increasingly high rate of intermarriage for Jews[1] and predictions of the decline of the American Jewish community, this is a surprising development. These young people are swimming against the tide.

Yet in New York City, Yeshiva University's James Striar School, intended for beginners in Orthodoxy, has an enrollment of more than two hundred. In Morristown, New Jersey, at Yeshiva Tiferet Bachurim, Lubavitcher *chasidim* ("pious ones," adherents of a movement emphasizing mysticism and loyalty to their leader, the *rebbe*) teach almost one hundred *ba'alei t'shuva* (literally, "masters of return"), as these people are called. In Far Rockaway, New York, Sh'or Yoshuv Yeshiva also enrolls almost one hundred students. Smaller schools are located in Monsey and Brooklyn, New York, in Los Angeles, and elsewhere. Lubavitch has opened a school for women in Minneapolis. Even traditional *yeshivot* (schools for advanced talmudic study) have begun to develop programs for these people. In fact, the schools intended for beginners have become so accepted by the Orthodox that their students include substantial proportions of Orthodox from birth who prefer them to traditional yeshivot.

Many large Jewish communities have programs for ba'alei t'shuva in yeshivot, synagogues, or both. In 1968 Rabbi Shlomo Carlebach, a

1. This percentage is the subject of controversy. Waxman (1981), relying on Massarik, puts the figure at 28.1 percent. Silberman (1985) relies on Lazerwitz to argue that the intermarriage rate is substantially lower, perhaps as low as 14 percent in the decade between 1960 and 1970. In any case, all of these figures are based on the National Jewish Population Study done in 1971, more than 15 years ago. The assimilation rate today probably at least approaches 40 percent. (See estimates by officials of the Federation of Jewish Philanthropies of New York *New York Times* 6 Feb. 1983, 45.)

Lubavitcher *chasid* and folksinger, opened "The House of Love and Prayer" for ba'alei t'shuva in San Francisco. In the early 1970s a chasidic rebbe in Boston developed a program for ba'alei t'shuva based in his synagogue, Bet Pinchas. By the late 1970s the Lincoln Square Synagogue on the upper west side of Manhattan had an outreach program for singles with an enrollment of twelve hundred men and women. Vancouver, St. Louis, Miami, and other cities have developed similar programs. Probably five to six hundred newly Orthodox have participated in full-time programs all over the United States, and thousands more have participated in part-time programs.

Even more striking is that more than seven hundred American Jews, men and women, currently study in yeshivot for ba'alei t'shuva in Israel. These yeshivot were founded by Americans for Americans and are staffed mainly by Americans. Their student population also remains largely American.[2]

This movement of return reaches far beyond yeshivot. A survey of Jews in the New York metropolitan area (Ritterband and Cohen 1984b) found that 24 percent of those who were highly observant (defined as those who would not handle money on the Sabbath) had been reared by parents who did not share such scruples. In fact, the parents of 10 percent of the highly observant did not even light Sabbath candles or practice the laws of *kashrut* (religious laws that forbid the consumption of certain foods and require the separation of meat and dairy foods and dishes).

The ba'al t'shuva represents a new phenomenon in Judaism; for the first time there are not only Jews who leave the fold—the by now expected behavior—but also a substantial number who "return." Further, most of these ba'alei t'shuva have returned not to Reform or Conservative Judaism, movements that have made a separate peace with the modern world, but to Orthodox Judaism, which seems to remain intransigently resistant to the demands of modernity.

That Orthodoxy retains its hold on those born into it is not surprising. Powerful factors support this attachment: the attraction of the value system, the rituals, and the festivals; early socialization into the world of Orthodox Judaism—even before one is aware of choices and alternatives; and ties to family, friends, and community. But what attracts those who were not reared in Orthodox families? What set of symbols, what ideas,

---

2. Yeshiva D'var Yerushalayim and Neve Yerushalayim for Women were founded by Englishmen, Rabbis David Refson and Boruch Horovitz. These schools originally drew a predominantly British and European student body.

what visions of social relations have pulled them out of their expected trajectory and onto this new course? What brought Judaism to their attention? What practices or beliefs are attractive to them, and which are difficult or even repugnant? What adjustments must they make in becoming Orthodox? Who are these young people, and how did they come to embrace their new religious beliefs? What is the meaning of Orthodoxy in the modern world? Answers to these questions give us a better sense of Orthodox Judaism's appeal and holding power in the modern world, where it is not reinforced by external social supports.

The Sociological Problem

The twentieth century should have completed the process of secularization that began in the late eighteenth century. But from Iran to the United States, one finds evidence of religious revival today. God was declared dead in the late 1960s, but before the next decade was out a major religious revival had begun in the heartland of modernity, the United States, with university students at its leading edge.

The student vanguard, drawn from the urban middle class, proclaimed their opposition to society and fashioned a counterculture. If this seeming contradiction of social background and ideological stance was not enough, the attraction of some to religious movements was an additional paradox. Durkheim's view that religion is a primary source of social cohesion (1915) implies that commitment to religion goes along with commitment to the dominant political and social values. The phenomenon of civil religions in modern societies (Bellah 1967) supports this view. It cannot, however, explain the rise of countercultural or sectarian religions and their appeal to urban, highly educated, middle class youth, who are usually perceived as being most susceptible to secularist perspectives.

Until recently, it was assumed that societies were being inexorably demythologized, rationalized, and secularized. Religion's continued existence was considered merely an example of the tenacity of old ideas, despite the inevitability of their eventual demise. Research focused on how religion managed to maintain strength in the face of the inexorable tide of secularization. Studies of religious conversion in the 1930s and 1940s (e.g., Fromm 1941. Cantril 1941; Hoffer 1951) often viewed it as an expression of the crippled personality, because only a "true believer" would wish to escape from the freedom offered by secular society to the restrictions of religious society.

In the past fifteen years, the widespread evidence of religious revival has given rise to a plethora of studies that seek to understand how religious revival and renewal occur in the face of secular society. The implicit questions of these new studies have been articulated by Heirich (1977): "How is a sense of religious grounding asserted in ways that lead various observers to take it seriously? What ingredients must it have? What must it be able to do? How is it brought to their attention? Under what circumstances does it become widely shared?"

Most of the studies that might be used to answer these questions deal with conversion to Christian groups and of necessity provide only partial data. Studies of Christianity have treated religion as a belief system (see Weber 1958; Glock and Stark 1966; Bellah 1967). Studies of Eastern and new religions have either treated them in the same way or dealt with them as a deviant form of religion (Lofland 1966; Lofland and Stark 1965; Bromley and Shupe 1979; Robbins and Anthony 1972).

This book describes and analyzes how a religion that emphasizes ritual rather than beliefs constructs its reality. It thus provides a strategic perspective for an exploration of some new, yet basic questions. I hypothesize that the return to Judaism is radically different from rebirth in Christianity, for the following reasons:

1. Christian rebirth requires belief primarily and ritual acts only secondarily. Judaism in contrast emphasizes acts, the performance of *mitzvot* (commandments).

2. Christian rebirth requires a single step of great import, a "leap of faith," a choice of "either/or," in Kierkegaard's terms. Return to Judaism involves the performance of many commandments, no one of which necessarily involves a decision on ultimate values. This difference may affect the process of recruitment to Orthodoxy, the types of people drawn to it, and the structure of organizations promoting commitment.

3. Judaism is practiced primarily in the home; Christianity, primarily at church. Thus Christian rituals are visible to potential newcomers who attend church. But to observe Jewish ritual one must enter the home; Judaism is learned only through intimate involvement in a Jewish family. Jewish ritual behavior is therefore much less accessible to potential new believers than is Christian ritual. Furthermore, as people may be hesitant to invite strangers into the bosom of their family, it may be more difficult to make institutional adjustments to accommodate sizable numbers of new believers in Judaism.

4. Judaism lays immense stress on the study of the religious literature. To preserve Jewish life, which was disrupted by national exile and persecution, Judaism has built a "homeland in the mind," a body of liter-

ature detailing the minutest aspects of religious life and its social context, which permits those familiar with it to judge the world by its perspectives and practices. Study and scholarship are essential elements of Judaism.

5. Jews are both a people and a religion, and this combination is essential to Judaism. The ethnic elements of Calvinism or Lutheranism or Catholicism are extraneous, but a large part of the Jewish religion consists of ceremonies that celebrate and recall national history. The Holy Scriptures of the Jewish people are also the history of the Jews. In Christianity the universal God is paralleled by universal man; in Judaism the connection of the universal God to the "chosen people" introduces an element of paradox that may in turn affect efforts to attract adherents.

6. Judaism is a minority religion in the United States and almost everywhere else. Even in Israel there is a strong awareness—given Israel's beleaguered condition since the founding of the state and before—that Jews are a minority in the world. Fear of majority reaction has inhibited efforts to proselytize in the past and continues to do so today. As a result Judaism has little experience with recruitment, and this affects efforts to reach out to other Jews.

Although choosing Judaism and joining a sect might seem similar because both groups are minorities, in fact there is an essential difference.[3] Sects reject many aspects of society, but their distinguishing mark is that they take religious values too seriously (Danzger 1987). They are essentially hyperconformists to the religious values of society, and this quality is what forces them to reject some aspects of worldliness. But Judaism, particularly Orthodox Judaism, requires rejection of some of the central religious values of society—that is, Christian values. Are Americans who choose to be Orthodox Jews thus choosing to be nonconformist?

7. Judaism as a religion that has undergone inquisitions, expulsions, crusades, pogroms, and, in our lifetime, the Holocaust is a problematic theological choice. Why would anyone join the religion of people who appear to be suffering Divine rejection? Most Christian groups claim to provide proof of Divine acceptance and favor, and they offer as evidence miracles or, not infrequently, the doctrine that Jewish suffering is proof of the truth of Christianity. Thus converts are recruited to a triumphant religion. But how shall we understand recruitment to a religion of the persecuted? And what can the place of miracles be in this recruitment?

8. Christianity is in its origins a countercultural religion. Its early

---

3. My article entitled "Towards a Redefinition of 'sect' and 'cult': Orthodox Judaism in Comparative Perspective" (*Comparative Social Research*, 1987) develops and clarifies these concepts as they are used here.

doctrine was born out of the new convert's rejection of their mother religion—Judaism. As a revolutionary religion, it required the overthrow and rejection of tradition and family for the sake of the new doctrine. Rejection of the old ways and the old relationships is a central conception. Thus Christianity explicitly permits rejection of one's parents as part of the process of conversion.

Judaism, in contrast, although prophetic and thus to some extent a challenge to the existing system, is a religion developed by a slow process of growth, accepting the old, revering it, and building on it. Rejection of parents is to be avoided at all costs, and rejection of past associations is a much more muted theme. How are relations to parents and friends redefined for the newly Orthodox? Is the rejection of former relationships a part of the process here as well?

In the analysis and description of the ba'alei t'shuva I focus on their *consciousness* rather than the subconscious psychological motivations of their behavior. I aim here at an understanding (*verstehen* in Max Weber's sense) of ba'alei t'shuva, of the motives they consciously perceive for their change, the decisive categories of their thought, and the specific stages of their involvement. We are aware that the stated motives may reflect a vocabulary bound to a particular social situation (Mills 1940); nevertheless, this approach permits us to see this change as the ba'al t'shuva perceives it. This understanding must come before any attempt at explanation.

Judaism, like other traditional religions, is most often practiced through habit. One learns it and accepts it while still a child. By the time mature reflection is possible, emotional ties to the rituals and social and familial ties to the community are so strong that questions and doubts are quickly banished from consciousness. But what is it like to confront its ideas and values and rituals for the first time as a mature person? And how is this sense of grounding "constructed"? The literature describing the phenomenon for reborn Christians says little about the process for Jews.

The ba'alei t'shuva are attracted to Judaism, but to what sort of Judaism? As we shall see, Orthodoxy is not monolithic; it is strained by differences in values, customs, and life-styles. The return of the ba'al t'shuva is not simply to Orthodoxy but to a particular view of Orthodoxy.

When a culture is intent on explaining itself, it provides teachers, as Orthodox Judaism does in its self-conscious efforts to attract new recruits. The teachers have their own perspectives and emphases reflecting different "party" views of the culture, and they may utilize or even develop different organizational structures to present their views. If return, as I argue, represents a choice among specific views of Orthodoxy, then to understand the choice requires a knowledge of the worlds of Orthodox Judaism presented by teachers, rabbis, and others eagerly engaged in attracting newcomers.

Thus I am interested not only in what is *learned* and also in what is *taught*. I therefore describe the efforts made by organized Jewry to respond to those who wish to learn more about it. I describe not only the outreach programs and organizations developed to assist in this recruitment, but also what is taught about Judaism, how it is taught, and who teaches it. Building a new belief system does not simply occur in the mind of the ba'al t'shuva, nor is it simply passed on by teachers to a tabula rasa. Instead, the efforts of each impinge on the other; each comes to know the other and makes adjustments appropriate to that knowledge.

In attempting to understand who the returnees are and why they return, I take into account not only their own views and explanations but how they appear to the organizations and people who try to attract and involve them in Judaism.

Some of the returnees are known as ba'alei t'shuva; others are known as simply "people lacking background." The different labels point to substantially different recruitment experiences. Further, hippie returnees are inducted into one type of Orthodox Judaism; mainstream into another. The process of transition may vary depending on the type of recruit.

There are also significant differences between male and female returnees. Orthodox Judaism requires gender roles somewhat different from those of the larger society, and some are surprising reversals of what is widely thought to be the Orthodox view. I examine how the woman returnee is perceived, the Jewish world she enters, and the aspects and experiences of this world unique to women.

The implications of being a returnee are particularly illuminated when Israeli and American returnees are compared. The critical differences in context—the former entering in the dominant religion of Israel, the latter entering an American minority religion—are obvious. Less obvious, but a point that nevertheless emerges distinctly from the data, is the different meaning that return has for each of them. For the Israeli it is a religious return; for the American, it is largely an ethnic return. The implications of this difference are profound.

Finally, the perception that the Orthodox community in Israel and America can reach out and attract numbers of modern and successful young people to its ranks and not be restricted to a defensive posture has implications for the future of orthodoxy. Not only has Orthodoxy been infused with a new sense of vigor and enthusiasm, it has also opened itself up to subtle change. Ba'alei t'shuva embrace some patterns of Orthodoxy and criticize others, and in the process they change the Orthodox community, forcing it to face the problems of the modern world in a new way. The Orthodox cannot shrug off the questions of the ba'alei t'shuva, for they are raised not by scoffers but by people with sincere interest. To maintain their integrity and the continued sense of the truth and reasonableness of their views, the Orthodox must respond. These responses reshape Orthodoxy itself.

Thus an examination of the kinds of answers given, the kinds of structures developed, and the kinds of relationships generated provides a view of the nature of Orthodoxy as it confronts and adjusts to the modern world. This book is, therefore, equally about ba'alei t'shuva and about the nature of Orthodox Judaism in the modern world and the relation of Jews to their religious lives.

Methodology

Data for this study are more than two hundred interviews and observations conducted over a period of several years, both in Israel and in the United States. These were open-ended interviews lasting from one to three hours each. I used an elite interviewing technique, following Dexter (1970). Interviews were conducted with deans, teachers, and students in yeshivot for ba'alei t'shuva. In addition, I spent hundreds of hours with students and teachers in the *bet midrash* (study hall)—the heart of these schools—at worship services, in the cafeteria, and in informal visits.

Student informants were often asked to provide additional information on the schools as a check on the accuracy of the information offered by faculty and administration. Deans were often asked for background information on students, primarily to enable me to select students of varied backgrounds for interview. All were asked to provide information on individuals, agencies, symbols, or events that played a role in the return of people to Orthodox Judaism, including unaffiliated people involved with ba'alei t'shuva, such ancillary agencies as the yeshiva section of the Student Authority in Israel, the National Council of Synagogue Youth, the Jewish Learning Exchange, and such places as the Western Wall and the Lincoln Square Synagogue in New York. All these places and people were visited. In no case was access restricted.

Several factors made my entry easy and facilitated rapport with subjects. First, I am a graduate of Mesivta Torah Vodaath High School in Brooklyn, New York, and I attended the Rabbi Isaac Elchanan Theological Seminary of Yeshiva University. These institutions have wide reputations in the Orthodox Jewish world, the former a more traditionalistic yeshiva, the latter the exemplar of the modernistic yeshiva.[4] I speak Yiddish and Hebrew, am familiar with Jewish law and the world of Orthodoxy, and am aquainted with key people and agencies. These credentials elicited trust among both modernistic and traditionalistic Orthodox.

In addition, I had met Rabbi Mendel Weinbach when were were both students at Mesivta Torah Vodaath High School. Rabbi Weinbach now serves as dean of the largest yeshiva for ba'alei t'shuva, Ohr Someyach. He welcomed me into his institutions, agreed to be interviewed for many hours, and encouraged colleagues and students to cooperate with me. I found no bar to interviewing any person I wished to interview. In a word, I was, and am, an insider.

My observations at the yeshivot thus started from an awareness of what to expect, what the routines are, what the values are. I am familiar with the authority of the *rosh yeshiva* (dean) and know how to read and understand a page of the Talmud. This awareness is critical to understanding the meaning of being a ba'al t'shuva, the authority of the rabbi, or the meaning of a given curriculum. This background informed the observations and the interviews conducted.

The research was conducted in several stages. In the first stage, from December 1975 to August 1976, I conducted interviews and made observations at the major ba'al t shuva yeshivot for both men and women in Jerusalem. On my return I conducted similar interviews in the United States. To check on the development of this rapidly growing movement, as well as to understand a number of questions about ba'alot t'shuva (female returnees) that had been raised in the preliminary analysis of the data, I conducted follow-up interviews with deans at many of the schools in Israel and made further observations during a five-week period in July and August 1982.

4. The terms traditionalistic and modernistic are "bracketed" as all yeshivot are traditional institutions in that they teach ancient laws and customs and accept the Divine revelation of Torah to Moses at Sinai and the authority of the Oral Law. Traditionalists also attempt to adhere to the customs and practices of a past they construct. Modernists attempt a fuller participation in society, limited only by *halakhah* (religious law).

The return visit also provided an opportunity to trace the changes, development, and problems encountered by ba'alei t'shuva in the course of adjustment, as well as to observe changes in the yeshivot and in Orthodoxy generally in response to the influx of ba'alei t'shuva. The research periods in Israel and the United States have provided a developmental and comparative perspective that may be unusual in the study of religious revivals but is crucial for understanding the *t'shuva* movement.

Preliminary findings based on this study have been presented at meetings of the Israeli Sociological Society (1976), the Association for Jewish Studies (1977 and 1980), the International Society for the Comparative Study of Civilizations (1986b), and the Association for the Sociology of Religion (1986a and 1987).

I
Origins
of
Return

Chapter 1

The Roots
of Return

The movement of return is a new phenomenon in Judaism. It did not happen in earlier periods because it could not; before one can return one must leave, and until modern times barriers between Jews and Gentiles were almost impermeable. Intermarriage was virtually impossible, as marriage outside the church or synagogue did not exist in many societies. Religious and legal strictures limited social intercourse— even commercial relations. To be sure, some Jews converted to other faiths, and some rejected all religion, but barriers between religious communities kept the number of apostates small, except where conversion was forced,[1] and kept alienated Jews within the community so that their children and grandchildren remained Jews.

Political emancipation shook the walls of the ghetto, allowing Jews to begin entering the wider society, and eroded bonds that held the Jewish community together. Jews could and did leave the community without making a conscious decision to forsake their religion. Wherever political emancipation reached, within a generation or two the trickle of Jewish assimilation into the larger society turned into a flood.

A brief examination of several examples of return occurring under substantially different circumstances will point up some of the require-

1. The Spanish Inquisition (1481–1492) led to the forced conversion of thousands of Jews. Many converts remained openly loyal to Judaism and were burned at the stake. Others, called *anusim* (forced converts) by the Jews and *marranos* (pigs) by the Spanish, hid their continued loyalty and attempted to reenter the Jewish community when possible. Their education provides an interesting comparison to that of contemporary ba'alei t'shuva (see Yerushalmi 1980).

ments for return and will also make clear the unique feature of contemporary return.

Models of Return

THE CLASSICAL MODEL

Probably the best known example of radical change leading to return to Judaism is that of Rabbi Akiva (50–135 C.E.), a great scholar, patriot, and finally a martyr. Akiva was an illiterate shepherd in his youth. His employer's daughter, Rachel, married him over her father's objections on the condition that he devote himself to the study of Torah. For many years they endured abject poverty while he studied at the academy. Eventually he became one of the outstanding teachers of his time (Babylonian Talmud (BT), Nedarim 52a; BT, Ketubot 62b).

Rabbi Akiva's story points to a problem faced by those who turn to Orthodoxy as adults: how and where to learn about Judaism. For Judaism had instituted a system of public education, but no provision had been made for those who had not had the opportunity to study as children.[2] Apparently, although Jews were still in their homeland and rituals and holidays had an element of *public* celebration that made them accessible to even the uneducated, some formal education was necessary even then for studying Torah, reciting prayers, and performing rituals.

In the diaspora, Jews built for themselves, in Heinrich Heine's phrase, a "portable homeland in the mind," a world of sacred literature. And this required still more education. But even the homeland in the mind could provide continuity only so long as integration into the larger society was barred by religious prejudice, Catholic dogma, and Islamic law. Modernity shattered these barriers.

A MODERN MODEL

From the time of the French Revolution and Napoleon's so-called Sanhedrin (1806),[3] it became possible in theory for a Jew to be a member of the

2. How many were as uneducated as Akiva is hard to estimate. Although there are numerous references to the *am ha-aretz* ("people of the land") in the Talmud, the term seems to encompass those who are lax in the observance of ritual purity as well as those who are ignorant of the law. A substantial portion of the population was probably illiterate. The majority spoke Aramaic, the language of the Targum (the authoritative first-century translation of the Bible), and some spoke Hebrew as well.

3. They were not a Sanhedrin in Jewish terms—that is, a supreme political,

society in which he resided and still retain his identity as a believer in a faith different from that of the majority (for example, no longer simply an alien living in France but a Frenchman of the Mosaic persuasion).[4] Once the barriers between Jews and others were lowered, the outflow from Judaism began and increased.

In Germany and other Western European countries assimilation continued unabated for over a hundred years with few indications of return. Franz Rosenzweig's articulate description of his return and his book *The Star of Redemption* (1921) were glimmerings of a new direction.[5] After World War I, with the help of the philosopher Martin Buber, Rabbi N. Nobel (an Orthodox rabbi), and others, Rosenzweig organized the *Freie Juedisches Lehrhaus* (Free Jewish House of Learning) and with Buber translated the Bible into German to facilitate the return of other intellectuals to authentic Judaism. Rosenzweig's school was a new organizational response to those Jews who wished to return to the religion of their fathers. Prior to its establishment individual guidance seemed adequate for those who returned. But now, perhaps because of the distance of assimilated Jews from tradition and even more because of their ignorance of Hebrew, formally organized education was required.

REVIVALS: CHASIDISM AND MUSAR

Although Chasidism (sometimes transposed *Hasidism*) was also a renewal movement, in this case the term *revival* would be more appropriate. Chasidim were strongly identified Jews. Chasidism emerged from Jewish despair. Jews had been decimated by the Chmielnitzki Pogroms (1648–1655), in which at least 100,000 Jews were killed, and had been betrayed by Shabbetai Tzevi, the false messiah, in 1666. Their abject spiritual state and their precarious physical state left them demoralized. Chasidism, a

---

religious, and judicial body—but simply an assembly of prominent French Jews convened by Napoleon to consider questions that would determine whether Jews should be eligible for French citizenship.

4. In America Jews were granted equal rights even earlier, with the Virginia Act of Toleration of 1786. This equality was reaffirmed in the Constitution, and Jews were granted the right to vote in national elections. But Jews in colonial and early Federal America constituted only a small segment of the world Jewish population.

5. Rosenzweig's adherence to Judaism was minimal. When a number of his Jewish friends at the university converted to Christianity, he too contemplated conversion. Determined in his words to convert "as a Jew," Rosenzweig attended an Orthodox synagogue on the High Holidays and then decided not to convert. He wrote *The Star of Redemption* while in the army in World War I.

religious movement that emphasized piety, mysticism, sincerity, and good deeds, was founded by Israel Ba'al Shem Tov (1700–1760). Directed at the poor and less educated classes, it breathed new life and optimism into them.

The less well-known but also important Musar movement was a renewal movement among the Jews of Lithuania in the second half of the nineteenth century. Its goal was to reemphasize the ethical aspects of Judaism and to ward off the inroads of Chasidism, which it was feared could lead to another spiritual disaster like the Shabbetai Tzevi affair, and *Haskala* (the Enlightenment), which threatened to secularize Judaism. The Musar movement failed to take root among the business people for whom it was intended; instead it came to be incorporated in the curriculum of many Lithuanian yeshivot. Its major emphasis was to provide strong emotional ties to religion—particularly in the areas of business ethics, avoidance of speaking evil of others, and compassion[6]—through meditation on teachings about these subjects in small groups of like-minded individuals.

A clear distinction is made within the Jewish community between Chasidism and Musar as renewal movements and the change exemplified by Rabbi Akiva and Franz Rosenzweig. In the parlance of the Orthodox world, the former is called *chizuk kirovim*, "the strengthening of those who are near"; the latter is called *kiruv r'chokim*, or "drawing close of those who are afar."[7] The sociological literature on religious revival in the United States does not by and large make such a distinction.

The Ideological Roots of Secularization and Assimilation

Jews have been unique as a people in their ability to maintain and pass on their ethnic and religious identity despite the lack of a homeland. Many have argued that this has been possible precisely because of their repres-

6. In the Navarodek school of *Musar* a technique was developed to expose the selfish, arrogant, and egotistic aspects of the person. It involved the breaking of social custom so as to incur rebuke—as, for example, requiring that one attempt to purchase nails in a drugstore or wear rags and attempt to mingle with well-dressed people.

7. The term *revival* is a rough equivalent of "strengthening those who are near." But missionizing for conversion is not the same as "drawing close those who are afar," as conversion involves a change from one religion to another. Nor are Jews *reborn,* a term that implies an earlier animalistic existence. *Return* best describes the Jewish experience.

sion. Excluded from the larger society, Jews had no choice but to maintain their commitment. They could not simply leave their religion, for that would mean joining those who attacked friends, family, and community. Therefore, as long as societies were static and boundaries between them impermeable, as long as religious hatred and persecution of the Jews continued, the existence of the Jewish people was assured.

From the Jewish perspective, this ability to endure in the teeth of adversity is evidence that Jews are a "chosen people." Persecution was an innoculation against the loss of courage. Jewish religious history presents Jews not as a triumphant nation but rather as a people brought to nationhood from slavery in Egypt: they were condemned by their lack of faith to wander the desert until hardened, their temple was destroyed, and they were exiled only to return, rebuild the temple, and reestablish themselves. In the process, they developed such institutions as the synagogue as well as a theology and faith tempered by adversity, which enabled them to persist despite the destruction of the temple a second time. They were even able to attempt to rebuild it twice more without losing faith. Each trial evoked a new and deepened response.

But whichever interpretation is preferred, clearly the hostility of the larger society contributed to Jewish continuity. When society opened to Jews, removing the barriers to assimilation, many began to leave Judaism.

The development of a secularist-humanist-rationalist ideology in the eighteenth century appealed to some Jews because it offered the hope of relief from the persecutions of the church. The science of Newton and the rationalism and toleration of Locke went hand in hand. Voltaire and the philosophes in France carried this further. The French Revolution articulated these values with the cry for liberty, fraternity, and equality. Napoleon followed and granted Jews the right to participate politically in society and to join with rationalists and Deists without betraying their people.

The result, particularly in Germany but also in France and England, was a wave of assimilation, intermarriage, and conversion. Science and the humanist-rationalist philosophy of that period slowly proceeded eastward throughout the nineteenth century giving rise to Reform Judaism, secular Zionism, socialism, Yiddish culture *bunds,* and other manifestations of secularism. In Central and Eastern Europe, however, outgroup hostility continued to shore up ingroup cohesion.[8] As the overwhelming

8. Ahad Ha-am (1856–1927), a Russian Jewish essayist and philosopher, wrote: "I try mayhap to give my weary eyes a rest from the scene of ignorance, of degradation, of unutterable poverty that confronts me here in Russia, and find comfort by

majority of Jews lived in this area, Jewish peoplehood did not experience large losses through assimilation and intermarriage.

Even Reform Judaism was less radical in Eastern Europe than in the West. In the absence of political emancipation, Jews in Eastern Europe had no choice but to identify as Jews. The Haskala movement affected only a small portion of the population and religious practice remained stable into the nineteenth century. Between 1914 and 1918 the displacement caused by the war speeded the breakdown of religious practice, making the population more susceptible to modernization and secularism. Orthodoxy had been practiced by the overwhelming majority of the Jews in Poland, but within one generation it came to be practiced by only about a third of the population (Heller 1977, 144). Despite increasingly virulent anti-Semitism, particularly in Poland, which led some Jews to defiantly reaffirm their Jewish identity, almost none found their way back to Orthodox traditionalism (Heller 1977, 208). Apparently, the poverty, superstition, and ignorance associated with Orthodoxy made it repulsive to those who had grown up in its bosom and had left it.

Whether a movement of return would have occurred eventually in Europe one cannot know, for the Holocaust swept that world away. Neither the assimilated Jews of Western Europe nor the secular and nationalistic Jews of Eastern Europe survived.

Jews in America and American Judaism

The Holocaust left a bereaved American Jewry as the most populous and powerful of world Jewries. A scant five years earlier they might have been considered upstarts, a refugee community first beginning to form its own identity. Now they were the center of world Jewry. Millions of American Jews or their parents had grown up in the European *shtetlakh* (small towns) and ghettos. Millions of others had been born in the great melting pot of America or bore children here. Tradition clashed with modernity. Orthodox Judaism seemed lost. And here the t'shuva movement began.

Sephardic Jews (Jews of Mediterranean and Arab lands) had come to

---

looking yonder, across the border, where there are Jewish professors, Jewish members of the Academies, Jewish officers in the army, Jewish civil servants; . . . [But I] . . . ask myself; Do I envy these fellow-Jews of mine their emancipation?—I answer, in all truth and sincerity: No! A thousand times No! . . . I at least can proclaim from the housetops that my kith and kin are dear to me" (quoted in Rosenberg 1965, 133–34).

North America from Brazil in 1654 before the period of Emancipation and Enlightenment. They practiced what Glazer (1957, 20) has called a "dignified Orthodoxy," that is, the Spanish aristocratic traditions of a Judaism that had not yet split into Orthodox, Conservative, and Reform.

In colonial times the settlements were an agglomeration of separate nationalities—French, British, Spanish, and Dutch—each with its separate territorial claims. Similarly, the settlements were populated by religious communities, Puritans in Massachusetts, Quakers in Pennsylvania, Catholics in Maryland, Anglicans in Virginia. These religious communities were often economically and politically separate entities, with their own governing bodies. Intolerance was rife. Religious life retained much of the segregated and ghettoized character it had had in Europe for centuries. To fashion these disparate groups into a single political body, a challenge of immense proportions, the Founding Fathers constructed a system of government that left much political power in the local community while guaranteeing religious freedom for all. The Constitution did not dissolve these separate communities. It simply guaranteed peaceful coexistence between them and provided the mechanisms for their eventual integration, a process that was completed only by the Civil War.

Thus the first wave of Jewish immigrants, the Sephardim, essentially came to an Old World in a new land, a land comprised of religious and political communities. In this circumstance, Sephardic Jewry retained its community structure and developed the first Jewish organizations in the country, gaining for Jews the same measure of tolerance provided for others. But the Sephardic community was small, numbering only two to three hundred in 1700 (Fishman 1973, 7).

REFORM IN EARLY AMERICA

By 1720 Sephardim no longer constituted the majority of the Jewish population; the majority of Jews were German born. They assimilated into American society, yet no movement of return developed. Ideological and social factors suggest why.

In the newly independent United States, about 70 percent of the whites were of English-Scottish descent, and perhaps 20 percent were German (Kiser 1958). The overwhelming majority of the population were Protestant. Jews numbered about twenty-five hundred to three thousand, only one tenth of one percent of the population. For more than half a century after the founding of the United States, a dominant English-Scottish population had an opportunity to develop institutions of government, education, and religion that reflected its values. By the 1830s and 1840s the Germans and Irish who had begun to arrive en masse had to adapt their cultures to fit the by-then crystallized Anglo patterns and values.

German Jews, whose settlements were scattered from the east coast to the Midwest, quickly absorbed the rationalism, secularism, humanism, and even the Protestantism of the larger society. Mainly artisans and small businessmen, they were heavily involved with the dominant population and uninsulated from assimilatory pressures.

In the first half of the nineteenth century belief in the power of reason and faith in natural law contributed to the democratization of society that was taking place in France, England, and the United States. The impact of such beliefs on religion could be seen in increasing skepticism, in the separation of church and state, and in religious doctrines that reflected increased respect for science and rationality. These new ideas contributed to the development of Deism, atheism, and Unitarianism in America and to the rapid growth of the movement of Reform Judaism.

Darwin's *On the Origin of Species* (1859) raised new questions for fundamentalist religion. Reform theologians welcomed these ideas and incorporated them into their framework. The story of creation was discarded, and a school of Higher Biblical Criticism, which reduced the Bible from Divine word to a concatenation of several primitive texts, was accepted. It became a central tenet of Reform Judaism that the *men* who wrote the Bible were fallible, and that religion, like science, was a series of progressions from a lower order to a higher. Orthodox Judaism, with its emphasis on the past, its ties to tradition, was in retreat.

In Europe, Reform had been limited by preexisting social and political arrangements, by habit and custom, and by the fact that the centers of Jewish learning and population remained under regimes where enlightenment had hardly reached and emancipation had not reached at all. And where emancipation did not reach, modernization and assimilation developed only slowly. In contrast, in America Jews attained full legal rights in the 1830s,[9] and for almost a half century thereafter encountered very little hostility. German rabbis in America promoted Reform Judaism, and the American movement adopted a more radical stance than its European counterpart, advocating a sharp break with traditional practices, including the laws of kashrut and *Shabbat* (Sabbath). The *siddur* (prayer book) was revised to reflect the Reform view of Judaism as an ethical, rational, and humanistic religion. Ritual behav-

---

9. Maryland revoked its official exclusion of Jews from public office in 1826. North Carolina and New Hampshire removed restrictions later (Fishman 1973).

ior in every area of life was discarded where, in the words of the Pittsburgh Platform, it did not fit "the views and habits of modern civilization." By the 1870s and 1880s Reform Judaism was almost synonymous with American Judaism. Of almost two hundred congregations, fewer than a dozen were Orthodox (Glazer 1957, 38.)

In 1885 Reform Judaism in America adopted a statement that came to be known as "The Pittsburgh Platform." Referring to the Bible as "reflecting the primitive ideas of its own age," it rejected Judaic religious ritual, emphasizing instead "universal culture." In place of Jewish nationhood, it substituted the notion of religious community, specifically stripped of the idea of return to a promised land.

Thus, although German Jewish immigrants numbered two hundred thousand by 1880, the organizational structures of a dispersed American Jewry could not provide a counterbalance to the assimilatory ideological forces that prevailed. The rationalistic and universalistic ideas of the age were adopted enthusiastically by Reform Judaism.

THE THIRD WAVE: EASTERN EUROPEANS

In 1881 and 1882, roughly concurrent with the closing of the frontier and the beginnings of industrialization in America, economic pressures and pogroms in Russia under Czar Alexander II started a flood of emigration from Eastern and Central Europe. Almost 2.5 million Jews arrived in the United States between 1880 and the end of free immigration in 1924. By 1925 there were approximately 4.5 million Jews in the United States out of a total population of 115 millon. Overwhelmingly, they resided in New York, Pennsylvania, Illinois, and Massachusetts. Jews were now a large, concentrated, and highly visible population (Fishman 1973, 34).

The third wave of immigration came from countries where emancipation had not reached, where Jews had remained ghettoized. For these people, Jewishness implied ethnic as well as religious identity. Old World societies had defined them that way, not permitting them to integrate into the rest of society even if they gave up their religion. They were not Russians or Poles of the Mosaic faith but Jews, no matter whether they were secular or religious.

In 1924, about forty years after Eastern European Jews had begun coming to the United States, the gates of immigration were closed. The last wave of immigrants divided into secular and Orthodox. Conflict between these groups was intense, sometimes coming to blows. Socialist and labor groups at times held marches and balls on Yom Kippur, specifically choosing to desecrate to the utmost this holy day of fasting.

By 1945 the majority of American Jews under the age of thirty were native-born. And although their parents or at least their grandparents were overwhelmingly likely to have been born in Europe and reared as Orthodox Jews, only a minority were themselves Orthodox.

THE SOCIAL AND POLITICAL CONTEXT

Some hostility to Jews had existed from their first landing in New Amsterdam, but in the context of the hostilities between Catholics and Protestants and among the various Protestant sects, this was not unusual. In any case, Jews were so few in number that they went almost unnoticed.

Toward the end of the nineteenth century, the rise of nationalism and acceptance of social Darwinism fed an emerging racism[10] that became much more threatening as the Jewish population grew. Hostility reached a peak in the 1920s. Membership in the Ku Klux Klan reached an all-time high, Henry Ford used his *Dearborn Independent* as a platform to attack Jews and to publish anti-Semitic literature, including the forged *Protocols of the Elders of Zion.* Father Coughlin's radio program, which consistently attacked Jews, had one of the largest audiences in America. Universities, led by Harvard, began adopting a *numerus clausus,* a quota system restricting the entry of Jews. After 1933 anti-Semitism in the United States paralleled Hitler's rise to Power. German American Bund organizations proliferated and followed Hitler's line. Charles Lindbergh created the America First organization, which blamed the Jews for the war in Europe and accused them of trying to involve America in it. Even after America's entry into World War II, anti-Semitic organizations and literature continued to grow,[11] despite and in part because of Jewish economic success. Only after the war, when the enormity and the horror of the Holocaust had become clear, did anti-Semitism recede.

Judaism and the Melting Pot

The second wave of immigrants, German Jews, had come to a homogeneous Anglo-Saxon, Protestant America shaped by rationalism and sci-

10. Darwinism was used to justify the restriction of immigration, the Jim Crow codes of the South, and the legalization of racial segregation (Hofstadter 1944). America developed its own style of racism, although the legal protections of the Thirteenth and Fourteenth Amendments provided a level below which one could not sink. But the looming threat of Nazism and growing anti-Semitism made these uncertain protections.

11. The number of anti-Semitic organizations in the United States reached its peak in 1947 (Forster 1950).

ence, where traditional community identities had been undermined politically by Federalism and philosophically by universalism. German Jews sought equality and attempted to remake themselves in the dominant mold, and they were largely successful. The third wave, in contrast, came to a heterogeneous America, to a melting pot filled with ethnic groups seeking to enter mainstream society. But Social Darwinism was taking hold, and racism was redefined to legitimate discrimination against Eastern Europeans and Jews. The ethnics responded by attempting to become American and abandoning Old World and old-fashioned ideas and styles. People were judged by their ability to speak English correctly and without an accent. Old-fashioned clothes, customs, and foods were shunned. One wanted to be modern, to be "American."

The guiding principles of integration were no longer science, rationalism, and Deism but rather the practical applications of Americanism: acceptance of the language, clothing, and life-style of Americans. To gain legal and social acceptance, immigrants had to abandon their ethnic identity and adopt the American way of life. For many Jews and other Eastern Europeans, this meant redefining themselves as part of a "religious" group—as Italian Catholics or Polish Catholics or Jews (Herberg 1960)—rather than an ethnic community with its own language, customs, and life-style.

A variety of options were open to Jews in America. Reform Judaism was available to those seeking both a radical change from the religious practices of the past and a new identity. This was too American for most immigrants, although their children could and did take this route. Various secular ethnic Jewish groups were open to those seeking a secular attachment; but as Jews began to shed their ethnic characteristics these attachments tended to be abandoned. For the children of Eastern European immigrants, Conservative Judaism became the major denominational attachment, with Reform the second choice. Attachment to Orthodoxy was also possible, but it was generally characteristic of the first generation or at best of a minority in the second or third generation.

CONSERVATIVE JUDAISM

American Conservative Judaism was born as a reaction to Reform, not as a dissent from Orthodoxy, and its adherents were the children of the Eastern European Orthodox of the third wave. In 1883, at a banquet celebrating the graduation of the first class from Hebrew Union College, nonkosher (*treyf*) foods were served, which caused a major scandal. The "treyf banquet," as it came to be known, and the adoption of the Pittsburgh Platform of 1885 set in motion a reaction that led to the founding of the Jewish Theological Seminary in 1887. At first the Seminary suffered from a lack of students and financial support. Solomon Schechter, appointed its leader in 1902, revived it, attracting the American-born sons of Eastern European Jews (Glazer 1957).

The Seminary played a central role in the growth of the Conservative movement, but it did not lead. Reflecting the egalitarian ethic that American Jews espoused, the Conservative movement was led by laymen. It was the congregation that determined the acceptable level of traditional observance or accomodation. The Seminary simply refined this and attempted to direct it by training rabbis. The changes that occurred were pragmatic or expedient. Unlike Reform, Conservative Judaism developed no clear ideological base for its position (Sklare 1972). This did not hinder its growth. In fact, it may have been a major source of the movement's vitality.

Conservative Judaism grew especially in suburban areas where Eastern European Jews settled. From the mid 1940s through the 1950s Conservative Judaism far outstripped Reform in growth, to say nothing of Orthodoxy, which seemed to be losing numbers at a remarkable pace.

ORTHODOX JUDAISM

The overwhelming majority of Eastern European Jews arriving in the United States in the third wave of immigration had been reared as Orthodox. Western European Jews had begun the process of assimilation, but because of pogroms, punitive army service, and economic discrimination, Eastern European Jews remained alienated from their host societies and largely isolated until World War I. The openness of America was a severe test of their commitment to Orthodoxy. Institutional structures were only beginning to be built. Ritual bathhouses were few and lacking in amenities. Supervision of kosher food was not well organized. Synagogues were by and large continuations of the European synagogues, as their names and local traditions indicated. Jewish education was chaotic and neglected; the yeshiva-day-school movement did not begin until the 1920s.

Writing at the end of the 1950s, Glazer summed up the position of Orthodoxy in America:

> Judaism is even more vulnerable to the unsettling influence of modernity than is Christianity. Judaism emphasizes acts, rituals, habits, a way of life. Christianity, in contrast, places more emphasis on beliefs and doctrines.

Judaism, in its popular form, in the version in which it was taught to the East European Jews who were the fathers and the grandfathers of the great majority of American Jews, tended to obscure distinctions between greater and lesser observances, to ignore doctrine even more than medieval Judaism did, to obscure the meaning of ritual. In effect, it taught a rigid set of rituals to cover one's entire life. The rigidity permitted no defense in depth, so to speak. . . . Once one had found . . . that it was more convenient to work on Saturdays, or to shave, or to abandon traditional dress, one had no body of doctrine to fall back upon that could explain what remained *really* important to Judaism—Indeed, the question was whether *anything* was really more important than the rituals established by God's word. Under this circumstance, an entire way of life disintegrated. (1957, 133)

A study of an eastern city with a population of 128,000 and a Jewish population of 8,500 painted a gloomy picture of the decline in strength of Orthodox Judaism (Sklare, Vosk, and Zborowski 1955). It described an immense loss for Orthodoxy in a single generation with gains for Reform and even greater gains for Conservative Judaism in that same period. Moreover, when the respondents (who were high school students) were asked, "What do you think you will be when you are married and raise your own family?" only one out of five children reared as Orthodox expected to remain Orthodox, whereas 62 percent of Conservative and 60 percent of Reform expected to remain with their denominations. Other community studies report similar findings (Polsky 1958; Goldstein and Goldschieder 1968).

Toward the end of the 1950s, then, scholars had largely written off Orthodox Judaism as an option for American Jews.

The Postwar Years: Glimmerings of a New Era

In retrospect one can see that by 1946 Eastern Europeans were beginning to accept themselves as part of American society. Synagogues established as Rumanian or Polish or Hungarian still flourished but had not been establishing new congregations for a generation. Orthodoxy, European in origin and loyalty, had been cut off from its roots and was on the verge of becoming Americanized. And fourteen thousand children attended Jewish day schools and yeshivot.

American Judaism as a whole was striking a new balance. Reform Judaism, which in 1885 had adopted a platform rejecting many of the fundamentals of Judaism, seemed to have second thoughts. In the Columbus Platform of 1937 it adopted a position that reinstated God in its theology and rejected the earlier radical references to the "God-idea." A new section headed "Torah" was introduced. And the Platform completely repudiated the earlier Reform view that Jews were a religious group only (Glazer 1957, 103).

The change in position undoubtedly reflected the greater hostility of American society toward Jews after 1885. But it also reflected the weight of Eastern European Jewry and its ethnic identity.

This identity was even further reinforced by the immigration of almost two hundred thousand survivors of the European Holocaust who entered the United States between 1944 and 1959 (Fishman 1973, 249). Many of them were chasidic Jews. In the aftermath of the unsuccessful Hungarian revolt of 1956, several thousand more came. As a result, by the end of the 1950s there was once again a first generation of Orthodox Jews in the United States, this time Holocaust survivors, wary of the non-Jewish world. They came to an America that by now had established an Orthodox base and the conditions for Orthodox life. They had lived the isolated life of the Jewish ghetto and not only sought it again but, because of changes in American society, were able to achieve this isolation.

Glazer and others writing at the end of the 1950s tended to see this group and all of Orthodoxy as a vestige of the Old World, capable of surviving only by insulating and isolating itself from the rest of America. As such, it might live for a while, but it could have no attraction for American Jews.

The Americanization of Orthodoxy, its success in establishing religious and educational institutions, the birth of the state of Israel, and the immigration of a wave of Holocaust survivors laid the institutional framework to facilitate return, although it was not foreseen at that time. In the 1940s one could see the beginnings of a return. By the 1960s and 1970s changed attitudes toward religion provided the impetus that permitted large numbers of religiously "lost" Jews to explore the possibility of return.

Chapter 2

Portals of Return:
Home and Synagogue

Orthodox Jews define themselves in terms of their observance of the laws of kashrut, the Sabbath, and family purity.[1] Because observance of family purity is a private matter between husband and wife and is not visible to anyone else, acceptance as a member of the Orthodox community tends to relate almost entirely to the practice of kashrut and Shabbat. Jews who observe both practices are considered to be Orthodox unless they define themselves as Conservative.

The laws of kashrut limit the kinds of food one may eat, but their effect is to limit also the persons with whom one shares a meal, where one may eat, and where one may travel. This affects not only leisure and business contacts, but also relations with friends and family members who do not observe kashrut. Similarly, the rules regarding Sabbath also forbid a variety of activities, from driving or riding in automobiles to making and receiving phone calls, on this day of rest.[2]

Those who become Orthodox, therefore, not only undertake a new way of life but also give up or at least subject to strain many of their most important ties to others who are not Orthodox, even parents and siblings. In sociological terms, becoming Orthodox involves an implosion of social relations until new ties are established. It is paradoxical that Orthodox Judaism, in which emphasis on family and community is a major source of cohesion and attraction to followers, should cause the estrangement of

1. These last laws restrict times when husband and wife may have sexual relations, style of dress, and such leisure activities as social dancing.

2. Halakhic observance of the Sabbath rarely occurs without observance of kashrut, as Sabbath observance apparently requires greater commitment. See Ritterband and Cohen 1984b; Heilman 1976, 6.

many of the newly Orthodox from their friends and family. Yet it does, and this tends to mark off those who become Orthodox from the "born again" of other faiths and even from Jews who have simply become more traditional or observant.

Whatever difficulty these observances represent for the newly Orthodox, they define the subject group clearly for the observer; the newly Orthodox are those who formerly did not observe the rules of kashrut or Sabbath and now observe both.[3]

Although the synagogue serves a number of essential functions, providing a place for public worship, a community meetinghouse, and a house of study, the most central aspects of religious practice occur in the home. On one hand, this has facilitated the transmission of Judaism, making it less dependent on public observance—an orientation that is critical for a minority religion and is probably an essential ingredient in the vaunted solidarity of the Jewish family. On the other hand, as I have noted, it has meant that elements at the heart of Orthodox Jewish practice are hidden from public view, making it difficult for newcomers to have an opportunity to learn them through observation.

The home-centered nature of Orthodoxy also presents a problem for recruitment to Judaism. Prayer meetings and preaching may be appropriate instrumentalities for Christian revival as Christianity is primarily church centered. But how and where can the Jewish returnee learn the essential rituals of Judaism, which is home centered? The observance of Sabbath and kashrut is learned in the process of socialization. Children see their mothers lighting Sabbath candles, sing the Sabbath *zemirot* (hymns) around the table with their parents, taste the Sabbath food themselves. The experience of Jewish life is not a story told to them by others. How can it be taught to adults seeking to learn about it? Can this experience be conveyed through books? Can a synthetic experience be constructed that will pass on the essence of the Sabbath, or is it possible to

3. The 1981–1982 survey by Ritterband and Cohen suggests that a third of those who identity themselves as Orthodox do handle money on the Sabbath and almost 10 percent do not observe kashrut. It also found that 3.4 percent of those who identify themselves as Conservative do *not* handle money on the Sabbath (Special computer runs, January 1987).

In this book we designate as "Orthodox" those who observe both kashrut and Shabbat. We use the Ritterband and Cohen category "highly observant" as synonymous with Orthodox, since 90 percent of their highly observant are Orthodox. We omit those who identify themselves as Orthodox but are not Orthodox in practice—the "sinning Orthodox," in the humorous and apt designation of a friend who belongs to this group.

experience it only in the bosom of family? The basic avenues for transmitting Judaism in traditional Jewish communities—home, school, and synagogue—all presuppose early training in Judaism. How can adults learn to be Orthodox Jews?

Marriage as a Portal of Return

Marriage is a portal to Orthodoxy for many, more often for women than for men.[4] By marrying someone Orthodox, one establishes a home consonant with the new commitment and avoids the conflict that might occur if one became Orthodox in a home where other family members were not observant.

Yet Orthodox Judaism's unique pattern of religiosity raises some questions. Schools for ba'alei t'shuva enroll about four times as many men as women. Yeshivot for those who are Orthodox from birth enroll more boys than girls. The synagogue is the preserve of men. And even in the home it is the men who lead the *seder* meal on Passover, the men who pray three times a day and observe other ritual commandments that mark the passing of seasons and festivals. If participation in religious services is taken as the mark of religiosity—as it is in those studies that find women more religious than men (Argyle 1959, 71–79)—then in Judaism or at least in Orthodoxy the men are more religious than the women. Yet my research suggests that women who marry Orthodox men tend to become Orthodox more often than men who marry Orthodox women.

Two factors seem to contribute to this pattern. The first is knowledge of rituals. Many women who become Orthodox come from homes where laws of kashrut were observed, although laws of Sabbath were not.[5] These women are familiar with the practice of kashrut, although before marriage they may not have been rigorous in its practice. This was the case for many of those who became Orthodox in the late 1940s through the early 1960s. Whether the new domestic roles of men and women have altered this pattern remains to be seen. In contrast, a man reared in a non-Orthodox home is probably not only unfamiliar with kashrut but with

4. No systematic data are available on this point. My statement is based on observation and interviews with couples.

5. In one modern Orthodox congregation of 250 families in New York City, two informants identified 25 women between the ages of forty and fifty-five who became Orthodox at marriage. Of these, 17 came from families that observed kashrut in the home to some degree (Danzger, field notes, 1980).

rituals of the home that require special blessings, prayers, and ritual practices typically neglected in all but Orthodox homes.

Second, although the man's religious role is the more visible, the woman's role in the home is more crucial to Orthodox life. A kosher home can be maintained if the husband is merely tolerant of the wife's religious practice; he need not become Orthodox for his wife to maintain kashrut in the home. If the husband is sufficiently tolerant, the wife may even keep the Sabbath. He may do as he pleases, but his wife will light the Sabbath candles and abstain from work.

But if an Orthodox man marries a non-Orthodox woman he will not be able to get by on her tolerance of his religion; he must have her cooperation. It is she who prepares the food, guarantees the kashrut of the home, and creates an environment conducive to proper celebration of the Sabbath. She cannot simply tolerate following the rules of family purity but must be an active participant, for it is she who must go to the mikveh each month.

A nonobservant wife, therefore, will probably have some familiarity with kashrut practices and will almost surely be under great pressure to change if her husband is serious about his religious commitment. A nonobservant husband is under far less pressure to change from an observant wife and is also less likely to be familiar with the required rituals.

Synagogue

Orthodox synagogues tend to assume that participants already have a knowledge of Judaism—that congregants can read Hebrew, have been trained in the use of the siddur, and can follow and participate in the services. Yet to learn Hebrew means learning not only a new language but a new alphabet. Even reading without comprehension is difficult. Prayer books do not generally indicate when one is to stand, sit, genuflect, or face the ark.[6] Most important, a congregant may attend the synagogue regularly but will not become a part of the community until he learns how to celebrate Shabbat and observe kashrut. Orthodox Jews hesitate to accept invitations to a home that is not kosher. Despite its limitations, the synagogue is available and does serve as a portal of entry to Orthodox Judaism.

6. In recent years Orthodox synagogues have begun purchasing siddurim that provide some of these instructions, a practice that addresses a need.

ENTERING THE COMMUNITY OF PRAYER

Until the 1940s most American Jews were immigrants. Young people born in the United States and not reared in an Orthodox home could still find relatives and friends who practiced Orthodoxy and could learn about Shabbat or kashrut through them, not simply by discussion but by participation in the observances. Even parents who had abandoned religion might be useful sources of information about religious practices and could demonstrate what should be done and how. But the bars to immigration after 1924 meant that by the early 1950s adolescents might well have parents born or reared in the United States who were themselves unfamiliar with Jewish religious practices. Perhaps only the grandparents who had abandoned their Judaism in America could recollect having practiced it. How then was entry into the Orthodox community achieved?

Halakhah requires that every male pray three times a day, preferably but not exclusively in a synagogue. The current custom is that males associated with Orthodox synagogues attend the Sabbath service on Saturday morning.[7] Because any man is eligible to lead the prayers or read the Torah in the synagogue service, some pressure to be capable of these activities exists. In large synagogues, where most worshippers are relatively passive participants and only a few are prayer leaders, these skills need not be developed; a man need only participate in the synagogue service on the Sabbath, when many participants are present, and can decline to lead the service without onus.[8]

For the man, there are two particular opportunities to learn these rituals: in preparation for the *bar mitzvah* and during the period of bereavement for a parent, when the *Kaddish* is said.

7. A substantial but smaller number attend the Friday evening service and the Saturday afternoon service. Weekday morning and evening services in modern Orthodox synagogues may be attended by only a tenth of the men in the community. The low attendance during the week is everywhere attested to in large synagogues by the use of the bet midrash as the place for prayers during the week. The bet midrash is far smaller than the main sanctuary of the synagogue. In the yeshivot, however, the place for prayers is almost as full during the week as on the Sabbath.

8. A supplementary mode of attachment to the synagogue is to participate in the management of its affairs through such activities as serving on committees and donating funds. This method cannot by itself provide full entry into the community but may be used in addition to participation in prayer. This approach is also often open to women in the Orthodox community and offers some participation in the synagogue life. Many women also attend synagogue services regularly on Sabbath and holidays.

Bar Mitzvah.   Children in Orthodox families generally receive sufficient religious training to be competent to participate in the Orthodox synagogue service. In many Orthodox synagogues preparation for the bar mitzvah (the ceremony in which a boy is inducted into adulthood) enables the child to lead the services and read the Torah at the service. In others the bar mitzvah boy also gives a sermon or a Torah lecture to mark his initiation into the community of study.

Conservative and Reform children also are ordinarily bar mitzvahed (or *bat mitzvahed* in the case of girls) and in preparation are often taught to read Hebrew, a process that may require their attendance at a local congregational school for two to three years. The result is the creation of a pool of young people who have begun to develop the capability to participate in synagogue prayer.

Attempts by rabbis or teachers (themselves often Orthodox) in Conservative or Reform congregational schools to encourage stronger ties to Judaism at times succeed so well that some students develop attachments to Orthodox Judaism. Those who seem especially eager to learn more about their Judaism may be referred to Orthodox institutions or personally tutored and guided by an Orthodox person.[9]

Mourning.   A second point of entry for males is the recitation of the Kaddish (a prayer sanctifying the glory of God, recited by mourners) by the sons of the deceased at each prayer service in the synagogue for a period of almost a year following the death of a parent. Theoretically, this brings the male children to the synagogue twice a day for prayer.[10] Practice often diverges from this normative requirement. But those who wish to honor parents fully as required by the halakhah may make efforts to attend the service twice a day for a year. In the course of this year they may be befriended by some congregant who encourages their participation in the synagogue and in the religion.

One respondent reported that he had always felt religious but had not had any Jewish education. His father died when he was thirteen, and he

9. In response to this, or perhaps simply to better articulate their views, Conservative religious schools often seek out nonreligious Israeli to teach Hebrew. This has its own dynamic. Secular Israelis have no involvement in the rituals that are still central to Conservative Judaism. The Conservative movement has not to this point been able to generate its own teachers. They are thus dependent on others who in their view are either over secular or over religious.

10. In the morning the *shacharit* (morning) prayer is recited. The afternoon *minchah* and evening *ma'ariv* prayers are recited at dusk. The three prayers require attendance twice daily.

attended the synagogue to recite the Kaddish. The men in the synagogue taught him the rudiments of prayer, and he used this opportunity to learn to be Orthodox. He remained peripheral to the community, attending services but not fully participating in Sabbath and kashrut observance, until he married an Orthodox woman years later. They sent their children to a yeshiva, now attend an Orthodox synagogue, and have become leading members of the congregation.

Another respondent, who was married and had three children when his father died, found entry more difficult. Attending synagogue to say Kaddish, he was befriended by Lubavitcher chasidim. They brought him wine, taught him to make *Kiddush* (a benediction recited over a cup of wine at the commencement of Sabbath and holiday meals), and persuaded him to attend synagogue. But he could not convince his wife to change. His home still is not kosher. He observes Sabbath to the best of his ability, often attending synagogue and occasionally taking one of his daughters along. More recently, as they have become teenagers, they have refused his invitations to join him, and he attends alone. In his home, the Sabbath is not marked by candle lighting or a festive meal. Although he persists in his commitment, he is not accepted in the Orthodox community nor does he consider himself part of it.

Formalization of the Synagogue as a Portal of Return

The synagogue was not designed to facilitate the transition of people from the nonreligious or non-Orthodox world to the world of Orthodox Judaism. But as the ba'al t'shuva presence became more marked, some synagogues and other institutions developed outreach programs. Even before the t'shuva movement began, the Young Israel movement was assisting people in their transition to Orthodoxy.

THE YOUNG ISRAEL AND THE MOVEMENT OF RETURN

The Young Israel is a synagogue movement with more than one hundred affiliated synagogues serving a membership of approximately thirty-five thousand families. Founded in 1912, it was developed primarily to provide an American Orthodox synagogue in a situation where most synagogues in the New World were simply extensions of the Old. The lower east side of New York, for example, had its Byalistoker shule, its Roumanisher shul, its Polisher shtieble, and many more of the same kind. The Young Israel was to be an *American* Orthodox synagogue, different from synagogues that carried on the traditions of the "old country."

For a time, it wavered in institutional affiliation between Conservative and Orthodox. Its earliest leaders were faculty of the (Conservative) Jewish Theological Seminary, and considerable numbers of seminary students were involved in its programs. By 1922 the newly established National Council of Young Israel had chosen to remain within the fold of Orthodoxy and bound to halakhah (Liebman 1965; Gartner 1973).

In this period many were drifting away from Judaism. Young people brought up in America were embarrassed by parents with foreign accents and clothing, European foods and style of life, old-fashioned ways and religion. The impoverished immigrant parents lacked education in the American culture. Children sought to escape this "ignorant" lower-class ethnic world and to become Americans. This conflict was exacerbated by governmental pressures and social demands on immigrant groups to acculturate. The Young Israel sought to bridge the growing social and cultural gap between parents and children by maintaining a commitment to halakhah while participating in American society to the fullest extent possible.[11]

To do this, Young Israel built a microcosm of the larger society within its own framework. Over the years Young Israel developed Boy Scout troops, athletic leagues, and sisterhoods. It developed an employment service to help Sabbath-observing Jews find employment at a time when discrimination against Jews in employment was legal and rampant and when even Jewish employers refused employment to Sabbath observers.

To bridge the gap between the Orthodox world and the larger society, the Young Israel sought the greatest leniency in halakhic rulings. The *mechitzah* (the partition between men and women in the synagogue) was as low as permissible. In a move away from tradition, women sat not in the balcony but, rather, on the same level as the men, although on the sides or toward the rear of the synagogue. At least into the 1960s, though not in the 1970s, social dancing was permitted in Young Israel synagogues. A unique feature of the Young Israel was its emphasis on youth, as its name implies. Its major goals were to hold on to defecting youth who couldn't relate to their parents and to attract newcomers. People in their twenties and thirties might be the leaders of the synagogue. Programs for children were developed for Shabbat afternoon. The young could have a *minyan* (prayer service) of their own, with their own cantor

11. That the Young Israel movement was designed to address these strains between parents and children can be seen in its motto, "and He shall turn the hearts of the fathers unto the sons and the hearts of the sons unto the fathers" (Mal. 3:24).

to lead the service and *gabbaim* (sextons). One innovation in particular, preaching the sermon in English, alienated the Orthodox rabbinate and the older generation of pious laymen, who were overwhelmingly European born and often lacked facility in speaking English. So radical were these moves that several yeshivot placed a ban on Young Israel (Sturm 1984).

Young Israel's attachment to halakhah distinguished it from Conservative Judaism. At the same time, its involvement in society and willingness to make some adjustments to American society, albeit within the frame of the halakhah, distinguished it from more traditional Eastern European synagogues that sought to rebuild the European experience in America. In the view of leaders of this movement the need to Americanize was imperative, for young people were already rejecting Judaism in droves. But abandonment of halakhah meant abandonment of the essence of Jewish life. The Young Israel sought to make it possible for the American-born to stay Orthodox while making Judaism appear modern. In essence what they were advocating was not modernization of Judaism—that was what Reform Judaism sought—but to appear modern while retaining the legal and normative underpinnings of Orthodoxy. I have called them "modernistic," modern in appearance but traditional at the core.

The American character of the Young Israel meant that the members had not been exposed to the life of the European shtetl, or attended the European yeshivot. Until the early 1960s the Young Israel members had probably acquired their knowledge of Judaism in *talmud torahs,* afternoon schools established to supplement public school education. Although talmud torahs did a creditable job of introducing young people to Judaism, teaching them to pray, to read the Torah, and to serve as cantors, as well as giving them some knowledge of Jewish law, they did not provide access to the world of Jewish learning—to the Talmud, the religious codes, and other works of Jewish scholarship. The talmud torahs could and did provide access to the community of prayer. At that time the Young Israel was a community of prayer with no pretension to be a community of study.

The Young Israel's period of development, from the 1920s through the 1950s, coincided with a period in which the talmud torahs were the predominant mode of Jewish education. Talmud torah students attended public schools and were very much a part of the larger society. The Orthodox Jewish community, represented by the Young Israel synagogues, were not strangers to the larger society, and thus the transition offered the newly Orthodox was not to a world cut off from society but to one that was thoroughly American.

Although the Jewish education of the Orthodox American was less advanced in the 1940s or 1950s than it became in the next decade, when American Orthodox started attending yeshiva day schools in substantial numbers, the educational gap between those reared and educated as Orthodox and the newly committed was nevertheless substantial. Young Israel synagogues sought to bridge it by introducing siddurim with English instruction, by making periodic announcement of page numbers for those who had difficulty following the prayer service, and by establishing sisterhoods and men's clubs for those who sought synagogue participation in ways other than through traditional study. By and large the Young Israel and synagogues like them were successful.

THE LINCOLN SQUARE SYNAGOGUE

The Lincoln Square Synagogue in New York, under the leadership of Rabbi Steven Riskin, has made major efforts to recruit to Orthodoxy and to accomodate the newly Orthodox. Since the early 1970s this synagogue has made kiruv r'chokim—bringing close those who are afar—a centerpiece of its work. The programs in this synagogue are built around the recurrent problems that ba'alei t'shuva face and attempt to provide solutions on an organizational level rather than through individual efforts.

Prayer. One of the most striking features of the Lincoln Square Synagogue is the beginners' minyan (now called beginners' service to indicate that it is not a minyan), initiated in December 1975. Theoretically, to pray in an Orthodox congregation one need simply enter the synagogue and join the other members of the congregation. In practice, this is very difficult. In fact, one of the most difficult religious acts for newly Orthodox is participation in the prayer service. Because it is the custom of Orthodox Jews to pray in Hebrew, newly Orthodox often feel unable to convey their own feelings. They find prayer boring and rigid, requiring far too much discipline and practice. They sometimes feel that learning prayer is an arduous task instead of a meaningful experience (see chap. 12).

Ephraim Buchwald, director of education at the Lincoln Square Synagogue, describes the beginners' service as follows:

> People are encouarged to come late to the services when they first start attending so as not to be overwhelmed by the Hebrew readings. We may be the only synagogue that encourages late coming. Parts of the prayers are read slowly so that all can follow. Also, at this service there is a lot of singing. And

we stop frequently throughout the service to explain the service and its structure.

Men and women sit separately at this worship service, and the mechitzah is lower than in our main sanctuary.[12] Despite this, more women attend than men.

People stay with the beginners' service for an average of about six months, and during this time I find there is a development of a sense of community of people. People become friends, see each other socially, visit each other, and really develop a sense of camaraderie. They feel they are on this religious journey together.

Q. How long does it take for people to have enough facility with Hebrew to participate in the prayers?

A. This varies. Many people come with some background and need to brush up on their Hebrew. But some know nothing, not even the Hebrew alphabet, so we provide tutors. Once they begin to read Hebrew they can follow the prayers better, and they continue to learn and practice as they attend the beginners' minyan.

Q. How many people get such tutoring each year?

A. It's hard to estimate. We tutor perhaps thirty each month, and others are tutored by their new friends.

Q. How many people attend the beginners' minyan?

A. I can tell you that our beginners' minyan is always full, and we have room for about fifty people. In addition, very often we have ten to fifteen people standing.

Q. How long does it take before they go on to the main minyan?

A. It varies depending on their previous education and also on whether they want to go on. Some develop friends in the beginners' minyan and don't want to leave. Others like our services because we explain more and sing more. Those who want to move on to the main minyan can probably do it in three months or so.

Q. Do many of those with little background go on to the main minyan?

A. Almost all do, although we have a few who continue to come to the beginners' service for years. We even have some who are Orthodox from birth who come regularly after they attend services elsewhere. They like the singing and the discussions of the services.

Q. How do you recruit people to the beginners' minyan?

12. The Lincoln Square Synagogue was founded as a Conservative synagogue, and in Conservative synagogues men and women sit together in prayer. Rabbi Steven Riskin, then a newly ordained Orthodox rabbi and himself newly Orthodox, persuaded the founding members to turn it into an Orthodox congregation. The synagogue's architecture with seats in the round and a low mechitzah reflect this attempt to reach out beyond the boundaries of traditional Orthodoxy.

A. We have a number of outreach programs, but one of our most effective means
   of getting people is by advertising that anyone may attend our beginners'
   minyan free of charge for the High Holy Day services. We run a shortened
   service, and we have hundreds of people come to that. That's how many of
   our new people come (see chap. 9).

One's first experience at the Lincoln Square Synagogue may not be the
beginners' minyan. It may be a lecture or a class in the Joseph Shapiro
Institute, an adult education program associated with the synagogue. And
one does not go directly from attendance at the minyan to other features
of Orthodoxy, such as the *kashering* (ritual cleansing of kitchen utensils,
sink, and stove, making them acceptable for use in the preparation of
kosher foods) of the kitchen. Rabbi Buchwald insists that before that
point is reached a person should be encouraged to attend classes at the
synagogue to learn more about Judaism.

One may start, then, either by attending classes and then joining the
minyan or by joining the minyan and then taking some classes. In the
meantime the individual will begin to observe the Sabbath. To teach him
or her how to do this, the synagogue offers two modes of learning. One is
by attending courses offered at the synagogue on the laws of the Sabbath
and the holidays. The other is by being a guest on the Sabbath in the
homes of some of the Orthodox members of the synagogue.

Both attending classes and being someone's guest for the Sabbath are
highly social activities that put young men and women together in a
situation where a friendship can easily be struck. It introduces them to
west side "yuppie" singles Orthodox society. It may well be that these
"accidental" characteristics of the group are a major attraction for those
who come to lectures and other synagogue functions.[13]

Updating developments in synagogue outreach in September 1987,
Rabbi Buckwald noted that the Lincoln Square Synagogue has received
such extensive media coverage since 1984 that it is no longer necessary to
advertise their programs. In fact, Lincoln Square Synagogue now encourages inquirers to attend beginners' services that are available in
many parts of the city: in Manhattan at Park East Synagogue, Kehilath

13. In 1980–1981, when Rabbi Riskin offered a series of lectures on Jewish singles, the ballroom had to be opened for the overflow crowd, which followed the
lectures over closed-circuit television. The synagogue itself holds six hundred people;
probably close to one thousand attended these weekly lectures. When a series on
Israel was offered in the 1981–1982 season, large crowds were again attracted but
there was no need for closed-circuit television; nor was the synagogue filled to
capacity. A headcount at one of these meetings, taken to be typical, showed about
three hundred and eighty.

Jeshurun, and Ohev Shalom, in Riverdale at the Jewish Center, and in Forest Hills at Chavurat Shalom and elsewhere.

In February 1988 twenty-five synagogues across the United States participated in a "turn Friday night into Shabbat" outreach program (*Cleveland Jewish News*, 1 April 1988). Orthodox synagogues in the United States are now coordinating their efforts at outreach under the guidance of national Jewish agencies.

Kashrut and social circles. One would imagine that kashrut would be an obstacle to becoming Orthodox, for observance of kashrut restricts one from taking advantage of the range of foods available in Manhattan. But Rabbi Buchwald reports that he often has to resist the entreaties of newcomers that he immediately kasher their homes. He urges them to take another course, to study a bit more first. Moreover, when Rabbi Buchwald does kasher a home he apparently does so with meticulous concern for every detail, beyond the strict level required. Rabbi Cohen is less concerned with these details. But the point of Rabbi Buchwald's efforts can be seen in this remark.

> In this community people sometimes push to have their kitchens kashered. I try to hold them back if I think they are not ready for it. But they want to have guests, they've made friends in the community and want to entertain them. Kashering a kitchen is like giving someone a seal of approval. It's almost as though the rabbi has said that now that it's kashered you can eat there. It's not so, of course. You still have to know whether the person is seriously committed. But some people think that's all there is to it.

Kashering a home may be done simply in an effort to find the social acceptability necessary for entry into the society.

The difference between Rabbi Cohen and Rabbi Buchwald in this respect is not simply a matter of interpretation of the law, although that may well be a factor, but of how each sees the function of kashering a home. In one view it simply facilitates a person's observance of the commandments. In the other view the person can get along well and probably can manage to eat kosher food without having the rabbi kasher the kitchen. But by kashering it the rabbi in effect allows the person to entertain others who are concerned with kashrut. Rabbi Buchwald hesitates to do this unless he is persuaded of the sincerity of the person. Rabbi Cohen, in contrast, seems to feel that one should make the transition to Orthodoxy as easy as possible.[14]

14. How sincere people have to be before they may be accepted has been controversial in Judaism for over two thousand years (see BT, Berachot 28a).

Integration and marriage. The process by which the newly Orthodox become integrated into the Lincoln Square Synagogue community, then, ordinarily involves their attending the beginners' minyan until they have learned the rudiments of prayer, spending *Shabbatot* at the homes of members of the congregation, supplementing this experience with classes, and preparing a kosher home under the direction and supervision of a rabbi.[15]

These steps are not the end of the process. Being a ba'al t'shuva—here meaning newly Orthodox—is a transitional status. Some other steps are necessary to become simply an Orthodox Jew.

The first of these is movement from the beginners' minyan to the main minyan (the prayer service in the main sanctuary). Surprisingly, Rabbi Buchwald notes that there is sometimes resistance to moving to the main minyan and that he occasionally has to push people into doing so. "Ba'alei t'shuva resist the main minyan because there is too much talking there. While they find the people at the main minyan warm and accepting, they are too social. The *davening* (prayer service) itself lacks a spiritual dimension. The sense of awe and respect for the prayers and for standing in God's presence is lacking. The ba'alei t'shuva are resistant to this and hesitate to join the main minyan."

Another answer was suggested by someone who had returned some years earlier. "Ba'alei t'shuva carry in some Protestant religious attitudes. They are high on religion and think it has to be expressed in terms of awe and reverence only. It takes a while for them to begin to see that it is also expressed in terms of warmth and love, even in terms of love for fellow Jews, which is why there is so much talking."

One is expected to continue attending classes and lectures. Ideally every Jew ought to devote time to the study of Torah. It is a religious obligation. At the same time for young people throughout the metropolitan area, including the Orthodox from birth, these classes are an opportunity to meet singles of the opposite sex.

This last point is important. Marriage is the factor that stabilizes and secures the ba'al t'shuva in his or her new religious commitment. In the view of the rabbis of the synagogue, if marriage does not occur the ba'al t'shuva will be unable to integrate into the Orthodox community. This is

15. The synagogue offers a number of programs for beginners, in addition. These include the "Beginners' Shmooze" (discussion group), Beginners' Newsletter, Beginners' Luncheons, Adopt-a-Beginner Program, and special holiday programs for beginners.

because the Orthodox community is a traditional community, and middle-aged members of the community generally also hold traditional family roles.[16] There are no accepted roles for middle-aged singles.

The Lincoln Square Synagogue therefore makes an effort to help men and women meet. Rabbi Buchwald reports:

> Young people meet at many of our functions. We try to make sure there are always opportunities for them to meet. For example, when Rabbi Riskin gives his public lecture series, we always follow that with coffee and cake in our ballroom so that there is an opportunity to socialize.
>
> We have a Purim party, which is a lot of fun, and young people come from all over the city to attend it; many of them are Orthodox from birth. We do the same at Chanukkah. On Simchat Torah we have a great festivity, and the west side is just jammed. People come from all over the city and from elsewhere. They rent rooms in hotels nearby. We provide meals to those that want it. They pay for the meals, but the cost is nominal. There are thousands of young people on the west side at that time, and there is lots of mingling.
>
> Q. Do you get involved with individuals as well, in trying to arrange meetings or matches between people?
>
> A. We do, but mostly it's done informally. We haven't formalized it yet, although we're thinking about it. There seems to be a real need for it.

The associate rabbis of the synagogue take a personal interest in helping people to meet and offering words of advice in the course of the rocky road of courtship. And Rabbi Riskin takes it as his personal duty to be involved in advising prospective marriage partners. He meets with the bride and groom and seriously interviews them, making clear the attachment he feels for his protégés.

One couple reported the following:

> Bob. Rabbi Riskin takes a special interest in his own people. When I wanted to marry Ellen he insisted I had to come to see him first.
>
> Q. When did this happen?
>
> Ellen. I went to see him to discuss arrangements for my wedding. I feel very close to Rabbi Riskin. He wanted to talk to Bob, to find out more about him.
>
> Bob. I was in the synagogue too, but he really didn't know me. He asked many questions. He is as protective as a father.

Once they marry and have children, the newly Orthodox tend to move to other neighborhoods, where they generally join modernistic Orthodox

---

16. In some synagogues only men are permitted to vote. Single women, widows, and divorcees are thus disenfranchised.

congregations and integrate without difficulty. Some join traditionalistic Orthodox synagogues, and since they are capable of observing the Sabbath and of keeping kosher, they are accepted, although there are some insider customs of traditionalistic Orthodox communities that must be learned.

Those who have not married for several years may leave Orthodoxy altogether, another reason the synagogue makes strong efforts to find appropriate matches. One of the rabbis at the Lincoln Square Synagogue voiced the view that the available women seem more attractive and accomplished than the men, a complaint widely heard among singles in other circles in Manhattan.

But whereas in 1979–80 Rabbi Buchwald expressed some discouragement over the difficulties involved in matchmaking, in September of 1987 he proudly claimed that ba'alei t'shuva tend to marry at a greater rate than the Orthodox from birth. He noted that the beginners' service celebrates about fifty marriages a year, almost as many as the entire Lincoln Square Synagogue community.

Ideally, at Lincoln Square men should be married by thirty at the latest, women even younger. Informants suggest that those over forty may attend the minyan and be invited to people's homes for Shabbat, but as they do not easily fit in with the rest of the community, they will not be sought-after guests nor will they find ready acceptance in other Orthodox communities. Instead, they tend to develop their own social groups.

Conclusions

The Lincoln Square Synagogue's programs are organizational expressions of experiences that are similar to the personal experiences of returnees of a generation ago. Becoming Orthodox means not only learning and accepting beliefs and practices. It also means becoming part of a community of people who support each other's common customs, beliefs, values, and life-style. One gains full acceptance only as part of a family. Family is the center of religious activity and the critical building block of community.

Religion provides answers to some of the ultimate questions: the meaning of life and death, of suffering, of pain and joy. Taken together, the answers provided by a given religion make up a system. This meaning system requires social bases or supports for its continued existence. Family and community provide these supports; they are "plausibility structures," social structures that support common values, customs, and beliefs (Berger 1967, 46). In Orthodox Judaism family is the central plausibility structure. Within the family the individual acts out the central roles and rituals of religion. Synagogues provide cohesion to a community of disparate and relatively independent units through common public prayer, celebration, and particularly study. The Orthodox from birth move from family to synagogue and community. This results in a community not of single individuals, but of families. The newly Orthodox are connected to synagogue and community first and through them to Orthodox family life.

Chapter 3

Portals of Return: Yeshivot

Although Judaism is transmitted primarily in the home, some formal education is also required, and Jewish communities have provided schools for the study of Judaism. In Europe such a school on the elementary level was called a *cheder* (literally, "room," as in a one-room schoolhouse). In cheders boys were taught the Hebrew alphabet, the five books of Moses, the prayers, the Prophets, the rudiments of Hebrew, basic Jewish law and history, customs and even *Mishnah* (the collection of rulings of the Oral Law). (Girls usually received no formal religious training.) Yeshivot were advanced schools in which *Gemara* (commentary on the Mishnah), as well as the legal codes and their commentaries, was taught. They were generally attended by men from teenage years until marriage. Yeshivot were schools for the intellectual elite, designed to enable those with superior capabilities to acquire the knowledge and technical skills needed to "swim in the sea of the Talmud," to become leaders of the community and experts in Jewish religious practice.

Katz (1971, 187) describes the cheder as supplementing the knowledge of tradition that the child absorbed from the family, the synagogue, and the street. The cheder was found everywhere in the traditional Jewish society. Even the Jew living in a remote village sought a tutor for his children or sent them to a teacher in a nearby town.

The subject matter taught in the cheder was the Pentateuch with a translation into the vernacular and with Rashi's commentary. Each week the pupils learned the biblical portion of the week, which was read in the synagogue that Sabbath, and if they did not finish it by the end of the week they skipped over the last few chapters. This material formed the basic layer in the national and religious consciousness of the entire community.

Cheder was subordinate to synagogue, so as to prepare the pupils to follow the congregational prayers and the reading of the Torah on the Sabbath. Synagogal needs overrode curricular considerations (ibid., 190). By attending cheder a child learned to master the rudiments of tradition and was able to join the congregation in prayer and carry out the essential rituals (ibid., 191).

In contrast, the aim of yeshiva education was to turn the pupil into a scholar with a thorough training in Talmud. This goal "could only be achieved by a minority who were capable of benefiting from prolonged study at a yeshiva" (ibid, 191). The yeshiva created scholars with the highest intellectual training. "No one who had not devoted several years to intensive study could follow a lecture on their level or a learned discussion between them" (ibid, 194).

In traditional Jewish communities the average observant Jew did not have yeshiva education. Here the *kehillah* (the community and its governing body) was regarded as the major institution fostering community values, and the rabbi was the religious authority. The cheder was the educational base for the plausibility structure (a network of people supporting one another's beliefs and values) that we have called the "community of prayer." The yeshivot provided an additional plausibility structure, a "community of study" for the elite.

As societies underwent modernization, religion came to be separated from the state. Similarly, the kehillah began to disintegrate under pressure from secularism on the left and Chasidism on the right. Yeshivot took up the responsibility for being the community-wide standard-bearers of tradition.[1]

In America, where education was open to all, yeshivot lost their elite character and lowered their standards. The community of study came to be a broad-based network of relations supporting religious beliefs and values, overlapping the network associated with synagogue prayer and rituals. This community of study developed a competing authority structure, with the rosh yeshiva rather than the community rabbi as the leading authority.

JEWISH EDUCATION IN AMERICA

At the time that the Young Israel was building, another crucial development was taking place in the American community, a radical change in

---

1. Chasidic rebbes represented a competing source of authority, a challenge to both rabbi of the kehillah and the yeshiva (see Katz 1971, 231–244).

the level and style of education available to American-born Orthodox Jews. European Jews coming to America were familiar with Judaism through their exposure to shtetl life and their education in the cheder. Some had even attended the great centers of learning, the yeshivot of Europe. Perhaps the lower east side or other settlements of Jews in America were similar to the shtetl. And perhaps even the cheders bore some similarity to those in Europe despite the vast differences in support from the social environment. Nevertheless there were almost no indigenous American yeshiva students.

Religious education in America went through several stages that paralleled the waves of immigration. During the colonial period Jewish education was provided primarily by tutors or in congregational schools that supplemented the general schools. In the 1840s German Jewish congregations began day schools so that their children could avoid the public schools, which had a strongly Protestant flavor. In these day schools secular studies were emphasized, and little attention was paid to Hebrew or religious subjects. Still later, as religiously neutral public schools began to develop, Sunday schools provided Jewish education; and by 1870 all the Reform day schools had closed.

In the Old World shtetl before World War I, entry to religious Jewish life was through home, synagogue, and the cheder. When Eastern European Jews emigrated to America, the cheder began to develop as a replica of the schools in the shtetlakh of Europe. But whereas in Europe a boy spent the entire day in the cheder, in America he went to public school and attended the cheder for at most a few hours, after school.

In the new environment of America the cheder did not work. Teachers were untrained; facilities were crude. With no community to reinforce the lessons of the cheder and the "American street" competing with and negating its teachings, children refused to attend or performed at minimum levels. The cheder proved incapable of providing sufficient motivation for the children to continue to study and practice Judaism.[2]

When the shortcomings of the privately operated cheder became apparent, the talmud torah, a communally operated afternoon Hebrew school, was established.[3] Girls also attended these schools. The curricu-

2. Students were often sent to school with the teacher's fee in hand, a practice demeaning to the teacher (see Philip Roth's description of the cheder in *Goodbye Columbus*, 1959).

3. Talmud Torahs had developed in some of the larger towns in Europe to provide education for orphans and the children of the indigent, who could not afford the tuition for the cheder. (see Zborowski and Herzog 1952). Similarly named

lum included Hebrew, history, Bible, customs, ceremonies, and prayers. The community talmud torah attempted to remedy the cheder's lack of facilities and its staff's lack of training and supervision.

By the 1920s Eastern European Jews were growing more respectable. Many had been in the United States for a decade, a generation, or even longer. Clearly the overwhelming majority were leaving Orthodoxy. Some were secularists or Yiddishists.[4] Others were Reform or Conservative. For a long period of time, to be Conservative was simply to be a committed shtetl Jew with a strong desire to be part of American society. Some, however, feared that the changes introduced by the Conservative movement went too far, and some of the American-born children remained Orthodox Jews. For whatever reason, despite losses to assimilation a small indigenous American Orthodoxy was developing. This could be seen most clearly in the growth of the Young Israel movement but existed in many other Orthodox synagogues as well.

Most of the Orthodox received their religious education in talmud torahs. These schools functioned until the early 1950s and then declined as Eastern European Jews moved from the thickly populated urban Jewish communities to the suburbs following World War II. Others received their religious training in suburban congregational schools that had begun to be established as early as the turn of the century. As the overwhelming majority of suburban synagogues were either Reform or Conservative, the congregational schools were overwhelmingly non-Orthodox.[5] Only the talmud torahs were bastions of Orthodoxy. From one perspective, the differences between talmud torah and congregational school were not substantial; both were afternoon and Sunday schools, peripheral to the life of their students. In neither type of school was *Talmud* studied, for the schools were seen not as training grounds for scholars but as means to prepare pupils for congregational prayer. The difference between them was in the mode of worship each supported.

---

schools had been developed even earlier in Turkey (*Encyclopedia Judaica*). The word *talmud* means study. The name *Talmud torah* does not imply that the Talmud (that is, Mishnah and Gemara) were studied there.

4. In the United States the Communist-oriented association for preserving and developing Yiddish culture was known as the Yiddisher Kultur Farband. A larger group of those sympathetic to its perspective, which saw preservation of the Yiddish language rather than Judaism as essential to the continuation of Jewish peoplehood, were commonly called Yiddishists.

5. Louis Wirth's discussion of the "second area of settlement" suggests an inexorable tendency for synagogues in the suburbs *not* to be Orthodox. (1928, chap. 12).

Conservative congregational schools provided educational support for participation in the Conservative synagogue. The use of Hebrew in prayer, for example, required that children learn Hebrew and therefore that they attend classes after school several days a week, often for two or more years, until they were bar mitzvahed, accepted into the congregation as an adult. For Reform congregations, where Hebrew was minimally used in the prayer service and where the services were conducted by religious leaders rather than laity, attendance at congregational school on Saturday or Sunday was sufficient for participation in the worship service.

For Orthodox congregations, where lay leadership of the services prevailed and traditional Hebrew prayers were used, still more rigorous training was required to facilitate the transmission of worship skills to the new generation. In fact talmud torahs provided twice the yearly number of instructional hours provided by congregational schools (four hundred hours versus two hundred). For all that, these schools aimed simply at training students for participation in the congregation.

But even talmud torahs were not fully capable of transmitting commitment to Orthodox Judaism. Many students showed only minimal interest in these schools despite efforts to improve the facilities, train teachers more effectively, and make the curriculum more relevant. Most students did not become Orthodox adults.

Yeshiva Etz Chaim (the forerunner of Yeshiva University) had been teaching high school and college-age students since 1886. At the beginning of the century, several new yeshivot intended for elementary school pupils were formed. In the 1920s beginning with Yeshiva Torah Vodaath a number of yeshiva high schools were organized. Students attended school from 9 A.M. to 6 P.M. Sunday through Thursday and to 1 P.M. on Friday. At least half the day was devoted to Jewish subjects—Hebrew, Bible, history, laws and customs, and prayers—and the rest to secular subjects. In addition, when boys were ten or eleven they were introduced to the study of Talmud as a major part of the curriculum.

In a short period of time vast changes took place in the structure of Jewish education. Cheders dominated the Jewish educational scene at the turn of the century. From the 1920s through the 1940s the community talmud torah and congregational schools were the mainstay of Jewish education. By the late 1960s the talmud torahs had been replaced by the congregational schools and yeshivot (day schools).[6] The most unusual aspect of the new elementary school yeshivot was that by providing both a

6. In 1967, 42.2 percent of the children who attended Jewish schools did so for

general and a religious education they effectively cut the child off from the secularizing influence of the larger community—at least during the school day. Religious educators hoped that this feature would reduce assimilatory pressures. And there seems little reason to doubt that the yeshivot have been more successful in transmitting Judaism than were the preceding institutions.

But the separatism central to the structure and success of the yeshivot cut students off from Jewish students in the public schools. Until the 1940s the attendance of many Orthodox children at the after-school talmud torah obscured this effect. But by the end of the 1950s a sharp increase in the number of students in yeshivot, together with a sharp decline in the number of students in talmud torahs as Orthodox Jews moved to the suburbs, led to a gap between Orthodox and non-Orthodox Jewish schoolchildren. Orthodoxy was emerging as a separate world of Jewish experience, cut off to some extent from other Jews, as well as from the wider society.

Yeshiva education took two directions. Influenced by the European model, it sought to educate scholars. In some schools, students were introduced to the study of Talmud at age ten, and within a year or so Talmud had become the major part of their curriculum. For a portion of Orthodox Judaism this emphasis on the study of Talmud grew through the 1950s and 1960s, resulting in a major expansion of higher yeshivot and further separation between the Orthodox and other Jews.

But many educators were sensitive to the danger of separating Orthodox from non-Orthodox children and attempted to fashion yeshivot that could bridge the gap between them. This concern gave rise to the day schools.[7] Started about a generation later than the first wave of yeshivot in America, these schools were open to both boys and girls. Presumably the aim was to go beyond preparing students for participation in the synagogue, but the further goals were unclear. What was clear was that a separate educational system was necessary. The Conservative movement began developing the Solomon Schechter schools, a day school system parallel to that of the Orthodox.

In America, then, the yeshiva had become a separatist institution used

---

one day a week, and 44.4 percent attended two to five days a week. Almost all the rest attended day schools.

7. These are also called yeshivot. As children attended these schools all day, they were also termed "day schools." The term day school is sometimes used to distinguish coeducational Orthodox schools from yeshivot for boys only. Day school yeshivot also placed greater emphasis on secular education than did yeshivot for boys only.

almost exclusively by the Orthodox for the education of their children. As time went on it became virtually the only educational institution for Orthodox children as the cheder and the talmud torah faded. On the elementary level, yeshivot primarily educated young children for participation in synagogue services. On the high school level and beyond, they provided training in religious scholarship and entry to the community where study was thought of, at least in part, as religious devotion rather than merely an educational experience.

New Strategies: Summer Camps, Torah Institutes, and Chavurot

The cheder was a traditional institutional response to the need to provide religious education for children. The after-school talmud torah and the elementary school yeshiva were uniquely American educational responses to the new context of the open society, but both were traditional in structure and curriculum.

In the post–World War II period, when few American Jews were European immigrants and many were second generation Americans, the problem of providing the experience of Jewish living—previously of little concern to those who had grown up in the ghettos of Europe with richly Jewish lives—now came to be seen as major. When it became clear that the formal educational structures of talmud torah and congregational school could not provide that experience, summer camps, Torah institutes, and *chavurot* were developed to fill this void.

Jewish educational camping began in 1919 as an attempt to continue the influence of Jewish school during the summer vacation.[8] Yiddish-language camps soon followed, and in 1941 the Hebrew-speaking camp movement began with the establishment of Camp Masad. In these camps kashrut was strictly observed, as were the Sabbath and worship service, although formal study was not a major component of camp life.

By the 1940s a number of yeshivot including Lubavitch, Torah Vodaath, and Chaim Berlin, as well as the Agudat Israel movement (traditionalistic Orthodox) all had summer camps designed specifically to transmit the Orthodox Jewish way of life to children. A major component of camp life was a program of formal classes for the study of the Pentateuch, the Talmud, and Jewish laws.[9]

8. The Central Jewish Institute founded the first camp, later known as Cejwin (*Encyclopedia Judaica*).

9. The first of the Ramah camps was founded in 1947 under the aegis of the

But summer camps were designed for youngsters aged six to sixteen. Nothing was available for people of college age until 1950, when Shlomo Bardin began using the Brandeis Institute (founded in 1941) on the west coast as a retreat at which young adults raised in nonreligious homes could experience Jewish living. Two years later Yeshiva University developed the Torah Leadership Seminars.

Unlike the other programs the Brandeis Institute and the Torah Leadership Seminars were for sixteen to twenty-two year olds who had little or no background in Judaism. These programs developed a nucleus of people, many themselves newly Orthodox, who became the leaders of those involved in attracting ba'alei t'shuva. They provided the ground for experimenting with programs and materials that could reach young people. But the seminars typically lasted for only four days, sufficient time to generate some enthusiasm and interest but not enough to be a basis for commitment. Those interested in becoming Orthodox had no opportunity to learn more or to continue living an Orthodox life.

Orthodox summer camps for children sometimes did provide a follow-up for the few non-Orthodox who attended them, particularly camps that were extensions of the yeshivot. At the end of a four- or eight-week stay at camp, those interested were encouraged to continue their education at the yeshiva during the school year. And as some of these yeshivot had dormitory facilities, observance of kashrut or Sabbath could continue. But for the young person of college age no facility existed to offer basic education. Anyone in the upper level of a yeshiva was assumed to have been attending yeshiva all along; knowledge of Judaism was assumed to be cumulative and was taken for granted. In effect such an attitude meant that a person could make the choice to be an Orthodox Jew (or have the choice made for him) only once, at the point when he was ready to enter the first grade of a yeshiva elementary school. Failure to make that choice at that time precluded further opportunity to learn how to be an Orthodox Jew.[10] Thus although the Torah Leadership Seminar and the Brandeis Institute represented new institutional responses to the needs of persons interested in learning about Judaism after childhood, they lacked a follow-up capability.

Jewish Theological Seminary to provide a similar camping experience with religious development at its center for children in the Conservative wing of Judaism (*Encyclopedia Judaica*).

10. In the late 1940s and early 1950s some yeshivot developed evening programs and storefront schools for high school students with little background.

Chavurot began as study group seminaries in the late 1960s.[11] Their development and growth paralleled those of the counterculture of the time.[12] The leaders of the first and most successful chavurah, Chavurat Shalom of Boston, were people who had spent time in the Ramah camps under the auspices of the Conservative Jewish Theological Seminary (Sklare 1974). For many the camp, not the observant family, was their only experience in Jewish living.

The camp style of life was closer in many respects to the communal styles of the youth culture than to the family styles of traditional homes. The experimental and experiential emphasis in the Ramah camps also paralleled these same emphases in the youth culture (Sklare 1974). The typical chavurah was a loose association of people who sought self-expression as well as intense involvement in Jewish life. It gave play to new forms and modes of worship, emphasizing the charismatic, emotional, and personal-growth aspects of Judaism.

Conservative Judaism did not develop a community of study—that is, a plausibility structure based on study as ritual. Hence the chavurah, an organizational response to return, came to be identified with the house of prayer rather than the house of study, as its beginnings suggested. This seems related to the nature of authority in the chavurah. Because it was not bound to halakhah, it could attempt forms of celebration in violation of rules followed by Orthodoxy. Thus it was not a path into Orthodoxy at all but rather a path into those forms of Judaism that did not accept halakhah as the final arbiter—that is, either Conservative or Reform Judaism.

The chavurah nevertheless had an impact on the return to Orthodoxy. Although few of those who spent time in a chavurah became Orthodox, many did learn of Orthodox practice through the *Jewish Catalog*. More important, the catalog, with its sympathetic portrayal of Jewish religious practice, made involvement with Judaism legitimate, and even fashionable. The notion of a living arrangement devoted to Jewish life, where

11. Mordechai Kaplan (1881–1986), the founder of Reconstructionism (an offshoot of Conservative Judaism that sought to reorient Judaism from salvation in the next world to salvation in this world), advocated establishing chavurot in 1943, and Havurat Shalom was established in 1946. Chavurot did not develop into a movement until the 1960s (Raphael 1984, 64; Reisman 1977, 7ff).

12. The connection between the chavurah and the counterculture can be seen in *The Jewish Catalog*, which describes itself as a Jewish *Whole Earth Catalogue*. Its three different versions (1974, 1976, 1978) were all written and edited by members of Chavurat Shalom (see also Sklare 1974).

worship and religious studies were pursued without concern for grades, facilitated acceptance of yeshiva as an alternative life-style.

Orthodoxy and the "World of the Yeshiva"

Orthodoxy is not monolithic. The Orthodox divide themselves into the *chasidishe velt* (literally, the chasidic world; more accurately, the chasidic community), the *yeshivishe velt* (the yeshiva community, or those who consider themselves loyal to the heads of yeshivot), and the so-called modern Orthodox.

Members of the chasidishe velt are identifiable by their style of dress, particularly black suits and hats, or the *streimel* (a hat trimmed with fur) and *bekeshe* (a black satin robe) for special occasions, as well as *peyot* (side locks) and untrimmed beards. Similarly, the members of the yeshivishe velt are often identified by their dark suits and fedoras and perhaps sideburns or, occasionally, trimmed beards. Not all of those who are part of these communities adopt their characteristic garb, but a significant core do, and the community is thus identifiable. The modern Orthodox seem not to be identifiable by dress, except that they wear hats or, for religious observances, kippot or skullcaps.

Identification with the chasidishe velt automatically means identification with a specific rebbe and his followers. One cannot be a part of this community otherwise. Identification with the yeshivishe velt does not ordinarily mean loyalty or attachment to one yeshiva, but it does imply that one has accepted the authority of the heads of yeshivot.

Sociologists classify authority structures of churches following the lead of Troeltsch (1931) as ecclesiastical (hierarchical), congregational (independent, lay-led, and democratic), or presbyterian (subject to the authority of a board of clerics, themselves equal). The structure of religious authority in the Orthodox Jewish community is quite different. Perhaps it can best be understood by reflecting that prior to modern times Jewish religious authority resided in the kehillah, the community, which through democratic processes appointed a rabbi and selected one or more community leaders who then saw to all community needs, including education, kosher food, religious courts, and representation to the government. Although the rabbi was elected by the community, once he was elected his power was based on his expertise in Jewish law. As Katz has pointed out (1971, 197) the yeshiva, if a community had one, was also subject to the authority of the rabbi.

In Europe, the structure of the kehillah was undermined by Chasidism, by Emancipation and Enlightenment, and by the upheavels of the Jewish population. The American Jewish community never developed a kehillah, nor did American rabbis ever exercise the authority held by their European counterparts.[13] A different structure of authority emerged in America, in which in some parts of the Orthodox community the sense of "we-ness" emerges from identification with Orthodoxy as a community of prayer whereas in other parts of the Orthodox community it emerges from identification with Orthodoxy as a community of study.

The distinction made here is not identical with that made in the Orthodox community. Although the term *yeshivishe velt* is more or less equivalent to what we are calling the "community of study," the latter term includes those who study but are not followers of the heads of yeshivot, whereas yeshivishe velt includes those who do *not* study but are loyal followers of the heads of yeshivot. The distinction is important because those with solid erudition in talmudic and sacred studies may differ substantially from the yeshivishe velt in their attitudes on such issues as secular education, the place of women, and the State of Israel. At the same time, many of those who consider themselves part of the ye-shivishe velt offer their loyalties to this world and identify with it in dress and customs while regarding study primarily as a devotion rather than as an instrument of education.

The yeshivishe velt consists not only of the scholars capable of independent talmudic study but of various levels of participation. The *gedolim* (great talmudic sages) are those with encyclopedic knowledge of the Talmud and the halakhic literature, who have earned world fame through their students, disciples, followers, and occasionally *responsa* (replies to questions regarding halakhah) and *novellea* (innovative interpretations of the Talmud). More than anything else, they are leaders of communities in a broadly political and religious sense. Next are the talmidei cha-chamim (disciples of the wise), some of whom may be as knowledgeable as gedolim but lack a following. Below that is the level of *b'nai* Torah or *b'nai yeshiva* (literally, sons of Torah or sons of yeshiva), who have

---

13. An attempt was made to establish a kehillah in New York City in the early twentieth century, but this ended in failure. Not even the various chasidic communities, such as Bobov, Satmar, and Lubavitch, or the German-Jewish refugee community of Rabbi Breuer could exercise the power of the kehillah in Europe, which often had government support and wielded powerful control in a closed society. In contrast, in the open society of America, leaving a community is a far more viable option for dissidents, and this limits community control.

studied in a yeshiva and are capable of following a lecture or discussion and often knowledgeable enough to study the Talmud independently. More important, as the appellation indicates they are followers of some leader or school. They take the roshei yeshiva as their religious authority rather than the rabbi of their congregation. In the world of the yeshiva the rosh yeshiva is the ultimate authority. The yeshivishe velt, then, consists of all of the above-mentioned types of students of the Talmud and their wives and children. It is not simply a colleagueship of scholars; it is a community.

Identification with this community manifests itself in dress, political attitudes, and attitudes toward culture and education. These values and norms are not halakhically prescribed; those who hold different views or who dress differently are still considered Orthodox so long as they adhere to the rules of kashrut and Shabbat. Many newly Orthodox gain entry to this community through ba'al t'shuva yeshivot.

Beginnings of the American Ba'al T'shuva Yeshivot

YESHIVOT

The yeshiva can provide entrance into the community of study for those reared in Orthodox families. The ba'al t'shuva yeshiva not only introduces the person to the world of learning, it also socializes him into the yeshivishe velt, with its unique emphases, customs, and practices, which are not necessarily limited to halakhah.

In fact, for the majority the ba'al t'shuva yeshiva provides only sufficient skills to enable the students to participate in prayer and to conduct their private lives as Orthodox Jews. During the typical period of study in the yeshiva (from a few months to about three years) students do not become capable of studying the Talmud on their own but may be motivated and prepared sufficiently to be able to enter a regular yeshiva. After several additional years of study the student might acquire the skills necessary for independent Talmud study. In any case, study at a yeshiva validates one's entry to the yeshivishe velt.

One wonders how yeshivot, institutions with a tradition of elitism, got involved in the recruitment of people to Orthodox Judaism. Even granting that yeshivot play a different role in America than in Europe, the world of yeshivot still constitutes a tiny community within the already small community of Orthodoxy and one that by and large cut itself off from the mainstream of society even more radically than did the rest of

Orthodoxy. How, then, did yeshivot come to reach out to others? What did these new recruits feel the yeshivot had to offer them? If one can join Orthodoxy through the synagogue, why go to a yeshiva? Approaching this question in a historical perspective will permit us to see the changing meanings and advantages of joining a yeshiva in the past few decades.

As early as the 1940s a number of yeshivot had already started to provide dormitory facilities for students with limited backgrounds in Orthodoxy. Dormitories had originally been intended to house students from Orthodox families who came from places outside of New York City. Yeshiva University had opened its dormitory in 1921 (Klaperman 1969, 146). By the early 1940s at least seven yeshivot had dormitory facilities, primarily for Orthodox-from-birth students from outside New York City. Once yeshivot developed experience in surrogate parenting of out-of-towners from Orthodox families, they saw no bar to offering these facilities even to those with limited educational background in Judaism.

One such group of students came not as a result of a recruiting campaign but as a result of attempts to raise funds for yeshivot in Central and South American countries. The *meshulachim* (fund-raisers) found that contributors to yeshivot in those countries were also concerned that their own sons receive a Jewish education that was not available to them. Several yeshivot, notably Yeshiva Torah Vodaath and Tomchie Temimim of Lubavitch in Brooklyn, recognized a need to admit a number of students from these countries. In addition to meeting the needs of their donors, the yeshivot were also enlarging their student bodies. But probably most compelling was the ideological reason. *Harbatzat Torah* (the dissemination of Torah), particularly among those who wished to learn it, was a great mitzvah. Indeed it was one of the raisons d'être of the yeshiva.

By the early 1950s, for example, students from Central and South America attending Mesivta Torah Vodaath in Brooklyn numbered about forty in a total enrollment of about three hundred. These students were not ba'alei t'shuva. Most of them were not at the yeshiva by their own choice but had been sent by their parents. Most were between the ages of thirteen and sixteen. By the accounts of the recruiters, the parents had been reared and educated in Europe as traditional Orthodox Jews, but many had lapsed in their practice and few had given their children a religious education. Most of the children, therefore, neither practiced nor knew Orthodox Judaism.

These students were viewed as "lacking background" rather than lacking commitment. They were assumed to be motivated by the same concerns and goals as other students at the yeshiva. No special programs were developed to introduce them to Judaism or to deal with the unique questions that would be raised when someone was introduced, for example, to the story of Adam and Eve at age fourteen rather than at age seven or eight. Yeshiva staffs assumed that all that was needed was the opportunity for these boys to attend classes, even before basic skills in reading and writing Hebrew were developed. Students were simply placed in lower grades until they had mastered the skills of these grades and then were moved up through the grades as quickly as their own development would allow. Within a year or so they would normally be put into classes only about a year below their age level, and after perhaps another year they might reach the grade level appropriate for their age.

The broad effect of school dormitories was to generate adjustments that were helpful to those with limited educational backgrounds. Some of the *rebbis* (teachers of religious subjects) had developed reputations as sympathetic and warm people who could be counted on for advice and assistance. The student who approached them could feel confident that they would be responsive to his needs rather than to institutional considerations or ideological position. Some rebbis came to be father surrogates, sought out for advice on a variety of personal issues. Families to which the boys were sent for the Sabbath meals became surrogate families, often developing strong ties with the boys. Jack M. was not atypical. He had his Sabbath and holiday meals at the same home from the time he was thirteen until he was twenty-one. He considered himself and was considered a member of the family, attending weddings and funerals and maintaining close ties with the family for years after he left the yeshiva.

As a result, when students from non-Orthodox homes entered yeshivot, a number of facilities were already in place. The schools had dormitories, cafeterias, student counselors, a few teachers who were sympathetic and would reach out to them, and a network of families in the neighborhood who were willing to take them in for Sabbath and holidays.

Another group of students from non-Orthodox homes also attended Yeshiva Torah Vodaath even earlier than the 1940s. These were students whose parents had themselves been raised in Orthodoxy and had practiced Orthodox Judaism until they came to America. Once here they found it impossible to earn a living without working on the Sabbath. Nevertheless, they still retained their strong ties to Judaism. They saw their work on the Sabbath not as a rejection of the religion of their fathers but as a painful necessity. For example, Mr. M. ran a grocery store, keeping it open on Sabbath and on religious holidays. He sent his sons to

Yeshiva Torah Vodaath from elementary school through high school. To give them the home background necessary for their continued Jewishness, he encouraged them to develop close ties with the family of a rabbi in his neighborhood whose sons also attended Torah Vodaath. The grocer's sons visited the rabbi's house regularly on Sabbath and the holidays, sometimes having their meals there. The grocer himself, a friendly man, developed close ties to the rabbi. The grocer's sons grew into Orthodox Jews and today still practice Orthodox Judaism. One was ordained as a rabbi. All send their children to yeshivot.

Although a sizable proportion of those whom the yeshiva took under its wing were sent by their parents, substantial numbers attended the yeshiva out of their own conscious decision. Indeed, many students attended the yeshiva over their parents' opposition.

Haskel K. lived at the edges of Williamsburg and had attended the Stone Avenue Talmud Torah for several years. Haskel's father was not Orthodox, although he had been brought up as an Orthodox boy in Europe. In the United States he had discarded religion. He was not opposed to it, he was simply uncommitted. Haskel's mother, on the other hand, was a deeply religious woman who kept a kosher home, observed the Sabbath, and taught her children all she knew about the practices of Judaism. One of the teachers at the Stone Avenue Talmud Torah took an interest in Haskel and, noticing his seriousness, suggested that he attend Yeshiva Torah Vodaath. Haskel had a checkered career at the school, which he found not only difficult but strange. Sometimes he performed well, at other times he did not attend. Eventually he came to take it seriously, went on to be ordained as a rabbi, became a businessman (a not uncommon pattern in Orthodox circles), married, and had children who are themselves Orthodox.

The early 1940s were a period in which yeshiva high schools and seminaries were growing, and some of the yeshivot with an infrastructure capable of supporting ba'alei t'shuva began to accept and educate so-called students of limited background. None were engaged in systematic outreach.

OUTREACH EFFORTS

By the late 1940's a change had begun to occur. Zalman Schachter describes Lubavitch efforts.

> During the Second World War the rebbe here in New York published three *kol korehs* [proclamations] saying its the days of the Messiah, the

golus [diaspora] is burning down. Lubavitch began to establish a string of elementary yeshivot first in the Bronx, then Bridgeport, New Haven,—Hartford was building its own yeshiva—Wooster, Springfield, Providence, Boston, that line; later in Rochester, where I was principal for a year, in Buffalo, and in Chicago.

We would wait in front of the public schools to pick up the kids during the release hour time for religious instruction. We'd tell them stories and sing songs and try to sell them on a talmud torah [after-school Hebrew school] or better on a day school. When we got the day school started we were the bus drivers, the nursemaids, and the teachers. For the secular stuff we got lady teachers who wanted to work part-time. The rest we did ourselves.

But I was not satisfied working the little *kinderlach* [children]. I wanted people to talk with. At that time, the Conservative movement had a Young People's League. But they weren't doing much. So we organized the Junior Cultural Council and started *farbrengens*[social gatherings] and taught them *niggunim* [religious songs] and to meditate—the chasidic word is *hitbodedut* [literally, to be alone, in solitude]. This was about 1949.

The college campus did not at first seem to be a fertile ground for their efforts. Until the post–World War II period those Jews who went to college generally chose a New York City institution, particularly the city's municipal colleges. But the end of the war also saw the end of quota systems against Jews at more prestigious colleges, and the G.I. Bill of Rights provided the funds for lower-income Jews to take advantage of this opportunity. The Orthodox community became aware of the scope of this change some time after, and thus it was only in the mid-1950s that Carlebach and Schachter thought to take their recruiting efforts to the campuses.

An interview with Shlomo Carlebach fills in another part of this developing outreach program.

> I worked for the rebbe for three years from 1951 to 1954. The rebbe sent me to yeshivot. I came from the Lakewood Yeshiva, and I was good in learning [Talmud study].
>
> Q. Why was he sending you to yeshivot where students were already Orthodox?
> A. To teach them Lubavitch Torah.
> Q. Did the yeshivot permit this?
> A. Unofficially. I would just hang around and talk to the students. I went to the big yeshivot in New York, Chicago, Detroit, Cleveland . . . and I talked about *chasidut*. I didn't stop anybody on the street and ask "Are you Jewish?" I became their friend first and only slowly talked about these ideas. I brought hundreds of kids to Lubavitch.

On Labor Day 1954 I decided to go to Atlantic City [then a Jewish resort area with several kosher hotels]. I talked to people and invited them to chasidut classes in New York. Saturday night I was walking on the board-walk and passed the Breakers, a kosher hotel. It was crowded with hundreds of people. I decided this is my thing. I took out a *sefer* [religious book] and was reading. Out of nowhere a boy and girl come up to me and asked "Are you a rabbi?" I said yes. They wanted to talk to me. They introduced me to their whole group. I don't know what I told them or what I sang with them, but at 4:30 that morning I rented a motel, brought out my *tefillin* [small black leather boxes containing portions of Scripture, worn by men during weekday morning prayers], and they put them on, one after the other. It was one of the holiest nights in my life.

Several such evenings convinced Carlebach that he had the ability to reach out to others. He and Zalman Schachter decided to try their hand at some of the campuses, where they knew substantial populations of Jews could be reached. Schachter describes it.

We were sitting around the rebbe's *tish* [literally, "table." In chasidic circles this refers to a festive Sabbath or holiday meal at which the rebbeh speaks to his chasidim]. It was *Yud Tess Kislev* [the nineteenth of the Hebrew month of Kislev, the day on which the first Lubavitcher Rebbe, Schneur Zalman of Lyadi, was freed from the Russian prison where he had been held on political charges. This is a major holiday for Lubavitcher chasidim]. The rebbe was talking about people in universities. I said to Shlomo who was standing next to me, "Next week is Chanukkah. Let's take the car and go to Boston; there's Harvard, there's B.U., there's Brandeis that just started. Let's see what we can do." I got about a dozen old sets of tefillin fixed and polished up and some old siddurim that included English translations. We had an accordion and an old tape recorder on which I had about an hour's worth of chasidic music, and we made it up to Brandeis and started our thing. Shlomo would tell the *ma'asehs* [stories of rebbes] and would wait for the few customers that would raise questions. Someone would say, "Do you guys believe in evolution?" And I would say, "Do we believe in evolution?" and start my own speil.

Q. How did you do this?

A. We just came into the cafeteria. They were having a Chanukkah dance and eating *latkes* [potato pancakes, a traditional dish for the holiday]. The lights were off. There was only a spotlight playing on the couples. The jukebox was playing. When we came in they turned the lights on. They wanted to see who these characters with beards were. There weren't so many beards around in those days except in Williamsburg and Crown Heights. I put on the tape-recorder. Someone unplugged the jukebox, we laid out our literature and just started shilling.

We did this many times at Brandeis and tried it at other places too. Shlomo would say "Chanukkah, Chanukkah. You lit the candles on the outside, but have you lit them on the inside?" It just opened things up.

In those days I was the music man, having set the Lubavitcher niggunim [melodies] to some words like "For the fate of my soul, I search for a goal, and I find none other than You." Shlomo hadn't yet discovered his singing and music thing. So people would hear, for the first time, something like a spiritual with an Eastern European melody, and a feeling of davening. This created a fine spirit and people wanted to know "What do we do next?"

At Brandeis . . . we told them that if—with instructions—you could put on and take off tefillin three times without problems the pair of tefillin are yours.

With the boys it was easy. With the girls we were stymied. We didn't know what to do, what to tell them.

Q. Did you do this sort of thing again?

A. Sure. It came to be expected. Word got out among the *shamosim* [sextons] in Fall River, New Bedford, Providence, Newport, and Boston to save old tefillin for us. The Hillel Director at Brown was sympathetic and it worked out to a once a month trip to that area. We tried B.U. and Harvard, but B.U. didn't have a Hillel House yet and sitting around the cafeteria didn't work well. You have to control the scene. At Harvard the Hillel Director couldn't see it as anything except lectures. So Brandeis was it for us.

The Lubavitcher community could also offer the opportunity to learn more about Orthodoxy without itself having to make major institutional adjustments. People who wished to learn were invited to the homes of the rebbe's followers in Crown Heights, Brooklyn. They would spend a Shabbat or a holiday there, and in addition to simply enjoying the hospitality and the experience of celebrating holidays in the Orthodox manner, they would attend the Lubavitch prayers, meet members of the community, and perhaps even meet with the Rebbe. Members of the Lubavitch community were eager to accommodate such people. A Lubavitcher informant put it this way. "They say that if you want to attract attention at Lubavitch and get people to fall all over you just drive up to the shul (synagogue) on Shabbos with a big cigar and then walk in. In a minute you'll have a hundred invitations. Everyone wants to make a ba'al t'shuva. If you just come to daven, no one will notice you."

THE DEVELOPMENT OF YESHIVOT FOR THOSE "LACKING BACKGROUND"

Lubavitch was the first to recruit among college students through Carlebach and Schachter. Because of its cohesion, size, and developed institutional structures, the Lubavitcher community could offer a range of social and integrative opportunities beyond those the yeshiva was capable of offering—a rebbe, a neighborhood, friends—in a word, *community* in the full sense. Lubavitch did not feel the need to open a ba'al t'shuva yeshiva until 1972.

In the interim, others had begun to develop schools specifically for those with so-called limited backgrounds, schools that would enable even those of college age to get a basic education in Judaism if they had none and would permit those with a bit of education to proceed further.

YESHIVA HEYCHAL HATORAH

Perhaps this story and the story of some of those who became Orthodox in the early 1950s is best told by a rabbi who now heads a major national Orthodox organization.

> I was a student at Heychal Hatorah from September 1952 to January 1955. When I came the yeshiva had been in existence for several years. [It was founded in 1948.] People who had no background and could hardly read Hebrew could come to Yeshiva Heychal Hatorah and be given teachers and classes in beginning Talmud or *Chumash,* the very beginning of Jewish education.
>
> The yeshiva was located in East New York, which had been a flourishing Jewish community but was declining very rapidly. We had about thirty students in the yeshiva. Not all were ba'alei t'shuva. There were some who came from Orthodox backgrounds. I would say it was about 75 percent ba'alei t'shuva and 25 percent people who had always been Orthodox. It was for post-high-school students, although there were one or two who were younger, and they finished high school by going to night school.
>
> Most of the ba'alei t'shuva were out-of-towners. One fellow I studied with was from Milwaukee. He was only fourteen years old, and he was going to high school at night. But he was one of the youngest people.
>
> The founders of the yeshiva, Judah and Jacob London were graduates of Yeshiva Chofetz Chaim of Brooklyn. Their parents' home in Williamsburg was open to all students in the yeshiva who couldn't return to their own homes for Shabbat. There was no dormitory; sleeping arrangements were made for the boys in different homes in East New York and Williamsburg, and they would have their meals at the Londons'. That was an important factor in keeping the boys in the yeshiva. They had a home in the Londons' home. Mr. and Mrs. London were truly generous and they were fully involved in this missionary zeal of the London brothers. Their unmarried sister and an aunt helped with this work.
>
> The yeshiva also provided meals. For example, I went to Brooklyn College at night as did many of the students, and there was supper for those who were part of that dormitory system. About a dozen or so ate at the yeshiva. I ate

there quite regularly because I never had a chance to go home to Borough Park before leaving for my college classes.

Tuition was very low. If you couldn't afford it you were not pressured. It's a mystery to me how they existed financially. They had some supporters. The students in the yeshiva were also sent out as teams to try to raise funds and recruit students to the yeshiva. I remember going one Sunday with an older student to the farmlands of New Jersey. We had a list of potential students and we visited their homes.

Q. What was the program in Heychal Hatorah?

A. We had classes in Chumash [Pentateuch] and *dinim* [laws]. But I can only recall the gemara. We learned chumash with more advanced students, and we caught on very quickly.

Q. What about study of Jewish philosophy or of ideas that might persuade students to become Orthodox?

A. We didn't formally study Jewish philosophy, but there were discussions with the Londons on religion or any other topic. And there was a lot of personal counseling. I was generally not involved in this but others were. For example, this fourteen-year-old boy from Minneapolis that I mentioned—I guess Rabbi London was sort of his father. He talked to them about everything. I think a lot of the religious molding occurred at the Shabbat meals at the Londons' house. I was told that these meals would take hours and at the meal there was discussion of all sorts of topics.

Q. What were the intellectual problems that students faced in becoming Orthodox?

A. Most students became *frum* [pious or religious] without much problem. It seems to me that when we came to the yeshiva we were 98 percent committed. A lot of the boys were sent by rabbis who had influenced them. They were already on the road to religiosity. At Heychal Hatorah the job was mainly to catch up in education rather than observance. You didn't find a fellow who was a *mechallel Shabbat* [violator of Shabbat laws] after he came in. But he might not have known a given rule. And after a couple of months they became very committed.

YESHIVA UNIVERSITY

While Yeshiva Heychal Hatorah remained small, Yeshiva University, building from a different base, succeeded in reaching a far greater number of people, and its recruits and teachers became the vanguard of those active with ba'alei t'shuva elsewhere.

In the period following World War II almost two hundred thousand survivors of the Holocaust (Fishman 1973, 249) came to the United States, among them many chasidim. They settled primarily in the New York City area. Several thousands more came in the wake of the Hungarian revolution of 1956. As a result American Orthodoxy suddenly found itself no longer at the extreme right of the Jewish religious spectrum; another group, the newly arrived East European chasidim, were still further right. At the same time suburbanization, which the Conservative movement had already experienced prior to the war, now became the mode for Orthodoxy as well.

Between 1945 and 1960 Yeshiva University and its Community Service Division (CSD) helped establish more than a hundred synagogues in the United States and Canada. These synagogues, situated mainly in the newly developing suburbs and in areas recently opened to Jews, included some of the wealthiest, most prestigious, and largest Orthodox synagogues. The Lincoln Square Synagogue of Rabbi Steven Riskin and the Montreal Synagogue of Rabbi David Hartman were among them. As new synagogues were founded, people turned to Yeshiva University for assistance in finding rabbis, cantors, and teachers. Yeshiva responded by developing programs to meet these needs.

Yeshiva University encouraged the development of congregational schools in the Orthodox community, and these schools often became the nucleus of yeshiva day schools. It founded the first yeshiva high school for girls in the United States in 1948, the Teachers Institute for Women in 1952, and the Stern College for Women in 1954. This last for the first time offered young women a college-level program combined with a Jewish curriculum (Klaperman 1969, 179).

When Orthodox rabbis turned to Yeshiva University in the early 1950s for assistance in teaching Judaism to young adults who lacked education in the fundamentals of Orthodoxy, Yeshiva responded by creating the Torah Leadership Seminars. The seminars lasted from three to ten days. The first one was held at the Yeshiva campus; subsequent seminars were held at the sites of summer camps after the camping season or at small hotels. The central experiential piece of the seminar was the Shabbat, celebrated in common with song, Shabbat food, prayer, and observance of the laws of Shabbat. The rest of the time at the seminar would be spent in groups with people like Steven Riskin or David Hartman discussing philosophical questions such as the meaning of the Holocaust, perhaps listening to chasidic tales and niggunim (religious melodies) sung by Shlomo Carlebach, or pursuing Jewish studies. The first seminar in 1955 attracted twenty-eight participants. Subsequent seminars often had more than two hundred participants. Attempts were made to hold the seminars twice a year and to have the same people come back again and again. The Torah Leadership Seminar was seen as a way not only to introduce young people to a Jewish experience but, by inviting them back several times, to create a bond that could be sustained so that friendly ties would remain and would encourage religious practices. If someone joined a yeshiva high school or chose to attend Yeshiva University after attending several seminars, this would make such a decision attractive to other seminar friends.

In 1956 Yeshiva University opened a program (which later became the James Striar School) "for those lacking background in Jewish studies." The first class had 43 students. By 1964 there were 264 enrolled in this program (Klaperman 1969, 183). Rabbi Morris Besdin, who was appointed director of the school in 1958, reported in 1981:

> Until recent years, students were almost entirely nonyeshiva students. They were mostly from talmud torah schools and congregational schools. Perhaps some of these students had a few years of elementary Jewish education, but nothing beyond that. At present, many of our students have come from yeshiva high schools.
>
> I once did a study of the students before the yeshiva influx changed the character of the student body. In the early years 90–95 percent came from nonyeshiva schools; about 20 percent of the students came from nonkosher homes, and although I never did a study of that, about 80 percent, I think, came from non-*shomer Shabbos* [not observant of the Sabbath] homes."

Rabbi Besdin argued that the dramatic change in the level of observance of students during the course of their stay at the school was suggested by the number of these students who became ordained as rabbis. "At the last *Chag Hasmikhah* [ordination celebration that at Yeshiva occurs every third year and had last occurred in 1980], of about one hundred students ordained I think about nineteen or twenty, approximately one in five, had been a student at JSS [the James Striar School]."

In the late 1970s a change occurred in the character of the student body at JSS. By the early 1980s about 50 percent of the students had a yeshiva background. A similar change has occurred at other ba'al t'shuva yeshivot. A tendency for the ba'al t'shuva yeshivot to recruit students closer to the mainstream of Orthodoxy appears to be developing, although elsewhere the percentages of students with yeshiva backgrounds are not as high as at JSS.

Several other institutions for ba'alei t'shuva bear mentioning. In 1967 Rabbi Shlomo Freifeld established Yeshiva Sh'or Yoshuv in Far Rockaway, New York. Begun as an extension of Yeshiva Chaim Berlin for some of the less able students and for those who wanted a smaller school with more personal guidance from teachers, the school began accepting students lacking background—often hippies. Within a year or two the yeshiva began to be known as a school for ba'alei t'shuva, as such students began to be called at about this time. The school grew for several years, reaching an enrollment of close to one hundred by the early 1980s. By the mid-1980s its student body also had undergone a change so that although the school continued to cater to ba'alei t'shuva it did so through its Tal Techiya Institute. Ba'alei t'shuva who had been at the school for several years had become part of the community—they married, entered an advanced yeshiva program, summered with their families at the school's summer campus in the Catskills, and sent their children to Sh'or Yoshuv's elementary schools. In essence the yeshiva became a community, attracting fewer new recruits but holding those who came for longer periods. This community also attracted some who were Orthodox from birth.

In 1972 Lubavitch established a yeshiva for ba'alei t'shuva in Newark, and the following year it moved the yeshiva to a newly purchased campus in Morristown, New Jersey. The student enrollment in the ba'al t'shuva yeshiva began with ten in 1972, grew to about eighty over the next several years, and stabilized at about that number. In Boston in 1973 Rabbi Levi Yitzhak Horowitz, known as "the Bostoner Rebbe," started a small yeshiva in his Bet Pinchas synagogue facility, which attracted from five to twenty students each year over the next several years.

In 1975 the Lincoln Square Synagogue also opened a yeshiva. It had much success with a six-week summer program under the leadership of Rabbi David Silber. The school, housed in an apartment on the upper west side of Manhattan, attracted about a dozen students. But yeshiva students were out of place in that environment. The school closed in 1978. Its experience was shared by other small ba'al t'shuva yeshivot in urban centers. Some supportive environment or community was necessary for their success.

Beginnings in Israel

Rabbi Mordechai Goldstein was drawn into dealing with people of little background almost by accident. He had come to Israel in 1964 with a group of other young men from the Yeshiva Chofetz Chaim, in an attempt by that yeshiva to strike roots there. The effort did not meet with much success, and most of the others returned to America. Rabbi Goldstein and three colleagues remained. Financially hard-pressed, they lived on stipends offered by the Harry Fischel Institute for Higher Torah Study in Israel and tutored younger boys in Talmudic studies.

Rabbi Goldstein recalls:

A rosh yeshiva came to me. He had a son who was on drugs. Naively, not knowing anything about drugs . . . , I said, "Torah can do anything. Why not?" I started to work with the boy, and I was successful. He used to eat treyfes [forbidden foods] on Yom Kippur. He's that type of boy. I was successful with him, and then other boys came by. I fell into this drug scene. I wanted to get help for these boys. They needed psychiatric help. I couldn't get any help from the government, so I had to face the problems myself. I was successful, but I didn't have the proper facilities or finances. But I did quite a lot of work, and I was involved. I accepted them for what they were. I gave them love. I didn't press them to change their long hair and clothing, because for some, this was important, all they had to hold onto.

But the facilities were shabby and inadequate. At first he shared quarters with Chevron, a poor yeshiva in a dilapidated area of Jerusalem. Following the Six Day War he was offered the use of some abandoned buildings on Mount Zion by the Ministry of Religion, to whom the care of these properties had fallen. The location, atop a historic mount near the Tomb of David and a short walking distance from the Western Wall, was strategic. Many of the tens of thousands of visitors who came to the *Kotel,* or "Western Wall," were eager to visit other historic sights and stopped at David's Tomb or wandered about the mountaintop enjoying the panoramic view of the Silwan Valley and the Valley of Hinnom. Some of these visitors were hippies in search of a religious experience. Rabbi Goldstein invited them to join him, and many did. This was the beginning of Yeshiva Hatfutzot-Har Tzion (Diaspora Yeshiva), the first of the so-called ba'al t'shuva yeshivot.

In 1967 Rabbi Noach Weinberg invited Rabbi Mendel Weinbach and Rabbi Nota Schiller, whom he had met as a student in Baltimore, to join him in attempting to develop a yeshiva for those new to Orthodoxy. But the school failed for lack of financial support.

In 1970 Rabbi Weinberg and some colleagues opened Yeshiva Magen Avraham in B'nei B'rak, Israel, a school for young adults interested in learning about Orthodox Judaism but lacking the necessary background. Magen Avraham was intended for Americans, and instruction was in English. Apparently there already were a few Americans seeking to know more about their religion. The choice of B'nei B'rak, an insular and pious religious community, as the location for the school was simply happenstance; support for the school came from a man who had family ties in B'nei B'rak. The school did not attract many students in part because of its location and in part because large numbers of potential students began arriving only after the Six Day War in 1967. Rabbi Weinberg left Yeshiva Magen Avraham and moved to Jerusalem.

"I started four other [outreach] organizations before attempting to start a yeshiva, but I met with too much apathy and despair. We had the information, and we tried to reach out. But it took too much energy for too little results. I looked for hard-core men, partners, dedicated people who felt the way I did about going out with our message. I finally decided, 'You've got to raise your own, make a yeshiva of your own and raise students who will go out with the message.'"

In 1972 Weinberg invited Mendel Weinbach to join them. Later that year Rabbi Carl Rosenberg, a businessman, arrived with Rabbi Nota Schiller, who returned from America. The men opened Shema Yisrael, not a yeshiva but a program for ba'alei t'shuva. For meals and dormitories the school used the rundown facilities of the old Navarodok Yeshiva in Sanhedria. In the fall of 1972 they opened Yeshiva Ohr Someyach in those temporary facilities. They attracted the interest of a number of people in the Mapai (Labor) Party, including Kaddish Luz, former speaker of the Knesset, who accepted the position of Chairman of the Board of Directors, Yakov Herzog, who became President of Israel in 1986, and other influential Israelis. The government was sympathetic to the idea and began supporting the school.

Noach Weinberg's leadership position was soon challenged by the other three, who were attempting to mold Ohr Someyach into a traditional yeshiva, differing from others only in that it dealt with ba'alei t'shuva. Weinberg, on the other hand, wanted "revolutionaries," fighters and workers for Judaism, not simply traditional *yeshiva bochrim.* If the Communists could succeed by using their techniques, then Jews had better develop their own effective techniques as well. "The only way we can survive," he argued, "is to go out there and get them [the atheists]. If we don't, they'll come in here and get us." Perhaps as a result of this difference of opinion Weinberg left Ohr Someyach in 1974 and set up his own school in the Old City—Aish Hatorah, or Fire of the Torah, a name that implies the revolutionary fervor Weinberg sees as the school's central purpose.

In the meantime, in 1970 the Hartman family approached Rabbi Mordechai Elefant, head of Israel Torah Research Institutes (ITRI), asking him to start a school for ba'alei t'shuva and offering to cover the costs. Rabbi Elefant chose Rabbi Chaim Brovender, a former student at the ITRI *kolel* (an advanced school for the study of Talmud for married men that provided them with a stipend) in Jerusalem. At the time Brovender, who had received his rabbinical ordination at Yeshiva University, was studying for a doctorate in Semitic religions at the Hebrew University.

The school soon outgrew the resources of the Hartman family as student enrollment increased. In 1973 Rabbi Elefant persuaded the Shappel family of Los Angeles to provide the financial resources for an expanded school, including a separate school for women. The institutions were renamed the Shappel Colleges of Jewish Studies for Women and for Men, respectively.

In the fall of 1973 Rabbi Yosef Krupnick was appointed associate dean of the newly opened Women's College headed by Brovender. This school started with eight students, enrolled twenty-five in the 1974 academic year, and had sixty in 1975. Part of this growth was a result of expanding the program to two years, so that a number of women who had been recruited in the previous academic year remained. By 1975 the men's college had reached an enrollment of ninety. This school, too, seemed well on its way to becoming an established institution.

The first of these institutions to establish a place for women was Har Tzion when it opened a women's division in its facility. At the outset, Rabbi Goldstein had simply attempted to provide a place where young men in search of religion, many of them part of the hippie and drug culture of the late 1960s, might study Judaism. Not infrequently, men and women in this counterculture traveled together. That some facility would have to be found for the women if the men were going to stay long enough to learn something about Judaism became apparent early. For Rabbi Goldstein, the solution was to house the women in a building a short walk away from the men's facility. There they slept, took meals, and were taught by the rabbi's wife. Rabbi Goldstein's solution, which may seem reasonable and even somewhat restrictive by the standards of American society—which at that moment in history was beginning to house men and women in the same dormitory buildings—was nevertheless considered problematic by the religious community of Jerusalem (which includes an ultrapious community) and scandalous by the yeshivishe velt.

This was a problem for other ba'al t'shuva institutions as well, and each solved it differently. The Hartman School, or "Brovender's," as it was more widely called, was opened in 1970 when the flow of hippies to Israel was at its peak. But Brovender's emphasis on the intellectual, his negation of experience, and his distaste for appeals to emotion placed him at odds with the hippies' worldview. Few came to him, and fewer stayed. His school was mainstream, establishment, in the mold of Yeshiva University, only more *mitnagdic* (opposed to Chasidism). Rabbi Noach Weinberg, then involved with the Shema Yisrael program for returnees, gave no thought to women and simply attempted to find accomodations for them until the men could be persuaded to drop the relationship. If women survived, they did it on their own, as house guests of someone willing to take them, or made their way to Har Tzion.

In 1972 Rabbi David Revson, an Englishman ordained at K'far Chasidim who held a doctorate in philosophy of religion, felt that the time was ripe to open a yeshiva for ba'alei t'shuva that would appeal to British and European students. He ran an advertisement in the newspapers announcing the opening of a new yeshiva. A substantial number of applicants were women, and Rabbi Revson decided to open two schools, D'var Yerushalayim for men and Neve Yerushalayim for women. (The names mean literally "the word of Jerusalem" and "the beauty of Jerusalem," respectively.) He invited Rabbi Boruch Horovitz of Manchester, England, to run the boys' school while he devoted his time to the girls' school. He felt that the latter task was the more difficult as there were no models for such schools, so that the curriculum would require substantial creativity. This school rapidly outgrew its facilities; by 1975 it had 130 students.

An ideological split almost led to the closing of Shappel Colleges in 1976. What remained of the former colleges under the auspices of ITRI was only the men's college in a truncated form, both in numbers and in program, serving an Israeli rather than American student population.[14] Rabbi Brovender left the school and set up two institutions outside of the ITRI framework, which are in fact the continuation of the earlier Shappel Colleges in terms of program, students served, and philosophy. These schools are now called Yeshivat Hamivtar ("yeshiva of the cutting edge"—perhaps a reference to their intellectual style) and Michlelet B'ruria (B'ruria College was named after Rabbi Meir's wife, known for her erudition, piety, intelligence, and her fiery willingness to challenge men's claim to superiority in knowledge and practice of Torah). In choosing these names for his schools Brovender was almost defiantly asserting his philosophic positions, which derive from a perspective similar to that of Yeshiva University rather than of the yeshivishe velt.

Although many new schools have been established for Israeli ba'alei t'shuva, since 1974 only one other attempt to establish a school for Americans in Israel was undertaken. This was a short-lived attempt by Ohr Someyach in 1978–1979 to establish a school for women. It will be discussed in chapter 5, when we deal at greater length with ba'alot t'shuva (women).

14. Subsequently, a women's school was also opened, and these instituituions are now known as the Darchei Noam-Shappel Colleges for Men and Women. The men's school enrolls about forty students; the women's school enrolls a smaller number.

Chapter 4

The 1960s and the Emergence of the Ba'al T'shuva

I n the half century after the close of mass immigration to America, American Jewry had made efforts to draw young people "of limited background" toward Orthodox practice. Although the effort had some success, the term *ba'alei t'shuva* was not used until in 1972, when five schools were founded specifically for ba'alei t'shuva.

Why were these newly Orthodox now called "ba'alei t'shuva"? What had changed the perception about newly Orthodox? What gave rise to these new institutions? Was there something about the students these yeshivot were attracting that led to a new label, "yeshivot for ba'alei t'shuva"? How were these schools different from those that served "students of limited background" in the 1940s and 1950s?

Upheavals and Reversals

ETHNIC IDENTITY IN THE 1960S

The civil rights movement of the mid-1960s had led to a strong sense of ethnic identity, not only among blacks but in other groups as well. For Jews, the new emphasis on ethnic identity had encouraged religious traditionalism.

Beginning in the late nineteenth century the doctrine of racism threatened Jews. Claiming a scientific basis, its proponents argued that some races were superior and meant to lead and that others were subhuman (*untermenschen*). Jews, Blacks, Asians, and southern and eastern Europeans were assigned to the category of inferiors. The effort of Jews to prove that they were the same as anyone else put Orthodox Judaism on the defensive because of its stress on the uniqueness of the Jewish people and the special rituals and foods that separated observant Jews from the rest of society. Reform Judaism, which emphasized the prophetic ethic of Judaism and rejected the ritual laws that separated Jew from Gentile, was ascendant. At this point in history demonstrating that Jews were not different from others was important, and it was the equality of Jews and the universalism of Judaism that Reform emphasized.

The emphasis on equality made natural allies of American Jews and blacks in the struggle for equal opportunity and civil rights. Reform Judaism was most heavily involved in this struggle because of its emphasis on the universalistic ethics of Judaism. Orthodoxy's emphasis on ritual and on the uniqueness of Jews seemed irrelevant, if not contradictory, to the notion of equality. Hence Reform and secular groups were the most active Jews—in fact, among the most active of all groups—in the struggle for civil rights.

What Reform and secular Judaism did not see, or perhaps were not distressed by, was the consonance between the value of equality and the desire to merge with the larger society. For a long time, this consonance did not seem to matter much to Reform and secular Jews. The Jewish rate of intermarriage was low, less than 4 percent before World War II (Kennedy 1944). The major threat to the Jewish people was posed by racists and especially Nazis. The right to be considered an equal become more critical, and the importance of the right to be different receded in the face of the physical threat. The threats posed by intermarriage still lay in the future.

Even before the turn of the century and until the mid-1960s, their common interest in equality and civil rights had made allies of blacks and Jews. If anything, the experience of the Holocaust made Jews even more sensitive to the potential destructiveness of racism and hence the strongest supporters of civil rights.

In 1964 and 1965, respectively, Congress passed the Civil Rights Act and the Voting Rights Act, which seemed at last to guarantee equality for all. The President of the United States, himself a Southerner, could declare, using the words of the Negro spiritual, "We shall overcome." Racism was everywhere in the United States in retreat.

Ironically, victory proved a dividing point between Jews and blacks. A splinter group in the black community, the Black Muslims, adopted a militant and separatist stance and began to attract the interest of other blacks. The Muslim character of this movement suggested an antagonism toward Jews through identification with the Arab world, and its leadership did nothing to discourage this interpretation. In 1967 Stokely Carmichael and others adopted the "black power" ideology of the Black Muslims and expelled whites—among whom were substantial numbers of Jews—from positions of leadership in the black civil rights movement. A highly vocal minority among blacks was now emphasizing militancy and separatism. The vision of the equality of individuals was being replaced with one of the equality of groups. One had to belong to a group, and group identity was critical. This was a view entirely at odds with that of Jews, who regarded equality as an individual, not a group, right.

More important, the ideological difference had profound social consequences. Some in the black community demanded proportionate access to jobs, schools, and the professions. This demand awakened fears among Jews of a quota system, like the *numerus clausus* used in the past to limit their entry into society. For the first time ideological differences, exacerbated by economic and status differences, drove Jews and blacks apart. Jews were teachers in schools where students were black, Jews were social workers serving a heavily black clientele, Jews owned retail stores in black neighborhoods. And, although the evidence rebutted the charge (Richard Cohen, Letter to the editor citing study by George Sternlieb, *New York Times,* 24 July 1970), Jews were accused of being the major slumlords in black ghettoes.

Riots in major American cities, starting in Los Angeles in 1963 and followed by New York, Chicago, and other cities in 1964 and 1965 and continuing through 1968, sharpened the confrontation between the former allies. To blacks it seemed that Jews were the oppressors. To Jews it seemed that blacks were the new *muzhiks,* and they were again caught in the vise between system and oppressed that they had experienced in Europe.

The black struggle for entry to the large society came to be perceived as an attack on Jews specifically. The largest cities in the United States, in which about 90 percent of the Jewish population were concentrated, experienced riots in which stores owned by Jews seemed to be singled out for destruction. Teachers, who in the large cities were disproportionately Jewish, were accused of racism. An outcry against the use of civil service examinations for tenure and promotion of teachers pitted Jews against blacks in a physical as well as political conflict. The trust and perception of common interest that had built up over a century were seriously damaged.

The radical change in the relationship between blacks and Jews in the mid-1960s had broad consequences for the relationship between the various Jewish denominations and society. As universalistic ethics had placed Orthodoxy on the defensive, the new emphasis on ethnic identity and uniqueness shifted the balance toward Orthodoxy. Secularist, socialist, and Reform Jewish philosophies that emphasized equality and the "sameness of all" were in retreat before a worldview that emphasized differences.[1] Granting legitimacy to ethnicity for blacks implied granting it as well to Jews. If so, then Orthodox Judaism won a measure of respect. If blacks could display symbols of their ethnicity proudly, could not Jews do the same? If one could wear a dashiki in public and eat soul food, why could one not wear a kippah and eat kosher "soul" food?

THE EMERGENCE OF THE COUNTERCULTURE

By the mid-1960s a second issue had begun to grip the consciousness and political processes of the United States: the Vietnam War. Techniques developed and honed in the battle for civil rights, techniques that had been given the sanction of the federal government in waging its war for civil rights against the states, were now turned against the federal government itself. Civil disobedience was used as a tool for resisting and reshaping government and the educational structure. And a federal government whose officials had sanctioned civil disobedience in the cause of black civil rights now found that it had legitimated the techniques of its own opposition.

The years 1967 and 1968 saw immense turmoil in the United States. The assassination of Martin Luther King, Jr., in April 1968 was followed by riots of blacks in scores of cities. By that time the Free Speech movement, led by Mario Savio of the University of California at Berkeley had reached universities and colleges across the United States, with violent confrontations between police and students on scores of campuses. The unrest spread to Europe. In Paris Daniel Cohn-Bendit (Danny the Red) led thousands of striking students and workers in protests against university and government policies. Universities were accused of being tools of the war-making machinery of government, their faculties of being more interested in research than in their students. Research facilities were burned and occasionally, as at the University of Wisconsin, bombed. Whereas

1. Alba and Chamlin (1983) report that identification with a single ethnic group (for example, Italian or Irish) has increased among college attenders. They find this surprising given the traditional interpretation of education as a force for acculturation and assimilation. They conclude that their "findings appear to corroborate the widespread claim of an ethnic resurgence in the last decades." If the Jewish experience is a guide, the defeat of racism and Nazism may have allowed renewed ethnic identity to flourish.

between 1957 and 1967 the universities had been respected institutions, providing leadership in the space race in response to Russia's launching of Sputnick in 1957 and serving as the moral voice of, and the recruiting ground for, participation in the civil rights struggle of the early 1960s, suddenly perceptions changed. Accepting government research grants was evil because the government supported a war that was judged unjust by half the population of the United States. Universities, churches, and even the family came under attack as establishment institutions. Rejection of the older generation was signaled with the slogan, "Don't trust anyone over thirty."

The establishment reacted sometimes with tolerance and understanding, but often with ferocity and violence. Student demonstrations at Chicago and elsewhere were met with police riots. At Kent State University three students were shot and killed by frightened National Guardsmen. The war in Vietnam dragged on with no end in sight. Young Americans began turning away from the establishment, away from large corporations, from industry and technology. They were ready for a life based on values rather than acquisition, concerned with who they were rather than with what they had. In these circumstances numerous minor themes in American culture came to be invested with tremendous importance. Rock music, long hair and beards, bright and informal clothes expressed rejection of the existing values. Music festivals such as the one held in Woodstock in 1968 drew scores of thousands of participants. Drugs, which in the early 1960s had been touted as "mind expanding," were now redefined as a means of dropping out of society. As the political struggle intensified, interest in charismatic and Eastern religions—religion in its nonestablishment forms—began to be manifested. In the summer of 1968 President Johnson was forced by the opponents of his war policies to announce that he would not be a candidate for reelection, the first incumbent president since Coolidge not to run for a second term. The Democratic nominating convention in Chicago became a media event with Yippies pitted against the Chicago police in violent confrontation. Vice President Hubert Humphrey narrowly lost the election to Richard M. Nixon.

Four years later, years of tumult, bombings, and violent confrontations between blacks and whites, pro- and anti-war demonstrators, army and students, Nixon won an overwhelming victory over Senator George McGovern in the race for the presidency. This victory signaled the end of the Great Society programs, and despite continued opposition to the war, a turning away from political involvement and revolutionary activities.

The counterculture had numerous and contradictory themes. Some groups like the Weathermen and the Symbionese Liberation Army were heavily involved in political opposition to the government and would resort to the use of violence to bring about its destruction. Others dropped out of society entirely, their attention focused inward on drugs or on the various new religions that began to flourish.

For a while the drug culture flourished. Timothy Leary's slogan, "Turn on, tune in, drop out," became the new watchword. But as the harmful effects of drugs came to be recognized, that movement too fell into disrepute. Religion, particularly Eastern religions with their antiestablishment qualities and their pacifism, seemed to support counterculture values. In addition they promised to provide psychological highs and mind expansion through such techniques as Yoga and meditation, without the potential dangers of drugs (Pope 1974; Glanz 1978).

These religions viewed the world as illusion, to be adjusted to rather than manipulated or mastered. This passive perspective, which in Max Weber's terms regards "man as vessel rather than as instrument," was consonant with pacifist political sentiments and with a nonintrusionist attitude toward the environment. Thus Eastern religions, with their view of the world as illusory in nature, their inward focus and concern for self-development, their pantheistic reverence for the life or soul in all things (which manifested itself in pacifist tendencies and vegetarianism), echoed the experience of students who had hallucinated when using drugs, who opposed a war that seemed both senseless and immoral, who wanted to reject a cruel, cold, and mechanical society and return to nature, emotion, and personal experience (Marcuse 1964). These perspectives fueled the antiwar movement, the environmental movement, the macrobiotic and natural-foods movement, and the self-discovery movement, all of which paralleled Eastern religions. At the same time these movements contributed to greater interest in Eastern religions, yoga, and transcendental meditation.

The college population was under intense pressure to react to what they perceived as a literal threat to life through the draft into the armed forces. Students were concentrated and thus easily reached; they were idealistic and at the same time at a stage of their lives when change and experimentation were possible and permissible. They lived in an age when economic concerns were not overriding—the age of Aquarius.

Jews, who attended college at three times the rate of the general population, felt these pressures strongly. Historically, Jews have been heavily involved in countercultural movements (Yinger 1982), and this one was no exception. Even prior to entering the college environment Jews held many of the countercultural attitudes regarding drug use, life-style, political radicalism, the future American society, and activism in left-oriented political movements (Piazza 1976). University experience enhanced most of these countercultural attitudes.

Some Jews in this milieu became involved in antiwar, environmentalist, and student-rights causes, and others in Eastern religions. As many as 6 percent of the followers of Reverend Moon's Unification Church, 12 percent of the Hare Krishna movement, and 25 percent of Zen Buddhists were Jews, although Jews constitute about 2.5 percent of the population (Melton and Moore 1982, 30). Similarly, Jews were heavily overrepresented in such radical political movements as Students for Democratic Society and the Free Speech Movement (Glazer 1970–71).

Involvement in Orthodox Judaism was another way of expressing an antiestablishment stance and at the same time coming to terms with ethnic identity. Which Jews chose increased Jewish identity and which other causes and solutions is not the focus of this study (see Stark and Bainbridge 1985); we deal here with those who did in fact choose Judaism in this environment. But it is important to note that Jews were heavily involved in the counterculture and that Judaism represented an alternative that was consonant with the predominant values of that day.

THE WAR OF REDEMPTION

The Six Day War is not called "the war of redemption," but that was its inner meaning for Jews. It was also an astonishing military victory. Attacked by the armies of Egypt, TransJordan, Syria, and Iraq, which were backed by a dozen other Arab states, with its standing army outnumbered more than ten to one, Israel shattered the Egyptian Air Force on the first morning of the war. Six days later, Israel's army stood at the banks of the Suez Canal. Jerusalem and the West Bank had been wrested from Jordanian troops, and Syria's heavily fortified positions on the Golan Heights, from which the Galilee had been shelled, were overrun. In less than a week, the military and political structure of the Middle East had been transformed. Israel had become a major military power.

What for the world at large was an extraordinary military victory was a gut-wrenching experience for Jews. In the weeks before the war Israel found itself isolated. Secretary-General U Thant withdrew the U.N. peace-keeping forces at Egypt's request, leaving Israel's borders exposed. France, England, and the United States, signatories of the 1957 TriPartite Agreement guaranteeing Israel's borders and its free passage through the

Straits of Tiran, refused to take action when Egypt blockaded the straits. Abandoned by the world community, Israel awaited the attack. Bomb shelters were cleared of debris and restocked. Civilians lined up to give blood. Graves were dug in advance of the war, twenty thousand in the Tel Aviv area alone.

The utter isolation of Israel in the face of the threat of destruction reawakened the terrors of the Holocaust in Jews everywhere. For two weeks Arab armies gathered, and the nations seemed to turn their backs. Nasser's stated war aim was not to compel Israel to return some portion of land but rather "to drive the Jews into the sea"; there was nothing to negotiate. Jews in the United States gave money, donated blood, and volunteered to fight for the Israeli army. Israelis and Jews found that they were each other's only reliable allies.

The war transformed Israeli and Jewish identity. In the preceding decade Jewish identity seemed to be splitting into two; Jews and Israelis, the former tied to the diaspora experience, the latter to the land (Herman 1970). Jewish identity might be religious, but Israeli identity need not be. A Canaanite sect of Israelis developed, claiming connection with the land, not the Jews.[2] So far had the sense of identity changed that the government of Israel felt it necessary to make the trial of Adolph Eichmann a show trial, to teach Israeli youngsters (and the world) about the Holocaust, which it feared was rapidly being forgotten.

The awful terror of annihilation that preceded the war forged anew the unity between Israeli and Jewish identity. Israelis and Jews everywhere believed they were at the brink of another holocaust, but this time they were not merely miraculously saved; they were redeemed. The religious symbolism of retaking the holy Western Wall after two thousand years was clear.

Israel's victory was interpreted in religious terms by secular and religious Jews alike. In June 1967 Yitzhak Rabin, then commander of Israel's Defense Forces (later Prime Minister of Israel), a secular Jew and a member of the Labor Party, said "The entire nation was elated and many wept when they heard of the capture of the Old City. . . . The paratroopers who conquered the Western Wall leaned on its stones and wept—an act so rare as to be almost unparalleled (Herman 1970, 214)." David Ben-Gurion, Israel's "old man," was photographed at the Wall in a kippah. Moshe Dayan, hero of the Sinai Campaign and Minister of De-

2. This is a reference to the ancient Canaanites who inhabited the land before the time of the patriarchs. They adopted that name to clearly dissociate themselves from the Biblical and Jewish experience.

fense in 1967, was quoted as having said, "Whoever was not religious became religious today." These events legitimated Judaism among secular and uncommitted Jews. (Rabin himself was said to have attended classes at a yeshiva for ba'alei t'shuva for a period in 1981.)

The changed perception of Israel by diaspora Jews lasted into the 1970s and probably beyond (Waxman 1981). Funds raised for Israel by American Jews dramatically increased after 1967. Immigration to Israel from North America, almost nonexistent in previous years, topped five thousand in 1969, 1970, and 1971, and continued at the pace of three to four thousand per year afterward. American Jewish sociologists argued that Israel had become the center of Jewish religious activity. In fact, Glazer claims that since 1967 Israel has become the religion of American Jews (Waxman 1981, 78).

In sum, the battle for black civil rights in the 1960s led to an affirmation of ethnic identity that caused the scale of values to slide away from the Reform and secular Jewish values of universalism toward Orthodoxy's particularism and ritualism. Opposition to the war in Vietnam in the late 1960s gave rise to a counterculture that rejected establishment politics, education, and religion and opened people up to alternative life styles. As Jews were heavily involved in the counterculture and its values, they were particularly open to change. The Six Day War powerfully brought home to Jews, even peripheral Jews, their connection to the Jewish people and provided an impetus to explore Jewish identity and Judaism as a life-style.

Perceptions and Misperceptions

BA'ALEI T'SHUVA: THE NEW PUBLIC PERCEPTION

The hippie ba'al t'shuva's presence on the American scene made it clear that a new phenomenon was occurring.[3] The radical transformations in

---

3. *Hippie* is a term used to designate the counterculture of the 1960s and early 1970s. Yinger (1982, 22) defines it as meaning opposed to the routine and conventional and, to some extent, to consumption. The emphasis is on community as opposed to the anonymous city, on peace and love as opposed to a society riven by conflict. Roszak (1968) emphasizes the hippies' opposition to technocratic society, citing opposition to "repressive rationality" (to the neglect of the importance of the irrational in human experience), bureaucracy, and society's exaggerated dependence on science as the only source of truth.

No single value defines the counterculture. Values varied at different times and from place to place. In Haight-Ashbury it was drugs; in Chicago, politics; in Wood-

appearance that new returnees underwent—from hippie to neo-chasidic—made visible a phenomenon that had been occurring for more than a generation and that had heretofore been dealt with as though all that was happening was that students with insufficient background were interested in yeshivot. Previously no thought had been given to the possibility that people were trying out new commitments and wanted guidance. Only when the widespread testing of values by the youth population became generally known and when thousands of Jewish hippies began drifting to Israel was this new phenomenon identified. The transformation in the appearance of these newly Orthodox hippies was dramatic, yet often involved a far less radical change than was required of those who had been "straight."[4] From the outside, hippies underwent the more radical transformation. The former hippie with long hair and layered, rustic, or antique clothes now looked like a chasid. This new image, so dramatically captured by photographs, recast the return to Orthodoxy.

While the mass media focused on the cultists, the Jesus freaks, the followers of Moon, and the Children of God, the Jewish media focused on the ba'alei t'shuva. It became clear that the newly Orthodox were not simply "people already committed but lacking background"; they were trying out and testing a new commitment. Media attention to these newly Orthodox therefore reframed the phenomenon and for the first time questions began to be raised as to how to deal with people who choose to become Orthodox.

How and why the new label of "ba'al t'shuva" came into being is

---

stock, music. Some of its values were even contradictory (for example, dropping out of society versus political activism). Yet, as Yinger points out, counterculture was a rejection of mainstream values. People could and did participate in this culture selectively. Those identified as hippies were not necessarily involved in the full range of countercultural values. Some adopted hippie styles of clothing and music; others went beyond this to include attitudes toward consumption or religion. Being a hippie, then, was a matter of self-definition as well as social definition.

In this chapter and elsewhere the term hippie refers to those who identified with this counterculture or were labeled hippies by others. In general people used the clothing style worn and elements of life-style, including preferences in music, as clues to identify hippies; those wishing to be so identified could adopt or affect these styles. Thus perception was critical here. It was important for the t'shuva movement that people *thought to be hippies* were becoming ba'alei t'shuva, particularly at a time when hippie culture was at center stage. The association suggested that youth who identified with the hippie culture might be interested in yeshivot.

4. Many hippies were seekers who had earlier severed their connections to parents and home, friends and jobs. For straights, such a change would have been much more difficult (see Balch and Taylor 1977).

unclear. As late as October 1983 the Executive Vice President of the Young Israel (modernistic Orthodox) objected to the term ba'al t'shuva, while a few months earlier the Bostoner Rebbe, a leader in the Agudat Israel, the traditionalistic wing of Orthodoxy, began efforts to establish an organization for ba'alei t'shuva.

Why this new label developed is suggested by Goffman's remark (1963, 58) that a change in name involves an important breach between the individual and his old world. This seems to be precisely the difference between earlier and later attempts to reach out to the nonreligious. The earlier strategy of outreach to "those lacking background" attempted to bridge the gap between the secular world and Orthodoxy and to provide an Orthodox microcosm of the world by developing Boy Scout troops and sponsoring dances and weekends that would attract nonreligious young people to the synagogue and eventually involve them in religious activities. Emphasis was placed on continuity with the past.

Outreach to ba'alei t'shuva was different. They were immediately confronted with a religious challenge. This approach, which demanded some rejection of the secular world, was much closer to the view emphasized by traditionalistic Orthodoxy (and was consonant with hippie countercultural values). Thus, the label ba'al t'shuva led to a new perspective on reaching out in the early 1970s.

COUNTERCULTURAL RELIGICNS AND ORTHODOX JUDAISM

Given the antiestablishment attitudes that underlay the newly developing religious sentiments, Orthodox Judaism had come to be seen as one of several viable choices. For hippies it seemed to have similarities to countercultural religions: its mysticism; its chasidim and rebbes, whose relationship paralleled that of disciples and gurus; its special kosher diet, a parallel to the interest in macrobiotic diets and natural foods; a unique style of dress; a far heavier emphasis on ritual than was found in established American religions, which was again paralleled by a similar emphasis in the Eastern religions to which hippies were attracted. The apparent congruences of these value systems may have seemed so attractive to those just beginning their return that the deeper divergences may have gone unnoticed.

Many of those attracted to Orthodoxy at this point were responding to some idealized conception that existed in their own imaginations. Orthodoxy was associated with and confused with Chasidism. But these returnees were not drawn to real Chasidism but their own vision of Chasidism. This can be seen in the special emphasis placed on aspects of Judaism that have parallels to Eastern religions. The unique way in which the parallels were translated suggested to some in the Orthodox community that "this was still a hippie trip, only one with a Jewish emphasis." For example, although *Kabbalah* (Jewish mysticism) was a part of Jewish traditional study, it was not part of the curriculum of the day schools or the higher yeshivot. Only in Chasidism was it stressed, and even there it was open only to those who, it was felt, had studied Torah sufficiently to have a mature understanding of it (generally men of middle age or older). Yet the seekers of religion in the 1960s sought knowledge of Kabbalah as a *first* step in their understanding of Judaism.

Macrobiotic food is another example. Kosher does not mean clean and it does not mean natural; it means prepared in accordance with Jewish ritual law. Chemical additives may make food unkosher, and Orthodox Jews therefore are careful about this. But if the additives are themselves kosher it makes no difference whether they are chemical or natural; the food is kosher. Similarly, mixing meat and dairy products together in food, on a plate, or at a meal is forbidden because this is symbolically "seething a kid in its mother's milk." But while such a practice may be interpreted as suggesting a sensitivity to animal suffering, it does not require vegetarianism.[5] Those committed to macrobiotic and vegetarian diets have often found sufficient symbolism in Jewish dietary laws to believe that these laws support the values underlying their diets. Because the Jewish laws and rituals are nowhere explained in terms of any fully authoritative philosophy, such beliefs are not easily contradicted. What is clear is that the food one eats is a *religious* concern in Orthodox Judaism as in some religions favored by the counterculture.

Hippie-Jewish dress style is still another example. Rather than being modeled after the clothing of modernistic Orthodox or even chasidic Jews, it was instead modeled after the hippies' idea of how European Jews

5. Interestingly, interest in macrobiotic food and vegetarianism has raised these issues to some extent in the Orthodox community as well. Whole wheat *challah* (Sabbath loaf) is no longer strange: *cholent,* a dish traditionally made for the Sabbath by cooking meat with beans, barley, or potatoes, may now be cooked with tofu and hence be vegetarian. One occasionally hears sermons alluding to the view that meat was permitted to man only reluctantly. In a recent book, *Vegetarianism and the Jewish Tradition* (1983), Lewis Berman argues that vegetarianism is endorsed by the Bible.

Similarly, hippie dress styles have influenced the *tallit* (prayer shawl) worn in the synagogue. One now occasionally sees a tallit worn with a bright colored *atarah* (headband). And one finds renewed interest in *Kabbalah* in Jewish study groups and adult education courses.

dressed at the turn of the twentieth century. This view, in turn, seemed to reflect Hollywood's notion as presented in *Fiddler on the Roof*—granny glasses, peaked caps, rough work clothes, and boots and beards, together with the uniquely Jewish religious garb, the *arba kanfos* and *tzitzit* (the "four-cornered" and "fringed" undergarment worn by men). The hippies wished to enter this highly ethnic world of the imagination, a world also in conflict with oppressive authorities.[6]

Jewish Responses to Jewish Hippies

Although the hippie group sought to enter this imagined Orthodox world, the existing Orthodox community in the United States was the one to which they turned. For the most part, the Orthodox community was closed to them. With few exceptions, notably Shlomo Carlebach, no one was willing or able to accept them *as they were*. Chasidic groups were generally suspicious of outsiders and unwilling to accept those whose religious practices were not identical to theirs. Even Lubavitch, which had by this time been involved in an outreach program, was not yet prepared to accept unreconstructed hippies. But one could not teach them to be Jewish unless they were first accepted into the community.

One might have expected that the Orthodox nonchasidic community would be able to reach out to hippies and accept them on their own terms. After all, the Young Israel movement had been attempting to make Orthodoxy attractive to young people for half a century, and Yeshiva University had more than a decade of experience with a school and seminars for the newly Orthodox. Yet yeshivot for ba'alei t'shuva began in Israel, bypassing existing outreach programs in America. Leaving aside that Israel itself contributed something that bridged the gap between hippie and Orthodox Jew, we turn first to the unique situation and values of modern Orthodoxy to understand why the very groups that seemed

6. A number of conflicts existed between Judaism, particularly Orthodox Judaism, and the counterculture, particularly in the area of sexual norms. Countercultural norms of sexual experimentation were in direct conflict with Judaism's emphasis on monogamy and strong family ties. Related to this is the place of women, although here countercultural values and norms were themselves contradictory, with women taking second place in many countercultural groups. A second area of potential conflict was the emphasis on self, or what has been referred to as the narcissism of the "me" generation. How these conflicts are handled will be discussed in chapters 11 and 12.

most capable of bridging the gap to those "lacking background" were unable to do the same for those who were ba'alei t'shuva.

"ESTABLISHMENT" ORTHODOXY

By the time the hippie religious movement developed, Yeshiva University had become an establishment institution. In 1956 when Yeshiva began its Jewish studies program it had no medical school, no school of social work, no graduate school of sciences. In 1957 the Russians launched their Sputnik space satellite, and within months the United States had started a crash program in the sciences. In the next decade universities, Yeshiva among them, experienced a period of tremendous expansion, facilitated by research and development grants from the federal government. By 1968 universities were seen as the core of the establishment and were experiencing bitter and violent conflict with their students. Yeshiva University could not be a portal to an alternative life-style because it was part of "the establishment."

Yeshiva University long had to walk a line between its identity as a yeshiva and commitment to Judaism on one hand and its university status and the requirement that it be nonsectarian on the other. It could not require attendance at prayers or observance of the mitzvot as a condition of enrollment as other yeshivot could. It was and is open to Jew and non-Jew alike. But it could and did require enrollment for at least some of its programs in a double program that requires Jewish study. (Many graduate programs are exempted from the double program requirement.) The double program requires Jewish study for half the day, from 9 A.M. to 3 P.M., Sunday through Thursday. College classes are conducted in the late afternoons, evenings, and Friday mornings).

In these circumstances, one could not expect the unanimous compliance with Jewish observances that one might find at other yeshivot. And for those who wished to be steeped in an atmosphere of Jewish study all day long, this was not the place to be.

At Yeshiva University, however, students could be instructed in religious practice—without the state's objection to this as religious indoctrination—through study of the literature of Judaism: the scriptures, the Talmud, and the Codes. Thus, rather than inform the student of the laws of Sabbath, the instructors taught him how to read the codes of Jewish law. But this program was long and difficult, particularly for those who came with absolutely no background, for it required that they learn the Hebrew alphabet and language, master the meaning of legal concepts, learn to read several types of script, develop an appreciation for the process of growth of Jewish religious law, learn to distinguish authoritative opinions from nonauthoritative ones, and confront other intellectual obstacles before they could determine the practice.

For those seeking immediate illumination, for those desiring to study kabbalah, for those who believed that religious illumination could be achieved through mind-expanding drugs, this path was simply too difficult, too laden with preparations. Nor did these people care about the college credits the university could offer. Therefore those whose interest in religion was sparked by the movement to Eastern religions and to religious experience through mind-expanding drugs did not seek this experience at Yeshiva University. Rather, they went to the East—to Israel—looking for a Jewish guru, a Jewish wise man and teacher there. The sort of student attracted to Yeshiva University was more likely to be mainstream, more interested in becoming Jewish precisely because Orthodox Judaism was becoming mainstream. They were not seeking to escape from society but rather seeking to enter it or, more likely, to remain in it.

Thus Yeshiva University's great strength, its ability to be part of mainstream America while being steadfastly Orthodox, proved a serious weakness. Its organizational involvements in state and federal government limited its ability to act. The perception that it was or desired to be mainstream put off those with countercultural values. One could argue that Yeshiva certainly recruited newly Orthodox, that it wrestled with questions of basic commitment for those whose commitment was uncertain. But one would have to concede that the transformation of students "lacking background" was not as dramatic as that of ba'alei t'shuva.

CHARISMATIC OUTREACH

The strategy of modernistic Orthodoxy was to reach out to the nonreligious by providing a microcosm of the larger world under religious auspices. The need to answer key questions of faith, although recognized, was not a systematic part of programs of outreach. The programs defined newcomers as people who simply "lacked backgrounds" rather than people who were struggling with their very commitment. This limited the possible responses.

In the late 1960s probably the only one on the American scene prepared to deal with such people in terms of their search for commitment rather than their lack of background was Rabbi Shlomo Carlebach, a Lubavitcher chasid. A charismatic personality, he was not an organizer and could not set up an institutional structure to further his work. But he attracted students to his religious happenings—prayer sessions, song fests, holiday celebrations—by the hundreds. His method was to person-ally assist each person in his or her search for Orthodox Judaism's truth. A core of young disciples gathered around him. They were there to learn from him rather than to work for him or with him. He cared for them. He helped to provide for them. He set up a synagogue. But the work was beyond his best efforts. He could not maintain contact with them. He led a number of his followers to Lubavitch. But unlike the newly Orthodox of earlier years, these people were older, sometimes more resistant to cutting ties to their hippie lives; many were not fully committed to becoming Orthodox and were searching and testing the waters. Lubavitch was not yet prepared to deal with them. To bring them along slowly enough to avoid alienating them before they experienced Orthodoxy would have required compromises that Lubavitch was not prepared to make.

For example, Carlebach felt that in order to have the opportunity to teach, to discuss, to celebrate religious rituals, even to pray at the outset it was necessary to permit men and women to sit together and participate together, to overlook their touching and embracing each other. "I plead-ed with the rebbe to let me do this but he wouldn't. But how could I tell the boys and girls, 'O.K. come in—boys on one side, girls on the other'? They wouldn't stay five minutes." As Carlebach saw it, thousands of young people were lost to Orthodoxy because of the inflexibility of Orthodox Jews. If the Lubavitcher would not compromise on their religious values, the Conservative and Reform synagogues were unable to compromise on their middle-class values. Carlebach claims that such synagogues often rejected his proposals to bring young hippies to them. The arguments were, "They'll make a mess. They'll bring dope. Who can tell what the boys and girls will do together?" Either way, American Jewish syn-agogues were unavailable to deal with hippie groups as they were—that is, as-yet uncommitted, willing to test the waters but needing someone to take the time and make the effort to persuade them. Organized American Judaism did not as yet recognize a need to deal with anyone other than those with insufficient background.

The Six Day War in 1967 riveted the attention of world Jewry upon Israel. With all of Jerusalem in Israel's hands the Western Wall, the holiest of places for Jews, was accessible, and Jews streamed there to pray, to make pilgrimage, or just to look. To some "the beginning of the redemp-tion" seemed to be at hand. In "the age of Aquarius," hippies found that messianic ideas were being treated with the utmost seriousness by some Orthodox Jews.

In the aftermath of the war, Rabbi Mordechai Goldstein was granted permission to open a school on Mount Zion near the Tomb of David in a quaint complex of buildings and gardens spreading out between monastaries and historical and religious sites. Har Tzion became a yeshiva for ba'alei t'shuva and caught the first waves of Western students who came to Israel. To live in the buildings the students had to reclaim the abandoned rooms, clearing them of debris and helping to decorate them along with the synagogue, study rooms, and open spaces. The yeshiva also relied on its own students for cooking and other chores (Beck 1977, 26–27).

Rabbi Goldstein's approach, like Shlomo Carlebach's, was to reach out to ba'alei t'shuva on their own terms. Har Tzion, he says, is *"mekabetz nidche amo,"* an ingatherer of His nation, which has been scattered. Rabbi Goldstein saw it as his duty to welcome and extend love to all, women as well as men, hippies as well as squares, drug users as well as straights. As a result, from its very beginnings Har Tzion was not a traditional yeshiva but a community. Goldstein became the Israeli counterpart of Carlebach, accepting hippies as they were, ready to work with them with no preconditions, requiring nothing from them—not that they cut their hair nor give up their girlfriends (although they could not continue to live together without marriage—separate quarters were provided), and it was rumored, not even that they give up drugs immediately. This last point was heatedly denied by Rabbi Goldstein, who insisted that he made every effort to eliminate drugs from his yeshiva.

Goldstein was willing to reach out to these hippies in language they understood, and to develop an institution to meet their needs. He said,

> People who are problems in their colleges have come to us from all over the United States—Zen Buddhists, Jewish boys. We've guided them and showed them. We're the first in the Musar movement to use, in our way, gestalt transactional analysis in order to develop the total personality. A person can grow. We've taken boys off drugs—heroin, cocaine, hard cases—and made them positive individuals in society. We've taken people who are homosexuals. These boys get married, and they now have children and are living a normal life—a Torah life. We face the problems, whatever problems that youth have. . . .
>
> When you meet a boy you should give him a kiss and a hug. He should feel that prayer is real prayer, feel that in sincerity and justice. In other words, give good vibrations. Instead of *talking* about what should be, they should actually *feel* there's a community, there's a warmth, there's religion in practice. There's respect for other people, for their rights. The learning is deep, sophisticated learning. And they should feel it's a real atmosphere. They should realize that Torah is a positive force that has answers—"Oh, Torah, Torah, teach me the way to live, the right way." There's a Torah

message from God, not ideas pushed into the Torah, but the Torah tells you what to do and the way to develop your total personality. And this is for everybody. We teach love between brothers, *ahavas yisrael* [love of all Jews], and we put on a little music. . . . We open our arms.

We talk straight, we speak clearly, and we open our arms, but we don't push the boy mentally into a box. He has to decide on his own to accept or not. We can have a boy here who doesn't believe in God. We can have a boy here who in the yeshiva premises keeps religion, but outside he doesn't. We don't push. We just plant the seed, talk straight, have a dialogue, open our arms, and have patience. You see and show love. You feel the vibrations and say, "Come forward." We don't compromise, but on the other hand we give the man his own validity, his own self-respect to move forward the way he wants to move. . . .

I fell into this drug scene and I wanted to get help for these boys. They needed psychiatric help, some of these boys. And I couldn't get any help from the government, so I had to face the problems myself. And given the law of averages, I was quite successful. I didn't have the proper facilities, the proper finances, but I did quite a lot of work, and I was involved. I accepted the boys for what they were. I gave them love. I didn't press them about their clothing, because for some of them it was an important part. They had to hold on to their long hair and clothing, and if I could somehow move them . . . I heard this story from Rav Sarna of blessed memory of Chevron Yeshiva: When Chevron came to Israel, to Yerushalayim, the Yerushalmis tried to throw them out of Jerusalem, and they moved to Chevron. Why? Because the Chevron guys had small hats and short coats. The Yerushalmis had large hats and long coats. So "Der Alte from Slobodka"[7] gave an example. He said, "I'm a professor. I'm taking a heart of stone and making a heart of a human being, of flesh. And in the middle of my operation you're telling me that the hat is too small and the coat is too short?" So I said the same thing. I'm in the middle of an operation, trying to save these boys. You're going to tell me their hair is too long? Or their garments . . . too hippie? It's foolish. So I let it go, and I thank the Lord, I was quite successful, guiding a lot of boys in their lives.

Goldstein's efforts resulted in his successfully attracting hippies, but they had two consequences that he did not anticipate. He had set out simply to accept problem students into his yeshiva, a small traditional school in borrowed quarters. But by his acceptance of nontraditional students, the nature of his institution came to be substantially modified. For example, a number of students at Har Tzion had professional experience playing with rock bands. With Rabbi Goldstein's encouragement

7. A well-known spiritual mentor in the Slobodka Yeshiva in Europe at the beginning of the twentieth century.

and financial assistance in purchasing musical instruments, an excellent musical group was put together. The group offered (and continues to offer) musical concerts on Saturday nights in an open square on Mt. Zion. The event is called a *melavveh malkah* (literally, accompaniment of the queen, as Sabbath is sometimes called). The concerts became a regular source of income and of publicity for the school, a means of recruiting new students, and a source of financial support for the members of the band. Most interestingly, traditional chasidic melodies were not played at this melavveh malkah. Instead, religious texts were set to rock and country music. At the same time, lighting and other techniques typical of rock festivals were used. For example, slides of scenes of Israel would be flashed on a screen above the audience while the music was played. Clearly, the student body had a major effect on the traditional musical mode of expression. What was elsewhere an ethnic or a religious expression, hardly capable of attracting the interest of those outside the religious community, was here being used to build bridges to a world that had been thought to be unreachable. The school attracted not only people with talent in music but also people prominent in other artistic circles. Thus the world of the yeshiva, a place for immersion in an ancient thought system, a place where popular music was not heard (and certainly not played), where popular books and even newspapers were discouraged, came to be invaded by modern styles and, while reforming others, came itself to be reformed.

Carlebach in the United States and Goldstein in Israel were demonstrating to the Orthodox community for the first time that it was possible to attract hippies to Orthodoxy, that sophisticated, world-traveled college students, students who had experienced everything the big world had to offer, "free" sex, drugs, *treyf* [nonkosher] food—things forbidden to the Jewish community and almost unknown in most Orthodox circles— were giving up all this freedom to become Orthodox. The initial reaction among the Orthodox to stories of hippies' becoming Orthodox was "Something must be wrong with them."[8] Some continued to doubt the reality of such changes for a long time after the first of the hippies joined Orthodoxy. But the successful transition of some hippies to Orthodoxy suddenly awakened the Orthodox to the possibility that what they had might indeed be attractive to others and gave it a powerful lift.

8. This says quite a bit about the way in which many Orthodox see their own commitment and raises questions about what the ties of Orthodoxy are for some of those who are "frum from birth" (born into observant families).

MODERNISTIC ORTHODOXY

Although the Modernistic Orthodox were in the forefront of attempts to provide a bridge between Orthodox and non-Orthodox Jews, their efforts were directed toward those who had taken the initial steps on their own. They were not bringing Judaism to the attention of the uninterested or persuading the uninterested of the truth of Orthodox Judaism, but simply facilitating the return of those already interested in Orthodox Judaism. This was the meaning of the work of the Young Israel in the 1930s and 1940s, of the yeshivot that opened their doors to youngsters from nonreligious families in the 1940s, and of Yeshiva University's camping programs, Torah Leadership seminars, and School for Jewish Studies.[9] Modernistic Orthodoxy was uncomfortable in the role of missionary. Only Lubavitch in the 1950s and early 1960s through Shlomo Carlebach and Zalman Schachter attempted to reach out and actually change people.

Perhaps modernistic Orthodoxy's hesitations derived from its rationalistic antifundamentalistic approach. Perhaps they derived from its endorsement of values of toleration for others within society, an endorsement that modernistic Orthodoxy found more necessary to the continued existence of Judaism than did the more traditionalistic Orthodoxy, which was more insulated from the pressures of the larger world.

MODERNISTIC ORTHODOXY'S HESITATION IN ISRAEL

Chaim Brovender's yeshivot, the Shappel Colleges, which were modernistic, could not reach out to ba'alei t'shuva in the same manner Goldstein had. Brovender's way was strikingly similar to that of Yeshiva University. Values and styles to which he was committed—democratic process, secular education, tolerance of others and their views—limited the response he was capable of making. In addition, his rationalism and antimessianism, which was so much a part of the world of the mitnagdic yeshivot, also placed him in a confrontational posture with the hippies who rejected what they saw as the rationalistic, bureaucratized, and disenchanted American society.

The following excerpts from interviews conducted with Chaim Bro-

---

9. Youngsters attracted to Orthodoxy through religious release hour programs in the public schools were a different matter entirely. They were too young to have undergone a change. They were simply being socialized into religion with the explicit or implicit permission of their parents, who allowed them to attend such programs.

vender in 1976, almost six years after he had started his yeshiva, reflect a revulsion at missionizing (characteristic of American Jews, particularly those who have been acculturated) and a strong suspicion of charismatic leadership, messianism and religious zealotry (the position articulated by mitnaggedim in their opposition to Chasidism).

> I have never seen myself as a person who could deal with what is generally called *chozrim b'tshuva* ["returnees in repentance," a phrase used in Israel as a synonym for ba'al t'shuva]. I never saw myself as being able to radically change the course of people's lives. The people who come to us are people who want to learn Torah. Now some of them have always wanted to learn Torah. I mean, they've been Jews all their lives. Perhaps their education has been weak, etc. Others have been radically changed—but not by us generally. We never considered ourselves a yeshiva for ba'alei t'shuva, as though this was a special subcategory of humanity that had to be dealt with in a special way. We considered ourselves a school that was prepared to deal with beginners in Torah, to enable them to continue and take their place among the ranks of the learners of Torah.
>
> The school began as a school for beginners, not for ba'alei t'shuva but for beginners. . . . We don't put up posters. . . . We have a magazine, but it's guaranteed not to get us into business. . . . I mean, there are no pictures.[10]
>
> If I thought I could, I would save the world. But I think I can teach somebody a *pasuk in chumash* [a sentence of the Pentateuch] or a line of Gemara [Talmudic commentary on the Mishna]. And that's what I want to do.
>
> Q. Why is the study of Judaism significant to those people? What makes it significant for them?
>
> A. I don't know what turns people on. I don't know what the chemistry is, and I don't care. Generally I think that it would not make me happy to see people turned on. There's probably a lot of charlatanism in it. There's probably a lot of exploitation of naivete—things that I can't stand, and I don't know how they can do it. But I admit that I take advantage of it. How do I take advantage of it? After this transformation happens, they find themselves in need of some place to learn, and they come to us. But I have nothing to do with making that transformation, and I don't want to get involved in it. I don't want the yeshiva to have anything to do with that because that is contrary to the learning experience. It's contrary to the notion of free investigation. It's nondemocratic and nonintellectual. It's not for me; it's not for the yeshiva. I feel the contradiction very strongly. If I would turn my boys loose on making other

---

10. In contrast, the Ohr Someyach magazine was designed to attract students to that school. It featured photographs, a bright and attractive cover, fiction, and poetry.

people Jewish when they themselves are beginners, they might become bigots. Because once you *have* to know the answer, one you *have* to know what to tell somebody, once you've *got* to convince them that you're right, then you can't be a talmid chacham anymore. You certainly can't learn anymore. You can't really study anymore. You've just got to know all the answers. You've got to always be right. If all those people who do that are assured *olam haba* [the world to come—i.e., heaven], I'm very happy. But it's not my thing. It's not what I'm interested in.[11]

Outcomes

Modernists are exposed to broad liberal education and professional training, which subjects them to pressures to defend the Orthodox life-style that separates them from others. Traditionalistic Orthodox generally avoid such education. Modernists are often subject to the pressures of the Christmas party, for example, as part of their occupational and professional experience; traditionalists tend to be employed in a restricted range of occupations in which Jews already dominate or their presence is already known and accepted. Democratic ideals, values of toleration, and suspicion of charisma, messianism, and emotional appeals restrict the recruitment efforts of modernists, who use these principles to defend their own integrity and their differences from the non-Jewish society in which they participate.

Thus although modernists reached out to others they did not actively recruit ba'alei t'shuva, particularly when recruitment seemed to require a dramatic change in personality. It was five years after Rabbi Goldstein founded Har Tzion that other yeshivot for ba'alei t'shuva began to open. During these five years the interest in traditional Judaism of seemingly lost Jews began to be recognized, and the image of ba'alei t'shuva among the Orthodox was transformed.

Organized Jewry in the United States and Israel was for a time incapa-

11. This was Brovender's position in 1976. By 1982 his school was engaged in active recruitment, in visits to college campuses, and the yeshiva included a new program intended for ba'alei t'shuva. He was much more at ease with this role and not inclined to question the validity of this activity. His students, however, were still not engaged in recruitment; nor were they encouraged to become involved. In 1985 he was joined by Rabbi Steven Riskin, who immigrated to Israel, and the schools began a more active outreach program. Why the school's recruitment policy changed is briefly explained at the end of chapter 8.

ble of responding positively to the hippie ba'al t'shuva. Chasidic and traditionalist Orthodox were too insular to reach out, modernists were too "establishment" for the counterculture, and this held even more strongly for Conservative and Reform Judaism.

Perhaps Carlebach and Goldstein awakened the Orthodox community to the possibility of attracting young, uncommitted Jews. Carlebach, more than any other individual, demonstrated that Orthodoxy could reach out even to the counterculture and could make Orthodoxy and Chasidism appealing. Goldstein developed the first yeshiva for ba'alei t'shuva. Starting as a traditional yeshiva, his school provided the students with the possibility of earning a livelihood, helped them make suitable marriages, assisted them in finding housing—in a word, became a complete community. This was not characteristic of traditional yeshivot.

These pioneering efforts to reach out to the ba'alei t'shuva *as they were* had three results:

1. People were being introduced to the Orthodox community while they still retained hippie life-styles, enjoyed rock music, hippie art, macrobiotic food, dressed in the hippie style, used incense and, occasionally, drugs. These hippie styles were recast in a Jewish framework so that tofu was used in *cholent,* the Sabbath *challah* might be whole wheat and the meal vegetarian, the music might be rock but the words would be traditional prayers and hymns, clothes might be hippie but a *tallit* (in the hippie style and colors) would be worn. On one hand, so long as this group continued to dress and behave as hippies they remained a separate community whose commitment to Orthodoxy was suspect. On the other hand, pride in the fact that hippies would freely choose Orthodoxy led to a measure of acceptance of them and their styles. Orthodox circles began to consider the possibility of reaching out to hippies and uncommitted Jewish youth as a means of countering those who were leaving Judaism for Eastern religions, cults, witchcraft, or radical politics.

2. Accepting hippies, including women, as they are with their own subcultural styles, gave rise to some separate communities of hippie ba'alei t'shuva. In the United States such a community developed around Shlomo Carlebach in San Francisco. In Israel it gave rise to a Carlebach community in Modi'in and to the Yeshiva Har Tzion, which constituted itself as a community. A number of yeshivot for ba'alei t'shuva have also developed community characteristics.

3. That some of the newly Orthodox hippies retained their own styles and lived as communities made their unusual (that is, Orthodox *and*

hippie) life-styles even more visible. They became media events. A wedding conducted by Shlomo Carlebach in Golden Gate Park, San Francisco, was featured prominently in a photo story in *Life* (26 Sept. 1969). Similarly prominent coverage was given to Har Tzion. As a result, the new label "ba'al t'shuva" came to replace the older labels "those lacking background" or "late starters." It was now clear that one of the problems that would have to be considered was how to deal with questions of faith, how to win a person's commitment. This was a problem that had not been faced in the past because the old label allowed the Orthodox community to assume that the person was committed and simply lacked training. The new label made it clear that commitment itself was an open question. And for a time the possibility that a mature person could make a commitment to Orthodoxy was itself questioned. These attitudes were overcome, but only slowly. And for those who remained hippie in their style of life, the suspicions were never completely stilled.

Some of the pioneers of Orthodox outreach suffered negative personal consequences that demonstrated the constraints on reaching out for Orthodoxy. Goldstein's school developed a reputation as a place where drugs were taken. Carlebach, who was a bachelor when he undertook these efforts and remained a bachelor into his forties, lost credibility when he was seen occasionally giving a young woman a hug or a peck on the cheek, behavior that was not problematic in terms of American norms but violated Orthodox norms. His friend Zalman Schachter is now associated with the Conservative Chavura movement rather than the Orthodox t'shuva movement. The yeshiva community of Jerusalem was and has remained suspicious of those who reach out to ba'alei t'shuva, and such people could easily find themselves rejected unless they develop a means of placing their attachment to Orthodoxy above suspicion. Yeshivot and programs for ba'alei t'shuva face a similar problem.

A review of the data indicates that there have been people who have returned to the fold of Orthodox religion historically, but the overwhelming majority of such people have appeared only in the past generation or two. A large number of such people have found the synagogue to be a portal of entry into the Orthodox community. A smaller portion of the population has used yeshivot as the portal of entry to the Orthodox community. This portal also provides entry into the yeshivishe velt, a community often more countercultural and parochial in outlook and stricter in ritual observance than the modernists.

Although the yeshiva has been a portal of entry for some part of the population since the 1940s, no changes in curriculum to accommodate its new role were undertaken until the 1950s when first the Yeshiva Heychal Hatorah and later Yeshiva University undertook to develop special programs for those of limited background. Starting in Israel in 1967, with a particularly energetic burst in 1972, a new type of institution was developed that came to be known as yeshivot for ba'alei t'shuva.

II
Institutions
and
Values

Chapter 5

The Ba'al T'shuva Yeshiva

With the growth of the perception that ba'alei t'shuva were something new, that something had happened that now made possible the return of those thought to be lost to Judaism, Orthodox Jews attempted to develop an institutional response to take advantage of this opportunity. In less than a decade yeshivot for ba'alei t'shuva became an accepted institutional form in Orthodox Judiasm.

Yeshivot for ba'alei t'shuva are a uniquely Orthodox response to renewed interest in Judaism and provide a strategic perspective on the nature of commitment to Orthodoxy. Interestingly, although about 85 percent of newly Orthodox American Jews enter the Orthodox community through the synagogue only a few synagogues have been developed as a specific response to ba'alei t'shuva (although some have developed outreach programs, see above chapter 2).

In Conservative and Reform Judaism the chavurah, or fellowship, became the new institutional response to renewed interest in Judiasm. The chavurah had begun in 1943 in the Reconstructionist movement (the radical wing of the Conservative movement led by Mordechai Kaplan) as small fellowship groups within congregations (Raphael 1984, 190). In 1968 Arthur Green, a young Conservative rabbi, founded Chavurat Shalom, the first commune-congregation, in Boston. This signaled a critical turning point in the development of the chavurah. Chavurat Shalom was a response to the youth counterculture of that time, and its structure and programs became a model for others.

Chavurat Shalom was initially designed as a seminary with the objective of training a new breed of rabbis and offering Jewish courses in a setting less formal and formidable than traditional educational institutions. The Commonwealth of Massachusetts gave the chavurah a charter as a nonprofit educational corporation, which had the coincidental advantage of making draft deferments available to a number of the members during the Vietnam War. Despite this feature, the seminary aspect of Chavurat Shalom never took hold (Reisman 1977, 8). It became instead a community of prayer, a synagogue with commune-like characteristics.

Soon other chavurot were established following the example of Chavurat Shalom. Within five years these chavurot, too, came to be synagogal structures, either attached to synagogues or independent synagogue-like communes, sometimes called *batim* (houses [Reisman 1977, 15]). Thus, although chavurot were revitalized under conditions of state accreditation and military exemptions that should have favored its seminary character, this response to the religious ferment of the 1960s became synagogal.

Orthodoxy, on the other hand, did not develop chavurot, even though the synagogue was a major portal of entry to Orthodoxy. Rather, it built seminaries or yeshivot for them. What made the yeshiva for ba'alei t'shuva an Orthodox rather than a Reform or Conservative response to the renewed religious interest of Jews? And what made the chavurah the response of the Conservative and Reform wings of Judaism?

AUTHORITY, COMMITMENT, AND THE STUDY OF TALMUD IN
CONTEMPORARY JUDAISM

Orthodox, Conservative, and Reform Judaism differ in religious practice. Orthodox Judaism requires the performance of many rituals, Reform requires few, and Conservative Judaism falls between the two. This difference affects the curriculum for religious training.

In Orthodoxy, religious honor and authority derive from the performance of religious ritual and from "learning"—that is, talmudic scholarship. Reform, on the other hand, is little concerned with ritual behavior and does not view ritual piety as a basis for authority. Its scholarship has centered on philosophy and theology, areas of Jewish thought that have been peripheral to yeshivot. In Conservative Judaism the study of Talmud and Codes is not as central as in Orthodoxy, and historical and sociological perspectives are important.

The chavurah posits a religious authority structure that is compatible with Reform and Conservative Judaism but not with Orthodoxy. The chavurah is a group of peers whose members, through their own decision, determine forms of worship and celebration. Though they may be guided by tradition and by halakhah, they do not feel bound by them. Most important, they need not be expert in Jewish law and tradition. Their philosophy sees the locus for the interpretative and adaptive mechanisms of Judaism in the community of Jews.

All branches of Judaism (for that matter, all religions with some holy scripture) require a system or institution to adapt the written religious laws and norms to changing contexts. This results in what has been called in Judaism the *Torah sheh ba'al peh,* the Oral Law. In the most traditionalistic view the entire Oral Law was given to Moses at Sinai, and all religious authority derives from this revelation. The only changes or modifications possible are those already implicit in the Torah or the Oral Law. In fact, a substantial portion of Orthodox Jews believe that there has never been any change or development of the halakhah in response to changed conditions.[1]

Reform Judaism sees the authority for adaption and change as residing in the conscience of the individual. It denies even the authority of the Written Law, the Torah, as it relates to religious rituals. For Reform, Judaism influenced by Hegel's and Darwin's view of history is an evolutionary process, continually reaching higher stages of development. The future rather than the past promises Divine revelation, and although the ethical imperatives of Judaism remain, each individual is to be guided primarily by his own conscience.

Conservative Judaism, seeking a position that affirms flexibility and change, if not within the framework of halakhah then at least with the guidance of Jewish tradition, claims authority for the Oral tradition. Nonetheless, its commitment to change and adjustment has required redefinition of the locus of the authority of tradition. Conservative Judaism has placed it in the Jewish people.[2]

Thus, the chavurah is compatible with both Reform and Conservative Judaism, whose members by their own decisions determine forms of worship and celebration. But the chavurah is incompatible with Orthodoxy, where religious authority is based on expertise in halakhah and piety.

Differences among the three wings of Judaism are most clearly seen in

1. Others disagree. See Berkowitz 1984; Grossman 1986.

2. The best expression of this view of religious authority can be found in Mordechai Kaplan's *Judaism as a Civilization* (1934). Kaplan, the founder of Reconstructionism, an ideology and a movement associated with but not identical to Conservative Judaism, taught at the (Conservative) Jewish Theological Seminary from 1909 to 1963 and exercised a powerful influence on the shape and ideology of Conservatism. His influence reaches well beyond the movement he founded.

the curricula of their rabbinical seminaries. In Orthodox rabbinical programs, knowledge of the Talmud and the Codes is emphasized almost to the exclusion of all else. Neither Jewish history nor philosophy nor even knowledge of the Bible (apart from the Pentateuch) is a part of the regular course of study. Students may learn some of these in prerabbinical studies at the high-school level. At Yeshiva University, they are part of the general college program. But even at Yeshiva University they are not a part of the program leading to rabbinical ordination. Nor will the study of the Talmud and the Codes aim to impart simply knowledge *about* the Talmud. What matters is not how the text came to be or the historical context surrounding it but the text itself. So much is this the case that in the 1960s even beginning students at Yeshiva University's James Striar School proudly wore T-shirts emblazoned "It. Not about it."

The Hebrew Union College/Jewish Institute of Religion (the rabbinical college of Reform Judaism), and the Jewish Theological Seminary (the rabbinical seminary for Conservative Judaism) emphasize instead historical and philosophical studies in their curricula. For Reform and Conservative rabbinical students, an emphasis on the historical contexts for the emergence of the sacred literature, the evolutionary development of Judaism, and the changing nature of halakhah undermines the relative importance of the study of Talmud and Codes.

Given the importance of halakhah for Orthodox Jews—and given that halakhah is not restricted to liturgy or special ritual occasions but provides specific rules for the conduct of the minutest areas of life—those who have the commitment or willingness to follow halakhah but not the requisite knowledge defer to and follow the more knowledgeable. This applies particularly to the ba'al t'shuva.

Thus difference between the Reform and Conservative and the Orthodox regarding new recruits may be illustrated by examining a specific ritual such as *Sukkot*. For the Orthodox, the Sukkot holiday requires that men take their meals and sleep in a temporary shelter whose only roof is a loose layer of leaves, thatch, or similar vegetation. A novice will have to be advised on the minimum and maximum size of the dwelling, on the materials that may and may not be used to roof it, on precisely what the obligation of "dwelling in the *sukkah*" consists of, and on whether or not one is relieved of this obligation in inclement weather. In all these matters those who have no knowledge are compelled by their own commitment to accept the authority of those more learned in the halakhah.

In contrast, if one celebrates Sukkot as part of a chavurah the details of the sukkah structure may be decided by the group itself. The sukkah may even be built indoors if the group prefers it, even though this would be contrary to halakhah. Further, just as the chavurah does not feel bound to follow the halakhic expert, so the members of the group do not feel compelled to follow the rule of the majority and may instead choose not to celebrate or to celebrate in a different fashion. My point is not simply that the community cannot compel compliance, for the Orthodox cannot do that either. But the community cannot even require compliance, as personal autonomy is the dominant value (Reisman 1977, 77–80).

These two conceptions of religious authority are so opposed that there seems to be no neutral ground. Thus, when the Pardess Institute, a ba'al t'shuva institution that developed out of chavurah origins, attempted to formulate an acceptable worship practice that would suit both the halakhah-oriented and the chavurah-oriented, neither group was satisfied. After numerous efforts failed, services were conducted according to the wishes of one group or the other on alternate weeks. Finally even that arrangement broke down, and prayer services became sporadic.

The Structure of the Yeshiva

What qualities set the ba'al t'shuva yeshivot off from other schools? What elements are essential to them, reflect the value systems they attempt to transmit, and provide insights into the world of the ba'al t'shuva and Orthodox Judaism? Although the structure of ba'al t'shuva yeshivot is similar to that of yeshivot generally, these features are new to the new recruit encountering a yeshiva for the first time.

SEX SEGREGATION

To the modern Western eye, a striking aspect of ba'al t'shuva yeshivot is that they are segregated by sex. Men study in some schools, and women in others. There are no coed classes or lectures. There is only one exception to this among schools for ba'alei t'shuva, and that is Pardess Institute, which does not call itself a yeshiva.

Yeshivot have traditionally been schools for men only. This pattern is consistent with the traditionalism of Orthodoxy. Consider that until recently religious seminaries of all faiths were open only to men. Consider also that Orthodox traditions are often crystalized into halakhah. (*Minhag Yisrael k'din*—Israel's customs are as laws.)

In addition, Orthodoxy especially emphasizes the separation of men and women in public religious activities. In synagogues men and women have worshipped in separate areas separated by a mechitzah for thousands of years, as far back as the Temple.[3] Furthermore, although Jewish women in antiquity were judges, prophetesses, and powerful queens, they have never played a significant role in Rabbinic Judaism, where the basis for power was legal scholarship. With few exceptions women have been excluded from houses of study. Rabbinic Judaism held to the view that only men were obliged to study the Torah and that Torah study was the most important religious obligation of all (*Mishnah Peah* 1:1). Women were completely excluded from this obligation.[4]

But simply to say that women did not attend yeshivot does not adequately convey the separation between men and women characteristic of yeshivot. Jewish law forbids a man to be alone behind closed doors with a woman other than his wife (or member of his family). Men are enjoined against engaging in idle chatter with women and are warned never to look with lewd intention on so much as the little finger of a woman. Social interaction between men and women is severely restricted. In the yeshivot these restrictions are emphasized as they are at no other time or place in the life of an Orthodox male.

The ba'al t'shuva yeshiva typically follows the lead of the general

3. For the origins of the women's gallery and a separate area in the Temple for women, see *Mishnah Sukkah* 5:2. The Conservative movement's removal of the partition and the introduction of "mixed pews," where men and women may sit together during prayer services, are considered the major causes of the break between Conservative and Orthodox Judaism.

4. Women are excluded from many obligations of Jewish religious law. The general principle is that commandments that are bound to specific times are not binding on women. Women are therefore not obliged, as men are, to pray at specific times of the day or seasons of the year or to perform other commandments similarly connected to time or season that involve positive acts. Women are, however, bound to abstain from forbidden acts even if these acts are time-related, as for example fasting on Yom Kippur. There are numerous exceptions to this rule (BT, Kiddushin 31a). Study, which is not tied to any given time, would be obligatory for women if the general rule were followed. In this case, however, an exception is derived from the statement requiring the teaching of Torah ("and thou shalt teach it to thy sons"), which is taken to specifically exclude daughters. Thus, although study is not time bound, women have been released from this obligation. The Mishnah (*Sotah* 3:4) cites a difference of opinion on this matter. Ben Azzai holds that "A person is obligated to teach his daughter Torah"; Rabbi Eliezer holds that "Whoever teaches his daughter Torah it were as though he taught her licentiousness." Although the reasoning behind it is refuted in a subsequent mishnah, Rabbi Eliezar's opinion has influenced the structure of education for women in Judaism. Higher religious education has not been available to women until modern times.

yeshivot in this matter. All yeshivot are severely restrictive by the standards of the larger society, although the extent of separation required varies. Embracing or kissing a woman who is not a member of one's immediate family is forbidden. Holding hands and social dancing are frowned upon. Even socializing and dating are to be avoided except for the specific purpose of finding a mate.

These customs are often known, even when not followed, by those reared in Orthodox families. But the ba'al t'shuva reared in an Americanized family probably has no awareness of these practices, which seem immensely restrictive. Whereas perhaps 85 percent of males and 50 percent of females in society at large have engaged in premarital intercourse (Robertson 1987, 252), in the yeshiva a handshake with a woman becomes problematic. This difference in attitude regarding the relation of men and women is one of the most formidable obstacles to recruitment, the more so as it is generally not well known in the larger community, even among those who attend the synagogue or have had bar mitzvah classes. The rules governing behavior between the sexes are generally taught when people are ready for marriage. Those who have not attended religious schools beyond bar mitzvah will not know them. Nor will the parents of ba'alei t'shuva. Paul Cowan's description of his own return to Judaism (1981) suggest that some of those who find the rules too restrictive may opt instead for Conservatism, even if they adopt the rules of kashrut and Shabbat.

From another perspective, the separation of sexes in the yeshivot acts as a screen, filtering out those who are unwilling to accept a discipline in social relations that is substantially different from their early experience. For those who have led relatively unrestricted sexual lives, precisely such restrictions may be attractive. They may provide order, the sense of discipline, and the hallowing of an act that had formerly been seen as self-serving or animalistic. In any case, although just what may be appealing in the new Orthodox norms of relations between the sexes is unclear, ba'alei t'shuva must wrestle with these norms and at least attempt to conform to them.

INTIMACY

Ba'al t'shuva yeshivot are small schools, with enrollments ranging from ten or fifteen to about three hundred. The typical school has between fifty and one hundred and twenty students. The smallest ones, with enrollments of twenty-five or below, are often affiliates of larger traditional yeshivot. The small size of most schools and the small classes, which rarely have more than fifteen or twenty students and frequently have as few as four or five, foster a sense of intimacy, emotional support, and warmth. Teachers quickly get to know the students as people. But intimacy also involves a loss of privacy. It provides opportunities for guidance but also possibilities for supervision.

Those already committed to Judaism may welcome guidance. But those encountering Orthodoxy for the first time may be asked to accept new restrictions and obligations before they are fully ready to do so. This group may see close guidance as supervision and repression. Schools that concentrate on study skills and mastery of texts and make an effort to provide students with more personal space, however, are sometimes said to lack warmth, close relationships between students and teachers, and sufficient direction for students.

Although some students clearly prefer warmth and intimacy and others prefer privacy, most are ambivalent. They want both and are unwilling to grant that each tends to be a negation of the other; the more intimacy, the less privacy, and vice versa.

While the small size of the schools fosters intimacy, the recruitment effort, which involves inviting passing travelers—potential students—to enjoy a meal or a night or a week at the yeshiva, introduces an element of transiency into the school that tends to undercut intimacy and warmth. Participants estimate that about 95 percent of those who come to the ba'al t'shuva yeshiva for a meal leave within three days. A student at one yeshiva looked around the dining room on a Shabbat at lunch and estimated that about 70 percent of the people in the room had been there for fewer than three weeks. In this regard, the ba'al t'shuva yeshiva is markedly different from the typical yeshiva.

Schools heavily involved in recruitment must maintain a high level of guidance and intimacy to achieve their own goals and avoid being overwhelmed by the students who are unsocialized in the way of life to which the schools are committed. Schools that do not provide close supervision compensate by not accepting transients. Intimate knowledge of the student is therefore achieved not by intense contact but by long-term and continuous contact.

SURROGATE ORTHODOX HOMES: DORMITORIES AND SABBATH HOSTS

Every one of the ba'al t'shuva yeshivot, with the exception of Pardess Institute, provides dormitory facilities for students. This is not simply an amenity; it is essential to the program of the yeshivot. Living in dormitories facilitates learning the daily routines of the prayers practiced by

Orthodox Jews. One can learn these routines in the classroom, but to observe and imitate is far more effective. A prayer of thanks is required on opening one's eyes in the morning; one's hands should be ritually washed upon arising, before one has yet taken "four steps"; the long and major prayers of the day are to be said before one has had breakfast. Breakfast itself requires familiarity with Jewish law and ritual, for there are rituals regarding consumption of the food, washing the hands before the meal, and the blessings to be said before and after the meal. At the close of study at the end of the day, a round of prayers is said before one lies down to sleep. All this—which is to say, a good part of ritual practices—would have to be taught formally were it not for the dormitory facility where students learn these practices by participating in them and observing others. And this is apart from the customs and laws of the Sabbath and the holidays, which are different from those practiced every day. One must learn to adjust to a day when lights are not turned on or off, radios and televisions are silent, the telephone is not answered, one walks and does not ride in cars—to a time when one does not eat bread or when one eats and sleeps in a hut.

In addition, the food must be kosher, which means that the foodstuffs themselves must be ritually acceptable, must have been prepared in the ritually required manner. The laws regarding kosher food and the preparation of kosher food are immense in scope and complexity. They constitute a fourth of the Code of Jewish Law. Rabbinical ordination is based on mastery of this part of the codes. Without the dormitory and without the yeshiva's kitchen, which provides kosher meals, the life of the ba'al t'shuva becomes immensely complicated. Moreover, an experiment in eating kosher food is an expense. The returnee must replace the dishes and cooking utensils in the home, buy two sets of dishes, pots, and other utensils. For Passover two more sets of dishes are required. The stove and ovens have to be ritually cleaned, and some food products replaced. In addition, the person must spend a considerable amount of time familiarizing himself or herself with the kosher products that are available and the laws pertaining to maintaining a kosher kitchen.

The kosher kitchen provided by the yeshiva removes the difficulties of eating kosher—which can be a major obstacle to those who wish to experience living by the standards of Jewish law. Thus, far more than an amenity, the kosher kitchen is essential for those attempting to begin the practice of traditional Judaism.

Rabbi Buchwald of the Lincoln Square Synagogue finds that a good deal of his time is devoted to advising newly Orthodox on how to keep a kosher home, on the kashrut of various products whose ingredients and arrangements with kashrut supervisory organizations are constantly changing, on which restaurants and hotels are kosher, and on kashering kitchens (ritually cleansing them so that kosher food may be prepared in them). Yet kashrut remained a problem, for as Rabbi Buchwald commented, despite his efforts he was aware that a number of congregants ate at places where nonkosher foods are served and ate foods whose kashrut is questionable.

Rabbi Morris Besdin of Yeshiva University said, in contrast, that he didn't think newly Orthodox students found it difficult to accept the laws of kashrut. Yeshiva University provides kosher meals for its students, and several small restaurants in the area provide kosher pizza, hamburgers, and the like. Student who want to can keep kosher with little difficulty.

In Israel kashrut is still less of a problem, as most restaurants and hotels serve kosher food. But eating out generally remains a problem in the United States except in thickly Orthodox neighborhoods.

The dormitory, then, is a functional equivalent of the home, providing first-hand experience with the practice of traditional Judaism, which is ordinarily open to observation only in the privacy of the home. Yet none of the yeshivot views the dormitory as providing sufficient experience in Orthodox life. All arrange for students to experience Jewish home life by visiting the homes of Orthodox Jews for Sabbath and holidays.

At the ba'al t'shuva yeshivot in Israel, students typically spend three Sabbaths at various homes and the fourth Sabbath at the yeshiva. The yeshiva makes a concerted effort to place its students, using its own deans, teachers, and supporters as the prime placements and relying on the assistance of friends of the yeshiva for additional placements. The dormitory supervisor or the *mashgiach* (dean of men, in charge of spiritual development) may have primary responsibility for these placements.

Students may be placed at different homes each Shabbat or assigned to a given family for Sabbath and for holidays. This, of course, will depend on whether they and their host family get along. If not, the student or the host family may ask for a change. If they do get along, the host family may become the student's adopted family, providing personal advice and assistance to him. They may become so personally involved with each other that the student is invited by the family to bar mitzvah and wedding celebrations and the family is invited to the student's wedding even if that occurs some time after he has left the yeshiva.

A home may have several students as guests for Shabbat, only one guest, or only an occasional guest. In general, deans and teachers at the yeshivot have several guests, most of them students who have just entered the school or are there for only a few weeks. The Shabbat is an opportunity for the faculty to get to know the students and to become aware of questions raised by encounters with Orthodoxy.

Students enjoy the Friday evening meal and the Shabbat midday meal at their host's home. Usually they return to the dormitory Friday night to sleep and again for a nap after the midday meal on Sabbath. The third Sabbath meal (*se'udah shelishit*), taken between the late afternoon prayers (*minchah*) and the prayers marking the end of Sabbath (*maariv* and *Havdalah*), is at the yeshiva with the entire student body gathered together. Songs, perhaps dancing, and a *d'var Torah* (a short Torah lesson) by one of the teachers mark this meal, as does, traditionally, a touch of melancholy over the imminent end of the Sabbath.

Because students return to the school to sleep, host families can easily accomodate several students. When the number of would-be guests exceeds the available host families in nearby Jerusalem neighborhoods, families in other areas may be asked to take a guest and provide sleeping accomodations. Proximity to the yeshiva is a prime consideration, and in all cases, of course, the host family must be Orthodox.

In the United States, similarly, students may be placed with families near the yeshiva. At Yeshiva University the school provides Sabbath meals and a program of song and study for students remaining on campus. In addition, the students run a service that arranges for Shabbat meals with Orthodox families in the neighborhood of the school.

THE TRADITION OF SABBATH GUESTS: SOME NEW PATTERNS AND PROBLEMS

The efforts by Lincoln Square Synagogue to provide Shabbat accomodations makes clear the problems that must be overcome in placing yeshiva students. Because Lincoln Square Synagogue is not a yeshiva, it has no dormitory. It has highly active programs, however, for those wishing to learn about Orthodoxy. Hence, it must provide sleeping accommodations for those wishing to participate in its Shabbat program who live beyond walking distance of the synagogue. In New York City this describes a substantial population of potential returnees. Members of the synagogue are therefore polled on their willingness to accommodate guests, who are screened by filling out an application form. In addition, the hospitality committee usually speaks to those seeking Shabbat accommodations, at least by phone, before deciding whether to place them. Nevertheless, potential hosts feel some hesitation. Some people fear that a guest may be a threat to the host family or may simply turn out to be a pest. And with nowhere else to go, the guest will be with them for the entire Shabbat, not only for the meals.

While having Sabbath guests (*orchim*) is an old Jewish tradition, potential recruits to Orthodoxy represent a new problem. In the past guests were Orthodox Jews. Potential recruits include some who are skeptical or simply curious. Inviting them to one's home leaves one feeling exposed and vulnerable.

For a long time the Orthodox community looked upon ba'alei t'shuva with suspicion. In an informal discussion of ba'alei t'shuva the rabbi of a prominent congregation in Jerusalem in 1976 remarked, "What's wrong with them? Why are they becoming Orthodox Jews? Are they normal?" To deal with the curious and those barely acquainted with the culture of Orthodox Judaism, a few people began to host large numbers of potential recruits for a Shabbat. During the second half of the 1970s numerous articles began appearing in the Israeli press and in the Orthodox press in the United States on ba'alei t'shuva. By 1982 so widespread was acceptance of ba'alei t'shuva in Jerusalem that having potential ba'alei t'shuva in one's home on Shabbat was something of a status symbol. At present in Jerusalem would-be hosts plead for guests, including those who need sleeping accommodations. One recruiter's late Friday night tours of Meah Shearim are sometimes accompanied by people eager to bring home a ba'al t'shuva. Two families in the Old City of Jerusalem invited large numbers of guests each week, packing into ordinary apartments as many as forty people. Many others invited five or six guests for a Shabbat. Although most of the people who offered their hospitality to visitors and the curious are simply Orthodox, a substantial portion were chasidim living in Meah Shearim, the most pious and insulated community in Jerusalem. This arrangement was favored by Baruch Levine, a former ba'al t'shuva who had begun his own recruitment program.[5] The very "otherness" of such homes, their mystery, was an inducement for people to come and visit. Before long young Orthodox people themselves decided that this was too good an adventure for them to pass up, and they too began to seek out such invitations for Shabbat meals. By the 1980s per-

---

5. Most yeshivot try to locate families whose religious convictions match those of the school. The practices may be new to the students, but the intention is to educate, not to shock. On the other hand, Baruch Levine and Jeff Siedel find placements in Meah Shearim and send the potential recruits to the *Toledot Aharon,* an extremely traditionalistic chassidic congregation. The heads of several schools claim to find this approach damaging to recruits and to the recruitment effort.

haps a third to a half of those accepting the offer to experience a Shabbat were in fact Orthodox, although they may be perceived by the Meah Shearim chasidim to be ba'alei t'shuva.

Schools for Women

Fewer schools exist for women than for men, and women's schools tend to be far smaller than men's schools. This pattern is surprising in light of the general pattern in the United States for women to be more involved in religion than men. Conceivably, this occurred because Orthodox Judaism emphasizes religious education for men but not for women. But raising the question with the deans of the schools produced a reaction that suggests that the answer lies elsewhere.

In the course of interviews conducted in Israel in 1975–1976, I was asked several times by deans of schools whether I had any findings that I could share with them. The interviewees were essentially asking to what use my data would be put. Would giving me free access to such information compromise confidences? Would I be reporting who said what about whom? In part to allay these doubts, on several occasions I informed interviewees of two of my general findings. One was that the overwhelming majority of ba'alei t'shuva had some Jewish background and training and were not starting from "ground zero," as the deans and teachers then believed. The second finding was the surprising imbalance of the ratio of men to women (Danzger 1977). At that time in Israel there were eight yeshivot for men and two for women. There was also one program for women in a men's yeshiva and the Pardess Institute, which accepted both men and women.[6] Furthermore, the total number of men at schools for ba'alei t'shuva was four times greater than the total number of women. Asked why they thought this pattern had developed, some of the deans speculated that women were less interested in religion than men.

This was suggested not only by those who believed that women were generally not serious enough to be interested in religious study but also by

6. Yeshivot for men were Magen Avraham, Ohr Someyach, Aish Hatorah, D'var Yerushalayim, K'far Chabad, Shappels, and Hatfutzot-Har Tzion (which had a small program for women). Women's schools were Neve Yerushalayim and Shappels College for Women. About fifteen women attended the Pardess Institute and a similar number attended the Hatfutzot-Har Tzion program for women. The Har Tzion program was more of an accommodation for the few women who wished to join than a separate school for women.

those who felt that Orthodoxy was too sexist to interest women. Rabbi Dov Begun of Machon Meir questioned these hypotheses. In his institute, he pointed out, there were about three women to every man.

Others suggested that perhaps parents had a more restrictive attitude toward women traveling abroad than toward men. This seemed to reflect the attitudes of some deans and perhaps some in the Orthodox community rather than those of the American student population they were trying to recruit. Furthermore, in America also men predominated at yeshivot for ba'alei t'shuva while women predominated at institutes and other part-time programs for the study of Orthodox Judaism. Yeshiva University had a separate school for newly Orthodox men but did not have a similar school for women, who were simply integrated into the University's Stern College for Women. Some separate classes geared to the needs of beginners were provided, but no separate school for beginners existed. Similarly the Lubavitcher yeshiva for ba'alei t'shuva (male) had close to one hundred students in attendance. In contrast, Beit Channa, their school for women, has ten to fifteen students. Furthermore, the several other yeshivot in the United States in the late 1970s were all designed for men rather than women. If the disparity were a matter of parents' reluctance to have their daughters travel abroad, why were so few facilities available for women even in the United States?

The possibility that women were not drawn to Orthodoxy was belied by the preponderance of women not only at Machon Meir in Israel but also at the Shapiro Institute for Adult Education of the Lincoln Square Synagogue. This institute, designed for those who wished to learn more about Orthodoxy, enrolled about two thousand students a year, about fifteen hundred of them women. Machon Meir had a similar ratio.

On the basis of information then available, some of the rabbis and deans concluded that the disproportion was a result of their own lack of awareness and effort to attract women. Perhaps in part as a result of their new awareness, several new schools for women were initiated. In 1980 Ohr Someyach founded Ohr Someyach for Women, and D'var Yerushalayim founded D'var Yerushalayim for Women.

But less than two years after opening its school for women, Ohr Someyach closed it down and instead developed an affiliation with Neve Yerushalayim, which had been founded in 1972 as a school for women. Neve retained its own name while operating under the aegis of Ohr Someyach Institutions. Neve expanded substantially, but principally through the growth of its Machon D'vora institute for women from Orthodox families. B'ruria too has expanded, yet it too now attracts a large proportion of girls from Orthodox homes. The School for Women of D'var Yerushalayim (founded as a men's school) now has a small student body (fifteen to twenty-five), primarily of Sephardic background.

Even the ba'al t'shuva yeshivot for Israelis, which began in the late 1970s and today number more than forty, are almost entirely men's institutions.

Despite efforts to increase the number of women attending the ba'al t'shuva schools, the situation has remained much as it was in the mid-1970s. Men greatly outnumber women at yeshivot for ba'alei t'shuva. We are left with the question of whether something about yeshivot makes them appropriate institutions for the education of men but not of women.

Yeshivot for Israelis

Although most of the yeshivot for ba'alei t'shuva are located in Israel, for a long time they were effectively closed to most Israelis. In every one of the early yeshivot for ba'alei t'shuva the language of instruction was English—even though the language of the Bible and of most Jewish source material is Hebrew or Aramaic, which is related to Hebrew. Overwhelmingly, the earliest recruits were from the United States and to a lesser extent from Canada, England, and South Africa. These students' lack of familiarity with Hebrew dictated that the language of instruction be English. One unanticipated consequence of this arrangement was that although some Israelis might have been interested in return, the programs effectively excluded them. From time to time an article appeared in an Israeli newspaper or magazine on former hippies who had found their religious and ethnic roots. These articles whetted the appetites of Israelis.

In 1976 several of the yeshivot for ba'alei t'shuva began outreach programs for Israelis. Orientation programs and study days were undertaken in conjunction with the armed forces and with other government agencies. But there were still no programs in these schools for Israelis, who had to struggle on their own as foreign students elsewhere might if they chose to enter the school.

In addition, several Israeli outreach programs were developed after 1976, but they were substantially different in structure and clientele from the ba'al t'shuva yeshivot. Rabbi Dov Begun's Machon Meir, an adult education program, was directed toward Israelis and open to both men and women. This part-time, evening program offered courses in Jewish thought, Bible, laws, and customs. Rabbi Adin Steinzaltz, a mathematician by training and a former ba'al t'shuva currently engaged in translating the Babylonian Talmud into Hebrew—an effort that has won him wide scholarly and popular acclaim—founded Shefa, a smaller organization directed toward Israeli intellectuals, artists, writers, and scientists rather than to the masses. It too was essentially organized for part-time study.

Ohr Hachayim, a yeshiva for Israelis in the Bukharin quarter of Jerusalem, came closest to the American yeshivot for ba'alei t'shiva but its students were quite different. Many students were former delinquents.[7] In fact, this yeshiva received wide publicity for its ability to rehabilitate wayward youth. In the language of instruction (Hebrew), the backgrounds of the students, their level of education, and the kinds of religious problems they encountered, Ohr Hachayim was sharply different from the American ba'al t'shuva yeshivot. Further, in the late 1790s the yeshiva's reputation for rehabilitating delinquents (see Cromer 1981) probably closed it off as an option for the bulk of the potential population. Much the same could be said for Migdal Ha'emek, a school founded for the rehabilitation of Israeli delinquents in the Lower Galil (one of the few outside of Jerusalem) by Rabbi Yitzhak David Grossman. Middle-class Israelis preferred the American ba'al t'shuva institutions despite the language barrier.

By the late 1970s a number of the ba'al t'shuva yeshivot had developed special programs for Israelis. In addition, Machon Meir developed a yeshiva for middle-class Israelis that closely resembled the American ba'al t'shuva yeshivot. At the same time traditional yeshivot began developing ba'al t'shuva affiliates, sometimes using their existing facilities. The Isra-

7. American hippies who used drugs were not considered delinquents. Instead they were socially defined as middle-class students or young people who had adopted a deviant life-style. In part this was a result of their not being considered addicted to drugs but merely users, which in turn was partially a result of their higher class status, which gave their actions a presumption of noncriminality (Lemert 1974).

The Israeli schools were proud to report that they had made returnees of former delinquents. This meant that the schools were effective in dealing with social problems and that religion had practical value. These stories served to attract funds and favorable attention to the schools. Only later when they came to be thought of as schools for wayward youth did they try to minimize this aspect of their work.

Interestingly, sects frequently engage in missions to those defined as criminal (drunks, drug addicts, and prostitutes) and to the lower class. Cults tend to appeal to the middle class (Stark and Bainbridge 1985, 404–5).

eli t'shuva movement had thus begun to take on a life of its own, with a unique character and structure.

Ba'al T'shuva Yeshivot in America

As discussed in chapter 3 the first attempts by yeshivot to facilitate return to Judaism began in America in the 1940s and 1950s and were aimed at those "lacking background." In the 1960s and early 1970s, as hippies began choosing to be Orthodox, ba'al t'shuva yeshivot emerged in Israel. Attempts were also made to establish ba'al t'shuva yeshivot in America at this time, including Rabbi Friefeld's yeshiva in Far Rockaway, established in 1968, Lubavitch's yeshiva Tomchei Temimim, founded in Newark in 1972, Bet Pinchas Yeshiva of Boston in 1973, and the Yeshiva of Lincoln Square Synagogue in 1976.

By the late 1970s several regular yeshivot had developed programs for ba'alei t'shuva and Israeli yeshivot for ba'alei t'shuva had begun to develop American extensions. Some of these took root as independent yeshivot. Yeshivat Chofetz Chaim of Queens, New York, for example, started with a part-time program. Within a few years this became Yeshiva Kesser Torah for ba'alei t'shuva.

In 1977 Ohr Someyach initiated an extension branch first in Yonkers and later in Monsey, New York. A number of Israeli ba'al t'shuva yeshivot opened branches in the United States soon after. Extension programs for ba'alei t'shuva were developed by the Israeli yeshiva Kol Yaakov in Monsey, by D'var Yerushalayim in Flatbush, and by Aish Hatorah in St. Louis. Under the auspices of Ohr Someyach a camp was founded in Connecticut. Extension courses for women were offered under the aegis of Neve Yerushalayim (the women's school) in Queens and Brooklyn. Yeshiva programs were also developed in Miami, Vancouver, and elsewhere. All these schools were quite small, even in comparison with the ba'al t'shuva mother yeshivot. The number of full-time students generally ran from ten to twenty, although for special programs that number might be several times larger.

American yeshivot for ba'alei t'shuva did not and probably could not grow as their Israeli counterparts did, because Israel offered a far more conducive atmosphere. Lubavitch continued to have a large measure of success probably because its yeshiva for baalei t'shuva, although isolated physically by its location in Morristown, New Jersey, nevertheless remained an integral part of the Lubavitcher community of Brooklyn. Marriages were arranged though that community, and the ba'al t'shuva and the yeshiva had the opportunity to draw on the full community resources. The James Striar School of Yeshiva University remained essentially a yeshiva for those lacking background even after the new public perception of returnees to Judaism as "ba'alei t'shuva" emerged. It did not attempt an active program of outreach.

The small enrollment at ba'al t'shuva yeshivot in America reflects the practice of encouraging students who want to pursue their interest in Orthodoxy to attend the school in Israel. That American schools survive at all, however, depends on their ability to recruit already committed students who have attended yeshivot in Israel to serve as teachers of beginners and to share faculty with the other institution in Israel. This institutional affiliation with the organization in Israel makes possible the existence of these institutions here.

One of the reasons for the greater success of ba'alei t'shuva yeshivot in Israel is the financial support they receive from the government of Israel, support that is not available in the United States, where yeshivot are funded by tuitions, which are often quite high. In the United States the expenses required are too great to be borne by the ba'alei t'shuva themselves, whose commitment to Orthodoxy is still tentative. In Israel the government covers a part of the costs, and as the cost of living is lower the American dollars that the students bring with them go a good deal further. The result of this is that ba'alei t'shuva yeshivot remain primarily an Israeli phenomenon, although their staff and students are American.

A second reason is that public recruitment to ba'alei t'shuva yeshivot tends to be seen as sectlike in Israel and as cultlike in America. By this I mean that in Israel these yeshivot are seen as hyperconformist to some of the values of society: they follow traditions of the majority too carefully (Danzger 1987). In Israel Orthodoxy is the religion of the dominant group's forefathers; one's parents or cousins, or at least grandparents, practiced this very religion. At worst, therefore, Orthodoxy is an anachronism. In America, Orthodox Judaism is a minority faith.

America is more accepting of synagogue outreach that tends to be modernistic in style and less confrontational. In addition, the more accepted pattern of outreach is through houses of worship rather than through seminaries or yeshivot. Yeshivot that attempt to publicly recruit are defined as cultlike—which is to say, of a faith that is not part of the dominant tradition. This deprives them of legitimacy and hinders outreach.

Chapter 6

The New Curriculum

The curriculum of the yeshiva historically has been predicated on the assumption that students have been reared in homes where Orthodoxy is practiced and have already been taught the Bible and the laws related to the everyday practice of Judaism. But what should the curriculum of the ba'al t'shuva yeshiva be? How shall such a student be taught Judaism? What should be the place of the Talmud and Codes in the curriculum? And what of the study of Jewish philosophy and theology, or the study of Kabbalah, the mystical knowledge of Judaism?

The Men's Curriculum

BAGS OF CANDY OR GEMARA

An excerpt from an interview with an advanced student at Yeshivat Har Tzion, the so-called hippie ba'al t'shuva yeshiva, provides some answers to these questions. This student was also a spokesman for the school in the absence of the dean, Rabbi Goldstein.

In response to a question about how students came to know the required religious practices, I had been informed that they started with Gemara (the complex discussions and explanations of the Mishna, which together with the Mishnah comprise the Talmud) and with halakhah.

Q. Wouldn't they start with a bit of chumash [the Pentateuch] or the basic mitzvot [commandments] or something like that?
A. No. Of all the things you can teach, Gemara is more important than anything else. Gemara is everything. It is Torah sheh ba'al peh [the Oral Law]. It's the real stuff. Everything else will follow. Chumash is not the primary learning of an adult Jew. *Torah sheh b'chtav* [the Scripture] is not of this world. In this

world it is Torah sheh ba'al peh, which is the harder way, not the sweet way; it's demanding. . . . But we also give them what the guys call "bags of candy." We always laugh about it. They themselves call other studies bags of candy after a while. The rabbi calls it that, too. He says, "Okay. Give out bags of candy."[1]

The discussion then turned to a certain rabbi often seen engaging young passersby in conversation. He was a genial man in his sixties with a snow-white beard, twinkling blue eyes, and red cheeks that made one think immediately of Santa Claus out of uniform. His conversations with tourists would focus on the historical site in which the school was located (the Tomb of David, near the Western Wall), the visitor's Jewish origins, or similar topics. The rabbi would often invite young people to have a meal or attend a class at the yeshiva. He was not officially part of the yeshiva, but in this way he was supportive of its work.

Q. Would these talks about the holiness of Jerusalem or the importance of Israel or of being a *cohen* [part of the priestly caste] be a bag of candy?
A. That's a bag of a bag of a bag. I'll explain. We send people to Rabbi N. almost like a bait. . . . I don't mean this in a derogatory way. We send people to him, and he's an expert. He knows all of Scripture backwards and forwards. I know more than one guy who met Rabbi N.; the rabbi would ask the visitor his Jewish name, the guy would tell him, and the rabbi would find it in the Bible. Something was happening, you see. Suddenly you see the guy is moving; he's interested. And then you get him inside to learn Gemara.

The importance of studying Gemara and as soon as possible emerges clearly from this discussion. Nothing else seems important, not the halakhah, not how to pray or read, not philosophy or even Kabbalah (even for the hippies), not even the Bible. The essence, the critical study, is gemara.

In advanced yeshivot the Gemara is not only the core of the curriculum, it is almost the entire curriculum. Even study for rabbinical ordination (*semikhah;* which, parenthetically, is not the purpose of yeshiva study)[2]

1. This term may have two meanings in this yeshiva. In the hippie culture, from which some of the students had come, it refers to drugs. In the Orthodox world it refers to the small packages of candies and nuts that are thrown at a groom or a bar mitzvah boy when he is called up to the Torah. Those using the term may be familiar with both meanings.

2. Study of Torah is to be undertaken *lishmah* (for its own sake) simply because it is a mitzvah, not for extraneous purposes. Even study toward ordination is sometimes facetiously considered not lishmah.

involves primarily mastery of Gemara, although ordination requires also a knowledge of the laws of "that which is forbidden and that which is permitted" (*heter v'issur*). But rabbis can be ordained without reading a page of the *Zohar,* the classic work of Kabbalah and with possibly only dim recollection of their childhood studies of the prophets. Rabbinical candidates are examined only in areas related to the practice of Jewish ritual.

This once again highlights Judaism's emphasis on the practice of the mitzvot in contrast to Christianity's emphasis on faith or belief. Statements of faith, creedal declarations, are not central to Judaism. One either is or is not an *observant* or a *practicing* Jew. Living the law and studying it in the Mishna and the Gemara also enable one to experience, through reconstruction of that reality in the mind, the life of Jews in their homeland almost two millenia ago. (Heine, sensing this aspect of the Talmud, called it "the portable homeland of the mind".) They also shape the individual into a "Torah personality," one who is creative and disciplined, emotional and rational, combining faith and reason—a personality so shaped by the Oral Law that all of one's actions reflect this perspective (Soloveitchik 1944).

HALAKHAH, KABBALAH, AND SEEKERS

Whereas halakhah spells out the norms that should be followed, Kabbalah deals with the mystical reasons behind the norms. This is not to say that halakhah does not also deal with the reasons for the norms. But the kinds of reasons provided by halakhah are rooted in historical events (for example, Passover), in practical and ethical consideration (such as equity), in custom, or simply in the fact that God has commanded it (Kant's "axiomatic imperative"). Kabbalah, in contrast, is rooted in metaphysical speculations regarding the nature of God, the world, good and evil, heaven and hell, angels, and the powers of evil. Beliefs regarding these matters have never been a matter of dogma as is halakhah; they are *soud* (secret), esoteric knowledge made available to only a few in close personal contact, not to be discussed in large lectures.

The omission of Kabbalah from the curricula of yeshivot is intriguing since kabbalistic notions are central to the Sephardic (Oriental) and chasidic communities. In many Sephardic communities a chapter of the *Zohar* is read every day, so that this central work of Jewish mysticism is widely known to all. Chasidim study the works of their rebbes, which include kabbalistic perspectives. Such books as the *Tanya,* written by Shneur Zalman of Lyadi, the founder of the Lubavitcher Chasidism, draw heavily on the *Zohar* and are studied by Lubavitcher chasidim as part of their daily study sessions. The Lubavitcher yeshiva for ba'alei t'shuva in Morristown, New Jersey, teaches *Tanya* to ba'alei t'shuva as part of the regular program of study. In this way, ba'alei t'shuva are exposed early on to kabbalistic ideas regarding such issues as death and life, the soul, the meaning of resurrection, the powers of the forces of evil, the relation of these forces to *tumah* (defilement), ideas about the messiah, and the end of days. But in other yeshivot these matters are touched on only in passing, if at all. They are never a part of the curriculum, never handled as separate subject matter or discussed in classes or lectures. When they are discussed, discussion is ordinarily on a one-to-one basis, following the tradition stated in the Mishnah (*Hagigah* 2:1).

In the late 1960s and early 1970s, many of the hippies who were potential recruits to Orthodoxy were also "into" meditation, astrology, tarot, new consciousness, the world as illusion. They may have heard rumors that Kabbalah offered a new Jewish consciousness, a meditation on holy words and letters that provided new experiences and offered the power to shape earthly events through spiritual forces. There is in fact a tradition that the great rebbes have been *ba'alei mofsim* (literally, masters of miracles), with the power to effect cures or to intercede with the Divine to bless a childless woman with children.

Nor is this belief restricted to chasidim. The Maharal of Prague, a sixteenth-century scholar and Kabbalist, is reputed to have used "the ineffable name," the special letters of the Divine name, to cause a *golem,* a manlike creature he had made of clay, to come to life to protect the Jewish community of Prague. The Maharal predates Chasidism by almost two hundred years. A major opponent of Chasidism, Elijah the Gaon of Vilna, was reputed to have dabbled in the miraculous elements of Kabbalah. Miraculous Kabbalah was widely accepted even by mitnagdic Jews (those who rejected Chasidism).[3]

3. The disappearance of kabbalism, particularly magical kabbalism, coincided with the expansion of science and the Enlightenment. The primary cause was probably the apostasy of Shabbetai Tzevi (1666), who after claiming to be the messiah and offering kabbalistic proofs that persuaded a substantial segment of European Jewry of the authenticity of his claim converted to Islam. His apostasy led to deep despair and a suspicion not only of messianism but of Kabbalah itself. Thereafter, kabbalists had to clearly distance themselves from doctrines associated with Shabbatai Tzevi. Nevertheless magical Kabbalah persisted in a muted form for more than a century.

In the late eighteenth century, Rabbi Jacob Emden accused Rabbi Yonatan Eybeshutz of being a secret Sabbatean on the basis of amulets that Eybeshutz had

Nor are other philosophical and metaphysical subjects considered systematically in the yeshivot. They are discussed when they are raised in the Talmud, but the Mishnah makes it clear that metaphysical speculations are not appropriate for public discussion. Yeshivot have traditionally defined this area broadly. For example, although Maimonides' halakhic work is a part of every yeshiva library and is discussed in lectures on the most advanced levels, his philosophic treatise *Guide to the Perplexed* is never covered in yeshiva lectures and is almost never to be found in yeshiva libraries. It is, in fact, off-limits to yeshiva students.[4]

Even Lubavitch, although it provides public classes and lectures on secondary mystical works such as the *Tanya,* nevertheless has made Gemara the central part of the study program for ba'alei t'shuva. At the Lubavitcher yeshiva for ba alei t'shuva in Morristown more hours are spent on gemara than on all other subjects combined.

How, then, are the interests of potential new recruits met, and how are they redirected? One answer is that some of their questions are handled in the discussion of the weekly portion of the Pentateuch and the related Midrash (a tradition of exegesis that goes back two millenia, to the time of the Mishnah). Often in the form of parables, the Midrash is used as the basis for interpretation of the Pentateuch. Other questions are dealt with in *hashkafa shi'urim,* lectures on general perspectives in Judaism, though these may be considered bags of candy, not serious subjects for study, by those who have learned how to study the Gemara. These lectures leave much room for innovation and philosophical interpretation.

Because study of philosophic ideas, Midrash, and Kabbalah are not systematic in the yeshivot, students do not have the tools to study these matters on their own. Even after years in yeshiva Kabbalah remains a closed book to the overwhelming majority of students. They cannot evaluate kabbalistic ideas. Particularly because the clarity of halakhic decision is lacking in Kabbalah and because ideas are often contradictory,

---

distributed to pregnant women to prevent miscarriages. The controversy that developed involved some of the greatest talmudic scholars of that day. It did not destroy the study of Kabbalah but forced it underground among the mitnaggedim who led the great European yeshivot. At the same time, science and the Enlightenment undercut its intellectual standing in the broader Jewish community. The last crushing blow was the destruction of Jewry in Eastern Europe, a major center for the study of Kabbalah.

4. Maimonides himself, in writing the *Guide,* made it clear that it was not intended for laymen.

philosophy, theology, and Kabbalah remain open to varying interpretations with no means for determining the correct interpretations.[5]

Kabbalah has thus been taken out of the realm of public study in Judaism and placed in the area of the private, where it can suggest no authority and confer no ranking, as no one is clearly aware of the gradations of knowledge among those who have studied Kabbalah. ("Miracle working," in contrast, is still a basis for authority in chasidic circles.)

The consequences of this for Judaism more broadly considered is that one may think almost what one pleases about resurrection, heaven and hell, the Messiah, the nature of God. In fundamentalist yeshivot, students and even teachers may insist that all the various statements on these matters in the Bible, the Talmud, and the Midrash be taken literally even when they appear to be contradictory. Nevertheless, these ideas are not the subject of public preaching and have almost no consequences for action.[6] The yeshiva student is not confronted with the obligation to believe in a formal credo but with the requirement to carry out the mitzvot, to act out a role. Some principles of faith have been formulated by outstanding rabbis of the past; for example, rabbinical Judaism asserted the doctrine of life after death, a major point of conflict between Sadducees and Pharisees. The essential body of Judaic belief has been variously summarized; the best known and most widely accepted of these summaries is the Thirteen Principles of Belief formulated by Maimonides. The principles reflect that Maimonides was a philosopher in that they are abstract and open to various interpretations.

Potential recruits often have questions about life after death and the nature of God, heaven, and hell. They may even have heard of Kabbalah and wish to learn more about it. The response of the rabbis is to provide some answers and attempt to deflect this religious curiosity into study of the Talmud. The teacher or recruiter will reply along these lines: "Your question is a good one. Let us sit down and study this and see what the Gemara has to say." The logic is that calculus cannot be taught to one who has not studied algebra and certainly not to one who has not grasped

5. Similarly, conflict over interpretation of scriptural passages has characterized Protestant Christianity, leaving interpretations and applications to the individual's conscience. In Judaism the prophetic writings are not normatively (halakhically) binding.

6. In modern times the consequence of differences in belief are to be seen primarily with regard to Zionism. For religious Zionists, the messianic idea is not only supernaturally miraculous; his coming may be hastened by the practical efforts of men. For the anti-Zionist religious, the Messiah is a supernatural concept, and human attempts to hasten his coming are simply sacrilegious.

the basics of arithmetic. The only way to get there is to learn the ideas step by step. To learn about Judaism one must be prepared to study it.

Some argue that even if Kabbalah could be taught publicly, the ideas expressed in the *Zohar* are too complicated to be grasped by the uninitiated. The serious student must make a serious commitment. And this will take time, at least a few months.

Responses of yeshivot differ in large part because of the different types of students they attract, each with his own sorts of questions. And yeshivot attract different types of students largely because they are led by different personalities with different conceptions of what is essential to Judaism. The relationship between the students and teachers is synergistic.

YESHIVAT HATFUTZOT-HAR TZION

Yeshivat Hatfutzot-Har Tzion came into being just as the hippie movement began to develop. In the United States Shlomo Carlebach, "the singing chasid," toured major college campuses in the Midwest, the South, and the Far West, trying to bring the message of Judaism to the students through his songs. At first he set traditional words to new melodies, melodies that were upbeat, reflecting the new Jewish sense of joy and confidence that sprang from Jewish acceptance in America in the 1960s and Israel's success in the Six Day War. His message was both religious and ethnic, in line with the themes of the hippie world. As his audience grew, his songs took on a folk character in the manner of Joan Baez or Bob Dylan, but his message was directed exclusively to Jews.

Carlebach's songs came to influence hundreds, perhaps thousands, of young Jewish hippies, many of whom ended up at Har-Tzion. Being part of the hippie world in that day meant, at various times and for different individuals, an interest in drugs, rock music, or mysticism. Drugs were banned from the yeshiva. Rock music was transformed and incorporated. How did the yeshiva respond to the interest in mysticism?

Carlebach himself was deeply involved in the world of Chasidism. Both he and his colleague in recruiting, Zalman Schachter, were part of the Lubavitch community. Their songs, their language, and the images and stories they told in conversations with hippies were full of mystical allusions.[7]

7. For example, at his concerts Carlebach would address his audience in the break between songs. At one gathering of forty to fifty young people in his synagogue Carlebach urged them to close their eyes as they sang the song *Od Avienu Chai* ("Our Father still lives"). Before beginning the song, he told the following

Hippies who found their way to Har Tzion hoped to be able to learn more about Kabbalah and chasidut, which many of them saw as the central object of deep learning. But what these hippies took for the deepest essence of Judaism was defined at Har Tzion as "a bag of candy"—an attraction, a lure, but not the core of Judaism. At Har Tzion, learning *Gemara b'eeyun* (in depth) is the core activity. Although Rabbi Goldstein reaches out to ba'alei t'shuva with love, he is not ready to teach them Kabbalah. His yeshiva's curriculum is a mitnagdic one. Aspects of Kabbalah are alluded to in *musar shmuesin* (informal talks on ethics and self-improvement), and students may study the *Mesillat Yesharim* (a handbook on ethical conduct written in the eighteenth century by Rabbi Moshe Chaim Luzzato and based in part on kabbalistic notions of the nature of man), but they will not study Kabbalah. Nor do they study chasidut in this yeshiva, which claims spiritual descent from Kelem and Slobodka, classical mitnagdic yeshivot.

YESHIVAT AISH HATORAH

While Carlebach and Schachter have influenced many of Har Tzion's students, who are former hippies, recruiters with other styles and religious perspectives have sent returnees to Aish Hatorah. The student body at Aish Hatorah reflects these recruiters' efforts. Meir Shuster is "yeshivish"—humble, self-effacing, persistent, interested in the individual. Baruch Levine and Jeff Siedel take an adventurous approach, urging potential recruits to experience something new. Rabbi Weinberg's approach is confrontational, demanding to know what the person understands of his Jewishness and why he hasn't bothered to explore it more deeply. In addition, some potential returnees simply fall in almost by chance. Aish Hatorah is well known for its aggressive recruitment program, so that it is often the place to which potential returnees are directed.

The majority of those who enter Aish Hatorah seem to be rootless young men interested in new experience, not religious seekers. These are simply participants in the secular youth culture, although a number of them had a special relationship to Judaism or curiosity about it. An invitation to meet a Jewish guru, to hear a lecture in a yeshiva, or to spend a Shabbat there could have some appeal, although it might not be much

---

story. Rav Nachman of Bratzlav once asked, "Why do we close our eyes when we say the Shema [the proclamation of the unity of God recited during morning and evening prayers])?" He answered, "We close our eyes in order to see God with our third eye."

more than curiosity or an interest in a free meal. Rabbi Weinberg's program is unique in that it represents an attempt to design a curriculum that challenges one's ground of meaning, and quickly and effectively transmits the basics of Judaism.

Although Reb Noach (as Weinberg is called by his students) is traditionalistic in dress, with full beard, black hat, and black frock coat, his program is not traditional. The program is part of what Reb Noach often referred to as "weapons development"—the development of programs and methods to counter secularism. He begins by teaching as first principle the knowledge of God—hardly innovative in other missionizing efforts but a radical departure for Judaism. He uses the Maimonidean code of law (not the *Guide to the Perplexed*), which is organized along philosophical lines and begins with the commandment to "know God." Reb Noach tries to reach out to ba'lei t'shuva by speaking to them in their own language about problems that he believes concern them. He has a three-month program for returnees in which they are taught in systematic order the mitzvot an Orthodox Jew must observe. The three-month program includes the study of portions of the Pentateuch, the siddur (prayer book), and the prophets in the Hebrew language (a struggle for most students), as well as the basic norms and rules of Orthodoxy and the philosophic discussions already described. At one time a party was given for each returnee with a festive "birthday cake" to celebrate his completion of the course. At the end of three months, the student is introduced to the study of Talmud.

LUBAVITCH

Lubavitch has been active in recruitment longer than any other group. In the 1940s and 1950s its efforts were directed primarily at schoolchildren during the religious release hour, a weekly period when public school students could choose to be instructed in their religion. In the late 1950s Carlebach and Schachter began their attempts to recruit on college campuses. At present Lubavitch in Israel is not highly visible in the direct recruitment of Americans. Their efforts there are directed toward Israelis—bringing Purim gifts and other goodies to troops in the field, arranging bar mitzvahs for the sons of fallen Israeli soldiers, or providing education to disadvantaged children. This has earned them respect among Israelis, so that some of those who are interested in religion seek out Lubavitch. (The accounts of many ba'lei t'shuva indicate that the personal efforts of Lubavitch in reaching out to individuals have had an impact on many returnees both in Israel and in the United States.) In the United

States since the early 1970s Lubavitch has used dramatic outreach techniques, including the use of "mitzvah mobiles," vans that drive through Jewish neighborhoods or appear at such events as rallies for Soviet Jewry or the Israel Day parade. Stopping passersby, the Lubavitch will ask men, "Have you put on tefillin today?" or ask women, "Have you lit Shabbos candles this week?" Men who have not are asked to enter the van, put on tefillin, and say a prayer. Women who have not are given a small brass candlestick. The Lubavitcher men offer no modern explanations for the wearing of tefillin or the lighting of candles. The tefillin are simply wrapped around a person's arm and placed on his head. The blessing for the tefillin and the *Sh'ma* are recited, and the tefillin are removed. The women are simply told how and when to light the candles and are given a transliteration of the blessing. In Israel the same procedure takes place at the Kotel and occasionally elsewhere, without the Mitzvah van. The Lubavitch are dressed in their usual attire, black suits and hats, untrimmed beards, and, occasionally, earlocks. They are unmistakably chasidim. They arrive on campuses in the United States in the same way. They may simply walk up to someone and ask if he has blessed the *etrog* on the Succot holiday or put on tefillin. Most of their efforts are not successful. Once in a while, someone does take them up on their offer. There is little effort at follow-up. Their approach seems to be to assume that the person will pursue it further in due time.

Lubavitch makes little overt attempt to reach out in the language or modalities of America. Its recruiters are people born and reared in the Lubavitch community. Although American born, most recruiters are not familiar with the language of the streets or university campuses. If there is music at their encounters or farbrengen, it is traditional chasidic music, developed by and for its own community and not intended as a bridge to the larger culture.[8] Lubavitch's program of study is not designed to communicate with American students or to take the students' American culture into account. Concessions to American culture in the curriculum are those required by necessity; for example, books on science and Judaism or modern philosophy and Judaism will not be used in any courses or even found in the library, but classes will be conducted in English rather than in the Yiddish traditional among Lubavitcher.

Interestingly, in the Lubavitcher ba'al t'shuva yeshiva Kabbalah and mysticism are a major part of the program although not nearly as impor-

---

8. Carlebach started as a recruiter for Lubavitch, but his innovative approaches resulted in friction and by the mid-1960s they separated.

tant as Gemara. The student is introduced to these ideas, beliefs, and values but as part of the study of chasidut, not explicitly labeled Kabbalah. Even at the entry level, ba'alei t'shuva in the Lubavitcher yeshiva in Morristown have an hour-long class on the *Tanya* each day and often spend additional time studying it in small groups. Paradoxically the one yeshiva that does provide some introduction to kabbalistic ideas does not use this to attract recruits.[9]

Early in the development of the Lubavitcher ba'al t'shuva program, the *Tanya* constituted the central subject matter of the curriculum. After some years, however, the amount of time spent on *Tanya* and chasidut was reduced and greater emphasis was given to Talmud, which is now the core of the curriculum. Given the importance of *Tanya* to Lubavitch and the probability that some of those attracted to Lubavitch are interested in Kabbalah or at least in *chasidut,* the move toward greater emphasis on Talmud seems puzzling.

It seems paradoxical that Har Tzion, which attracted hippies who may have been interested in Kabbalah and mysticism, nonetheless emphasizes study of the Talmud following a traditional model; that Aish Hatorah, which designed a unique curriculum for ba'lei t'shuva, emphasizes rational approaches to religion rather than faith and emotion and offers no studies in mysticism; and that the Lubavitch community, whose philosophy is based on mysticism and Kabbalah, offers nothing by that name in its yeshiva and has modified its curriculum to emphasize Talmud more and chasidut less.

We note in passing that yeshivot closer to the mainstream of Orthodoxy and middle-class status have traditionally placed emphasis on the study of gemara rather than Kabbalah. Not surprisingly, Ohr Someyach, Brovender's yeshivot, and Yeshiva University also place the study of Gemara at the center of their curricula.

At Yeshiva University, in the past the writings of such Jewish philosophers as Maimonides and Albo had their place in the college curriculum and indirectly illuminated talmudic studies as well, but the works of kabbalists were never discussed. This has changed. While the works of Maimonides and other philosophers are discussed, mystical literature is also discussed. At Brovender's yeshiva in recent years lectures have been

9. The limits imposed by the Mishna (Hagiga 2:1) inhibit Lubavitch from presenting this material as Kabbalah to ba'alei t'shuva. This again demonstrates that Lubavitch are inward-looking and that even in their outreach programs their efforts are not directed at bridging the gap between themselves and newcomers.

offered on *Likkutei Maharan,* the writings of Rabbi Nachman of Bratz-lav, and on the *Netivot Olam* of the Maharal of Prague. At D'var Yeru-shalayim, *Mikhtav me'Eliyahu,* the writings of Rabbi Eliyahu Dessler, are discussed. Each of these works is mystical, with underpinnings in Kab-balah. All these yeshivot have become somewhat more receptive to Kab-balah, although their clientele may be less interested in it than are students at Lubavitch or at Yeshivat Hatfuztot-Har Tzion.

Action and Study

That religious acts rather than beliefs are the core of Judaism raises several questions. First, are these acts merely mechanically performed, or do they contribute to the formation of a meaning system and a set of beliefs? If the latter, how does this happen? Second, if acts are the core, why the emphasis on study? Finally, is the study of Gemara understand-able simply as a way of acquiring knowledge for the performance of religious acts?

UNDERSTANDING THROUGH THE ACT

In Judaism's philosophy of education, acts come first, and beliefs and commitment follow. This position is stated succinctly in *Sefer Hakhinukh* (literally, *The Book of Education*), purportedly written by Rabbi Aharon Halevi of Toledo in the thirteenth century.

> Know that man is formed by his actions. His heart and all his thoughts follow after the actions he engages in, whether they be good or evil. Even if a person's heart is totally evil . . . if his spirit is awakened and he puts his effort and his activities diligently in Torah and the mitzvot, even though he does not do it for the sake of heaven, he will immediately turn to the good, and from having acted with no concern for God he will come to act for His Name. And because of the power of his actions his evil inclination will die. *Because the heart is drawn after the deeds.*
>
> And even if a person is totally righteous, and his heart is straight and innocent and desires Torah and Mitzvot, if he is involved constantly in foolish things . . . he will turn, after a given time, from righteous hearted-ness to being totally evil. For *a person is formed by his actions.* (Sixteenth Commandment, emphasis added)

This lesson is taught in many ways in all yeshivot. For the more ad-vanced students the words of the *Sefer Hakhinukh* may be used. But even young children are taught that in observing the commandments one must first do and then understand. They are taught that just as Jews responded at Mount Sinai when accepting the Torah, saying, "We will do and we will listen" (Exod. 14:23), so in observing the commandments, the ritual actions are required first. Explanations may follow, and they may be accepted or rejected.

This perspective was demonstrated at a t'shuva meeting in an Orthodox synagogue in Queens, New York in spring 1987. The featured speaker was Uri Zohar, a former Israeli television personality who had become Orthodox in 1977, had since been ordained as a rabbi, and for some years had been a leading speaker at meetings for return to Orthodoxy. In the lecture Zohar addressed the question of what is a Jew. He insisted that to be a Jew one had to *act* like a Jew, and that meant observing the commandments of the Torah as defined by the rabbis. In the question and answer period following the lecture, a member of the audience suggested that Zohar's position left no room for the importance of faith, for belief in God; all was simply action. Zohar insisted that concern with faith and belief was a Christian concept. Suppose, he said, one compares two people. One calculates that there is a 50 percent chance that God exists and has revealed His law to Israel at Sinai, and as a consequence—as "insurance" against the possibility that this might be true—he observes the commandments of the Torah. The other professes complete faith in the existence of God yet does not observe the commandments. Which of the two is the good Jew? He insisted that without a doubt the rabbis and sages would choose the observant Jew, not the believer.

In presenting this argument Zohar was articulating the perpective of many yeshivot for the newly Orthodox, in particular Yeshivat Aish Hatorah in Jerusalem. In this view, Orthodoxy can be a rational choice. Faith is not essential. But how than is commitment to Orthodoxy developed?

Social-psychological studies cast light on this question. Role-playing, for example, has been shown to influence opinion change (Janis and King 1954). People who pretend to take a role advocating a point of view come to accept this view. Those who passively listen to or read about a point of view are far less likely to do so.

Festinger (1962) and others (Festinger, Riecken, and Schachter (1956) have demonstrated that actions involving expenditures or commitments are often rationalized after the action has been taken.[10] The less the

10. Festinger (1962) reported that people offered two equally attractive objects tend to value the one they keep more highly after their choice than before it. The more costly the choice or the fewer the rewards for it, the more powerful the efforts to rationalize it. This has come to be known as "the theory of cognitive dissonance."

Psychologist Roger Brown sums up this theory as follows: "If action cannot be adequately accounted for by factors other than a favorable judgment, then there is a very great need to make the judgment favorable in order to justify or explain the

external pressures (such as coercion or remuneration) to justify behaviors or value choices, the more will the activity or value choice be seen as sufficient justification for the action. Furthermore, the more costly the action or value choice in terms of time, expenditure, or conflict with other values, the greater will be the weight attributed to the chosen values or actions. In this way the person reduces the "dissonance" of the choice. In other words, a person who makes a choice or by action demonstrates a commitment will then rationalize that choice or action to himself or others. The thought process of justification occurs *after,* not before, the choice or act of commitment.

Zohar's description of his own experience with prayer is a paradigm of this response. "The first time I tried to pray I wrapped myself in a prayer shawl, I faced the wall so nothing would distract me and tried to speak words of prayer. But I couldn't. I felt I was talking to the wall. I felt foolish. I just stood there and wished for a long time that I could experience the feeling of prayer. And then it came to me and I could pray in sincerity and not feel foolish."[11]

In yeshivot, then, the object of the curriculum is not to learn *about* the rituals but to learn to *perform* the rituals. That the person first performs the action and only afterward speculates on its inner meaning may provide a psychological impetus to accept an explanation and allows the development of a range of explanations, as the act, not the explanation, is primary.

STUDY AS AN ACT IN ITSELF

If action is required and beliefs and meaning are only accidental characteristics, then ritual would seem wooden and empty. Yet Jews attribute meaning to rituals, and Jews have beliefs. How are the rituals given meaning? The answer is by study.

---

motivation for what has been done. . . . The poorer the excuse for an action, the greater the need to make it 'rational' by means of attitude change" (Brown 1965, 585).

11. This is also consonant with Eliade's (1959) explanation for why ancient religions began with rituals and only later developed the myths and beliefs that explained them. Himmelfarb (1975, 615) has demonstrated that action is more important than belief in predicting religious involvement. Based on a factor analysis of data gathered from a sample of Jewish adults in Chicago, he concludes that "in some respects the more efficient measures of religious involvement for American Jews are behavioral rather than ideational measures." He further notes, "This is especially interesting because the literature on Christians concentrates predominantly on ideational measures—particularly orthodoxy (doctrinal beliefs).

To be sure, one studies to know how to perform the commandments. But many rituals could be taught more easily through observation. Moreover, why spend many hours in study when one simply wishes to *behave* as an Orthodox Jew? In fact the majority of the newly Orthodox never study at a yeshiva. If knowing the rituals is all that is required, why study the Talmud? Anyone who is familiar with the Talmud knows that the digressions, minority opinions, logical distinctions, and the often ambiguous conclusions sometimes leave students at all levels without a clear sense of what the final ruling is. Why then is Talmud the major part of the curriculum at the ba'al t'shuva yeshivot?

In part the answer is that study itself is an ultimate value. A person who studies is religionizing, is involved in a holy act that gives him a sense of worth. The fact that time was spent in study is enough (see Heilman 1983).

The head of one yeshiva described it as follows: "Religious experiences are fairly universal, whereas this notion of being able to learn and turning that into a religious experience is somewhat unique to Judaism. The notion that there is a Torah which God gave us and that by learning Torah you somehow involve yourself in this process of the giving of the Torah and delving into the will of God is fairly unique."

Study facilitates the performance of rituals, and it is a religious act in itself. Beyond this it has the latent function of providing an opportunity for reflection on the meanings of rituals and commandments. It gives ritual acts a surprising elasticity of meaning, so that contrary to the assumption that the acts are wooden and crumble when tested by modern ideas—an argument that Glazer (1957, 69) offers to explain the decline of Orthodoxy in America—ritual acts provide the space and forms on which to reflect and draw meaning. Constructing a new meaning system may take time, and during that time ritual practice and religious commitment may indeed decline. But they need not remain empty. Ritual acts provide opportunities to develop meanings, and study groups are the plausibility structures that support these meanings.

How does one get from study, seemingly an individual act, to group-supported meanings? The structures of study provide the answer. Although individual study often occurs, great weight is placed on group study. The school on various levels and the public reading of the Torah in synagogues provide opportunities for communal learning.

More interesting are the informal study groups for the study of Talmud, such as those described by Heilman (1983). These groups develop into powerful plausibility structures, not only mentally recreating the life and times of the Bible, the Mishnah, and the Talmud but also providing an opportunity to reflect on the meaning of the rituals, to reinterpret them in light of the experience of the group, and to develop a new bond.

In the ba'al t'shuva yeshiva this development occurs with particular clarity. Students are taught the rituals and norms of Judaism and spend time deeply involved in study. They are soon reflecting on the meaning of the rituals. As we shall see, some explanations offered have a surprisingly modern cast.

Interestingly, in yeshivot different subjects are typically studied in different structures. Jewish philosophy is most often studied alone, the Bible sometimes alone and sometimes in groups, and the Talmud most often in groups. This difference suggests another important consequence of study, the construction of religious authority.

Typically, a teacher (rebbi) offers a *shi'ur*, or lecture, which covers a page of the Talmud. A student may read the page and related commentaries with the help of the teacher. The teacher will then elucidate and comment on the arguments presented. The Talmud's style of argument is question and answer, and it lends itself to question and answer by teacher and student. The teacher may ask students a question the Talmud itself asks, and the student may give an answer provided by the Talmud or by one of the commentaries, with or without being aware that others have suggested it. Giving the answer in the latter case indicates that the student has fully understood the discussion, as does asking a question that the Gemara or a commentary asks. Both a *guteh kasha* (a good question) and a *guteh teretz* (a good answer) are highly valued. A shi'ur in Talmud, then, typically requires more active involvement by the student than a college lecture.

The character of talmudic study is evident in student preparation and review. Talmud is studied with a *chavruta*, a study partner. The students correct each other's mistakes, try to explain the argument to each other, and sometimes find themselves gesticulating and shouting at each other. A bet midrash, or study hall, is not at all the silent contemplative place one might expect. It is full of shouting and vociferous argument, a marketplace of ideas, not an ivory tower. A ranking system based on scholastic abilities is built, and at the apex of this system is the rosh yeshiva, the head of the yeshiva, the leading teacher and scholar. The scholar becomes the authoritative interpreter of the laws and rituals, and the group becomes an authority structure. Yet scholarship alone is not sufficient; piety is also required, as the emphasis on ritual practice suggests. In essence the scholar-saint is the leading authority.

STUDY AND COMMITMENT: SUMMING UP

Judaism's approach to religion is experiential. Acts or religious practices constitute the core, and carrying out these acts—that is, playing the role of practicing Jew—leads one to become Jewish in soul or personality. In this framework, study has two objectives. One is to learn the halakhah, the rules that should be followed. Simple observation or experience of Judaism, although important, may be insufficient in new circumstances. Study, which teaches the principles behind the action, is therefore also important for action.

Study is also a religious act. To study is not simply to learn and know but also to religionize.[12] For this reason yeshivot—places where one practices Judaism as well as learns to practice it—spend so much time on study.

Beyond this, study is an opportunity to develop a plausibility structure, a network that supports the common meanings in ritual and at the same time facilitates a search for additional interpretations and understandings of the meaning of rituals.

The Curriculum for Women

In many respects, ba'al t'shuva schools for men and women in Israel are similar. Both tend to be small, to have a transient student body, to offer some kind of dormitory facility, to be located in Jerusalem, and to have been created for American students, with Israelis brought in only as an afterthought. But the curricula at schools for men and for women are vastly different, deriving from differences in male and female religious status and obligations. For example, men have particular obligations regarding prayer and rituals on Sabbath and holidays. Women have unique obligations to dress modestly, light the Shabbat candles, maintain kashrut in the home, and observe the rules of family purity.

12. Outside of yeshivot only a minority of Orthodox Jews are involved in study circles. Those who observe kashrut, Shabbat, family purity, and required prayers are "good Jews" even if they do not study. Those who also study are further honored for the additional hours they spend "religionizing."

Perhaps many Orthodox Jews are content to rely on the rabbis to provide explanations when necessary, much as laymen are confident that scientists have rational explanations of puzzling phenomena. They implicitly rely on a system that legitimates some ideas as truths. This trust is expressed by the term *emunat chachamim*, "belief in the sages." Instilling this trust is one of the critical tasks of yeshivot.

Whereas men's yeshivot focus almost exclusively on the study of Gemara, Gemara is considered unnecessary for women. Between the wars, when advanced schools for women were developed in Europe, their purpose was fostering practical studies to enable Jewish women to better conduct a Jewish home and to provide vocational training for girls. The model for the schools for ba'alot t'shuva seems to be the teachers' seminaries for women that developed in the United States after World War II.[13] These in turn had modeled themselves after the interwar European schools. The American seminaries emphasized study of the Pentateuch with the medieval commentaries, the prophets, and dinim (the laws related to Jewish observance), particularly those related to practices in which women might be involved. Modernistic seminaries might teach *Makhshevet Yisrael* (Jewish thought), including classical and contemporary Jewish philosophy. Although some of these seminaries might have offered classes in Mishna, they did not offer classes in Gemara. Many women attended because they wanted to continue their education in Judaism, not because they wanted to be teachers. This paralleled the pattern of men who studied at higher yeshivot even when they had no interest in a career as a rabbi.

Kashrut, Shabbat, and family purity are essential practices of Orthodox Judaism and are halachically as much the woman's obligation as the man's (and in practice more the woman's responsibility). How is it, then, that women learn enough Judaism to be adequate in a half year while men must study for a year or two? Can an adequate grasp of Judaism be developed in six months?

The women's programs seem to indicate that it can. Women are apparently adequately prepared without knowledge of the Talmud, which does not directly teach the rules and norms of Orthodoxy. But why is Gemara not taught to women?

WHAT IS NOT STUDIED

Traditionalists believe that women should be educated in Judaism but that their training should be limited to practical matters.[14] Yet in a tradi-

13. In the United States the Herzliyah Teachers Institute, the Teachers Institute of the Jewish Theological Seminary, the Beth Jacob Teachers Seminary, and the Teachers Institute for Women of Yeshiva University provided education for women at an advanced level.

14. The wife often knows the application of the laws—how specifically to salt the meat or prepare the food so that it conforms to the kashrut or Sabbath laws; the husband may know these things only theoretically.

The gap between theoretical and practical knowledge is caricatured by the story

tionalist school for ba'alot t'shuva much time is devoted to the study of the prophets, philosophical questions, and the Bible as well as to dinim, the practical laws. Some philosophical discussion is necessary as ba'alot t'shuva are confronting Orthodoxy for the first time and have questions that must be addressed. Yet the philosophical materials thought necessary for ba'alot t'shuva are not a major focus of study for ba'alei t'shuva.[15]

Furthermore, although women are taught practical laws, they are not educated in the methods and sources of the law. Thus they may be taught the specific rules that apply to Shabbat, kashrut, or family purity, especially those rules that they will have to apply daily. But they are not taught to trace the developments and extensions of the laws to new situations even when these cases impinge directly on activities for which they are responsible.

Women are not simply being taught things that are practical while men are taught the philosophical or theoretical, for part of the women's curriculum is devoted to the philosophical while part of the study of Talmud and Codes is indeed practical. A more accurate generalization seems to be that women do not study the Talmud but study anything else, practical or philosophical. This position reflects the ideal role of the husband as the religious authority within the family. Beyond the family, whereas most men do not wield authority in communal affairs, women may not (Novak 1984). Perhaps women are dominant in the domestic role and men in the communal role (Zborowski and Herzog 1952), and talmudic study is preparation for the latter.

PRAYERS

Public prayers are occasions for men to religionize. Men learn the rituals of prayers by observation. Women do not participate directly in these public prayers.[16] They may not be counted as part of the minyan. They

---

of the rabbinical student who, when shown a chicken's gizzard regarding which he had studied many laws of kashrut, exclaimed, "So this is the holy gizzard!" See also Zborowski and Herzog 1952.

15. Interestingly, the Mishnah's statement that "study is not the essence but rather deeds are" (Avot 1:17) implies that study for men is also practical in the sense that it leads to observance. There are a host of similar statements in the Talmud—for example, "He who learns in order to do [good deeds] . . . is granted the possibility of learning and teaching, observing and doing (Avot 6:6).

16. In many communities, women were not taught to pray at all, although they had the obligation for certain prayers—for example, blessings before and after meals, and the lighting of the Sabbath candles. The lack of instruction for women often led to their substituting prayers in Yiddish.

cannot lead the prayers. Yet because women in the larger society typically pray, many of the ba'alot t'shuva expect to pray regularly.

The schools for women have not developed a uniform ideological position on this issue; the modernistic have generally allowed more public religious expression for women than the traditionalistic. At Pardess Institute some of the prayer services are conducted without the traditional mechitzah, and women participate in prayers at these times together with the men. But even there women do not lead the services or read the Torah. At the Lincoln Square Synagogue, women, with the acquiescence of some leading Torah scholars, formed a prayer group.[17] In ba'alot t'shuva schools on the Sabbath or on holy days a minyan of men are invited to the school for public prayers, while the women pray behind the mechitzah. At other times the women will pray alone.

The place of women in prayer may turn some away from Orthodoxy. Those most likely to be turned away by this often have strong Conservative or Reform Jewish backgrounds with these movements' concomitant strong commitment to women's rights. This seems to produce an ideological basis for opposition to Orthodoxy. The unaffiliated and those with antiestablishment views, such as hippies, see the place of women in Orthodoxy as less problematic.

A CURRICULUM IN DOMESTICITY

At the Shappel College for Women (Brovender's), a modernistic school that stresses advanced study for girls, the associate dean was both proud and amused to inform me that one of the administrative problems the school faced was controlling the use of raw ingredients in the school's kitchen. The girls, who prepared their own meals in the kitchen, used so much flour, oil, and eggs to bake cakes and other dishes, which they then gave away, that the cost was becoming a serious drain on the school's budget. Despite the rigorous program of study at Neve Yerushalayim and its emphasis on an intellectual approach to Judaism, the halls of the school were covered with posters announcing sewing classes and dress

---

17. The term *prayer group* was used rather than minyan, which carried the sense of official public prayer. The prayer group, in which women lead the services and read the Torah, has since been emulated in other communities. This is done, however, without those key elements of service that indicate that it has official standing. For example, the blessing for reading the Torah is not recited in such groups; nor is the *Kaddish* repeated. Men cannot fulfill their religious obligations of public prayer by attending such prayer groups, and thus men rarely attend, even behind a mechitzah.

sales. Visits to the sick, help for the poor, and other acts of kindness were also central to Shappel's, so much so that the Friday program was devoted entirely to such activities. This not only provided an opportunity to do a mitzvah of a nurturant and womanly sort, but for those who might be helping a poor housewife with several children get her tasks done on Friday, it also provided an opportunity to observe preparations for the Sabbath first hand.

Marriage was so important a factor that it would emerge at the slightest consideration. When one girl attending Neve was asked, "What is the most difficult problem you find in accepting Orthodoxy? What philosophical or ritual issue do you have to struggle with?" she answered, "I'm really thinking hard about whether I should cover my hair after I marry." (Deciding whether to cover one's hair implies actively choosing the community with which one will affiliate as well as one's religious practices—whether she will be a part of the community that attends the theater or the movies and goes swimming with men and women together or chooses a community that avoids these and similar mixed activities.)

Every one of the schools for ba'alot t'shuva has people who attempt to find suitable marriage mates for the girls. At Neve Yerushalayim a woman teacher takes this task as her prime responsibility. The schools act in loco parentis, some more and some less formally, in interviewing prospective mates. A similar arrangement exists at the men's schools. The difference is that at the men's schools "learning" and becoming a talmid chacham are the major goals. At the women's schools the student is learning to become a Jewish woman, wife, and mother.

The following excerpt from a conversation with three British girls who had come to Neve for the summer months in 1982 provides a sense of this. In a joking manner one said, "I've come to Neve because I want to find a *chasan* [a husband]." "That's what we're all here for," said the second. Nods and laughter all around.

Q. Will the people at Neve really help you to find someone?
A. Well yes, they really do, but I hear the housemother will not even talk to you about it unless you're here for three months.
  Second girl: I believe it's more like six months.
  First girl: Well, I guess I'll just have to find someone on my own. (Laughter.)

WOMEN'S ROLE

The schools for ba'alei t'shuva, whether for men or for women, teach not only a literature and a set of norms and values but a role. Scholarship alone is not the goal. Some students are quite sensitive to this.

One young man left Brovender's yeshiva to study at Ohr Someyach because, he said, "I didn't just want to know how to learn or to be able to do the mitzvot. I wanted to be a yeshiva bochur [a traditional yeshiva student]." Apparently at Brovender's students don't look or sound sufficiently "yeshivishe."

For women the role of yeshiva bochur is not only grammatically impossible (*bochur* literally means lad) but also untraditional. A woman cannot be a traditional yeshiva student.

The dean of the D'var Yerushalayim School for Women—a small school founded in 1980 primarily for Israelis from Sephardi backgrounds who had turned away from Judaism and now sought it out again—put it this way:

> If you teach a boy Torah, he knows Torah. If you teach a girl Torah, you build a home. The "Yiddishe momma" of years past is a true thing. The feeling of Judaism is passed on by the mother. Traditionally, knowledge was passed on by the father. Feeling was passed on by the mother. That's what we're trying to do for these girls—to renew in them the will to strive to be Jewish. When they start tasting it, they can pass it on.

> Q. Are you saying that what they are taught is the traditional role of a woman?
> A. That's the main thing. She has to be taught Judaism and her role as a Jew. We feel a girl should not study all day. She needs her feet on the ground, to be involved with family, to work.
>   I heard of two girls who were visiting someone for Rosh Ha-Shanah and asked their hostess, "How are you preparing for Rosh Ha-Shanah?" She answered, "I made gefilte fish, and I made a chicken, and I made a *kugel* and so forth, and I've cleaned the house." The girls were dumbfounded. They expected her to say that she studies two hours a day, that she davens three times a day. That's what they are expecting and hoping for. And they are turned off a bit. They scorn and laugh at their hostess, and that is very wrong, because a very important part of Rosh Ha-Shanah is making the fish and making the chicken. That's an important part of family life. Some schools feel that a girl should study all day because she missed religious instruction for eighteen years and has to make up for it. We feel our girls are much more balanced religiously.

The view expressed here is a traditionalistic Orthodox statement on the appropriate role for women. It clearly conflicts with the liberated woman's view of the appropriate woman's role. It also conflicts with the view of women's role held by other schools for ba'alot t'shuva.

In fact, in radical distinction to others Brovender's modernistic Orthodox school, B'ruria College, even offers women the opportunity to study Gemara. B'ruria has even established an advanced program called

"Kolelet," a radical name as it implies a parallel between this program and the kolel program in yeshivot (the program for married students who have reached the most advanced level in the study of Talmud).

Even Neve Yerushalayim, considered a traditionalistic school for women, seems to contradict the position taken by Rabbi Tucker, the dean of D'var Yerushalayim for Women. According to Rabbi David Revson of Neve Yerushalayim:

> Girls have huge needs to mother, to bring up family and forget everything else. I find myself pushing girls to study, to make something of themselves.
>
> Sometimes radical feminists undergo radical transformations. I was talking to a group of young people at Yale one evening and spotted a girl wearing a sweatshirt which said, "If we are going to send men to the moon, let's send them all." We met afterward and I said, "You must be Jewish." She asked, "How do you know?" I answered, "No one else would wear that sweatshirt." She's here now, and I have trouble keeping her here. I keep telling her, "Stay. Don't marry yet. You can do something for Yiddishkeit." If she wants to further her education we'll help her. Of course if she wants to marry we'll help her; I help people as they need to be helped.

What lies behind the conviction that women should continue to develop themselves is the view that men should spend several years studying in a kolel after marriage and that women should be prepared during this period to contribute to the support of themselves, their husbands, and even their children. The women at Neve seek out such a relationship. To declare that one's fiance will spend several years studying at a yeshiva after marriage has become a source of status.

At Yeshivat Hatfutzot-Har Tzion a woman may have to support her husband's study for an even longer period. Some students have been at the yeshiva eight to ten years or more. By this time most husbands have found work—usually part-time—while their wives continue to contribute to the support of the family, considering it an honor that their husbands continue to learn. On the surface the pattern that seems to be emerging suggests women's liberation. In fact it seems closer to that of the Eastern European shtetl (see Zborowski and Herzog 1952).

That Har Tzion students, many of whom began their search for religion as hippies, have adopted this role is no surprise, since women in the hippie culture typically play the role of supportive wife and mother. Although women have been at Har Tzion since the late 1960s, no formal classes or schooling in Judaism have been developed for them. Rabbi Goldstein's wife teaches the women in informal classes and on a one-to-one basis. She is the mother of ten children and has little outside help save that offered by the girls attending Har Tzion. The arrangement seems almost designed to socialize the women into the role of Jewish wife and mother.

Brovender's B'ruria College seems to offer a contrasting model for Jewish women. Here women are trained in Judaism through the use of classical texts. They learn to master the texts and to engage in independent study. B'ruria is unique in that it enables women to study Gemara, traditionally the preserve of men.

But, interestingly, some women leave B'ruria for other schools because they wish to become traditional Jewish women, just as men may leave Hamivtar to become yeshiva bochurim. An interview with a student at Nevei illustrates this tendency. This student had attended Brovender's school for women and was entirely positive about it. She felt she had gotten an excellent grounding in Jewish sources and methods of study. Her training had been so good that she was now a counselor and tutor at Neve. Her teaching made it clear that she had mastered some of the difficult commentaries on the Pentateuch. But when asked why she had left Brovender's she replied, "They taught Gemara there, and I thought that girls shouldn't study Gemara." Although she was eager to learn, she felt this activity would not enhance her status as a Jewish woman and suggested that the desire to study Gemara derived from feminist rather than religious values.

But even B'ruria does not neglect the core role of Jewish women, that of wife and mother. It too attempts to help its women students find a suitable mate.

THE CENTRAL ISSUE FOR WOMEN

Some potential recruits see the role of women in Orthodoxy as a problem. One young woman, explaining why she had no interest in learning to be Orthodox, reported her observations of an Orthodox family. "The husband said that Jewish men put their wives on a pedestal. But he was sitting here at the Sabbath meal while she was running in and out like an obedient servant, bringing the food and taking care of the children." Another said, "Sure, there is a division; men have their mitzvot and women have their own unique mitzvot. But why is it that men's mitzvot like davening relate them to God, while women's mitzvot, like kashrut and Shabbat, basically end up being service to men?"

Yet some women do choose to become Orthodox, apparently attracted by the role of wife and mother in the traditional Orthodox family. For those who become ba'alot t'shuva this attraction outweighs the differences in what men and women learn, how they pray, or which commandments they perform. The overwhelming sense is that these women want family, and in the traditional Orthodox Jewish sense. Somehow the role of Jewish wife and mother is rewarding enough to outweigh all other considerations.

One young woman who became Orthodox summed up her view as follows: "My grandfather was Orthodox. And the best memories I have of my childhood are those of the family coming together at his home on Passover and celebrating the holy day together. I want to have that for myself and my family."

Chapter 7

Value Conflicts

Judaism in the United States supports some of the values of the larger society, but it also professes some uniquely Jewish values that run counter to those of the larger society.[1] In this respect all three wings of Judaism are countercultural. For a nonpracticing Jew to become Reform or Conservative is in a sense a countercultural act; to become an Orthodox Jew is even more so, for Orthodoxy, by requiring observance of the laws of kashrut, Shabbat, and family purity, distances its adherents from and puts them in conflict with American society.

Viewed from the outside, Orthodox Jews constitute a single community bound together through their practice of kashrut and Shabbat, which sets them off from others and limits their participation in the broader society. But the Orthodox themselves distinguish three subcommunities: chasidic, "black hat" (or yeshivish), and modern. These subcommunities differ in styles of worship and dress, religious organizational affiliation, and secular and religious educational styles. Both the regular yeshivot and the ba'al t'shuva yeshivot associated with these subcommunities articulate and exemplify these differences.

The character of the chasidic community and its distinction from other Orthodox subcommunities have been explored in a number of studies and novels.[2] The distinction between black hat and modern Orthodox is

1. For a discussion of some of these differences and of Judaism's transformation in the United States into a religion espousing the "American way of life," see Herberg 1960.

2. For community studies of Chasidism in America, see Poll 1962 and Rubin 1972; for chasidic leaders, see Buber 1947, 1948 and Wiesel 1972. For a novel dealing with the relation between chasidic and "modern" Orthodoxy, see Potok 1967.

much more subtle. With regard to the issues affecting ba'alei t'shuva, chasidic and black hat yeshivot usually take the same position. We shall therefore focus on the distinction between black hat and modern Orthodox.

DRESS STYLE

The ideal black hat yeshiva student wears a black suit, a white shirt with no tie, and a black fedora. In contrast, modern yeshiva students wear informal clothes—perhaps slacks and a sweater, perhaps even jeans and running shoes, a brightly colored or dark shirt, and a knitted skullcap (*kippah seruga*). Yeshivot where most of the students are dressed in this way are sometimes designated kippah seruga yeshivot. The black hat yeshivot are what has been called strictly Orthodox or traditional. The kippah seruga yeshivot are sometimes called modern.

All yeshivot are traditional institutions, not only in the sense that the institution itself and the material studied are old or that the way of life they inculcate has existed for a long time but also in the sense that the essential goal of these schools is to maintain and continue traditions. We prefer, therefore, to call the former "traditionalist" and the latter "modernist."

Although by custom Orthodox men wear some head covering, neither black hat nor kippah seruga are historically authentic. Between the wars, European Jews, including yeshiva students, dressed in the style of the country in which they were located. (The chasidim were the major exception; their styles of dress today follow the styles chasidim adopted at the turn of the twentieth century, with black, long-jacketed suits and large-brimmed, black felt hats.) The differences between the styles of dress at the two types of yeshiva are based not on halakhah but on community practices. Nevertheless, in traditionalist yeshivot the impression pervades that this formal style of dress is the traditional dress of yeshiva bochrim, that it holds an element of historical authenticity.[3]

3. Photographs of students at major yeshivot between the wars clearly demonstrate that this is not so. Furthermore, the wearing of black, so strongly favored in the chasidic and yeshivish groups, is counter to views on dress expressed in the Talmud. The Talmud specifies that a *talmid chacham* should dress in white clothes without stains and without patches (BT, Shabbat 114a). Black clothes are regarded as a sign of mourning and distress (BT, Hagiga 16a). The Mishnah (Midot 5:4) states that a priest found unfit to serve in the Temple should clothe himself in black and leave the Temple. If found fit, he should clothe himself in white. The Talmud

Again, modernistic yeshivot are not modern. Yeshiva University, whose motto is "Torah and Science," does not offer courses in biblical criticism, nor does any other yeshiva. Yeshiva students everywhere are taught that Moses received the Torah at Mount Sinai, not that it developed and evolved over the course of a thousand years. Miracles are accepted, with the difference being that the modernists try to understand miraculous events naturally where possible, particularly in the Midrashic or interpretive literature, whereas the traditionalists prefer to see miracles wherever possible.

Differences in clothing styles, however, are often used to identify community boundaries.[4] While their garments stigmatize chasidim and black-hat yeshiva students in the larger society, within the subgroup they enhance the status of those who wear them. The dress style indicates the wearer's willingness to identify himself as part of a counterculture, in effect to declare that his commitment to the group is so great that he is willing to stigmatize himself. A newcomer may be admonished *not* to wear such clothing as it may be inappropriate to his status, a sign of arrogance rather than commitment.

This perspective sheds light on the anomalous pattern of yeshiva clothes. Both modernist and traditionalist yeshiva students wear head covering. Both wear tzitzit (a fringed garment worn by Jewish males), and many in both groups wear beards. These practices are based on halakhah and custom. But the distinctions emerge precisely in those areas in which there are no specific religious requirements.

The dean of one of the black hat ba'al t'shuva yeshivot put it this way: "They [the modernistic Orthodox] are looking to do as little as possible.

---

reports that when Rabbi Akiva had to inform a colleague of the latter's excommunication he clothed himself in black (BT, Baba Metzia 59b). The most negative view of black clothing states, "If one wants to sin, let him clothe himself in black, and repair to a place where people will not recognize him" (BT, Kiddushin 30a, Moed Kattan 17a).

When one considers that there is less talmudic authority for wearing a head covering, which is universally accepted among Orthodox Jews, than there is for wearing white and avoiding black clothing, then the peculiarity of wearing black is all the more striking. Other than that black clothing was sometimes mandated by hostile authorities as a way of stigmatizing Jews, there seems to be no basis for this custom.

4. Goffman notes that militant programs of all kinds can be served by the device of self-stigmatization, which cuts them off from the larger society. He quotes Poll's statement that chasidim wear their traditional garments so that "they may refrain from any possible sin" (Goffman 1963, 101).

Only what is required. Our boys want a life of holiness. Their question is always, 'How can I do this in a holy way? How can I act in a holy way?' And they want to do the same thing with their clothes and their food and the way they celebrate Shabbos, everything. They don't ask, 'Do I really have to do this?' They're not looking to see how they can get out of it."

One ba'al t'shuva, commenting on another ba'al t'shuva group, said: "They are still hippies. They are hippies who also have a Jewish trip. They have other trips too. They meditate; they are vegetarian or eat macrobiotic food or practice yoga exercises. And they are also Orthodox Jews. But it's not their main purpose in life. It's not what they are. It's just another one of the things they do. You can see that they are the same people. They are still wearing hippie dress, their faces haven't changed."

This student himself wore a black *kapote* and hat, untrimmed beard, uncut peyot (sidelocks) perhaps a foot long, which he allowed to hang down during the davening and rolled back into curls under his hat when he was finished. His white shirt had no tie, in the style of the most religious, and at the completion of the morning prayer service he donned Rabbenu Tam's tefillin.[5] Implicitly he was asserting that to be Orthodox one must make oneself into a chasidic Jew. One's total appearance must change in the process.

This informant is suggesting that the willingness to dress in a manner that stigmatizes is an excellent indicator of commitment. He is not concerned only with the halakhic or normative requirements of dress. Rather, he wishes, by his dress, hair style, and even demeanor, to indicate that he rejects the standards and styles of those who are not part of his world and is fully willing to accept the rejection and even contempt of the world. Thus the clothing is a measure of his convictions and commitment precisely because it is stigmatized in the larger society. The more the clothing or the behavior stigmatizes, the stronger the evidence of commitment.

The distinctions in dress that divide the yeshiva world into two communities are not as sharp as we have portrayed them. "Blue hat yeshivot" are more formal and traditionalistic than the kippah seruga yeshivot but less so than black hat yeshivot. At some kippah seruga yeshivot the students wear jeans and sandals, whereas at others the students wear slacks but not jeans and if they wear sandals they wear them with socks.

Dress style differs subtly in the girls' schools as well. In some the

5. At the close of the morning prayer service, after Rashi's tefillin have been removed, a second pair of tefillin is worn briefly—typically by elders among chasidim—who seek to perform an additional pious act.

teachers cover their heads with a *tichel* (kerchief); in others they wear only wigs. The more traditionalistic wear kerchiefs down to the forehead, allowing no hair whatever to show; the less traditionalistic wear wigs; the still less traditionalistic wear kerchiefs but will allow some hair to show. The first group may wear high-necked dresses, long skirts, and black stockings. The second group wear high-necked dresses and long skirts, but their stockings are in natural colors; the third may not wear stockings in hot weather but will not wear slacks. The differences in dress are subtle, but they permit each community to recognize its own members on the basis of dress.⁶

The differences go beyond styles of dress. Traditionalists and modernists have separate rabbinical and political associations. The Rabbinical Council of America (RCA) draws members primarily from Yeshiva University, a modernist yeshiva. Rabbis of Young Israel synagogues are predominantly members of the RCA and are also Mizrachi (modernists) supporters. Members of the Igud Harabonim are drawn primarily from traditionalist yeshivot and are supporters of Agudah. In Israel religious groups are also divided into different political parties, and the party system reaches into all areas of life. Parties own banks and newspapers, compete for and control government ministries, sponsor school systems, build their own housing developments, and run summer camps, kibbutzim, and moshavim (see Fein 1967).

These associations tend to maximize differences between groups by adding a political dimension to existing ideological differences. Leadership, funds, and followers become points of competition.

Issues Separating Traditionalist and Modernist Yeshivot

The principal points of conflict between the two yeshiva communities involve Israel, secular education, and the role of women. On each of these

6. In July 1982 accusations by the Agudat Israel party (the major supporter of traditionalistic Orthodoxy) that El Al Airlines was not observing the required laws of kashrut and Shabbat led to a reorganization of work schedules to eliminate these violations, which reduced pay for some workers. Airline personnel went out on strike in protest and in retaliation attempted to bar Agudat Israel supporters from flights while allowing Mizrachi (modernists) to board. Men wearing dark suits and hats were assumed to be Agudah supporters and were blocked. Those wearing the kippah seruga were assumed to be Mizrachi supporters and were permitted to board. For women the distinctions were much more subtle. The word was that women whose blouses were buttoned at the neck were Agudah supporters; those whose topmost button was open were assumed to be Mizrachi.

issues, the traditionalist yeshivot reject more of the values of the larger society than do the modernist yeshivot.

ISRAEL

From the beginning of Jewish history, love of Zion was expressed in a predominantly religous framework. Through the millenia, whenever groups of Jews came to live in what is now Israel their motive was religious—attachment to the promised land. The late nineteenth century saw the emergence of a new thrust, political Zionism, an attempt to build a state in the ancient homeland. Led by Theodore Herzl, this movement was secular in its outlook at its inception and remained a predominantly secular movement with a religious wing, the Mizrachi.

Although religious Jews felt powerful ties to the land of Israel, few joined the Zionist movement. Zionist leadership was secularist and anti-religious and viewed Jewishness as a national rather than a religious identity and Judaism as outmoded and tradition-bound. Yet most religious Jews did not oppose Zionism. As time went on, conflict intensified. Between the wars, the traditionalist Agudat Israel—a political party *and* a religious movement—and most of the chasidic rebbes in Europe actively opposed Zionism and Zionists, condemning those associated with it. Opposition was framed in fundamentalist terms: the promised land was to be redeemed in the days of the Messiah; until the Messiah came, men were to do nothing to achieve that promise, for human action would suggest that men, not God, were to be the source of redemption, and this would be heretical. This position reflected the perception that the messianic dream was being secularized by Zionism, an attitude still held by a small portion of the chasidic world, particularly the Neturei Karta group in Israel, the Satmar group in the United States, and some yeshiva groups such as Brisk Yeshiva (mitnagdic) in Israel. These three groups see Zionism as another Shabbetai Tzevi—a false messiah, so to speak, but a secular one.

At the same time, in some religious circles political Zionism came to be seen as the very fulfillment of the messianic promise of redemption. For Rabbi Kook, the first Chief Rabbi of Israel (1920–1940), then Palestine, and his followers, the beginnings of the building of the state represented the *atchaltah d'geulah,* the beginnings of messianic redemption. Thus the issue was joined in the religious camp. Some people saw building the land of Israel as a mitzvah of the highest order; others saw it as heresy. These perpectives came to characterize Agudah and Mizrachi, respectively. The issue was one of the most divisive in Orthodoxy from the beginning of the century until the end of World War II.

The Holocaust destroyed whole communities and support systems on both sides of the issue. It also cut the ground from those who opposed a political Zionism. Differences nevertheless remained. Agudat Israel only reluctantly came to accept the state of Israel. Agudists came to Israel, settled and helped build it but rejected Zionism, held positions in government bureaucracies but disclaimed responsibility for policy, ran for and were elected to the Knesset but held no ministerial posts because they claimed the state did not follow the teachings of the Torah. Mizrachi served in every cabinet, sought to give religious expression to national events such as Independence Day, willingly served in the army, and even organized yeshivot where students combined religious studies with army service.

In the yeshivot, these symbolic differences were considered important and principled. Traditionalistic yeshivot in Israel and in America did not sing the Hatikvah (the Israeli national anthem) at ceremonial occasions, did not celebrate or even mention Israeli Independence Day, and rejected the prayer services established by Mizrachi groups to mark the day. Most of the yeshivot favored Agudah. There were some exceptions, notably Yeshiva University in the United States and Mercaz Harav in Israel. But their pro-Israel, pro-Mizrachi stance, rather than legitimizing Mizrachi or Zionism, undermined the very legitimacy of these schools among yeshivot.

In Israel rejection of the state conflicts with the core values of the society, and the countercultural symbolic rejection is exacerbated by the traditionalistic yeshivot's resistance to service in the army. The armed forces are the single most respected institution in Israeli society.[7] Yet traditionalistic yeshiva students, by their use of the deferments granted to seminary students, often avoid service in the army or use the deferment to postpone service until they are past the age for active service.

In contrast, to the modernistic yeshivot the state represents "the beginnings of messianic redemption." Service in the armed forces has the nature of a religious obligation. Students at *hesder yeshivot* (literally, yeshivot in the arrangement), who fulfill their military obligations by

---

7. Youngsters who fail to serve are dishonored. So widespread was this attitude that juvenile delinquents, who were rejected by the army because of their criminal records, considered it a breakthrough when they were offered a rehabilitation program that would make them acceptable to the armed services.

spending alternate periods of time on active duty and in the yeshivot,[8] came to be idealized as the model of the Israeli soldier, replacing the soldier-kibbutznik ideal of the early statehood period. They played a major role in tank units in the Yom Kippur War of 1973 and in the Lebanese War.[9] Traditionalistic yeshivot resisted this arrangement.

SECULAR EDUCATION

Yeshivot g'vohot (higher yeshivot, for those of college age and older) in America can be distinguished by their attitude toward secular education.[10] Most yeshivot are suspicious of college, some forbid their students to attend at all, and most place some restriction on the number of evenings or hours per week that students may attend. Among yeshivot g'vohot in the United States, only Yeshiva University in New York and the Hebrew Theological Seminary in Chicago provide both a secular and a religious education. The difference in attitudes toward secular education is a major source of conflict between traditionalistic and modernistic yeshivot in America (Helmreich 1982).[11]

The conflict had its origins in the European yeshivot of the late nineteenth century. While secular studies were taught at the yeshivot of Samson Raphael Hirsch and Azriel Hildesheimer in Germany and the Tahkemoni yeshiva of Mizrachi, other yeshivot, fearful of assimilatory pressures, forbade the study of secular subjects. In 1893, for example, during a period of administrative harassment and pogroms aimed at forcing Jews to flee Russia or to assimilate, the Yeshiva of Volozhin closed its doors rather than agree to the demand by the authorities that Russian be taught.

In America yeshivot seemed to be on the brink of accepting college

8. Considered equivalent to the practice of having military units serve in Nahal (pioneer military kibbutz groups) to fulfill their military obligations during peacetime.

9. In the Lebanese War, they suffered so disproportionate a number of casualties that the leaders of the hesder yeshivot met with Menachem Begin, and only his promise to restructure their personnel concentrations so as to avoid similar disasters persuaded the roshei yeshivot to continue.

10. This section draws on the work of William Helmreich (1982), particularly pp. 194–265.

11. Helmreich distinguishes "strictly Orthodox" and "modern Orthodox" yeshivot in America primarily by their attitudes toward secular education and makes almost no mention of their differences with regard to Israel. In Israel the central issue is attitudes toward the state and army service.

education. In 1928 Yeshiva College was established. In 1946 Yeshiva
Chaim Berlin and Yeshiva Torah Vodaath jointly submitted an application to the Regents of New York State for a college charter.[12] At about
this time Yeshiva Ner Israel in Baltimore entered into an arrangement
with Loyola University whereby its students were offered advanced
standing toward a B.A. degree. The Chaim Berlin-Torah Vodaath effort
was abandoned soon after. Some of the participants suggest that this was
due to the resistance of Rabbi Aaron Kottler, an outstanding scholar and
a charismatic personality who was opposed to secular education
(Helmreich 1982, 47–50).

Jews were reeling from a fifteen-year war of extermination against
them by Nazi Germany, which professed to represent modern scientific
knowledge. The leaders of modern Western culture, to whom Jews had
looked for relief from oppression in the preceding century, had watched
without protest. The moral legitimacy of secular knowledge and science,
as well as their agencies, the colleges and universities, came to be questioned. Even though the overwhelming majority of students at all yeshivot
attended college, Rabbi Kottler's followers argued that secular education
had no intrinsic value and was not to be honored or taken seriously.
Helmreich quotes a yeshiva student's assessment of industrial psychology: "What can they do? They can tell you where to put the toilet paper?"
If college was valued at all, it was as an instrumentality, a means to an end
and not as an end in itself.[13]

12. At that time only 15 percent of college-age students in the population at large
attended college (Trow 1966, 441). Once Jews were integrated into the larger society, their rate of college attendance tended to be about twice that of the general
population, and this probably was true in the 1940s. At present about 60 percent of
the general population attend college. Helmreich surveyed the alumni of a yeshiva
that opposed college attendance and found that only 14 percent of the students who
attended yeshiva between 1933 and 1978 did not attend college (1982, 275). As this
survey includes those who attended yeshiva when college attendance was far less
popular, it is probable that in the recent past almost all yeshiva students with the
exception of chasidim attended college.

13. The general argument is that the atmosphere at a secular college is not
conducive to religious observance, that heretical ideas are sometimes discussed in the
classroom, and that college attendance takes time away from Torah study. At some
yeshivot even limited attendance is prohibited; at others students can attend on a
limited basis, usually two nights a week, and a few permit students to attend college
four nights. A significant number of students ignore these rules.

Yeshivot press students to avoid heretical ideas. Thus courses in the behavioral
sciences, especially psychology, anthropology, sociology, and needless to say, philosophy, are to be avoided (Helmreich 1982, 223). On the other hand, Yeshiva Univer-

A still more radical countercultural value has developed in recent years with the emergence of the kolel, where men who are married and have families are provided with stipends by the yeshiva to continue their studies of Talmud. The first such yeshiva was established by Rabbi Aaron Kottler in Lakewood, New Jersey, in 1943. Throughout the 1940s and 1950s several other yeshivot established kolels, but the number of students attending was small, perhaps fifty to one hundred, according to Helmreich. Today more than one thousand students study in *kolels* in the United States and perhaps ten times that number in Israel, where the students include many Americans.[14]

Although most kolel students leave after a few years to earn a livelihood and support their families, some stay in the kolel for five or ten years or even longer. In their view a life of study in a kolel is the highest vocation a Jew can pursue. But this means that to survive they must depend on the school's small stipend, on public assistance such as welfare or food stamps, on the salary their wives may earn, or on the support of parents and in-laws. Sometimes yeshiva students seek large dowries as a means of support during their years of study in the kolel. This style of life runs contrary to the work ethic and is a source of substantial conflict between prospective kolel students and their parents, as well as with the values of the larger society.

In recent years modernistic yeshivot have also established kolels. But the commitment of modernistic yeshivot to secular education, their view that secular studies have a legitimate place in the education of an Orthodox Jew, and the tendency to limit kolel study to a few years make these kolels more compatible with the values of the larger society. They are seen as places for advanced study of Talmud, not as opportunities to escape from the world.

THE ROLE OF WOMEN

All religions define and limit the relationship between men and women. In the Moslem world, the woman's veil, her restrictions in the harem, and occupational limitations in traditional societies effectively curtail contact

---

sity's position is that secular education can contribute to and deepen religious understanding. Helmreich calls secular education a "crucial issue" that distinguishes Yeshiva University from other yeshivot.

14. The *Yearbook of Religious Zionism, 1983–1984* claims 9,302 full-time married students in kolels and 4,601 half-time students. There is some evidence that many students may register at more than one school full-time to collect stipends. The more accurate figure may be much lower (23).

between men and women. In the Christian West, many of the barriers separating men and women have broken down in the post-industrial period. Occupational segregation is under challenge, clothes and hair-styles are often unisex, educational institutions that just a few years ago were reserved either for men or for women only have become coeducational, and courtship patterns have also changed radically. Whereas a century ago courtship might have been chaperoned or regulated so that men and women could not be alone together, today a period of cohabitation before marriage has become almost an accepted part of the courtship process. On the whole Orthodox Judaism has resisted these changing standards of the larger society, but here again substantial differences exist between modernist and traditionalist yeshivot.

Orthodox Judaism claims a long tradition for the separation of men and women in worship, going back to the Second Temple in Jerusalem, where men worshipped in one courtyard and women in another. That tradition is preserved in Orthodox synagogues today, where men pray in one area of the synagogue and women in another.[15] The issue of the separation of men and women in the synagogue, more than any other, brought about the schism between Orthodox and Conservative Judaism in the United States in the early part of this century.

The tradition that yeshivot are schools for men only also goes back millennia. The early academies were not simply schools but legislative and judicial bodies deriving from the Sanhedrin, which could by majority vote decide issues of law or institute new law. The public and authority functions of these academies made them an inappropriate vehicle for the education of women, whose religious functions in the ancient world were private and domestic (Novack 1984). Yeshivot g'vohot today remain institutions for men.[16]

Halakhah specifies numerous restrictions on interaction between men and women outside of the family; listening to a woman singing is considered sexually arousing and is to be avoided. Men are forbidden to gaze lustfully at women, to be alone with a forbidden woman who is not a close relative, particularly another man's wife, to make love to one's wife during her menses and for a week afterward—even to kiss and embrace

15. In larger synagogues women are often accommodated in a balcony, following a tradition dating to the Second Temple.

16. Although the Jewish Theological Seminary (Conservative) does not claim to be a yeshiva, this tradition is so strong that the Seminary admitted women into its rabbinical program for the first time in September 1984 only after a bitter controversy (*New York Times,* 6 September 1984).

her with sexual intent until she has purified herself by a ritual bath (mikveh). Women are required to dress modestly, although the meaning of modest dress is not specified. It has also been "religious custom in Israel" (*Dat Yisrael*) for women not to wear their hair loose and flowing but to cover it with veils, kerchiefs, caps, hairpieces, or wigs.[17]

In all these areas the traditionalist and modernist yeshivot agree. Beyond this the two types of yeshivot differ substantially as to the degree of separation required.

Traditionalists believe that even touching a woman's hand is forbidden. Modernists draw the line of the forbidden at the concept of lust and do not avoid handshakes. Traditionalists consider social dancing forbidden, whereas some modernists have permitted it.[18] Traditionalists consider that it is forbidden for men and women to swim in a pool or at a beach together; modernists have in the past not considered this forbidden. Traditionalists often sit apart from their wives at weddings and other celebrations; modernists have men and women seated at the same table. Traditionalist wives have either covered their hair completely with a kerchief or have worn wigs; modernist wives have either worn their hair uncovered or worn small hats.

The degree of separation of men and women required by traditionalists

17. The custom is based on the discussion of the *sotah*, the wife suspected of being unfaithful to her husband. The Torah specifies that if she has met alone with another man over her husband's objections she should be subjected to a religious ordeal (Num. 5:11–31). As part of her ordeal the priest will "loosen her hair," which implies that a married woman's hair is bound up or covered and that a loose woman's hair is loose (BT, Ketubot 72a). The Talmud therefore concludes that those who fail to bind or cover their hair violate "Jewish custom" (Dat Yisrael). If divorced, they leave without a *Ketubbah* (a monetary divorce settlement). In America until recently many Orthodox women, even in traditionalistic families, did not cover their hair. Their reading of the law was that such practice was not a religious offense but an infringement on wifely duties, so that if the husband did not object uncovering one's hair was of no consequence.

The woman's covering her hair was almost abandoned a generation ago. The *Arukh Hashulkhan* (a work by a leading Torah scholar, Rabbi Yeheil Michal Halevi Epstein, 1829–1908) had ruled that "in our day hair can no longer be considered sexually arousing" (chap. 75, paras. 6, 7). This ruling, too, once widely accepted by the modernists, is slowly being rejected as more of the modernist women cover their hair.

18. Social dancing was permitted in some Orthodox German Jewish schools between the wars, and some rabbis have argued that halakhically it is not forbidden. It was widely accepted by modernistic Orthodox synagogues in the United States until the 1960s.

is often resented by women, who believe that separation implies an inferior status. Some men also find these customs and laws burdensome, as separation imposes limits on men's activity as well as women's. It is often the men who wish to engage in social dancing or swimming or to meet alone with a woman or touch a woman's hand. In fact, according to halakhah the *man* is obligated to avoid these behaviors; no law forbids a woman to gaze lustfully at a man or to listen to a man sing. These halakhic restrictions are even more limiting than the patterns of traditional nineteenth-century America, where courtship was conducted under the vigilant eyes of parents.

While modernists have pressed for minimal restrictions in this area, traditionalists have extended limits to new areas. For example, at Orthodox weddings in Europe there was no social dancing, but there was also no mechitzah separating the men's and women's sections at weddings. Currently at traditionalist weddings, a mechitzah is erected.[19]

The two groups are similar in their view of the role of women in the nonreligious area. Traditionalists permit and may encourage their wives to go to work to help support the family. Their women may receive a secular education and may dress in the latest modern (but modest) styles.

Conflict in a Modernist Yeshiva

One would imagine that modernist yeshivot, which try to minimize distinctions between men and women and offer women higher religious education, would be prefered by ba'alot t'shuva. They provide elements of traditional family life and at the same time allow for greater personal freedom and an education more in line with that of modern women. Yet a major upheaval in Shappel's College for Women in spring 1976 suggests how complex this issue is.

In the fall of 1972 Shappel's admitted twenty-five women into its program. It offered courses in Chumash (Pentateuch), Prophets, Mishnah, dinim (laws), and Jewish thought (*makhshevet yisrael*). Its approach was similar to that of Shappel's College for Men. Heavy emphasis was placed on acquiring the tools for independent study. The commentators'

19. The Mishnah (Taanit 4:1) describes the Fifteenth of Av and Yom Kippur as days when "The daughters of Jerusalem went out in borrowed white clothing and danced in the vineyards saying, 'Young man, lift up your eyes and see whom you choose for yourself'" while admonishing the young men to choose character and family line over beauty. Clearly the men saw the women dancing, not a mechitzah.

methods of analysis were taught, as well as the commentaries themselves. Students did not simply learn Rashi (the classic commentary on the Pentateuch), they learned to examine Rashi's comments so as to understand the questions he was addressing. They were taught to distinguish among the different sources that Rashi quotes—to note, for example, that when Rashi cites two alternate interpretations of a verse, he is satisfied with neither—and to attempt to understand what each interpretation lacked. They were taught to examine the source that Rashi used to interpret a verse, to note what he included in his commentary as well as what he excluded, and to try to understand why some parts of a source might have been excluded. Each of the different commentaries was examined for style of analysis, contrasting, for example, the Ramban (Nachmanides), whose modern psychological approach is combined with mystical interpretation, and Seforno, who offers classical philosophical interpretations.

The staff of the school included people who could articulate Jewish values and communicate their commitment as well as their knowledge to women who had little knowledge of Judaism. The director of the school was Rabbi Yossi Krupnick, a man in his early twenties, son of a rebbi at the Yeshiva Rabbi Jacob Joseph High School in New York City.

The master teacher at Shappel's for Women, who taught most of the courses when the school was still small, was Rebbetzin Malke Binah, a young American woman married to a teacher at Yeshivat Ha-Kotel. Her husband is the son of the rosh yeshiva of Netiv Meir, a religious Zionist school in Jerusalem reputed to be one of the best yeshiva high schools in Israel in both secular and religious studies. Thus, the school's administration and teachers should have been above reproach on religious matters.

In the spring of 1976, following the Passover holiday break, a number of girls went on strike against the school, claiming that it was not religious enough and demanding changes in policy and personnel. These students charged that on a school *tiyul* (camping trip) to Eilat some of the food was not kosher. Further, the striking women alleged that during the tiyul the armed guards who were required to accompany their bus had gone swimming while the girls were swimming. The staff flatly denied the first charge and explained that the guards were swimming a distance from the girls and in any case were not under their authority. Some months later in an interview in the United States the leader of the striking women elaborated on these charges. She alleged that at the Purim celebration the men had made offensive off-color jokes but were not admonished by the staff present. The merits of the charges are impossible to determine. But clearly several of the students resented this institution's liberalness and wanted it to take a more frum (pious) position with regard to food and in particular with regard to the separation from men.

Prior to the upheaval, although the school permitted and encouraged the women to say grace after meals together and to sing the Sabbath zemirot (hymns) at the table, some of the women had refused to do either on the ground that this was unseemly. They had also taken to wearing their hair in braids, following the custom of the people of Meah Sh'arim (the most traditionalistic section of Jerusalem). The school administration had been puzzled as to how this last custom had come to be adopted. When I asked about this practice this same informant explained that she had introduced it. She had been assisting a family in Meah Sh'arim as part of her Friday program of *g'milat chassadim* (acts of kindness) and noticed that unmarried women in the area wore their hair in braids. Told that this was Jewish custom she began to persuade other women in the school to follow this example. She also told me that the women in the school would not sing grace after meals because they did not want to expose the rabbis present to *kol isha,* a woman's voice, which may be forbidden. (She was aware, I discovered on further probing, that many authorities believe this rule applies only when one voice is heard, not when many women sing together, but she felt that the more stringent interpretation of the rules should be followed.)

My informant, the initiator of much of this conflict, was not a hippie who had recently left one cult to join another. She had been raised in a neighborhood thickly populated with Jews. She had attended the local congregational afternoon school attached to a large and vibrant Conservative community. Her brother and sister had attended as well. She had visited Israel several times before coming to Shappel and had attended a private out-of-state college for a year before switching to the local college, which had a substantial portion of Jewish students. This school served as a training ground in her decision to try to learn about Orthodoxy. She was not a dropout seeking to make a countercultural statement but someone seeking "authentic" Jewish values. Her acceptance of clothes style and other extra-halakhic customs as symbols of Orthodoxy seems based on an inability to distinguish variations in custom from essential practice. This is a problem often faced by those new to a culture.

The result of the protests was that Rabbi Mordechai Elefant, head of ITRI, who had initiated the Shappel Colleges for Men and Women, felt compelled to demand the resignation of Rabbi Krupnick, the director of the school, and Rebbetzin Binah, the master teacher. Rabbi Brovender thereupon resigned as head of the Shappel colleges. Within a year he had set up his own college for men, Yeshivat Hamivtar, and followed with Michlelet Bruria for women. Shappel's College for Men continued under a new director, and the women's division was closed.

Apparently the pressures exerted by other yeshivot compelled Rabbi Elefant, who had initially selected Rabbi Brovender to head the schools because he appreciated his modernistic style, to seek a more traditionalistic approach. While Rabbi Brovender's schools meet a need and continue to grow, they are somewhat alien in the yeshiva environment in Israel. Rabbi Brovender continues to wear his kippah seruga, but as a rosh yeshiva in Israel he is under pressure to wear the black hat and suit.

Convergences and Symbolic Differences

Differences between traditionalistic and modernistic yeshivot have emerged only in the twentieth century, and some differences, such as in clothing, have developed only in the last generation or so, perhaps suggesting an impending schism. Yet there are also growing convergences among the yeshivot.

Leading roshei yeshiva and others strongly opposed to secular education have succeeded in delegitimizing college and university education in part of the yeshiva world. For some yeshiva students the delegitimization of secular education probably discourages or at least delays their forsaking the yeshiva world. Yet even roshei yeshiva may have such education.[20]

A similar pattern has developed with regard to Israel. As we have noted, the early rejection of Zionism was based in part on the view that at the "end of days" God would gather in His people once again; humans had no right to reestablish the Jewish community in Israel. The Holocaust and the establishment of the state of Israel made this position moot. To entirely reject the state of Israel, which protected Jews and supported religious education and yeshivot was difficult; but secular Zionism and

20. This results in some interesting labeling. Rabbi Joseph B. Soloveitchik of Yeshiva University is "blemished" in the eyes of some for his doctorate in philosophy from the University of Berlin, as was Dr. Samuel Belkin (an outstanding Torah scholar and president of Yeshiva University) for his doctorate in classics from Brown University. If one mentions that the Lubavitcher Rebbe, Rabbi Menachem Mendel Schneersohn, has a degree in engineering from the Sorbonne or that Rabbi Isaac Hutner studied at the University of Berlin—this is a sign of their breadth of knowledge.

nationalistic patriotism could still be rejected. Unwillingness to fly the flag, to sing the Hatikvah, and to celebrate Independence Day remain the outward manifestations of this position; but for the most part traditionalist yeshivot no longer question cooperation with the state.

The crucial conflict remains avoidance of service in the army by students at traditionalist yeshivot. In Israel, where service in the armed forces is expected of all and women serve also, this has led to particular bitterness against traditionalist yeshiva students, and in turn the students justify their unwillingness to serve by denying the legitimacy of the state.

Regarding the separation of men and women and conspicuously religious clothing styles, the modernists have changed in the direction of the traditionalists. B'nai Akiva youth are now much more careful in their observance of the laws separating men and women in the dating situation. Married B'nai Akiva women cover their hair with a kerchief much more frequently than a decade ago. B'nai Akiva men are quite often bearded and wear their tzitzit outside their shirts so that they are visible to all. They continue to wear the kippah seruga and informal clothes, but they seem more ready to accept halakhic interpretations regarding relations between the sexes than in the recent past. They seem to be aiming at a claim for greater symbolic legitimacy by adopting these practices.

In the ba'al t'shuva yeshivot, both perspectives tend to converge. Newcomers, still in jeans, mingle with older students, making it difficult to identify a yeshiva by dress. The past experience of the newcomers gives them an ease in their relationship with women that is uncharacteristic of traditionalistic yeshiva students. Moreover, most ba'alei t'shuva have had some college or university training before entering the yeshiva, and some (particularly hippies) may have dropped out and rejected this education, making it unnecessary for the yeshivot to resist secular education. Further, because their students and a substantial portion of their staff have had such education, they can speak in the language of these secular studies. Neither denying nor affirming the value of secular education, they can simply ignore it. The yeshivot for ba'alei t'shuva may even encourage a student to finish his or her education. Only when they are pressed for an evaluation of secular education will it become clear that it is not regarded as a value, only as an instrument.

The major point of contention revolves around attitude toward the state of Israel and service in the armed forces. The acid test of attitude toward Israel is service in the armed forces. Several ba'al t'shuva yeshivot have programs for Israelis, almost all of whom have served in the armed forces, remain on active reserve, and are called up several times a year. For many of the American students in these yeshivot as well, the Israeli army is a religious and ethnic symbol in the wake of the Holocaust. Students entering the yeshivot are in search of Jewish identity, and the threat to Israel from military attack by hostile forces makes it hard to deny the obligation to serve.

In the wake of the Yom Kippur War of 1973, a sense of depression and aimlessness hit Israeli society. Israelis refer to it as a "spiritual earthquake." From the high of the victory of 1967, when many believed that Israel's security problems had been solved for generations to come, they fell to the depths in 1973, when once again they feared that they might lose the war and be annihilated, as it appeared might happen in the first weeks of war. Major values of Israeli society came to be questioned, and this became the critical event that generated the t'shuva movement in Israel. In an effort to find some ground for an ideological society whose values were being shattered, the government turned to the ba'al t'shuva yeshivot, which had experience in reaching out and explaining the position and values of the religious community. A program of *toda'ah yehudit* (Jewish knowledge) that involved the ba'al t'shuva yeshivot put even traditionalistic ones in an almost unparalleled position as morale builders for the armed forces.

Paul Laster, a member of the administrative staff of Ohr Someyach, describes the process:

> I was a major in the United States Army doing public relations work in Virginia. I wasn't raised as a practicing Jew, but I had a strong Jewish identity. In 1977 I decided to visit Israel, and when here I joined the Israeli Army. Given my experience, the Israeli Army put me in a special programs project. At that time the army was looking for programs that provide a sense of inspiration and motivation for the men. They had already started some contacts with the ba'alei t'shuva yeshivot before I came. I got interested in the yeshivot myself and came to visit them again and again and became more religious as time went on. At the same time, I was in charge of the toda'ah yehudit programs. These programs were supposed to give soldiers, who were most often very ignorant of their Jewish roots, some sense of what Jewishness was all about so that they would know what they were fighting for. I kept sending more and more of the army groups to the ba'al t'shuva yeshivot and especially to Ohr Someyach. There were Americans here, and I could talk their language, could understand them. But my commanding officer got a little annoyed at me. He wasn't religious minded, and he felt I was pushing my own views. He began making life difficult for me, and finally I resigned from the army and came here to Ohr Someyach to work for them full time.

A coincidental conjunction of several factors—the erosion of Zionist socialist values, the development of ba'alei t'shuva yeshivot in the early 1970s as a result of the growth of the counterculture, the American connection to the ba'al t'shuva movement, Israel's loss of confidence following the Yom Kippur War of 1973—all made ba'al t'shuva yeshivot an appropriate choice for the army in its search for commitment-building institutions.

In turn, as institutions receiving government support for educational outreach programs, yeshivot could not refuse this request from the army; nor would they, for bringing their message to the soldiers was an opportunity they sought. Moreover, the army was coming to the yeshiva; at times, the yeshiva did not have to leave its own turf. The yeshiva was to do the teaching, to set the rules. Yeshivot held, correctly for the most part, that these factors effectively protected them from co-optation and assimilation into the army and national culture. Nevertheless, the arrangement helped break down the barriers between the two worlds. As early as 1975 Ohr Someyach hung in its entry foyer a photograph of a combat wing of Israeli Air Force jets on which the wing officer had inscribed his thanks and appreciation for the warmth and cordiality with which the yeshiva had received his crew and the strongly favorable impressions the few days at the yeshiva had left on them.

By 1982 several other letters of thanks and photographs of army groups had joined the first at Ohr Someyach's new campus in Ma'alot Daphne. In the summer of 1982, with the war in Lebanon still raging, army service by students at regular yeshivot had become a major issue. Whereas in 1975–1976, in almost a dozen interviews with staff and students at Ohr Someyach the army had hardly come up, in 1982 it was the subject of intense and extended discussion. The exemptions from service for yeshiva students led to bitter accusations by the mass media of draft dodging. The yeshivot, particularly the traditionalistic yeshivot (by 1982 Ohr Someyach and other yeshivot had programs for Israelis), were said to be persuading Israeli army reservists to shirk their duty.

The yeshivot were under pressure and could ill afford to lose government approval, not only because they were financed in part by the government but primarily because the issue of service in the armed forces challenged the very legitimacy of their existence. How could they reach out if they were perceived as takers but not givers?

In discussing this issue Rabbi Mendel Weinbach said:

We're doing our part. I've made *aliyah* and live in Israel. I serve in the army. The boys in our yeshiva serve. How can someone living in South Africa or England or America tell me what to believe or that I have to say *Hallel* (a prayer of thanks, which is part of the holiday liturgy and recited by religious Zionists on Independence Day) or salute the flag? Does that make me a better Israeli? Why must I do it your way? I'm meeting all of my obligations as a citizen. Maybe I'm not Peres or Shulamit Aloni's kind of Zionist, but why is their attachment to Israel better than mine?

And according to Weinbach, a high-ranking military officer visited Yeshivat Ohr Someyach as the head of an investigating commission and reported "that we were doing a great job."

Thus in 1982 the participation of traditionalist ba'al t'shuva yeshivot in that central institution of Israeli society, the armed forces, pushed them toward the mainstream of Israeli society. At the same time the "sacredness" of the army was sullied by its invasion of Lebanon and by its failure to prevent massacres in Sabra and Shattila. The sacredness of *chalutziut* (pioneering land settlement) was undermined by the terrorist acts committed in 1982–1984 by members of Gush Emunim. At the very moment that forces in society were secularizing sacred values, the traditionalist ba'al t'shuva yeshivot were pushed by other forces—the Zionist inclinations of their student body, their connections to government agencies, the programs of outreach for the armed forces, their attachment to Begin—to modify their own position. As a result the principled differences that distinguished traditionalist and modernist ba'al t'shuva yeshivot have narrowed. As Mendel Weinbach put it: "We are *sh'khorim* (black hats). But we are sh'khorim nekhmadim (lovable black hats)."

In fact they seemed to be so considered by Israeli society. Banks, insurance companies, airlines, and other major industries offered their workers educational retreats in a variety of settings—at universities, kibbutzim, and ba'al t'shuva yeshivot such as Ohr Someyach, among other places. Substantial numbers of workers chose to spend a day or two at a yeshiva, attending seminars, meeting with the staff and students. The mass media regularly ran stories on the ba'al t'shuva yeshivot, and most of these stories were favorable, focusing on the Americans, South Africans, or others who have found their Jewish identity in the yeshivot or on the Israeli delinquent youth who have been rehabilitated by the yeshivot. Ohr Someyach, Lubavitch, and other institutions like them seem to have become lovable black hats because of their connection to the army and because their outreach programs seem to express toleration and concern for others.

More recently, some air force pilots who became ba'alei t'shuva have refused active duty, raising questions about yeshiva support for the State. The availability of draft deferments to those in ba'al t'shuva yeshivot has led to the charge that some Israelis are using these schools to dodge the draft. In addition, since 1984 the parents of some young people who have become radical ba'alei t'shuva have begun to organize against recruitment. Claiming that their children have abandoned them when they entered these yeshivot, the parents have raised charges of "brainwashing." Although there have been no court cases involving snatchings, such as occurred with the followers of Reverend Moon and others in the United States in the 1970s, public discussion has been generated by this opposition. The two issues—refusal of active duty in the army on grounds of attendance at a yeshiva and the objections of parents in cases where young people have rejected them after becoming Orthodox—have resulted in a change in relations between ba'al t'shuva yeshivot and the army. On 17 June 1988 the *Jewish Press* reported that Defense Minister Yitzhak Rabin had "banned partisan activities by religious activists in army camps. His order followed complaints by parents" that recruiters for ba'al t'shuva yeshivot have influenced their children and led many to relations with their secular families.

Rabin ordered that soldiers shall not be allowed to visit such yeshivot as part of their army service and that spokesmen for these yeshivot no longer be invited to carry out their activities in army camps. This was a clear break with the policies that had invited such exchanges, which had begun more than a decade earlier.

It is not likely that the complaints of parents by themselves could have caused this breech of relations. The more likely cause was the resignation from active duty of a number of pilots and other personnel. Parents' complaints were probably the excuse to act in a situation that had a long and problematic history is Israel—the exemption of large numbers of traditionalistic yeshiva students from service in the armed forces. The ba'al t'shuva yeshivot at first seemed removed from this controversy, as many of their students had already served. But when some resigned their commissions and claimed religious exemptions, the ba'al t'shuva yeshivot lost their immunity from these accusations. In fact, in challenging the army, one of the most sacred institutions of Israeli society, the yeshivot risked their character as sectarians of the majority—hyperconformist to the dominant religious values—and came close to being redefined as cult, that is, promoters of nonlegitimate religious values.

The promoters of outreach are also faced with an enduring underlying dilemma. While their outreach programs (and their early connections to the army) have earned Lubavitch and the ba'al t'shuva yeshivot a special acceptance in Israel and among Orthodox Jews in the United States, at the core the groups' acceptance of others is more limited than some of their

actions seem to suggest. Contradiction is inherent here. To declare "we
are all the same" weakens commitment to the special way of life. To
declare "we are different" makes recruitment difficult. The conflict is
sometimes resolved by telling outsiders one thing and insiders another.
That strategy, however, leaves the groups open to charges of deceit.
Failure to reaffirm the core values that distinguish the group from others
results in the loss of the group's identity. Perhaps this explains why
Lubavitch has publicly declared on several occasions that Israel is not the
atchalta d'geulah (the beginnings of redemption), as Rabbi Kook and
religious Zionists hold. These public declarations are in all likelihood
directed primarily at Lubavitcher themselves, reminding them that they
are different.

Ohr Someyach's outreach program in Givat Ada apparently ran into
this same dilemma. A school was established to educate children of nonreligious families, but the children of Ohr Someyach yeshiva students
attended a separate institution. Here again the outreach program led to
the problem of reconciling the group's unique commitment to outreach
with the feeling that the children from nonreligious homes may limit the
level of religious education and standards of religious behavior that their
own children may achieve. Setting up a separate school raises the question
of whether the standards the group seeks to achieve can indeed be
achieved by the bulk of Jewry or must remain specific to a small, separate
group, a point that undermines the claims of the ba'al t'shuva movement.

The dilemma for modernists is less severe here, as they see themselves
as part of the larger community and accept Israel as the "start of redemption." Their dilemmas originate elsewhere, as we shall see.

Chapter 8

The Hidden Conflict: The Basis of Religious Authority

In chapter 7 we noted that dress styles identify different subcommunities of Orthodox Jews, which hold different attitudes toward Israel, secular education, and relations between men and women. Here we argue that these differences in attitude reflect a larger consideration.

Some observers (Leibman 1965; Singer 1976) have argued that these differences derive from the fact that traditionalists are world-rejecting sectarians whereas modernists are world-accepting denominationalists. But this leaves some questions unanswered. World rejection implies asceticism, yet none of the Orthodox subcommunities rejects wealth or luxury. Furthermore, traditionalists explain their behavior as reflecting *yiras shamayim,* "fear of heaven," not ascetic rejection of the world. To put it another way, within the traditionalist community, dress style is a symbol of identification with the community, not of world rejection.

We suggest, instead, that the critical feature distinguishing the modernist from the traditionalist is *the nature and scope of the authority to which each is committed*. Traditionalists allow their leaders authority in political and personal matters, and the leadership attempts to exercise authority beyond the specifics of halakhah. They achieve this by developing powerful communal ties and customs. Modernists, in contrast, seek maximum scope for personal decision making, and their leadership limits its authority to halakhah. Communal ties and customs are weaker among modernists. This difference in authority and control gives rise to other distinctions such as those in dress and attitude. Unlike the other differences between the Orthodox communities, this one is not clearly articulated, and the communities themselves are not fully aware of them. We shall attempt to demonstrate that it is crucial to explicate how this difference is taught and to assess its impact.

Religious Authority

Religious authority has been a particularly intriguing and intractable problem in the sociology of religion. Max Weber introduced the Greek word *charisma* into the lexicon of sociology to designate one of three legitimations of authority, that which is based on the claim to a special "gift of grace." (The other two are traditional authority, which refers to the "eternal yesterday," the basis of the claims of kings, and rational-legal authority, the basis of bureaucratic authority.) Charisma has come to designate not simply a legitimation of power but the very basis of the power wielded by religious leaders. It has been defined as normative power, in contradistinction to coercive power, which characterizes the polity, and remunerative power, which characterizes the economy (Etzioni 1961). Claims to charismatic power are validated by the commitment of followers. To understand charismatic power, one must understand the basis for normative commitment.

In the past sociologists have often described religious leadership and authority by using organizational models more appropriate to the study of economic or political organizations. Thus the sociological literature on religious authority is replete with references to the organizational structure of religion, drawing distinctions among episcopal, presbyterian, and congregational (that is, hierarchical, collegial, and independent local) clerical authority structures. These concepts have been used to classify and compare religions in terms of sects and ecclesia, or perhaps in attempting to see how authority structures evolve from one type to another (Harrison 1959).

The symbolic-interactionist approach to the construction of the grounds of belief and commitment suggests a new direction in the exploration of religious authority. Religious authority may use coercion to force compliance or may offer remuneration or other rewards in exchange for compliance, but its essential power derives from the normative commitment of its adherents. This commitment develops in the course of socialization and is supported by a plausibility structure (that is, a community of others who maintain the same symbols and offer one another support of their common symbol system). In essence, the world we see, the emotions we feel, the mental prison bars that contain us and produce compliance to authority are ideas in our own minds. They must continually be rebuilt anew, or they disappear. Examining the nature of this commitment and how it is built is therefore critical.

The importance of this issue can be seen if one considers that Judaism in all three of its wings seems to be congregational; its authority structure should therefore follow the Protestant model. That it does not and, moreover, that differences in religious authority among these wings do not begin to be explained by the structural approach suggest that the meaning and locus of the commitment to normative authority must be examined.

RELIGIOUS AUTHORITY IN JUDAISM

The nature of religious authority, the conception of what guides a Jew's actions, differs for each of Judaism's wings. For Reform Judaism the source of religious authority is the ethical and universalistic teachings of the prophets. Because conscience is a reflection of the Godhead for Reform, the ultimate authority is man's own conscience, guided by the moral and ethical teachings of the Bible.

Conservative Judaism finds the core of religious authority in Jewish peoplehood—the culture, customs, and practices of the Jewish people throughout the ages. Judaism is a tradition that includes not only the Bible, the Talmud, and the Codes but also the practices of Jews, the traditions of "catholic Israel,"[1] the entire "civilization of Judaism."[2] The ultimate source of religious authority for Conservative Judaism is the Jewish people and its tradition.

Orthodoxy views the halakhah as the essence of Judaism. Conformity to these norms (which include traditions and community practice), decided on by a majority of scholars in the past and codified into religious law, is obligatory. Religious authority is to be found in the Codes and Responsa, the body of legal decisions and precedents. Not surprisingly, therefore, the focus of Judaic studies for Reform is philosophy, for Conservatism is history, and for Orthodoxy is Talmud.

But if halakhah is the source of authority for all Orthodox Jews, why are there differences among the Orthodox? The answer is that even a detailed legal system needs interpreters. In Orthodoxy the question is "who shall be the interpreters of halakhah?" For chasidic Jews, the rebbe, the scholar-saint of the community, the person those knowledge and holiness set him above others so that his decisions, behaviors, and advice

1. Solomon Schechter's phrase denoting *all* of the Jewish people.
2. Mordecai Kaplan's descriptive term (1934) for the essence of Judaism.

are to be followed, is the interpreter. In the case of the rebbe, saintliness is manifested not only by saintly behavior but occasionally also by reputation as a ba'al mofsim (literally, a performer of miracles) or more frequently a *po'el yeshu'ot* (literally, a provider of salvations), whose prayers affect the higher spheres and who is aware of heaven's plans for men.

The eighteenth-century opponents of Chasidism (mitnaggedim), who founded the great European yeshivot, insisted on the primacy of halakhah and the technical halakhic expertise of the pious person[3] as the bases of religious authority. In the past two or three decades traditionalistic yeshivot have been claiming that the basis for religious authority is not only halakhah but also *da'at Torah,* "the Torah perspective."

Both modernistic and traditionalistic yeshivot are committed to halakhah, including norms regulating dress, sexual relations, diet, work, and ethical behavior. Regarding the authority of contemporary rabbis, modernistic and traditionalistic yeshivot differ. The traditionalistic refer the student to the da'at Torah of the gedolim (great talmudic sages), arguing that gedolim may address any issue, halakhic or nonhalakhic, and claim the authority of Torah.[4] Traditionalists argue that even if modernists do not violate halakhah in any way, nevertheless the modernistic stance is in violation of da'at Torah. Modernistic yeshivot reject this view.

3. A rabbi's reputation for personal piety is an important factor affecting acceptance of his halakhic decisions. The rabbi's authority derives from his role as both scholar and saint (Carlin and Mendlowitz 1958).

4. This formulation leans primarily on Rabbi Elchonon Wasserman (1875–1941), who claimed da'at Torah as the moral authority for his opposition to Zionism, Communism, and secular education and for his views on other contemporary issues. Those claiming the authority of da'at Torah also question the legitimacy of modernistic yeshivot. Rabbi Wasserman was rosh yeshiva at Baranowicz, Poland, and the leader of Agudat Yisrael, the traditionalistic and at that time anti-Zionist Orthodox party. See Helmreich 1982, 68–69 for a discussion of the traditionalistic view of da'at Torah.

The response that modernistic yeshivot make to this attack is that (1) even on halakhah, gedolim are not infallible; (2) if there is room for legitimate differences of opinion on halakhic matters, where gedolim are expert, they cannot be infallible in areas where they possess no special expertise (for example, on whether the Soviet Union will respond to public pressures for Jewish immigration); (3) gedolim differ on major issues such as Zionism and secular education. (See *Hamevaser,* the student publication of Yeshiva University, 11 Jan. 1984, citing Rabbi Moshe Feinstein's introduction to his *Igros Moshe.* Rabbi Feinstein [1895–1986] was the most highly regarded *posek* (halakhic decisor) in America in the post–World War II period and a gadol accepted by modernists and traditionalists.)

RELIGIOUS AUTHORITY AND POTENTIAL RETURNEES

Religious authority is a special problem for ba'alei t'shuva, whose situation requires that values be articulated fully and quickly "lest the potential recruit misunderstand and leave." Although they tend to accept the binding authority of the Bible, the major intellectual problem they face concerns the authority of the oral tradition (*Torah sheh ba'al peh*), which involves humans in determining the scope and application of Divine laws. In yeshivot for ba'alei t'shuva the issue is twofold: (1) What authority do the oral law and extensions of the laws of the Bible have? (2) What authority do contemporary rabbis have, and does rabbinic authority extend beyond the specifics of the Codes?

Yeshivot respond to the first question by teaching students the Talmud, which elucidates the connection between biblical and rabbinic law. The oral tradition claims authority contemporaneous with the Revelation at Sinai, and the Talmud applies and explicates the oral tradition. For example, the Pentateuch forbids work on the Sabbath, but apart from the lighting of fires, it does not define "work." Yet there must have been a tradition as to what constitutes work. The Talmud defines the nature of work through a process of biblical exegesis. The Talmud's candid style does not hide from the students disagreements over the nature of the tradition and its applications.

The Talmud wrestles with a paradox: on one hand it holds that the oral tradition starts with the Revelation at Sinai; on the other hand it presents disagreements, extensions, and new applications of the law. The Talmud distinguishes between laws based on "tradition from Moses who received it at Sinai" and those parts of the law developed by rabbis. The Talmud insists on the Divine nature of the law and at the same time on the authority of the rabbis to continue to develop and shape halakhah. The law is Divine in its source, yet humans develop and extend it,[5] and disagreements arise about elements of the law.

This paradox is not openly addressed, but the entire thrust of the Talmud is to attempt to resolve apparent inconsistencies and disagreements by seeking the reasoning behind contradictory statements that might explain how both could apply or by demonstrating that they derive from different but equally valid traditions. The underlying message of the

5. By and large this issue is not confronted in Orthodox yeshivot, although it is addressed by such innovative thinkers as Rabbi Joseph B. Soloveitchik at Yeshiva University and Rabbi Eliezer Berkowitz at the Hebrew College of Skokie. See the latter's *Not in Heaven*, 1984.

effort is that this tradition has been taken seriously since the beginnings of rabbinic Judaism and must be taken seriously by those who would follow it now. Yeshivot believe that studying the Talmud powerfully demonstrates to students the authoritativeness of the oral tradition. In this all yeshivot, modernist and traditionalist, are in agreement.

How are the different views of authority taught in modernist and traditionalist yeshivot? The answer to this lies not in what is taught but in *how* it is taught.

The Study of Talmud and the Construction of Religious Authority

A typical page of the Talmud consists of a Mishna, a statement of a law or custom, and some dissenting opinions. In the Gemara the opinions are elaborated on, examined, and compared to related and contradictory rulings. Any given page of the Babylonian Talmud[6] also presents annotated comments by Rashi and questions by the Tosafists (twelfth- to fourteenth-century commentators on the Talmud and particularly on Rashi's interpretations) on the issues raised either by the text or by Rashi. Emendations refer the scholar to textual variations; addenda refer him to appropriate legal decisions in Maimonides' code, the *Mishnah Torah,* and Rabbi Joseph Caro's code, the *Shulkhan Arukh.* At the back of the standard Talmud text one may find thirty or forty other commentaries and annotations of the Talmud.

The Mishnah itself is in Hebrew, the Gemara in Aramaic; Rashi, Tosafot and other commentaries use a unique Hebrew script unlike that used by the Gemara. The annotators and commentators often use unfamiliar abbreviations. The entire text is unvocalized and unpunctuated. The style of writing is telegraphic if not cryptic, the logic of argument is often complex, and a single logical sequence may extend for several pages. All in all, to read and analyze a page of Talmud is a formidable task requiring a knowledge of Hebrew, Aramaic, and several scripts, styles of thought, and styles of argument, as well as the subject matter. It takes a highly intelligent and devoted student several years to master this task and

6. Roughly contemporaneous with the Babylonian Talmud, a separate set of discussions of the Mishna, known as the Jerusalem Talmud, was developed in Palestine. This work elaborated in particular the religious laws pertaining to the special sanctity of the land of Israel. It was less relevant for Jews living outside of Israel, who favored the Babylonian Talmud, which is studied in yeshivot everywhere.

many more years to master a sufficient portion of the Talmud to become familiar with major issues and perspectives so that he can arrive at decisions in uncharted areas.

In the past, the typical Orthodox Jew studied Chumash, Mishnah, and laws, but in-depth study of Gemara was left to the scholarly elite (Katz 1971). At yeshivot for ba'alei t'shuva, young men are introduced to the study of Talmud within weeks and sometimes days after their arrival. Because the ba'al t'shuva yeshivot attempt to compress into a few months a process that normally takes years, nuances in instruction that would go unnoticed in regular yeshivot may be observed.

APPROACHES TO THE TALMUD AT BA'AL T'SHUVA YESHIVOT

Traditionalistic. There are striking differences between modernist and traditionalist yeshivot in their respective *approaches* to the study of Talmud. Surprisingly, the modernists first attempt to teach the student to master the text, whereas traditionalists are more concerned that the student comprehend the logic of the arguments.

Rabbi Mendel Weinbach reports that at Ohr Someyach (traditionalistic) students are presented almost immediately with abstract and complex issues, leaving the task of mastering the text for a later time.

> I'll start by presenting to the students the major ideas of the Gemara's discussion. For students who have just come in and who don't have the background I won't use a text, but I'll present the Gemara and the Rashi and Tosafot. We'll be doing a kind of mental acrobatics, moving from one view to another and to the commentaries. But we really don't cover the text.
>
> They may have the same Gemara a few months later, when they've become acquainted with the language and can follow the argument inside the Gemara. If they are around long enough they may even have it a third time, when I cover the Gemara, Rashi, Tosafot, and other sources inside. It's not always the same people that go through all three levels; it depends in part on how much they knew when they came in. There are three levels of shi'urim (lectures), and as they advance they learn more of the text and more on their own.

In regular yeshivot Gemara is also studied on several levels. For the first few years students study Gemara using only the Rashi commentary. Similarly, laymen studying Gemara typically read only the Rashi commentary. Tosafot is generally reserved for advanced classes at yeshivot. Yet in Ohr Someyach and other traditionalistic ba'al t'shuva yeshivot students are introduced to the questions raised by Tosafot soon after they start their studies. They are involved in highly abstract discussions of talmudic points before they have mastered the text.

Modernistic. At Yeshivat Hamivtar (modernistic) students first spend a number of weeks studying the language of the text itself and the simple meanings of the words. They are then ready to move to the next higher level, the structure of the argument on the page. Only after several months of wrestling with the text at this level do the students proceed to the logic of the argument as it is presented on the page as well as in commentaries and discussion elsewhere in the Talmud.

For example, at Yeshivat Hamivtar the text was *Pesahim* 8a; the students were beginners in the program. The point under consideration in the Gemara was where one is *not* required to search for leaven prior to Passover, when all bread and leaven are forbidden. The Mishnah states, "All places where leaven is not brought, do not require a search." The rebbi asked what was the implication of stating this point negatively and what differences might be implied had the statement been framed positively (that is, "All places to which leaven is brought must be searched"). The logical implications of the difference between the two statements were considered. Continuing with the text, the Gemara cites two contradictory statements and resolves the contradiction with the phrase: "this . . . refers to . . . and this . . . refers to . . . " But neither "this" is specified, leaving to the student the task of determining which of two contradictory statements is intended by the first "this" and which by the second "this." The rebbi noted that the consistent pattern in the Gemara was to address the second problematic statement first and then return to the first. The students, made aware of this pattern and others like it, find that the task of understanding a section of the Gemara is considerably eased.

Rashi's different version of the text and the implications of the difference were carefully noted. While the Gemara before the students asks, "What do the words *all places* teach us?" Rashi's version says, "What does the word *all* teach us?" In Rashi's text, the Gemara's question is clearly addressed to the term *all* rather than to *places.*

Proceeding through the text, the teacher asked the students for the translation of each word. Various translations were considered, as well as the implications of each for the structure of the argument. In the course of the discussion, students were asked to formulate their own questions or answers without looking at Rashi and then to see how Rashi interprets the text. Similarly, in studying the Tosafot the rebbi tried to encourage students to see how Tosafot differed from Rashi.

A potential confusion in the text illustrates his technique. The unvocalized text reads "if a MTH divides a house . . . further search for leaven is required." Vocalized one way (*Meetah*), the phrase refers to a bed that divides the area within a house. Vocalized another way (*Mateh*), it refers to a stick or a staff. The student reading the phrase was uncertain about the correct reading. Rather than provide the answer, the rebbi prodded the students to draw the logical conclusions of each interpretation. An animated discussion ensued. "Staff," it was argued, implied that a slight object would not divide a room, but a large one might; "bed" implied that even a large, heavy object does not divide a room and further search was still required. The rebbi was not as interested in the correct answer as he was in whether students were learning to apply the logic of the Talmud to the problem. He complimented the students on their ability to consider the implication of each interpretation, briefly demonstrated why bed was the correct reading, and went on.

This approach gives the students confidence that they can deal with the texts. They are asked to hold Rashi and Tosafot in abeyance until they have at least attempted to understand the text on their own. They are not there to learn what Rashi or Tosafot think; they are attempting to understand the Gemara. After they have tried it themselves they turn to the great interpreters of the Talmud to see what others have said. In a sense, this approach puts them on a footing with the commentaries in the great enterprise of interpreting the Talmud. It not only provides the student with skills in interpreting and understanding the Talmud but also builds the feeling of being a colleague of Rashi and Tosafot and other commentaries, although admittedly a junior colleague, rather than simply a student.[7] Nothing to this effect is stated in the process of study.[8]

7. In distinguishing the styles of study of the two yeshivot one needs to be mindful that Ohr Someyach and other yeshivot must catch the interest and loyalty of the student as quickly as possible, lest the student simply leave. Some of these students are people who have been met at the Kotel or at the bus stop by recruiters and invited to a meal or a Shabbat at the yeshiva.

Yeshivat Hamivtar, on the other hand, has until recently been reluctant to attempt to persuade the uncommitted. In the early 1970s Brovender evidenced almost a distaste for this task, although lately his views have softened. Students at Hamivtar are not ordinarily drop-ins but have committed themselves to study for six months to a year. This program, then, was based on the assumption that there will be sufficient time to teach, and that the student's interest is already there.

The programs of Ohr Someyach and Hamivtar are thus not fully comparable. Yet they do reflect the difference between the modernist and traditionalist approaches.

8. This difference in approaches to the study of Gemara is far less apparent at regular yeshivot than at ba'al t'shuva yeshivot. Students at regular yeshivot will have learned the reading and translation skills at much younger ages, beginning at age ten.

Approaches to Other Subjects

Differences between yeshivot can be seen in their approaches to other studies as well. Charismatics redirect the life of followers in a wide range of areas, and relationships are not ordinarily limited to a specific role. This implies an emotional attachment on the part of the follower to the charismatic. *Mitnagdut* was born in the eighteenth century in opposition to the charismatic power of the early chasidic rebbes. The opposition was rooted in the concern that Chasidism might represent another false messianic movement, similar to the Shabbetai Tzevi movement a century earlier. Lithuanian yeshivot attempted to remove charismatic power entirely and replace it with rational-legal power in Orthodoxy.

Both Ohr Someyach and Hamivtar are yeshivot derived from this mitnagdic tradition. Hamivtar (modernistic) appears to actively discourage emotional involvement or at least intellectualize and cool it. Ohr Someyach (more traditionalistic) also takes pride in its "rigorous, nonemotional approach." But Ohr Someyach does stir the emotions to create attachment toward roshei yeshiva.

BIBLE AND LITURGICAL POETRY

A lecture on Deuteronomy at Ohr Someyach focused on God's intimate relationship with the Jewish people and the need to feel this relationship strongly. Thoughtfully, articulately, and paying careful attention to the text and the meaning of the words, the teacher attempted to demonstrate God's feelings for the Jews and the kind of reciprocity that should be sought. Explaining Deut. 1:31, which refers to God's carrying the Jews "as a father carries his son," he suggested that to experience this reciprocal emotion, it would be useful to think of moments of longing or sadness, moments when a loved one leaves. He described his recollection of his grandfather about to enter the operating room to undergo an operation. "He was a simple man, not very learned but strongly believing in God. With his yellowed hand he grasped mine. I was still a young man,

---

Over the next several years emphasis will slowly shift from the text to the logic of the argument, as the students become more capable of grasping the intricacies of the discussions. The subtle differences in attitude that lead to differences in the conception of religious authority are harder to demonstrate, although they are there. For an illustration of the approach to a page of the Talmud in a traditionalist yeshiva, see Helmreich 1982, 98–103. For a discussion of Talmud study in informal study groups outside the yeshiva, see Heilman 1983.

in my teens. He started saying *viduy* [a confession of sins]. Then he pressed my hand and was taken away. I never saw him alive again."

The teacher pointed out that this incident is an example of an event one might think of to develop a feeling of attachment to God. The students, many of them university graduates, seemed caught up in the example. A student turned to me to say: "He is really able to make the Chumash come alive."

At Hamivtar, by contrast, preparation for the fast of the Tisha B'Av[9] was relatively unemotional, although it offered an ideal situation to provide socialization to the emotional aspects of Judaism. Here the discussion focused on *Kinot,* the poems depicting the cruelty of the enemy and the sufferings endured by the Jews when the Temple was destroyed. The rebbi identified four themes of the poems: the suffering of the Temple, of the congregation of Israel, of the gedolim, and of individuals. The discussion in part was devoted to demonstrating that this was the general organization of the book of Kinot, as well as the organization of many individual poems. Care was taken to translate each word that might be difficult to understand. The author of each kinah discussed was identified, and the rebbi explained the symbols embedded in the Kinot. For example, regarding the statement "The lions trampled Jerusalem," he noted that the lion was the insignia of the Tenth Roman Legion, which conquered Jerusalem. No attempt was made to make the students experience the poem, although many opportunities existed. For example, one kinah depicted the situation of the son and daughter of the High Priest Rabbi Yishmael, who had been sold into captivity. The kinah describes their masters discussing the beauty of the slaves, one describing his maidservant as being as beautiful as the moon, the other his slave in even more laudatory terms. The two captives, unaware that they were brother and sister, were locked in a room at night for the purpose of breeding more slaves. In the morning, when they recognized each other, they committed suicide. The kinah appeals powerfully to the emotions, but the rebbi added nothing to it, did not elaborate it beyond translating the words themselves.

To assume that emotional attachments to the sanctums and heroes of Judaism are not developed at Hamivtar would be a mistake. The process

9. Tisha B'av, which occurs in midsummer, is the day of deepest mourning in the Jewish calendar. It commemorates the destruction of the First and Second Temples (586 B.C.E. and 70 C.E., respectively) and the fall of Betar following the revolt of Bar Kokhba (135 C.E.).

is simply more subtle. To suggest that there are levels of emotional attachment would be more accurate. Chasidism provides the most emotional experiences in close communal life, prayer, song, dance, and even study. Attachment to the rebbe is restrained only by the framework of halakhic rules. Traditionalism provides less emotional connection to particular leaders and to a particular community, but these ties are still there. Modernism offers still weaker emotional and communal ties, but only in comparison with the first two. Its emotional ties and community connections are still far stronger than those of other branches of Judaism, but the relative emotional coolness provides greater freedom of action.

HALAKHIC DECISIONS

How students learn the halakhically required behaviors for different situations also distinguishes modernistic and traditionalistic yeshivot. This difference was illustrated by Rabbi Brovender's response to the question of how students learn which ruling is to be followed.

Q. What do you tell someone who comes to you with a question about halakhah?
A. We don't tell him what to do.
Q. But then how does he know what to do?
A. We have him look it up himself.
Q. But how can a person who is just beginning look up something? How will they know the sources? How can they read the material? How is the newcomer here supposed to learn about whether or not he can turn on a light on Shabbat or when he is supposed to wash his hands? Do you have them look it all up?
A. No. When it comes to telling a person that turning a light is forbidden on Shabbat we simply tell them that. That's easy enough to follow. I'm not talking about that. I'm talking about a situation where someone wants to know the *reasons* for something, or the point of view to follow where there is a difference of opinion. I'll tell them where it can be found and have them read it themselves.
Q. And if they can't?
A. Then I'll help them. But I don't give them the answers. That's something they have to work out for themselves.

Consider, in contrast, the following quotation drawn from the introduction to the English translation of the *Mishnah Berurah* (the authoritative halakhic code of liturgical and holiday observances) by Rabbi Aharon Feldman, a rosh yeshiva at Ohr Someyach. "IMPORTANT ADVICE: *No one should ever on his own decide a halakha problem from*

*a printed text without first consulting a proper authority. This is true for
any work and especially for the Mishnah Berurah.*"

Ohr Someyach is expert in modern styles and techniques of communication, as is evident from their publications, programs, and staff. They
are aware that independence of thought is an educational buzzword. That
one of their roshei yeshiva so clearly communicates students' dependence
on "proper authorities" suggests that there may be another issue at stake
here. That issue is the nature of religious authority.

Modernists take the approach that the authority of the halakhah is to
be found in the persuasive logic of the arguments themselves. Traditionalists assert that the authority resides in the person of those who have
already mastered the materials, that to decide solely on the basis of logic is
to miss the values and emotions that undergird perspectives. To argue
that one or the other of these approaches is more modern is not possible.
All one can say is that the emphasis of the modernistic approach is on
logic and halakhah, on the law rather than the individual. The consequence of this approach is to place greater weight on the need to persuade
the individual. The approach values independence at least in the sense
that the authority for religious decision does not reside in someone else. It
places individual conscience at the center of decisions.

This modernist approach is not new. It is in fact characteristic of the
Mitnaggedim of Lithuania. It is a tradition of study with scientific elements at its base. Gather the precedents, generalize, apply to the specific.
Avoid turning over authority to another. All this characterized the Mitnaggedim in their opposition to the chasidim and particularly to the
charismatic qualities of the rebbe, which they feared would lead to a
renewal of the conditions that made possible Shabbetai Tzevi's messianism.

More than anything else, the mitnaggedim feared emotionalism, religious enthusiasm, charismatic leadership (hence the Yiddish phrase "a
kalte misnagged," a cold mitnagged), and sought to substitute logic,
rationality, and *halakhah* as the guides for Jewish life.

The traditionalist yeshivot have solid precedent for their perspective as
well. For them the application of halakhah to new areas requires not
simply logic but that the leader be steeped in Jewish learning and Jewish
life, so much a "Jewish soul" that his decision represents the path that
halakhah would take if specific guidelines existed. The deciding factor,
then, is not the logic of the argument but the quality of personality or soul
of the people making the decision. For traditionalists it is important that

one turn to a *gadol* for a decision, not simply because a gadol is expert in the area, but because he will reflect the Torah view.

Although the modernists also accept the gadol, they do so because of his superior scholarship. If in a given decision the gadol cannot demonstrate the validity of his view on the basis of a scholarly or logical argument, they are under no obligation to accept it. Such a perspective limits the gadol's authority in areas of life not covered by halakhah. The traditionalists argue that the claims of the Torah personality cannot be ignored in any area because they carry da'at Torah, the religious perspective. Modernists argue that da'at Torah is itself a recent creation and did not exist in classical religious tradition. There is also the problem of what the decision should be in an area where the views of gedolim clash.

The Rosh Yeshiva as a Charismatic Authority

A TRADITIONALISTIC VIEW

Traditionalist yeshivot drew their circle small and excluded modernist yeshivot from their yeshiva world. One would imagine that Yeshivat Hatfutzot-Har Tzion, which reached out to hippies in their terms and language and permitted them to retain their style of dress and other customs, would provide its students with the broadest personal latitude— that its approach would be similar to that of modernist yeshivot. Yet Yeshivat Har Tzion drew that circle even smaller, so that for a number of years all its teachers were former students of this yeshiva.

A former ba'al t'shuva and student who served as a rebbi in the yeshiva describes it.

> We present a highly specialized and specific tradition in learning Torah, which we learn from our rabbi, who learned in turn from his rabbi, etc., etc., which we say is our *masorah* [tradition] from Sinai.
>
> Our primary goal is to make students who will master the system of learning and will perfect their character and perfect their *midos* [virtues] and become gedolim, talmidei chachamim, and completely dedicate themselves to Torah.
>
> Our rabbi has a highly specific discipline in learning Torah, which he received from his teacher. His goal is to pass this on to his students. . . . *He received the tradition from a rabbi (we claim this is the essential point of what we're doing, to receive the Torah from a teacher, from a rabbi, from the living man)* [emphasis added], so that the values he teaches are the true

value judgments of Torah and not a man's own trip. . . . If a man doesn't have a connection with the giving of the Torah at Sinai, which is a handed-down method and tradition, where is he? He's on his own. It's like a guy flew in from Mars and found himself in a library of books. What the rebbi teaches is oral law; this can only come from a live man. . . .

The student all his life has his rebbi, wherever he is. . . . The rebbi may leave, but he always . . . leaves a little slap. [This means] they don't even have to be next to you physically. You always have the "little slap" once you're trained. And that's the little thing that keeps you in line, so that you don't stray from the source of Torah.

It sounds funny, right? I'll tell you something interesting. When my rebbi has his rebbi, who is the rosh yeshiva of Chofetz Chaim, come to visit in Israel—maybe once a year—he comes to the yeshiva and speaks to us, and I see always the same thing. Rabbi Goldstein, my rebbi, . . . takes in every word, I mean literally, no doubt about it. He goes to make sure that it's straight from the source. Rabbi Goldstein's son is studying at Yeshivat Chofetz Chaim. All the classes at this yeshiva are taught by Rabbi Goldstein and his older students. That's also part of our method—to hand down the tradition. Even though we are very happy to have people come in and teach us many things, what we're most interested in is that people will receive the Torah that was supposed to be handed down to them.

We have respect for the Torah and for the rabbis, which expresses itself in the way we learn. For example, when we find a difference of opinion between Rashi and Tosafos we'll say they're not asking a kasha [question] on Rashi. We say, "Do you think Rashi didn't understand what was being asked, that a student could have asked a question that Rashi couldn't answer? Do you think for one minute that when Tosafos asks a kasha Rashi didn't think of the same objection?" They [the authors of the Tosafot commentary] are little pipsqueaks [by comparison], they are Rashi's little grandchildren.[10]

So, we say, what could Rashi have known so that, despite the kasha Tosafos asks, he said what he did?

We say that a person without good midos [virtuous behavior] cannot learn Torah straight. He can't see straight. And learning is [primarily the learning of] the midos [character]. In this yeshiva, we're very careful that we don't separate learning from the midos. That is not to say . . . that we're sitting and learning musar [ethical teaching] twenty-four hours a day. But in the learning of Torah, the learning of Gemara, the rabbi takes the responsibility to insure the growth of his students, to be responsible that his students will grow and not stagnate and that they won't just get an external look at Torah, but they'll really be people of Torah. The rabbi takes the responsibil-

10. In fact, some of the outstanding tosafists *were* Rashi's grandchildren.

ity to make sure that they're growing in their midos and their character. We have a close student-teacher relationship, which we believe is extremely important.

We're able to work more easily with people who haven't developed bad habits in Torah and learning, which means, for example, a person moving his own idea all the time and not able to hear the Torah . . . or listen to a teacher. A guy who learned a method before has a very hard time.

We demand total discipline in the yeshiva. I don't mean in terms of tyranny. . . . I remember once some guy came in complaining to me that he [Rabbi Goldstein] doesn't want people to learn; he wants disciples. I said, "Yes, that's a hundred percent correct. We're not a bet midrash [study house]; we're a yeshiva." We claim that we're one of the few yeshivot in the world, which means we have a group of people who are here together to learn Torah *from a rabbi,* who are *pilpul chaverim* [colleagues in the study of complex talmudic arguments], who grow together in learning Torah, like the Maharsha [a talmudic commentator], like the Ba'alei Tosafos [the writers of the Tosafot commentary].

This student is not simply insisting on the importance of rooting the oral tradition in the Revelation at Sinai. Indeed, that is something no yeshiva would deny. The emphasis here instead minimizes the legitimacy of students or scholars coming to conclusions about laws, practices, or ethical positions on the basis of *their own* reading of the appropriate talmudic texts. Yet using one's own *sevarah,* or reasoning, has substantial legitimacy. It is the major style of argument of the Talmud itself. It has typically characterized mitnagdic yeshivot in the past. This rosh yeshiva, himself a student of a mitnagdic tradition, nevertheless presses a claim for the authority of the teacher over reason, an argument that has been more typical of Chasidism.[11]

The emphasis on receiving the Torah from "a teacher, a rabbi, a living man" underscores this point. The rosh yeshiva's respect for his own rebbi and his attentive attitude, his concern that if he doesn't hear it from his teacher he may falsify tradition, represent the attitudes his students are expected to adopt with regard to him and his teachings, which in effect turn him into a charismatic leader.

11. This argument has a long history in Judaism's attempt to maintain its traditions. In attempting to grapple with the contradictory positions found in the Mishna, the Gemara uses two approaches, historical and logical. Some sages have preferred the former, others the latter. The Talmud at times refers to this as a conflict between Sinai (tradition) and *Oker Harim,* an uprooter of mountains—that is, logical argument.

Respect for the living tradition is also a justification for the exclusion of all other teachers. They may have different traditions. Perhaps theirs are not "from Sinai"—that is, authentic. There is an implicit suggestion that only this rosh yeshiva or his students are legitimate teachers.

The argument that Rashi must have been aware of the questions the Tosafists raised regarding his interpretation but nevertheless persisted in his interpretation implies that Rashi's view is deeper than it appears; this again buttresses the perspective that authority or tradition is not to be taken lightly. This view is supported by a statement in the Talmud that is often repeated in yeshivot. Referring to earlier generations of teachers, the Talmud states, "If we are as men, they are as angels, and if they are as men, then we are as donkeys." Thus, the Har Tzion view is not simply an argument for tradition but an argument with the explicit support of tradition. The assumption that the sages do not err in their interpretations of religious laws and texts is sometimes referred to as *emunat chachamim*, belief in the sages. Applied to the positions taken by sages in nonhalakhic matters, this belief gives their pronouncements in these areas the legitimacy of da'at Torah, a position that we have already indicated is fraught with problems, as gedolim often disagree. Here we see that emunas chachamim, even as it relates to the interpretation of a text, may be problematic. For if we believe that Rashi did not err, then we must believe that the Tosafists erred in raising questions about Rashi's position. Those who hold strongly to the position presented above are not too troubled by the logical problem. Essentially, they simply require that all the classical texts and commentaries, as well as contemporary gedolim, be treated with the utmost respect or reverence. Humility must be the rule, for they are angels while we are at best men and possibly no more than donkeys.

The concern for midos refers not simply to character or virtue but to an attitude of humility and obedience to religious norms and authority. Moreover, it is expected that if these midos are learned they will be manifested in behavior and in dress. The student with midos should appear shy, even timid, and should dress in a formal style; his entire demeanor should reflect his identity as a "yeshiva bochur."

The "bad habits in Torah and learning" that make those raised as Orthodox less preferred as students relate to independence of thought, as is clear from the emphasis on "total discipline in the yeshiva." That there are other approaches is admitted by reference to the contrast with the bet ha-midrash, where everyone has a right to his own perspective. This student argues that in a yeshiva this is inappropriate, for here the rosh yeshiva's relation to students is not that of "first among equals" or even that of expert to novice, but rather that of saintly Torah personality, an incarnation of Torah itself, as it were, to those who would learn.

REJECTION OF CHARISMA AT A MODERNISTIC YESHIVA

Rabbi P. of Yeshivat Hamivtar puts immense stress on the study of the text to make the student capable of learning on his own. He cannot understand why anyone would go to hear someone talk about a point in the Torah when he has the opportunity to read the works of Maimonides, one of the greatest minds in Jewish history, or the *Likutei Maharan,* excerpts of the sermons of Rabbi Nachman of Bratzlav, a great chasidic rebbe.

As he does attend lectures by prominent teachers of Talmud the statement was puzzling. Why he preferred the written word came out later. Discussing the yeshivishe velt Rabbi P. remarked that everyone wants to know what everyone else is doing in order to do the same thing. Everyone wants to be part of the community, and they all act the same way to prove it. They go to the rosh yeshiva, and he tells them when to marry or go into business or whether they should study secular subjects. They have no life space of their own, but this is what many of them want. He (Rabbi P.) has many unanswered questions. But he prefers unresolved questions to the certainty of a follower. He wants the freedom to think for himself.

Interestingly, despite the mitnagdic approach this modernistic yeshiva does not reject mysticism. The *Likutei Maharan* are studied even though Rabbi Nachman of Bratzlav was a founder of Chasidism, a charismatic who claimed to be a reincarnation of Rabbi Shimeon Bar Yochai (the founder of Kabbalah) and of the Ari (Rabbi Isaac Luria, the great medieval mystic) and whose doctrines emphasize the role of the *tzadik* (saint; literally, righteous one) as the great soul necessary for man's redemption. The answer seems to be that only the timeless elements remain in the writings of the gadol. Contemporary issues are not addressed directly. This leaves the student with the possibility of drawing on the gadol but retaining greater personal freedom.

HISTORICAL POSITIONS ON RELIGIOUS AUTHORITY

The very nature of halakhah, which vests authority in the laws and not in man, provides substantial support for the modernist position—not simply in the philosophical sense but in the sense that actions are justified in terms of the accepted rules.

Discussions of authority in halakhah often cite the dispute between Rabbi Eliezer ben Hyrcanus and Rabbi Joshua ben Hanania and his colleagues, in which Rabbi Eliezer attempted to support his point through a series of miracles. Even when a heavenly voice confirmed the view of Rabbi Eliezer, Rabbi Joshua refused to concede, arguing that the Torah "is not in heaven" (BT, Baba Metzia 59b). The story demonstrates that in the view of halakhah one follows the rule of the majority even if the minority view receives Divine confirmation, for God Himself accepts the rule of the majority. The implication is that in halakhic decisions logical persuasion outweighs charismatic power.

But one can find support for the traditionalist view as well. In his *Introduction to Seder Zeraim*, Maimonides quotes the Mishnah (Eduyyot 8:7), which states: "Controversies between the Academy of Shammai and the Academy of Hillel began when the students did not serve their teachers [meaning did not live with them, serve all their needs and get to know them well][12] sufficiently. At that point, controversy developed in Israel and the Torah became as two Torahs."

Maimonides goes on to point out that the prophet Elisha deserved to succeed Elijah because he had "poured water on the hands of Elijah" (that is, served him). Interestingly, Rabbi Joseph B. Soloveitchik of Yeshiva University, whose forebearers were leaders of mitnagdic yeshivot and who is considered a proponent of mitnagdut, has argued that the Torah sheh ba'al peh is to be found in the personality of its scholars and teachers (lectures, 1955).

If this position has historical precedents, it also has historical problems. Foremost is the possibility that the charismatic leader may be antinomian. This was the case for Shabbetai Tzevi and is true also of Chasidut, at least in the early stages of some chasidut. Elijah the Gaon of Vilna (1720–1797), one of the greatest talmudists and spiritual leaders of modern times, opposed precisely this charismatic antinomianism.

Reform's antinomianism, which has also troubled Orthodoxy, is seemingly based on rationalism alone, but in Gershon Scholem's view (1972) a closer look indicates a connection not simply to modernity but also to Kabbalah and mysticism. Of course there are differences between the views of traditionalists and Reform. Reform is not at all bound by halakhah, whereas traditionalists claim to accept halakhah and argue that da'at Torah may add to the obligations of the Jew but not detract

12. Interestingly, Rashi (BT, Sotah 22a) interprets the phrase "serve their teachers" to mean "have knowledge of the rationale behind the halakhic ruling." This view, which carries halakhic weight, supports rational-legal, not charismatic, authority. It also suggests a need to further examine the questions of how and when one view or the other came to be accepted.

from them. Reform represents what traditionalists see as the danger to normative Judaism: rule by men rather than by laws. They do not see da'at Torah in a similar light. Of note, at present the modernists press for rule by law rather than rule by men, following the mitnagdic tradition. Thus the formerly traditional argument is the basis for the modernists' view of halakhah, whereas traditionalists hold some views that characterized the modernizers (not modernists) of a former time—Reform Judaism.[13]

All this suggests a need to reconsider Weber's legitimations of authority as we seem to have here a type of rational-legal charismatic.

THE DEAD REBBE AND BA'ALEI T'SHUVA

Differences in attitude toward religious authority probably explain why of all chasidut today (Lubavitch excepted) the Bratzlaver chasidut in Israel has the greatest attraction for ba'alei t'shuva. Bratzlaver chasidim are known as chasidim of *Der Toteh Rebbe* (the dead rebbe). Unlike other chasidic groups, which select a new rebbe when their rebbe dies, Bratzlaver chasidim have never chosen any successor to Rebbe Nachman (1772–1811), preferring the symbolic position that Rebbe Nachman continues to lead them. Perhaps ba'alei t'shuva prefer this chasidut because death has stabilized the charismatic and mystical powers of the rebbe and made it possible to examine them with cooler emotions. The rebbe can no longer evaluate new situations or go beyond his written word, only the messages that already exist have authority. The words of the rebbe can be weighed for those elements in it that are timeless rather than bound to the specific context in which they were made, and this may add to their sacredness. Yet the individual is free to interpret this message by his own lights and thus gains a measure of additional personal space.[14] Other chasidic rebbe, by contrast, can and do make determinations in everyday situations that their disciples feel compelled to follow.

13. Conservative Judaism has also denied the authority of halakhah as a binding standard for all and has argued instead that Judaism is a civilization and that the base for religious authority is too narrowly construed if it is restricted to halakhah alone. Instead the entire life of the Jewish people must be considered.

14. While this holds for most of those who have a passing acquaintance with Bratslaver chasidut, a very different dynamic operates for those who have joined the group. Such people often become followers of charismatic leaders within the Bratslaver group and seek direction in all areas of life. Some of these people are Israelis who were formerly delinquents or petty criminals and are now eager to abandon their former identity.

Halakhah and Charisma

The charismatic, the person capable of articulating the deeply held convictions of a normative community and reaching its members on the deepest level of meaning, plays an important role in religion. He interprets and applies the values and norms in new and challenging situations, giving life and power to them and providing moral satisfaction to members of this normative community. Religions need such people, particularly in periods of change and crisis, to direct and focus their values and norms and infuse them with new meaning. Without this, the commitment of members may dry up, leaving them woodenly following the norms, yet ready to break away should their convictions be seriously challenged.

In periods of stability the contribution of charismatics may seem unimportant. But stable social structures maintain outward signs of conformity. Inner convictions are not tested, and charismatics may be ignored or suppressed. Stable religions in fact often appear to feel threatened by charismatics. Dostoyevski has described this powerfully in his portrait of the Grand Inquisitor (1955). Christianity has had its Joans of Arc, and the Catholic Church has institutionalized charisma in religious offices and insulated it in religious orders. In this manner it has used organizational techniques to regulate charisma while using it.

Protestantism has sometimes had more difficulty with the centrifugal and factional pressures introduced by charismatics, which have often resulted in the creation of new denominations. Yet the existence of new denominations often relieves the mother group of the charismatic's threat.

Historically Judaism has attempted to control charisma normatively, with the halakhah itself providing a limit. But Judaism too needs its charismatics, and at times crises have given rise to messianic leaders and movements. The seventeenth-century struggle with Shabbeteanism led directly to mitnagdut, opposition to early Chasidism. This conflict has all but disappeared since World War II, but three perspectives on the relation of halakhah to charisma remain: (1) the chasidic view gives the charismatic leader, the rebbe, the greatest scope of authority. Halakhah places limits on that authority, but the authority may be exercised where it is not limited halakhically; (2) the mitnagdic view held by modernists today allows the smallest scope for the charismatic power of leaders and greatest latitude for individuals to decide their own actions; (3) the traditionalist perspective diffuses charisma among a group of leaders, leaving it to the various communities to determine who these leaders shall be and often to dismiss those who disagree with their standards no matter how pious or learned they may be.

The view currently associated with the modernists is not necessarily oriented toward change or progress. On the contrary, it may well be a restraint on those who propose radical change. Similarly, the charismatic is not necessarily pro-change; in contemporary times this power has been exercised to promote radical traditionalism, which ritualizes activities and style of dress that were formerly not traditional. Halakhah and charisma have remained in constant tension and oscillation in Judaism, with sometimes one and sometimes the other a source of change.

Charismatic power diffuses beyond the narrow confines of scholarship into all roles of the followers. Chasidic leaders deliberately exercise charismatic power. Differences in dress set off chasidim from traditionalists and modernists and restrict their interaction in the larger society. As a result, chasidim tend to deal with societal pressures by forming segregated communities; traditionalists and modernists tend to cope by segregating work and religious roles. Thus chasidim are not only more involved with the charismatic leader but also more dependent on the community supporting him.

Institutions and Values Reviewed

Ba'al t'shuva yeshivot are new institutions for Judaism. Although a movement of return has been underway in Judaism since the 1940s and earlier, yeshivot for ba'alei t'shuva developed only in the late 1960s and early 1970s. These institutions were the response of Orthodox Jews to the interest in Judaism of hippies and other members of the youth counterculture of that period. These new institutions have very much the same curriculum and structure of regular yeshivot. Yet they have made adjustments to accommodate students who knew little about Orthodox Judaism, were unfamiliar with Hebrew, and above all whose very commitment to Orthodox Judaism was the major problem to be wrestled with. In addition, many of these new students expressed countercultural values, and the relation between these values and the yeshiva values was explored.

At the time when yeshivot were recruiting hippies, the countercultural aspects of the yeshiva may have provided a unique opportunity for recruitment. When Carlebach successfully attracted large numbers of hippies to his religious happenings and when some of them began to seek out "wise Jewish teachers" in noticeable numbers so that Yeshivat Hatfutzot-

Har Tzion came to be seen as a hippie ba'al t'shuva yeshiva, others also began reaching out to hippies and religious seekers. The new yeshivot that were developed followed the lines of the yeshiva world from which they sprang; some were modernistic in approach and others traditionalistic.

Although all yeshivot are essentially traditional in curriculum and in program and teach the same sacred literature and religious commitment in similar ways, those that are more radically countercultural make the claim that they are more traditional than others. We have signified this difference between yeshivot by calling some "modernistic" and others "traditionalistic." Differences in this respect have a profound impact on how they recruit, whom they recruit, and what the new recruits become.

Comparing the values of these two types of yeshivot with those of potential recruits, one can't help but notice that whereas the values of modernistic yeshivot were more congruent with those of the straights, the values of traditionalistic yeshivot were more compatible with those of the hippies. Religiously restricted diets and ethnic identification found both modernistic and traditionalistic yeshivot in accord with the counterculture. Such elements of ethnic and hippie culture as styles of dress and hair were adopted in the wider society, making it easier for anyone to wear a kippah or a beard.

But the values of the hippie counterculture had a number of other similarities to the value system of traditionalistic yeshivot. Traditionalistic and chasidic styles of dress simply added the justification of "ethnic roots" to countercultural styles. For some hippies, therefore, the transition was easier than for straights. Traditionalistic yeshivot's rejection of secular education was not problematic for hippies. Many of them had already achieved high levels of education or had themselves dropped out of schools, leaving the traditionalist perspective on secular education moot. As for the traditionalistic yeshiva ideal of spending years studying Torah in a kolel and forgetting about entering a profession or earning a living, this too was in line with the hippie view that one ought to drop out of society.

Chaim Z., a hippie who had spent ten years at Yeshivat Hatfutzot-Har Tzion, described this type of transition in 1982: "I was experimenting with life. I wanted to be all I could be. I lived in the Bronx and used to go to parties where we would smoke pot and play music. Then I came here. I want to continue to learn, to continue to develop myself in Torah."

To those like Chaim Z., Israel was the promised land. Here were rabbis and leaders of their faith justifying their view that they need not work but instead should devote themselves to the study of Torah. Their wives and parents or the state could support them. Their previous view that self-support was at best a minor obligation that took a back seat to the obligation to experience life was modified so that the first obligation was to grow and develop in Torah. But work was still not a prime moral imperative.

The attitude of traditionalist yeshivot toward Israel, denying respect to the state of Israel, as distinct from the land of Israel and the people of Israel, was also congruent with the hippie's attitude toward the state. Hippies rejected the government, particularly the "corrupt Nixon presidency," while accepting the land of America and the American people.

The hippie perspective was more congruent with the traditionalistic notions of gedolim and of da'at Torah than with the notions of halakhah, legal precedents, or the weight of persuasive argument and written codes characteristic of authority in modernistic yeshivot. Da'at Torah in essence is a claim to charismatic authority, the authority of the person rather than the rational-legal system. For hippies who sought wise men, the traditionalistic rosh yeshiva was not only a wise-man-guru but a Jewish guru. Ethnic roots and charismatic leadership were embodied in one.

The yeshivot were not flooded with hippies. Many came to look, but for most of them the rigid regimen of the yeshivot was too tough to take. The discipline of the Orthodox Jew was at odds with the relaxed, laid-back, experimental perspective of hippies. Of the small group who entered and remained at yeshivot, most had to drop their hippie styles within a matter of weeks or months and adopt yeshiva styles that, while compatible, nevertheless required a change.

But the hippie movement also legitimated the countercultural values of yeshivot. It made yeshivot more acceptable to a large group of young people who, while not hippies, were sympathetic to hippie goals and styles. Yeshiva values could be presented as contemporary, even fashionable. Traditionalist yeshivot could thus appeal for the first time to the most with-it part of society, the hippies.

With regard to the status of women, the perspective of traditional yeshivot was consistent with the hippie perspective, although the traditionalist yeshivot were probably more egalitarian in their outlook than the hippies. Reports on a number of communes indicate that women were assigned the roles of cooks and housekeepers and the care of children while men did or did not do what men traditionally have done or not done (Conover 1975). At their core, hippie values apparently combined traditionalism with sexual license. In this respect the traditionalistic yeshivot offered women an advantage. Their commitment to traditional men's and women's roles at least offered the women some protection from being exploited and then abandoned when vulnerable with child.

The separation of men and women in Orthodox Judaism may well have been a major obstacle to recruitment for all yeshivot and schools for women. Carlebach attracted a broad spectrum of students to Passover seders, Sabbath celebrations, and melavveh malkah singalongs. Carlebach found it impossible to separate the men and women. Those who came to these happenings, while interested in Judaism, were probably less interested than those who actually attended a lecture or a meal at a yeshiva. And estimates are that 90 to 95 percent of the latter left immediately afterward.

Of course other elements of the unique life-style of the Orthodox presented in the yeshivot may have turned off these potential recruits. From interviews conducted with those who left, the major problem appears to have been in accepting religious discipline in all areas of life.

In Jerusalem in 1975–76 one saw men in the hippie community wearing beards, dashiki, and colorful Georgian *yarmulkes* and women wearing long dresses, often of denim, long-sleeved, multicolored blouses, and bright kerchiefs down to the forehead, covering long hair that flowed behind. The hippie style of dress met all the requirements of halakhah for modest dress. But style of life, particularly in the area of separation of the sexes, set them off from Orthodoxy. One saw men and women proceeding hand in hand to the Kotel for prayer, a practice totally alien to the Orthodox. And one came across apartments shared by two or three unmarried hippie couples, who lit Sabbath candles, sang the Kiddush, went to pray, but nonetheless maintained an unorthodox and un-Orthodox living arrangement.

These of course were not the hippies who were enrolled in the yeshivot, although some of them probably entered yeshivot later on. In the yeshivot that hippies attended, separation was maintained. But although strict sexual rulings were a severe limit on recruitment, some of the young countercultural people appear to have accepted sexual separateness and may even have sought it out as a means of rejecting their former lives.

As the years go by and the counterculture of hippies fades from the scene and as the ba'al t'shuva yeshivot become more accepted in Orthodox Jewish circles, a number of changes have slowly developed. Brovender's yeshivot for men and women, for example, have begun reaching out and attempting to recruit new students, despite the earlier rejection of this approach. His earlier hesitancy to recruit has probably been quieted by the apparent success of such efforts by others. Most of the ba'alei t'shuva recruited have been balanced and stable people who have remained committed to Orthodoxy in enough numbers to make an impact. But the kinds of recruits have also changed. Brovender could not bring himself to recruit hippies in part because their values were not his. But he can and does appeal to mainstream students, which most of the current recruits are.

Although broad changes in the values and conditions of the larger society and the effort at outreach seem to be pressing both traditionalistic and modernistic ba'al t'shuva yeshivot in the same direction, the differences in dress, in other symbols, and in attitudes should not be regarded lightly. They signal an underlying and not fully articulated difference in the conception and scope of religious authority. They define different plausibility structures, which is to say different belief communities within Orthodoxy. They have implications for the community that the returnee joins and for what the returnee may become.

III
The
Returnees

Chapter 9

Recruitment

A survey of Jews in the New York metropolitan area found that almost a quarter of Orthodox Jews are new to Orthodox practice (Ritterband and Cohen 1984b). If the Orthodox indeed constitute 11 percent of the Jewish population (see also Lazerwitz and Harrison 1979), estimated at about 5,500,000, this would suggest an Orthodox population of about 605,000 and a newly Orthodox population of about 150,000 (table A–1). These estimates may be high, as we are using practice rather than denominational identification to describe Orthodoxy, and more likely 6 to 9 percent of the Jewish population observe kashrut and Shabbat (Tobin and Chenkin 1985). And if getting a clear sense of the number of observant Orthodox is hard, being precise about the number of newly Orthodox is still harder. Nevertheless, as these are the only available data we will use them, keeping in mind the limits of the same. Defined in terms of observance, then, the number of newly Orthodox is about 100,000.

Some may nonetheless argue that the figures of newly Orthodox presented here are too high, as many of those identified in the sample may come from traditional families. That argument misses the point. What defines Orthodox Jews is their observance of kashrut and Shabbat. These practices can produce an implosion of social relations that does not occur even when numerous other rituals have been practiced. Even a move from observance of a number of traditions to the practice of kashrut and Shabbat involves a qualitative religious change.

I should emphasize that despite the number choosing to be Orthodox the data do not suggest that Orthodox Judaism is growing. The survey indicates that although one in four parents were Orthodox in practice only one in ten respondents are Orthodox (table A–1), a substantial loss in the last generation. Put another way, this survey found 158 who are newly Orthodox and 952 who were reared in Orthodox homes but are not Orthodox. These data appear to contradict the view of those who argue that Orthodoxy is retaining its numbers (Cohen 1983, 51). Some might argue that the losses occurred in previous generations and that the recent revival of Orthodoxy has stemmed these losses. This would mean that the table compares the cumulated losses of several generations to the gains of a single generation, masking recent gains. If so, then we would expect to find that newly Orthodox are concentrated in the younger population. But the data in table A–2 suggests no significant difference in age between the newly Orthodox and others. The newly Orthodox population does not appear to be younger than the rest of the population.

Again the data could be said to demonstrate that people of all ages are becoming Orthodox but return is a recent phenomenon. My research does not support this view, as I have found that the middle-aged returnees also became Orthodox in their youth or early adulthood. Furthermore, the movement has been underway for more than a generation.

Yet although the movement started some time ago, the period of greatest growth has occurred since the 1970s. In fact the movement was so small that it was unnoticed in the 1950s, even after it was underway. Given the relatively short period since the movement began, the numbers suggest that the tide is no longer running in one direction and the future may hold greater gains for Orthodoxy.

We turn now to the characteristics of the newly Orthodox. Are they the less educated and the poorer classes, who perhaps use religion as a crutch, or are they young, urban professionals? Although they are not a particularly young group, the latter view is more accurate. The survey finds no significant difference between them and the larger Jewish population in level of general education. As a group they are neither more nor less educated (table A–3).

By contrast, the newly Orthodox differ significantly from others with regard to Jewish education (table A–4). The newly Orthodox have a significantly higher rate of attendance at Hebrew schools and at yeshiva day schools. This suggests that the newly Orthodox come from families that are more interested in maintaining ties to Jews and Judaism than the Jewish population at large. Furthermore, a significantly larger proportion of the newly Orthodox are foreign-born (table A–5). In these respects the newly Orthodox are similar to the Orthodox (see also Lazerwitz and Harrison 1979).

A striking finding derived from the survey data is the predominance of women among the newly Orthodox. Although almost 41 percent of respondents to the survey were men, they constituted only 25 percent of the newly Orthodox. In contrast, the proportion of newly Orthodox who are women was substantially higher than their proportion of respondents (table A–6). As we shall see, Orthodox family life seems to have particular appeal for women. But this pattern of men selecting women less religious than they are who may then adopt their husbands' practices is also consistent with the pattern of intermarriage between Jewish men and non-Jewish women (Mayer 1985). It finds an echo in the chasidic community when chasidic men marry nonchasidic women (Levy 1973).

I am unable to develop further generalizations about the newly Orthodox from random population surveys. Jews constitute only 2.5 percent of the American population, Orthodox Jews roughly ten percent of Jews, and even the first figure is more than the percentage of expected statistical error in most surveys. To identify the Jewish population in the New York survey the researchers used a variety of techniques including computer-generated randomized lists of persons with Jewish surnames, who were then reached by telephone. This technique was used in order to reach all Jews, including the nonaffiliated. But the Jewish population tends to cluster, with different subcommunities—some of them Orthodox, others Conservative or Reform—living in different areas. This means that one cluster may not be the same as another. One must therefore examine different subcommunities.

The ba'al t'shuva yeshivot represent a source of data on major clusters of newly Orthodox. There one may find and examine an easily accessible concentrated population of newly Orthodox. From there, one may, as we have, find leads to other concentrations of newly Orthodox and to the agencies and individuals involved in recruitment. Many of those who enter yeshivot have previously begun their return in synagogues or elsewhere.

By rough estimate based on extrapolation of attendance during the years of this study, approximately 15,000–20,000 students have attended ba'al t'shuva yeshivot (including Yeshiva University's James Striar School and other schools for those lacking background) since their inception. This number includes a substantial portion—perhaps a third to a half—who were Orthodox from birth. Several thousand of these were Israelis attending American ba'al t'shuva yeshivot. Thus, possibly as many as 10–15 percent of the newly Orthodox have attended yeshivot for the newly Orthodox. In addition, the data in table A–4 suggests that many newly Orthodox were sent to regular yeshivot and day schools by parents who were not observant.

In one important respect the population identified by the survey and the population in the ba'al t'shuva yeshivot are different. About three-fourths of the students in yeshivot for newly Orthodox are male, in contrast to the survey group, which is predominantly female. But with regard to education, social class, and even age (for reasons explained above) other data on the yeshiva population (Aviad 1983; Kovacs 1977; and Levine 1980) suggest that the populations are similar.

Given their size and their substantial portion of the newly Orthodox, close examination of ba'al t'shuva yeshivot is not simply strategic but essential for understanding the movement. Yet to stop there would be to miss much of what goes on. I have therefore studied not only yeshivot and their students in America and Israel but also respondents who did not attend yeshivot, men and women, young and middle-aged, and the people and agencies that assisted them in their return. In this chapter I examine recruitment, particularly as it occurs in Israel. There it is most open and fully developed, and a significantly larger proportion of newly Orthodox visit Israel than do other Jews (table A–7). To understand the process of becoming Orthodox we start with the perspective of the new recruit and his family.

RETURN: AN UNANTICIPATED DEVELOPMENT

Typically, the sequence of roles in a person's life is anticipated and prepared for. The twelve-year-old boy anticipates his young manhood, learns about it, and seeks role models. Parents, friends, and neighbors, as well as relevant organizations, anticipate the coming change in status, attempt to inform the boy of how to play the role of young man, define when it shall begin and how it shall be done. Certainly people do not march through this sequence in lockstep. But there are many ordered sequences, particularly in areas most crucial to defining a person. Thus there are educational sequences (elementary school, high school, possibly college and professional training), marital sequences (courtship, marriage, widowhood), developmental sequences (childhood, youth, adulthood, middle age, old age), occupational sequences (novice, young Turk, old hand, retiree).

But the ba'al t'shuva disrupts the anticipated ordered sequence. Whereas religious convictions were peripheral they now become central. This reorders life's priorities, requiring the adoption of a new rhythm of life with no work on Saturdays, the adoption of a new holiday calendar celebrating a different set of events, the eating of different foods (and scrupulous avoidance of other foods), and the developing of new friends. It may even require a different mate than was anticipated earlier. In these ways, becoming a ba'al t'shuva may be radically different from becoming a reborn Christian. Although Christian rebirth may also require sharp changes in patterns of life, they are not likely to be so radical because, as we have seen, Christianity requires belief primarily and action only secondarily and because to become Christian in America is to emphasize dominant cultural themes whereas to become more Jewish is to estrange oneself from the mainstream and to embrace a different set of values, rituals, and life-styles.

The ba'al t'shuva thus moves on an uncharted and unexpected course. Parents and friends anticipate a given progression—college, job, marriage—and most people move through this sequence as expected. The ba'al t'shuva has also been socialized into this sequence, not into the role of a practicing Jew. His every encounter with Judaism is fresh. He sees it with an adult's eyes and subjects it to critical if not cynical scrutiny. His Orthodoxy is unlike that of those reared in Orthodoxy, who have learned to accept behaviors and beliefs in unquestioning childish innocence that carries over to adulthood.

Just as Orthodox Jews continue in their practice in part as a result of the momentum of their childhood experience and social pressure, so most people reject this different practice as a result of their socialization to the dominant set of values and their desire to conform to the expectations of peers. Separating the force of this momentum and the power of the social bonds that tie one to continued rejection of Judaism from the experience of encountering Judaism is difficult. That experience may be positive but not sufficiently powerful to overcome the social ties. Or the symbols and values of Judaism themselves may drive off potential returnees.

The essential attractiveness of Jewish rituals, values, and symbols has been under scrutiny from within Judaism for over a hundred years. Reform Judaism in particular (but also Conservative and to a far smaller degree Orthodox Judaism) has attempted to eliminate "crude" or "primitive" rituals and to introduce more appealing ones. But what is attractive to people, what is unattractive, and why remain an enigma. The ba'al t'shuva offers a unique opportunity to view Judaism with mature eyes, unclouded by the social ties and presocialized attitudes that help keep the Orthodox from birth within the fold. Although Jews have learned through millennia of experience how to unfold Judaism for the young, the ba'al t'shuva challenges them to do this for adults. In the process, Judaism is itself articulated and clarified.

Recruitment to Orthodoxy

From the perspective of some Christian Americans, and even some American Jews, Orthodox Judaism is as strange and as deviant as a cult. And although such new religions as the Unification Church of the Reverend Sun Myung Moon recruit among the "heathens," recruiters emphasize those doctrines in their theology that are compatible with and familiar to prospective recruits. In contrast, that Jewish recruitment is carefully limited to Jews[1] considerably eases the problem of first approach for Jewish recruiters. Yet while the sense of being part of the same community may produce a feeling of commonality, the symbols, rituals, and rhetoric of Orthodox Judaism are likely to be foreign to the prospect. Furthermore, the Jewish recruiters espouse a minority faith.

ENCOUNTERS IN ISRAEL

Jerusalem serves as an excellent recruiting ground for ba'alei t'shuva because it is the location of the holiest Jewish places, the Temple Mount and the Western Wall, the last remnant of the wall surrounding the Temple Mount. It has a central place in Jewish prayer, ritual, and song. For Jews it is the concrete evidence of Jewish life during the period of the Bible and the prophets. If Israel is the place where Abraham, Isaac, and Jacob walked, where Joseph and his brothers dreamed and quarreled, then Jerusalem is the place from which David and Solomon reigned as kings, and the Temple Mount is the place where, in that legendary era, Jews came to pray and to celebrate their festivals and where they died in their struggle against Roman armies. Thus Jerusalem is the holy city without peer, the Temple Mount is the holiest place in the world for Jews, and the Western Wall near the Temple Mount is one of the most popular recruitment sites.

The Central Bus Terminal is a more difficult recruitment spot than the holy sites. Prospects are not engaged in behavior that could be construed as religious; they are simply disembarking or embarking. But just being a Jew in Israel suggests some sense of Jewish identity. The recruiter may identify the person as a tourist on the basis of overhearing a few words of

1. The efforts are never directed at Christians. As a minority in the United States Jews are hesitant to offend the sensibilities of others. In addition, Jewish tradition has long held that only Jews are obliged to be Jews, that righteous non-Jews have no obligation to become Jews, although they may join if they wish. Finally, the fact that Jews have not engaged in conversion efforts in the past has produced a sense that such efforts are in extremely bad taste. These historical and social constraints are widely held by Jews. Reform Judaism's new position that Jews ought to reach out to and convert non-Jews has generated great controversy among Jews.

English or even on the basis of dress. "Nice day, isn't it?" or "Have you been waiting long for the bus?" is an effective ice-breaker. Conversation may continue for a brief period seeking further identification—"Are you from the Coast? From Chicago?" But to pursue this line too far might be perceived as an invasion of the prospect's privacy. If initial probes elicit highly positive responses, indicating the prospect's openness and receptivity, they may be continued—"Would you like to spend a Shabbat with a Jewish religious (or Orthodox) family (or group)?" Or "Have you been to a yeshiva? Would you like to visit us and join us for lunch?"

The purpose of this conversation is as clear as is the nature of the group involved. In contrast to the Unification Church and other groups that have been described as cults using surreptitious and deceptive techniques in recruitment (Lofland 1966, 1977), Orthodox Judaism typically recruits openly. The prospect knows what he is getting into. In fact, the dress and style of the recruiter declares this even before the invitation is offered. One of the most successful recruiters in Jeruselem, Meir Shuster, wears typical traditionalistic garb: a black suit, with the required out-of-style narrow lapels, a white shirt, a dark tie, a black narrow-brim felt hat, and a scraggly and unkempt beard. An invitation to hear a lecture at a yeshiva and have lunch there or to spend a Shabbat with a religious family is unmistakably an invitation to sample this style of Judaism.

Perhaps one in five or one in twenty accepts the invitation. There are no reliable data. Acceptance depends on the recruiter, the environment, the kind of people approached. Some of those who accept the invitation may have a greater interest in religion than others. But many refuse simply because they are previously engaged; at another time or place, they might accept such an invitation. And many of those who accept do so primarily out of a spirit of adventure and a willingness to try something new. In fact, the appeal to the "hippie types" may be couched in these terms. Those who pride themselves on being adventurous may find it embarrassing to be unwilling to participate. "Come on, you've been to India and Afghanistan, to ashrams and monasteries, and you mean to tell me you haven't got the curiosity to visit a yeshiva?" Given the hippie's self-image such an appeal is difficult to refuse.

THE KOTEL

The Western Wall is the premier location for recruitment. No matter how secular the Jew who comes to the Western Wall, how skeptical, ignorant, or hostile to religion, one's presence there permits others to assume that one has some interest in what it is to be a Jew. The central aspect of that place and that experience is Jewish. An invitation to participate in Jewish worship at the Kotel is therefore natural and almost expected if one is Jewish. Recruiters do not suggest that one share a Sabbath meal or visit a yeshiva out of an interest in Judaism alone; the appeal is also couched in terms of experience and adventure. And whereas people might be irritated by such an invitation if it were offered elsewhere, at the Kotel it is often accepted as appropriate. How can one take offense at being invited to participate in a Jewish experience? The site gives the recruiter an implicit right to that assumption.

Friday evening at the Kotel, a well-known tourist attraction, provides a special opportunity for recruitment. Various chasidic groups come to pray, students from the nearby Yeshivat Ha-Kotel have a custom of dancing down to the Kotel, and hundreds of the curious come to watch hundreds of the observant at their prayers. Those who have come to watch and nothing more wander about among the worshippers, cameras in hand, paper coverings (supplied by the ushers) on their heads, occasionally snapping pictures despite repeated reminders by the ushers that picture taking is forbidden. Others watch from behind a three-foot elevation in the Kotel plaza that marks off the place of worship from the tourist area.

Long pants and shirts are required for men; skirts and modest blouses or dresses for women. A head covering is required for men and for married women. Beyond that, the worshippers dress in any manner they please, from chasidic garb to shirtsleeves or army uniforms. Worshippers may approach the Kotel and pray in their own manner, in their own words, or join whatever group they please. Men pray on the north side of a movable wall (a mechitzah) and women on the other.

Torah scrolls, necessary for public prayer, have been placed in arks built into the walls of a gigantic tunnel-like enclosure to the north of the Kotel plaza. Men thus have access to the scrolls, and the scrolls are protected from the weather. Prayers at the Kotel are not said in unison. Instead, individuals standing in the plaza utter their solitary prayers, or small groups of individuals join together in the traditional minyan or prayer quorum of ten men or more. Men with similar religious traditions will form a minyan. (Women do not form a minyan but pray as individuals.) Sephardim (Oriental Jews), Ashkenazim (European Jews), chasidim, modernistic Orthodox, and yeshiva students typically pray in their own groups.

The Kotel plaza is simply an open plaza with a few *bimot,* or large lecterns, for spreading out the Torah scroll when it is read. Groups form and re-form. People wander from one prayer group to another, and the prayer groups themselves constantly shift places, especially during the day, in an attempt to escape a sometimes blazing sun. But on Friday evenings in summer the Kotel plaza is cool and shadowed. The groups come on a regular basis, and a pattern is discernable. In the northeast corner, nearest the Torah scrolls, chasidic groups gather—Bratzlaver chasidim in the enclosed area, Belzer and Vishnitzer at the northeastern corner right up against the Kotel. Other chasidic groups also cluster close to the Kotel. To the south and closer to the women's section are yeshiva minyanim and in particular the Yeshivat HaKotel of B'nai Akiva. In the center and south of the prayer area are scattered *balebatishe minyanim*— prayer quorums of ordinary people. Some will be minyanim of Sephardim, Jews from the Arab lands. Others will be Ashkenazic, following the traditions of European Jews. The prayer traditions are somewhat different, and the cantillations and melodies are substantially different. Any minyan must choose to follow one or another tradition, not both.[2] But individuals from one group often pray in the quorum of the other group, following the other group's customs. The area for prayer is thus not one where formal, organized, and decorous services are performed. It is rather an area where people are either engaged in solitary prayer or join small groups of their own community in intimate prayer circles. If one wishes to start a prayer circle one need only call out "minyan" or the name of the given prayer (that is, "minchah" for the afternoon service or "ma'ariv" for the evening service) until ten men are gathered and public prayer can commence. One may then be the reader of the prayer or of the Torah or have one of the honors in prayer—such as being called up to the Torah or carrying the Torah out and putting it away—if the others in the group acquiesce. One may bring along one's own group to be assured of these honors, as is typically done at bar mitzvot or on the *aufruf* (Sabbath preceding the marriage) of a bridegroom. The variety and informality of prayer styles lend an air of casualness to the atmosphere, despite the intensity of prayer of some, and allow tourists and gawkers to wander among the worshipers. Some get so carried away in greetings of friends that the sanctity of the place and the intensity of emotion it engenders are challenged by continual encounters with the irreverent and people are distracted from prayers by the opportunities to socialize.

For all the informality and variety, public prayers—that is, prayer services by a minyan—are always Orthodox. They may follow the tradi-

2. The Sephard liturgy of the chasidim is something of a compromise but follows Ashkenazic cantillation and pronunciation. The pronunciation of vowels distinguishes groups from each other but does not distinguish liturgies. Hence people with different pronunciations may pray in the same minyan.

tion of any community, but they all follow the halakhah. Although no official prohibition prevents anyone from praying as he wishes, the separation of men and women in the prayer area precludes Conservative and Reform prayer services. Conservative and Reform Jews are thus left with the choice of either praying as individuals or joining one of the Orthodox minyanim in public prayer.[3]

Beyond the prayer area and marked off from it by an elevation of about a meter is the Kotel plaza, where various national ceremonies are conducted. For example, commencement exercises for paratroops in the Israeli Defense Forces are conducted in this area, ceremonies celebrating the unification of Jerusalem are held here, and even such non-Israeli Jewish organizations as the Shomrim Society of the New York City Police Force appear in dress uniform at their ceremonies here. But for the most part this area is the space where people meet friends and socialize, where tourists take pictures, and where children wander by on foot or in strollers.

In this area Conservative and Reform Jews form their own prayer quorums and engage in public prayer. Conservative Jews, particularly teenagers, may chant a good part of the service in Hebrew. The service at times is indistinguishable from the Orthodox except that men and women pray together with no separation between them. Reform Jews, particularly adults, may pray in the same areas as Conservative, but the style of prayer is noticeably different. A few songs may be sung in Hebrew, but the prayers will be said in responsive fashion entirely in English. Typically, Reform teenagers coming to the Kotel in groups cluster near the southwestern corner of the plaza, where they hear lectures on the history and archaeology of the Kotel, participate in responsive reading of texts from the prayer service or from the Bible, read aloud from the works of poets, or present something of their own, depending on the leader and the occasion.

The distance of these groups from the Kotel carries a message. They may come up to the Kotel to offer their own prayers, to kiss it, or to leave messages in the crevices between the great ashlars. But they must do so as individuals, leaving their group and its customs behind. Confronting the holiest of Jewish places in this manner raises questions about the legitimacy of the Conservative and Reform modes of religious expression in the minds of some of the young people. Physical distance from the Kotel

3. Conservative and Reform Jews could also have men and women pray in separate groups at the Kotel. But to my knowledge this has never occurred.

Position of Prayer Groups at Western Wall (aerial view)

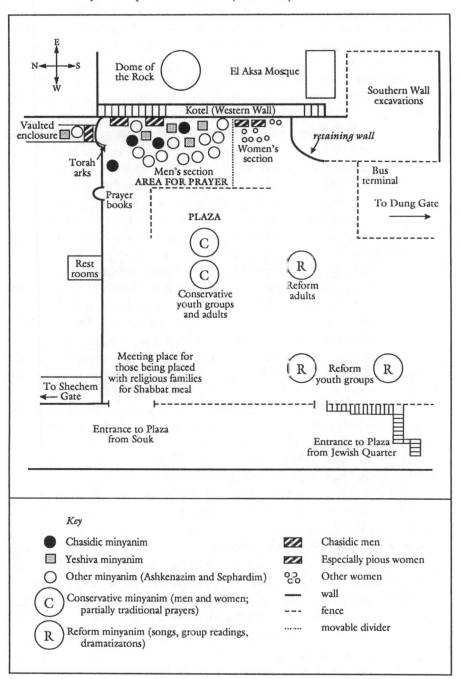

Key

● Chasidic minyanim

▨ Yeshiva minyanim

○ Other minyanim (Ashkenazim and Sephardim)

Ⓒ Conservative minyanim (men and women; partially traditional prayers)

Ⓡ Reform minyanim (songs, group readings, dramatizatons)

▨ Chasidic men

▨ Especially pious women

Other women

— wall

--- fence

······ movable divider

implies a spiritual distance from the center of Judaism as well. Beyond that, the very mode of praying in the prayer area and the dress and manners of the people there reflect chasidic and Orthodox shtiblach (small chasidic congregations), not the style of the affluent synagogues with their decorous manner of worship. The expected religious experience often turns out to be a confrontation with a strange religious practice almost foreign to the young Americans who come to discover their heritage.

Occasionally one sees attempts to bridge the gap. A group of men and women from a Reform temple in the United States stands near the center of the plaza and under the direction of their tour leader—in this case their rabbi—sings in Hebrew, "Heveinu Shalom Aleichem."[4] Or the leader of a group of teenagers leads them down the steps to the southwestern corner of the plaza and on entering not only puts a kippah on his head but also pulls tzitzit out from under his shirt and lets them hang freely in the manner of the very Orthodox. In this place, this group's worship services seem torn by feelings of marginality. The experience seems to be a powerful demonstration that Orthodoxy is central, holy, attached to the ancient symbols, and authentic, while Conservative and Reform Judaism are removed and peripheral, that although one may become more involved in Judaism this must be done as an individual Jew, not as a Reform or Conservative Jew. Remaining with one's group will leave one at the periphery. The positions of groups at the Kotel plaza seem to reflect the Orthodox view of Judaism.

Confronting Judaism's holiest place in this manner at times leaves the young non-Orthodox Jew with a desire to learn more about Judaism, to experience it. Sensing this, some of those at the Kotel have taken to inviting individuals to their home for a Sabbath meal. And yeshivot for ba'alei t'shuva have come to use this place as a recruiting ground.

For the yeshivot, the pattern started almost accidentally. Young men from Yeshivot Hatfutzot, still in their hippie attire (their customary style), went to the Kotel. With the camaraderie of fellow countrymen far from home, already connected by opposition to the establishment, they met others like themselves. An invitation would follow. Within weeks, the realization that this plaza could be a rich source of recruits turned the accidental encounter into a planned effort at recruitment. By the early 1970s a number of other institutions were involved in this.

4. Literally, "We bring peace unto you." This is often the opening hymn at the late Friday evening service in Conservative and Reform synagogues. It is not a part of the traditional Orthodox Friday night prayer service.

Even after the passing of the hippie movement from the scene and the end of the travelers and seekers, the custom of inviting young people home for a Sabbath meal continued to grow. By 1981 and 1982 it had become so formalized and had reached such proportions that it was being led by two young men who publicized the practice at coffeehouses and through distributing literature. Each Friday night they placed about one hundred and twenty young people for Shabbat. In addition, several people began to invite many guests regularly to their homes for Shabbat. (One, Rabbi Shienberg, invites thirty-five to forty-five people to his home in the Old City each Friday night for a festive Sabbath meal. He does the same for the Sabbath midday and late afternoon meals.) Given the informal nature of the effort, numbers are unavailable, but probably more than two hundred young people are accommodated each Friday evening (apart from those accommodated for the midday and afternoon meals).

Given this phenomenon, yeshivot located within walking distance of the Kotel have a distinct advantage in recruiting students. In fact, Yeshivat Aish Hatorah, in the Old City of Jerusalem, takes advantage of its location by opening its facility to young men who would like to experience Judaism a bit more fully. Baruch Levine, Meir Shuster, some of the students at the school, or even Rabbi Weinberg himself will invite young men at the Kotel to join them for the Sabbath meal. They are even able to offer guests lodging for Shabbat.

Other yeshivot benefit from being in close commuting distance from the Kotel. Although Neve Yerushalayim and Brovender's yeshivot are more than an hour's walk from the Kotel (D'var Yerushalayim is also a substantial walk), these places—in fact, any point in Jerusalem—are only a short taxi ride from the Kotel. On any day other than the Sabbath, Levine, Shuster, or others may invite a group to the yeshiva for a lecture or a meal. They can reach Neve Yerushalayim, at the opposite end of the city, by taxi in about fifteen minutes. This recruitment advantage is one of the main reasons the ba'al t'shuva movement has centered in Jerusalem.

AN INVITATION TO SHABBAT

The single most widely used recruitment device is to invite likely recruits to a home for the Shabbat meal. Most potential recruits that have been "picked up" at the Kotel or at the bus station are sent to homes of the traditionalistic Orthodox, those more likely to wear formal dark clothes and less likely to have a college education.

This seems paradoxical. One might have anticipated a preference for modern Orthodox homes, in which the Western visitor would not experience so much culture shock. Modernistic Orthodox, more familiar with the larger culture than traditionalistic Orthodox, might get along better with visitors, know how to present Judaism, be more sensitive to the concerns and interests of the visitors. But the staff of the traditionalistically oriented ba'al t'shuva yeshivot feel more comfortable with traditionalistic Orthodox and believe that their goals and views of life are more fully supported in such homes—as in fact they are. This, then, becomes the primary consideration. The ability to articulately present Judaism to visitors is only a secondary consideration.

Nevertheless, concern that the host family be able to communicate and not be too extreme tends to make yeshivot shy away from placing visitors with the chasidim of Meah Shearim, a section of Jerusalem populated by the most traditional, including those not only opposed to the secular world but hostile to the state of Israel.

The Shabbat as drama. Interestingly, one pair of recruiters, Baruch Levine and Jeff Seidel, does send its visitors to homes in Meah Shearim and offers a tour of the district. Although the deans of several of the ba'al t'shuva schools believe that this practice turns people away from serious consideration of Orthodoxy as a religious life alternative and present Orthodoxy as a quaint if not bizarre sect of Judaism, visitors flock to Levine seeking Shabbat placements and join his tours of Meah Shearim. Many become sufficiently interested to try a yeshiva for a meal or a few days and perhaps to stay for a longer period, becoming ba'alei t'shuva.

Baruch Levine is himself a ba'al t'shuva who studied at Brovender's yeshiva and at Ohr Sameyach. A slim, good-looking fellow in his middle twenties, he has a full black beard and dresses in a black suit and hat. But the cut and style of his clothing set it off from chasidic dress. His style is fashionable, even urbane. His attractiveness is not lost on the young women, who speak of him as "*very* cute," "really good looking."

Levine, Jeff Siedel, and several assistants come to the Kotel plaza on Friday well before sunset. They wander about the southwest corner of the plaza, approaching young men and women who by appearance and dress seem new to the experience. The Kotel plaza has an informal ambience; one may go up to a stranger and strike up a conversation. Asked whether they would be interested in having a Sabbath meal with an Orthodox family, some accept, some refuse, and some hesitate, as in the following conversation overheard between Levine and two young men with backpacks.

First Male. I've already paid for a room tonight, and I won't be able to get back there if I go with you. The buses don't run on Sabbath.

Levine. You've come to Israel for an experience, not for a hotel room. You rented your room so you could have that experience. But now that I'm offering you another arrangement, are you going to let the fact that you've paid for your room stand in your way?

Second Male. His logic is ironclad. He's right.

Levine then sent them to his apartment in the Old City to change from their shorts to long pants so that they would look "respectable" at the Sabbath meal.

By the end of the evening, Levine, Siedel, and their associates had placed about fifty young men and women at various homes for the Sabbath meal. They claim to have placed an additional hundred or more earlier in the day. Nor are they the only ones engaged in this activity. Meir Schuster places another twenty to thirty (mostly men) each Friday evening. As has been noted, Rabbi Schienberg invites thirty-five to forty-five people to his home for the Shabbat meal, and Michael Kaniel, a former New Yorker, educated at yeshivot, whose magnificent apartment overlooks the Kotel, may have several guests in addition to the ten to fifteen sent to him by Levine.

For women, this experience can be a harsh turn-off from further interest in Judaism, as indicated in the following account by a young woman who was already Orthodox but was in Israel studying at one of the yeshivot for women ba'alot t'shuva.

> After we finished davening at the Kotel, Baruch's group dropped off each of us at our host's place. The wife, her mother, a little boy, and three little girls were there. We chatted for a little while. She wanted to know all about us, who we were, where we were from. After about half an hour, the husband came home. I don't know whether he had been at the Kotel or some other shul. He didn't greet us. He didn't talk to us. He came in, said "Gut Shabbos," and started pacing up and down and davening. Then he made Kiddush [benediction over the wine]. He washed [ritual washing of hands], and we all did also. We made the Motzi [blessing on the bread] and began to eat. He didn't talk to us at all during the meal. He said a few things to his wife. She kept running in and out to the kitchen. If this were my only contact with Orthodox Jews, I'd never be Orthodox.

But the young men I interviewed at Ohr Someyach in the summer of 1982 had a uniformly favorable reaction. They marveled at the warmth and hospitality of their hosts. They enjoyed playing with the children. The wives might engage them in pleasant conversation, and the husbands would try to teach them. Communication might be difficult if they didn't know Yiddish or Hebrew well enough, but there was a sense of inclusion, of being welcomed.

Interestingly, men (who are not placed with the same hosts as women) rarely if ever notice a negative attitude toward women. One reason for this is, of course, that the men are not slighted. Another reason is that chasidic women may engage in friendly conversation with women.5 Male visitors therefore simply perceive that both women and men are open and friendly. Female visitors find the women friendly and interpret the chasid's unwillingness to communicate as an insult.

After the Sabbath meal, a group, consisting of perhaps seventy to eighty young men and women, tours Meah Shearim. This tour is well publicized in hotels and coffee houses, and the group may be somewhat younger than those that Levine places in homes for Shabbat. Some youngsters of high school age on tours with various Zionist and religious organizations who have a "free shabbat" in Jerusalem join him. Levine divides the group into separate groups of men and women just before they enter Meah Shearim. This, he explains, is simply in deference to the religious sensibilities of those they are about to visit. There is some grumbling, particularly among the younger girls, who have come with a mixed group of boys and girls and are a bit frightened by the separation. Most quickly comply, and those who object have no choice. They proceed to the Toldoth Aharon, the synagogue of an extremely insulated chasidic group. This week the rebbe is not there. Some other arrangement will have to be made for the men to hear some words of Torah. The group enters the large, old-fashioned synagogue. About 150 to 200 chasidim sit at several long tables arranged as a single line. Beer and boiled chick peas are on the tables. Each of the chasidim wears a striemel (a fur-trimmed hat) and a gold bekeshe (a long satin jacket). Most wear a bright checked or striped cummerbund *gartel* (literally, a girdle or belt). An elder is addressing the group in Yiddish. The visitors do not understand. They are not greeted, and no one interprets for them. Small groups of chasidim are engaged in conversation even while the elder is speaking. He stops. The chasidim begin a song.

The women have been taken upstairs to the gallery. A heavy latticework blocks the gallery completely from the men's view and makes it difficult for the women to see into the synagogue. The chasidim sit under the overhang of the gallery, so that in any case the women cannot see them. When the men and women meet outside the synagogue, several of the women express their annoyance at having seen nothing.

---

5. This derives from the saying in Avot, "Do not converse much with women," and from a series of laws restricting male relations with women. These laws, as we have noted, restrict the males, not the females.

The men's group is once again separated from the women as the men file into the ground floor apartment of a poor chasid, entering through a back yard. The living room is lit only by a few candles, for the chasid will not use electricity on Shabbat. About forty-five young men crowd into the room, where soft drinks and cakes are arranged on a table. The chasid is dressed in the manner of the Toldot Aharon chasidim—bearded, head shaven, flowing sidelocks framing his gaunt, handsome face in the candlelight. He continues singing a chasidic niggun (tune) softly as the men file in. A number find seats, and the rest stand in hushed silence. The chasid's two young sons, about four and six years old, stand near him. He stops singing. Utter silence. He pauses, opens his eyes, which had been closed while he sang, and says, "Gut Shabbos." It is electric. The answer, "Gut Shabbos," comes back in unison. Another pause. He starts speaking in perfect British-accented English. The surprise is almost palpable. He talks of the beauty of the Sabbath and tells a story of a king who had sent his disobedient son into exile. Years passed, and the king sent his servant to call the prince back. When the prince saw the servant, he was reminded of his father's house, which he had almost forgotten. But now the yearning and longing for it almost overcame him. "So it is with us. We have been cast out from Eden. Shabbat reminds us of that state of mankind. We feel it and yearn for God. [In Hebrew] 'Refresh me with apples . . . for I am sick with love,' from the beautiful Song of Songs. The longing for God overcomes us."

He and his wife, he says, will be going to Natanya, a seaside resort, for a week—their first vacation in two years. He looks forward to dangling his toes in the water. A quotation from a Wordsworth poem on the beauties of nature closes his little talk. With that he rises, makes Kiddush, and offers wine and the trays of cake and soft drinks to all, reciting the blessings for each aloud and in a clear voice so that everyone can recite the blessings with him. A few more minutes are spent in a discussion of Shabbat and love, then the visitors leave. The entire episode takes no more than ten or fifteen minutes.

Outside the young men comment to each other on how powerful the experience was, how generous this chasid was to give them all this food. He did not know them. The generosity was particularly impressive given the man's obvious poverty.

The group walks back to meet the group of girls, who had been left standing in an alley during the entire time. A number of the girls have already returned to their hotels. Many of the girls are furious when told of the experience the boys have just had.

The group continues on, with Levine describing the life of the community as they proceed. He places great emphasis on the warmth and the sense of community in Meah Shearim. Stopping in front of one home he tells of how he had once brought a group of young men to a chasid's home unaware that the man's wife had given birth the previous day. When she looked out the window and saw the group of women visitors in the street, she invited them all to her home and insisted that they eat the refreshments she had prepared to celebrate the birth. The story emphasizes her sacrifice, generosity, and hospitality.

Continuing through the streets, the group encounters signs, some in English, with slogans like "Zionism is diametrically opposed to Judaism" plastered and occasionally painted on the walls. The impact of those signs that they could read is strongly negative. Many of the young people in the group are there because their parents, committed Zionists, have sent them. Many are themselves committed Zionists. At the last point in the tour, Levine sums up the experience, stressing that all the visitors had descended no more than three or four generations ago from the same type of people they had encountered that evening. "Find your roots and identify with your roots," he admonishes them.

The experience, an adventure with a series of unexpected twists, had taken one final turn. The strange society the youths had experienced, which was so different from them and so warm and giving, was indeed their own roots. Although the experience may have shaken some of the youngsters, for most it remained a superb piece of theater, a piece in which they were not only audience but actors. For a few, it left a powerful impression, especially for those who had come to Israel to learn about their religion and were already enrolled in one of the ba'al t'shuva yeshivot. For them it seemed to reduce the strangeness of Judaism by presenting it as warm and accepting although strange, to the point of being almost bizarre.

For the women, the experience was far more negative, and few women, even those in the ba'alot t'shuva institutions, seemed moved. At best, it did not turn them off too much. The argument that this was their own roots, roots that they were seeking, made it hard for them to reject it.

The deans of several ba'alei t'shuva yeshivot expressed sharp disapproval of this approach. As they saw it, it exposed people to an extreme view of Judaism that was more likely to turn them away than to attract them. But viewed another way, the experience is a screening process. Those who were attracted to Orthodoxy would be a self-selected group that would not be deterred by difficulties encountered in the acculturation process. Not many are attracted to this style, and those who are are likely to be interested in distancing themselves as much as possible from their former selves. These represent a small group, often with problems of personal identity. For the most part ba'alei t'shuva instead seem to seek continuity with their earlier lives.

The shock approach makes the person encountered aware of the "otherness" of the religious experience. A respondent at Har Tzion told me that what caught her attention was that while she was taking a drink of water Rabbi Goldstein came along and said, "You didn't say thanks." "To whom?" the respondent asked. "To God," Rabbi Goldstein replied. That was the beginning of a conversation that led to her joining the group. Rabbi Revson pointed out a student he had met on a plane flight. They had been talking, and he came to know that she was Jewish. When the meals were served, she was given a nonkosher meal. Rabbi Revson offered her part of his. She refused. He left his meal untouched. When she asked him why he wasn't eating he replied that he couldn't eat when he saw a Jewish person eating nonkosher food. He did not eat for the entire flight. Some weeks later he received a letter from the young woman inquiring about Neve. She wrote that she was so impressed by his action that she was determined to find out more about her religion.

These encounters are not as extreme as the experience in Meah Shearim. But all of them involve a combination of the unexpected, an experience that seems to mark something off as wholly other and at the same time provides a warm, human tie.

The Shabbat: Rituals and symbols in the Jewish home. The unique aspect of Shabbat is its symbolic core. It is a celebration that combines the warmth and love of family with religious symbolism. The Shabbat meal is as rich in symbols as the Passover seder, and in typically Jewish fashion this celebration is embedded in the family.

A person accepting a Sabbath invitation is likely to be placed in the home of one of the rabbis involved in recruitment. But the rituals, symbols, and observances are the same in simple religious households. The prospective recruit will be asked to arrive before the start of Shabbat at sundown. The family may still be occupied with preparations—cooking the Sabbath meals, cleaning the quarters, bathing and changing clothes. The guest is invited to wash up but is basically left to his own devices. The crescendo of the bustle increases until just before sunset, when all activity ceases. It is Shabbat. Lights have been turned on or off for Sabbath, a metal shield is placed on the stove burners, some burners have been adjusted and pots arranged on them to keep food warm. Neither lights nor stove will be adjusted throughout the Sabbath.

The pleasant bustle, the aroma of the cooking, even the lighting of the candles may be familiar. The sudden quiet that descends on the household with the lighting of the candles may be surprising. But adjusting the lights and the stove and the admonition that one may not turn lights on or off or cook on the Sabbath frequently come as a complete surprise. If explanations are sought, the answer will not be philosophical; it will be simply that this is forbidden on Sabbath, that the Torah requires it.

On returning from the synagogue, the greeting "Shabbat Shalom" (Sabbath Peace) or "Gut Shabbos" (Good Sabbath) is exchanged. The family sits down at the table and sings the hymn "Peace unto you, ministering Angels." Proverbs 31, "A Woman of Valor," is either sung or recited. The table has been set with two *challot* (twisted breads), which are usually covered with a cloth embroidered with Sabbath themes. A decanter of wine, a cup (often of silver), and a salt cellar will also be on the table. The bread knife will be hidden under the challah cloth. The table will be covered with a clean tablecloth. All this is required and will be found everywhere. Candles, lit at the onset of Shabbat, are frequently placed on the table.

Each element carries its own religious meaning. According to legend, on Sabbath one is accompanied home by two angels, a protagonist and an antagonist. If upon entering the home one finds the table set and prepared for the Sabbath, the family changed and bathed, then the protagonist blesses the home, and the antagonist is compelled to answer "amen." Should this be a home where there is no Sabbath, the antagonist curses it, and the protagonist must answer "amen." Therefore, when on returning from the synagogue one finds the table set and the family ready one greets these angels with song, saying to them, "Peace unto you, ministering angels" and requests, as the song continues, "Bless us with peace, angels of peace," concluding, "Go in peace, angels of peace, angles of on high, sent by the King of the king of kings, the Holy One Blessed be He." "Woman of Valor" is recited in gratitude to the woman of the house, recognized as the "essence of the home," its critical center and being. Her intelligence, her work throughout the week, her love, industry, and charity are praised. In Jewish tradition Friday night in particular is a time for the husband to express his love for his wife. Kiddush, the ceremony of sanctification of the day, follows. The man of the house fills his cup to the brim with wine and recites verses of Genesis, proclaiming that "in six days God created heaven and earth, and he rested on the Seventh day." The blessing is made over the wine, and a blessing of thanks for having "chosen us and bestowed the Sabbath upon us" is recited. All those at the table then take a sip of wine.

Each person then ritually washes his or her hands by pouring water twice over each hand from a large and unchipped cup without a spout. A short prayer is recited, "Lift up your holy hands and bless the Lord," as is the benediction, "who has made us holy with his commandments and who has commanded us to wash our hands." When all are seated, the husband lifts the cover off the challah, passes the knife over both loaves, and cuts one in half. Taking a larger slice of challah, he dips it in the salt and makes the blessing over bread. A slice of challah is then passed to each member of the family and guests; each dips it in the salt, recites the blessing for bread, and eats a bit of the challah. Not a word is uttered from the time a person washes his or her hands until some challah is eaten. Conversation then resumes, and the meal commences.

The first course consists of chopped fish in aspic (*gefilte fish* in Yiddish, *dag memulah* in Hebrew; literally, filled fish). This appellation is derived from the way the fish is served when most elegantly presented, with the mixture formed into a fish shape and covered with the skin of the fish. The dish is almost universally served; fish, meat, and wine are considered essential for the festive celebration of the Sabbath. But Jewish law forbids one to pick bones out of fish on Sabbath. This recipe of filleted and ground fish with bones removed facilitates the proper celebration of the day and avoids the possible religious-legal violations.

A soup course and a chicken or meat entree will follow. A kugel, or pudding, of noodles or potatoes will also be served as a recollection of the manna, the miraculous food eaten by the Israelites during their wanderings in the desert. If tea is served, the hot water is poured into the cup *before* the tea essence is added, and tea bags are not used. Instead, some previously brewed concentrated tea is poured in to flavor the water. In this manner one avoids "cooking" or brewing the tea, which is forbidden on the Sabbath. If lemon is added, it will not be squeezed into the tea; the slice is put into it and perhaps squeezed with the spoon when it is already in the cup to avoid violating the Sabbath by squeezing juice.

Between courses zemirot are sung. These are songs extolling the beauty and pleasure of the Sabbath. The meal concludes with grace after the meal.

The Sabbath noon meal follows a similar pattern: Kiddush over wine, the ritual of washing hands, the blessing of the bread, the use of two challot, symbolizing the double portion of manna received by the Jews when wandering in the desert, the salt, associated with the Temple altar (Lev. 2:13), zemirot songs, and so forth. Chopped liver or chopped egg and onion salad may be served. Again, these foods are served for religious reasons. The main dish may be *cholent,* a hot dish placed in (or on) the oven before the start of the Sabbath and served during the day. The dish may include beans, barley, potatoes, rice (any or some combination) and meat or meat bones. After being simmered for fifteen hours or longer, it becomes a thick porridge. Each community has its own recipes (Hungarian Jews may use beans, Polish Jews potatoes, Sephardic Jews rice), but some form of this dish is traditional, as it is the only way to provide hot food on the Sabbath, when cooking is forbidden. Moreover, this dish carries the message that the Samaritans, who forbade hot food on the Sabbath, were wrong and the Pharisees, who permitted it, right. The dish makes a political statement about a controversy two thousand years ago.

A third meal, called the se'udah shelishit, literally third meal, follows later in the day. Generally it is taken only by men, as it occurs in the synagogue between the late afternoon and evening prayers. More often than not it is simply a symbolic meal. Frequently the meal is nothing more than a slice of challah dipped in salt. Again two challot are used. Occasionally some fish is also available, and beer may be served. Zemirot are again sung. At the third meal, more commonly than at the earlier two, some lesson on a religious topic is offered. Among chasidim, this is often the moment for a moral story about some great rebbe. Again, the meal is concluded with a recital of the blessing for food.

Immediately following the meal, evening prayers are conducted. At the end of these prayers, a Havdalah, or separation ceremony, marks the end of the Sabbath. This ceremony consists of a declaration of trust in the Lord's salvation. "Behold, the Almighty is my salvation, in Him will I trust and I will not fear. . . . I lift the cup of salvation and bless God." This is followed by a blessing over light; a taper lit at the start of the ceremony is held aloft.

The extent to which the Sabbath meals have symbolic meanings is little known. Even those brought up in the practices accept many customs as simply traditional, unaware that any symbolic significance attaches to them. To those experiencing an Orthodox Shabbat for the first time, only a few rituals, perhaps the lighting of candles or the Kiddush or some traditional foods, are known. But as the meaning of each of the symbols is explained, the Sabbath meals may come to have a character similar to the Passover seder—not merely a meal but a dramatic reenactment of a variety of biblical passages, rabbinic experiences, and philosophy. Newcomers may find it difficult to digest so much symbolism along with a meal. But the hosts need not press these explanations; it is perfectly acceptable for all simply to enjoy the food and customs without troubling guests to understand it all. Unlike the Passover seder, tradition and custom for the Sabbath meal de-emphasize the explication of meanings. Sabbath is a time for joy, for the enjoyment of good food and drink, song, and love.

Further, participation in these symbols by guests is minimal. While the guests will be requested to wear a kippah (if male) and to ritually wash their hands and may be encouraged to sip the Kiddush wine and taste the challah, little else will be required. Should a guest refuse to eat, he or she has not withdrawn from participation in the celebration of the Sabbath. The hostess may press, but primarily out of pride in her own food; she does not perceive the guest's refusal as an indication of his rejection of Judaism—or his participation as commitment. This attitude is conveyed to the guest, often wordlessly, and the guest then understands that none of these actions is a commitment.

Not even the wearing of kippah or the ritual washing of the hands is a commitment. It is simply a social amenity. "When in Rome, do as the Romans do." The sign of commitment is the guest's willingness to accept further hospitality of this sort. Will he come for another Sabbath? And if yes, then what of another, and another?

New experiences will wear thin. The symbols and rituals come to be taken for granted. The restrictions associated with Sabbath may become more confining as they become a part of a routine. Not to turn on a light when one is in the dark, not to cook food when it is cold, not to light a cigarette, not to travel become unbearable restrictions. Something else must be built beyond this. Something must continue to draw the individual so that commitment seems worthwhile and the restrictions not onerous. For many Orthodox families the Sabbath becomes so central to their lives that, as one woman put it, "I think that even if I didn't believe in God, I'd still want to have Sabbath. I love it. It's a day I look forward to all week."

If Orthodox Jews define themselves in any way it is as shomrei mitzvot (observers of the commandments). And the litmus test of Orthodoxy is not Passover or any other festival, not kashrut, not even prayer, but Shabbat. It is assumed that if one observes Shabbat fully, then one's observance of the others is adequate.

Recruitment in Israel and in the United States

The description of recruitment in Israel makes it clear that there are substantially different patterns for recruitment in Israel and in the United States, even in recruiting Americans in both these places.

In America the Young Israel developed programs aimed at maintaining the Orthodox commitment of youngsters and reaching out to the non-Orthodox. The technique for achieving this involved building a microcosm of the larger world in the Orthodox community, including sporting leagues, scouting, dances, and other recreational activities, and providing a meeting ground for the Orthodox and the peripherally committed.

The process of recruitment entailed involving peripherally committed people in the recreational activities of the Young Israel synagogues. This often resulted in the development of friendships. As a result, these new people might begin attending synagogue services, be invited to friends' homes, learn to understand Orthodox people and the Orthodox style of life, and eventually begin to consider this commitment seriously for themselves. No special techniques were used to pick up or hook potential recruits. The programs existed in Jewish neighborhoods and were open to all Jews.

The typical path of such returnees might be the following. A youngster attends public school and becomes friendly with another who attends the Young Israel religious school. The Young Israel youngster invites the unaffiliated schoolmate to a scout meeting or a ball game. If they are young adults, it might be to a dance or picnic. New friends are met; social ties develop. The new recruit visits the homes of others, learns about kosher food and Shabbat, and recognizes that to be fully a part of the group he or she must adopt the same practices. If parents are resistant, participation continues to be peripheral although the recruit may attend services at the synagogue. If the commitment is serious, then when one marries one chooses an Orthodox mate and sets up a home that is kosher and Sabbath observing. At this point one has fully entered the Orthodox community.

This technique addresses the problem of how to get the new recruit to adopt a pattern of life that might result in being cut off from friends and family and requires knowledge of rituals practiced primarily within the family. This is achieved by first establishing new friendship ties or even a new family and then adopting the observances that Orthodoxy teaches.

Yeshiva University offers a camping and school experience through its summer camp and its colleges for those lacking background. Potential recruits are generally made aware of these programs through a congregational rabbi. This experience represents not so much outreach as accommodation by Orthodoxy to meet the interests of those seeking it out.

The National Council of Synagogue Youth was founded by Yeshiva University as part of its Community Service Division, designed to assist the work of Orthodox rabbis in congregations. As part of this effort, it developed a national council of local synagogue youth groups. The activities of this group are similar in purpose to those of the Young Israel groups described above. This organization also has basketball games, outings, and game nights. Reflecting the more openly ethnic and religious trends of the 1970s, it also has more specifically religio-social activities. A Saturday night singalong of religious songs is labeled a melavveh malkah (an "accompaniment of the Queen," a reference to a post-Sabbath meal celebrated to extend the Sabbath's joy). The informal arrangement of having a friend stay at one's home for the Sabbath has given way to the camplike atmosphere of having a hundred or more youngsters put up at homes in a neighborhood so that they may celebrate the Sabbath together at what has come to be known as a *shabbatone*. Similar gatherings occur on religious holidays.

These programs are directed mainly at maintaining the interest of young people, particularly adolescents, who are already members of synagogues; at the same time those whose attachment to Orthodoxy is peripheral may become involved. Some of those who manifest an interest in Orthodoxy are encouraged to attend an Orthodox summer camp, attend Yeshiva University's schools, or enroll in one of the yeshivot for ba'alei t'shuva in Israel.

Probably the best known recruiting program is that of the Lubavitcher chasidim of Crown Heights, Brooklyn. This group recruits through a wide variety of programs, including the public schools' religious release hour, shabbatones, and street encounters. The strategy here is to confront the person directly with a religious act and challenge him or her to participate in the religious rituals.[6] Its recruiters may be seen in brightly colored vans asking people whether they are Jewish, and if the response is affirmative, offering the women candlesticks for Sabbath lights and religious literature. Men are asked whether they have worn tefillin that day and offered help in putting them on, or on the Sukkot holiday they are asked to hold and bless an etrog (citron) and a *lulav* (palm frond) in accordance with the custom of that holiday.

6. Interestingly, Lubavitch in Israel does not take a confrontational position. It has no yeshiva in Jerusalem, where the major work of recruitment occurs. Its programs in Israel—bringing Purim gifts to the army or providing bar mitzvah celebrations to children whose fathers were killed in the army—are low pressure and seem aimed more at generating good will than at making converts.

The Lincoln Square Synagogue started as an effort to bridge the gap between Orthodoxy and Conservatism. Apparently, this effort made the synagogue attractive to potential recruits, especially the large community of single Jewish professionals living on the West Side of Manhattan. The "beginners' minyan" was a radical innovation in Orthodoxy. For the High Holy Days, special services for beginners were opened free of charge to the public, again an innovation for Orthodoxy, as these services are often a major source of funds for synagogues.

Following the lead of Lubavitch, Lincoln Square Synagogue undertook publicity campaigns on the west side. At the Chanukah holiday, which occurs around Christmastime, volunteers offer a Chanukah gift to passersby—perhaps some candles to be lit in honor of the holiday, a *dreidel* (top) with which to play some holiday games, or a recipe for making latkes (potato pancakes), a traditional holiday dish. The gift also includes a list of the synagogue's activities and an invitation to participate. On Purim, a carnival-like holiday, *hamantaschen* (poppyseed pastries in triangular shape), cookies, and candy are distributed by costumed volunteers, with similar messages enclosed in the gifts.

In addition, undoubtedly important in gaining new recruits was a series of lectures, concerts, outings, parties, and the like for young singles. Topics were geared to Jewish singles. One year, for example, a series of lectures dealt with sex and the Jewish single, a relevant topic for this group.

The strategy for this program was somewhat different from that of the Young Israel and the National Council of Synagogue Youth. The target population was young, single Jewish professionals, people who are independent of family, who seek new relationships, for which the synagogue's programs provide a framework.

The Jewish Education Program offers classes in Judaism to Jewish children attending public schools during the weekly religious release hour. This program is essentially made possible by the cooperation of the public schools, which provide the release time hour. The young instructors, typically students at yeshivot, use the classroom time for biblical stories and songs and attempt to induce children to participate in other activities under Orthodox auspices, such as outings or picnics and, more recently, in the shabbatone Sabbath weekend.

There are also a few yeshivot for ba'alei t'shuva in the United States: Sh'or Yoshuv in Far Rockaway, Lubavitch's Tomchie Temimim in Morristown, New Jersey, Kol Ya'akov, a branch of an Israeli school in

Monsey, New York, Bet Pinchas in Boston, and others. But none of these yeshivot engages in recruitment.

Recruitment in Israel follows a different pattern. It is more often confrontational, as are the programs in yeshivot, particularly at yeshivot heavily involved in recruitment like Noach Weinberg's Aish Hatorah. Potential recruits are pushed to defend their beliefs, and they are often hard-pressed to do so.

Programs directed at Israelis follow a similar strategy. Rabbi Elbaz, the head of Ohr Hachayim Yeshiva, often leads a parade, complete with band, into poor neighborhoods. The band and marchers attract attention. The rabbi then delivers a sermon calling on sinners to return to Judaism. His techniques have attracted widespread attention, and he now has an annual t'shuva rally during the Ten Days of Penitence, the days between Rosh Ha-Shana and Yom Kippur.

Some programs in Israel do not follow this strategy. The *Gesher* (literally, bridge) organization, as its name implies, seeks to bridge the gap between the secular and the religious. Some of the yeshivot for ba'alei t'shuva completely eschew recruitment of the newly religious, preferring to deal only with those who have already made a commitment to Orthodox Judaism.

COMPARISONS BETWEEN ISRAEL AND AMERICA

Recruitment to Orthodoxy in America follows a bridging strategy; that is, recruiting efforts are directed toward building a microcosm of the larger society under religious auspices and offering popular social events, such as dances or ballgames to attract potential recruits, although there is no attempt to hide religious affiliation. Underlying this approach is an attempt to narrow the gap between Orthodox Judaism and the outside world by emphasizing the compatibility of the two.

In Israel, a confrontational style predominates. Recruits are challenged to defend their secular ideologies or accept religious beliefs. They are challenged to give up drugs and promiscuous sex, to observe holy days and other religious commandments. Little effort is made to reach potential recruits on their own grounds or to offer social activities as a means of drawing them closer. Some schools may reach out to hippies and try to accept them as they are. Har Tzion in particular did this for hippies, and ba'al t'shuva yeshivot make an effort to be accepting of others' styles. But in Israel no attempt has been made to reach out to others in terms of their culture—for example, to have a rock concert or a camping trip under religious auspices so that social ties can be established before religious themes are introduced.

Yeshivot for ba'alei t'shuva function differently in the United States and Israel. In general, in the United States students enter yeshivot only after they have developed an interest in or commitment to Judaism. In Israel the yeshivot themselves are often recruiting agencies, the front line where the battle for the individual's commitment occurs. Those who want to address these "first questions of commitment" will find them not in America but in Israel.

"Bridgers" tend to be modernists, to have denominationalist attitudes of tolerance and respect for other faiths. "Confrontationists" tend to be traditionalists, to hold the sectarian view of having the only truth. Sectarians may tend to adopt a more confrontational approach because this is more consistent with their generally countercultural perspective. Denominationalists accept other religious and secular expressions as legitimate, which pushes their outreach in the direction of finding common ground, emphasizing their trait of acceptance.

That the bridging strategy predominates in the United States while the confrontationist strategy predominates in Israel seems to be related to minority versus dominant status. Judaism's minority status in the United States inhibits efforts at recruitment. Jews do not fear suppression; too many other groups recruit for that to be a concern, from Christian evangelists to cult groups. Nevertheless, there remains a sense of embarrassment at attempting to recruit to Orthodox Judaism in public.

Judaism's majority status in Israel means, to paraphrase Plato, that Jewish values may be found in the public arena "writ large." These values are reinforced by public celebrations, holidays, rituals, and values. For example, the Israeli Army issues only kosher rations and has rabbinical supervision of its kitchens. Polls indicate that the overwhelming majority of the Israeli population supports this arrangement. Saturday, not Sunday, is the day of rest in Israel. Christmas and Easter are not celebrated. Passover, the High Holy Days, and Sukkot, the Feast of Booths, are celebrated by the people and observed by government agencies. Radio and television, newspapers and magazines devote time and space to the holidays.[7]

7. There was widespread comment that it was in a sense fortunate that the War of 1973 began on Yom Kippur, because on that day everyone was home, the roads were empty, and the reserves could be immediately summoned and dispatched. For an analysis of the impact of Judaism on Israeli society and government, see Liebman and Don-Yehiya 1983.

Value congruence is an important factor affecting the choice of recruitment strategies. Sectarians do not reject the values of society so much as they *overconform* to some religious norms while ignoring others and condemn society for its failure to behave as they do (Danzger 1987). Sectarians share the religious tradition and values of the dominant religion but differ regarding some aspects of it. This formulation, of course, fits sect groups and fundamentalists on the American scene.

Minority religions, which derive from clearly different religious traditions, in contrast, cannot confront the majority with their norms. When they openly attempt to recruit, they are met with hostility and often labeled cults.

In Israel, strongly countercultural Orthodoxy is considered sectarian. That is, it has a place in the constellation of religious values, although many find it objectionable. A group voicing these same values publicly in the United States might be defined as cultlike. In Israel, with the exception of those groups that reject the state, they are considered sectarian.

Chapter 10

Why They Return

Why do people change their attitudes and beliefs and become Orthodox Jews? Answers to this question are suggested by the actions of those who become Orthodox, the groups they join, and the stages by which the process occurs. The reasons the returnees themselves offer to explain their behavior are important data for understanding how they see their own actions and how they are viewed by others, but they may not be sufficient to explain why they changed.[1]

A person's reconstruction of the events leading to his return reflects the pattern that he has learned is appropriate. Events or stages that have no

1. Answers to such questions as "How did you come to be attracted to Orthodoxy?" or "Why did you become a ba'al t'shuva?" are usually framed in terms of motivation or attitudes. But motives are understood differently by social scientists than by the public at large.

When one's actions belie the words used to explain the actions (as when revolutionaries claim to be robbing the rich to further the revolution but use the booty to live the high life), the motives offered may be questioned. When they are meant to deceive others they are termed lies. When they are perceived to deceive the self they are called rationalizations. In both cases another motive is sought based on the evidence of the actions. But whether a motive in fact explains the act depends on whether the society is willing to accept it as an explanation. As C. Wright Mills (1940) has taught us, "What is reason for one man is rationalization for another." The difference depends on whether the group to which one is relating is willing to accept it.

Thus individualistic, sexual, hedonistic, and pecuniary vocabularies of motives are acceptable in twentieth-century urban America. But we would be skeptical of a billionaire businessman who claimed religious motives for his business conduct, because such motives are not *now* accepted as business motives. Similarly, a medieval monk who wrote that he gave food to a poor but pretty woman "for the salvation of his soul" would probably be disbelieved in the twentieth century. Demonic possession might be a satisfactory "motive" for action in the medieval world;

place in prevalent paradigms of return pass unnoticed. Other experiences, which at the time of their occurrence were hardly noticed or felt, may take on new and weightier significance so as to be consistent with acceptable patterns of return. This is characteristic of all of us in a variety of situations, not only of ba'alei t'shuva. We construct a biography of our occupational development, our marriage, our very selves in much the same

---

it is not in ours. Nor would a Freudian or Marxist interpretation of behavior have been accepted in the medieval world.

Max Weber defines motive as the meaning that appears to the actor or the observer to be an adequate ground for his conduct (Mills 1940, 906). The motive, or reason, for an action is not the same as the cause of action. Motives are justifications of actions.

This approach to motives, which is widely accepted in social psychology, suggests that we will not find a motive or motives to explain why a person becomes a ba'al t'shuva any more than the motive for voting Republican or Democrat can be fully explained by the voter's description of a candidate's attractiveness. In both cases the dominant theoretical perspective in social psychology would suggest that we look instead toward group affiliations, position in the social structure, or past experiences that have left their mark on the individual. Social class, income, and education are excellent predictors of voting tendency, even though the voter may not be aware of their impact on his behavior.

Experimental evidence demonstrates the extent to which situational factors affect a person's actions. College students subjected to group pressures deny the evidence of their own eyes and agree with a group's definition of the length of a line (Asch 1958). People obey authority even when no sanctions are applied or threatened and will attempt to administer painful, even dangerous electric shocks to others at the simple but firm request of a person in authority (Milgram 1964). Whether a person helps another in distress varies with whether the person is alone or in the presence of someone else. In one experiment 70 percent of subjects attempted to provide assistance when they were alone, but if another person present ignored the cries only 7 percent tried to help (Latane and Rodin 1969).

Identity is itself viewed as an amalgam of responses of the individual in various situated activities (Alexander and Wiley 1981). Attitude is a problematic concept with implications for behavior that are not entirely clear. If anything, it is viewed as a dependent variable emerging from the pressures exerted on the individual that force compliance as a result of sanctions or that he espouses in order to remain a member of a group. Kelman (1961), who has developed this view of attitudes systematically, holds that some attitudes are internalized and, once internalized, are partially independent of social structure. But internalized attitudes seem to constitute a small part of the attitude set. From Kelman's perspective, most attitudes are simply reflective of the pressures of social structure.

Social psychologists generally view attitudes as dependent factors caused by other factors rather than as independent factors that cause behaviors. Studies indicate that attitude changes may occur if one changes one's group or simply plays a different

manner. These reconstructed biographies are referred to in sociology as "accounts" (Scott and Lyman 1968). They are stories that "account for" our present situation.

These accounts are not false or intended to mislead, although indeed they may at times mislead. But even when they are intended to be faithful accounts of a person's progress from the past to the present or explanations of how one came to be a ba'al t'shuva, the *explanation must be accepted by others in that social situation, and only certain accounts are acceptable.* Much of the welter of past experience will be overlooked in the construction of the biography. The account is thus a reflection of the group's values and self-perception, as well as the individual's.

The Rhetoric of Return

INAUTHENTIC AND AUTHENTIC RHETORIC

In January 1975 the Young Israel of Hillcrest, Queens, sponsored a Friday night forum on "Returning to Judaism," at which Sara, the daughter of Rebbitzin Esther Jungreis, chaired the forum and two newly Orthodox Jews described how and why they became Orthodox. One of the returnees was a young, pretty girl of about eighteen or nineteen. The other was a young man of twenty-three or twenty-four. After some brief opening remarks, the young woman was introduced as a former "Jesus Freak" who had been "saved" by Rebbitzin Esther Jungreis. She rose and told her story.

She had grown up in Miami and had known nothing more about her Jewishness than that she was Jewish. On hearing that the Rebbitzin was holding a Jewish revival meeting in Miami, she and three friends, also Jesus Freaks, determined to challenge the Rebbetzin with their new-found religion.

The disruption they caused during the meeting led to a discussion

---

role. The most convincing explanation for this is the theory of cognitive dissonance, which says that people justify their actions after the fact by attributing value to their choices that they themselves did not hold prior to the actions.

This brings us once again back to the perspective that the stated motives of people are less explanations of their behavior than rationalizations. Festinger (1962) and Mills (1940), though starting from different perspectives, seem in complete agreement on this.

afterward, which continued into the night. In the next several days, she, her friends, and the Rebbitzin met for many hours of heated discussion, much of it centering around the martyrdom of the Jewish people for their religion and the Holocaust experience. Toward the end of these sessions, the Rebbitzin invited her to come to New York to continue the discussions, and in a few more days she "became convinced of the Truth." She called her parents who cried for joy over her new-found commitment.

In closing, she said, "I found *Ha-Shem*.[2] I was at peace, I felt great joy. I felt Ha-Shem was in me, that He loved me and cared for me." Turning to the audience she said, "You have to find Ha-Shem, to feel His love, to let Him come into your heart."

Somehow this struck a false note with the audience of modernistic Orthodox ranging in age from fifteen to about fifty-five, with most in the thirty-five to forty-five age bracket. Many were professionals, both men and women. Those who were more involved and educated in Judaism were particularly skeptical of the young woman. They doubted that she would long remain Orthodox.

The young man followed with a description of his return. He had become friendly with a neighbor who was Orthodox. His neighbor's practices intrigued him. He enjoyed the warmth and family life that accompanied the observance of the Sabbath and the holidays. Slowly he began some of these practices himself. His neighbor, while not affiliated with Lubavitch, admired the group's welcoming approach to other Jews and suggested that he contact Lubavitch to learn more about Orthodox Judaism. Through his neighbor and Lubavitcher tutors he has learned about Orthodoxy. He currently observes the laws of Shabbat and kashrut and continues to study with Lubavitch.

This young man's talk was accepted by the audience as the story of someone who would probably remain Orthodox. Somehow his story was authentic while hers was inauthentic. Her story attaches her to Ha-Shem; his attaches him to the Jewish people, to community. Her story speaks of the sense of being loved by God; his speaks of study, of growing knowledge and awareness of Jewish law and practice. Her transformation was swift; his was slow. Finally, his story leaves him a beginner, one still learning from others. Her story places her in a position to proclaim a message to others, to be a leader.

Both, of course, are telling their own stories as they knew them. Inquiry

2. Hebrew for "the Name," a reference to God, whose name is ineffable.

several years later revealed that both had remained Orthodox. But whereas her story was acceptable in Christianity, it was not acceptable in Judaism. The audience considered it false because it did not fit into the patterns of accepted motivation for Judaism. Ba'alei t'shuva who tell such stories describing their motivation meet with incredulity. The repetition of such stories is discouraged, and a different account or biography of return is constructed, with neither the community nor the returnee aware of this process.

The following excerpt from a paper by a graduate student in sociology (Kramer 1972), himself a ba'al t'shuva, describes the leader of a ba'al t'shuva settlement established on an old deserted kibbutz, referred to here as "K."

Reuben M. is a ba'al t'shuva and his wife is a convert to Judaism. Reuben M. once ran a radio station in the United States, and his public voice makes itself obvious after one speaks to him for a few minutes. He is a professional and has succeeded in gaining the sympathy and support of the Israeli public and the Jewish Agency. Contributions come in the form of voluntary labor from nearby settlements, individual financial donations, and, recently, government aid to his ba'al t'shuva kibbutz. He and his settlement have appeared in all the Israeli newspapers, plus French television and foreign publications in many parts of the world. Reuben doesn't care what is said about him as long as he is publicized. According to the newspaper clipping collection I saw at "K," he has been quite successful.

Not only does Reuben utilize his charisma for the outside world, but he manages "K" with it internally as well. He strictly prohibits promiscuity and drugs, which has resulted in his expelling a few people. Other people have left because of dissension with Reuben. His personality is overpowering and what he says goes.

Most of the people in "K" at first are willing to submit to his charisma since usually they are too unsure of themselves and their new Judaism to assert themselves about anything. Later as people pull themselves together some find Reuben's charisma unbearable.

As inevitably happens when a yippie [politically activist hippie in the 1970s] establishment is too hippie, people go elsewhere. Two couples have married in "K" and both have left to continue learning in a more stable religious environment.

The most unusual aspect of "K" is Reuben's ignorance of Judaism and his unwillingness to admit it. He speaks with a general sense of jubilance about Torah and mitzvot, but after a few minutes it becomes obvious that he has only the most rudimentary idea about what he's saying. At one point I corrected him on something he plainly misunderstood; he countered by telling me to go and learn. He continued talking, and several knowledgeable yeshiva students again corrected him. He countered this by saying that today Judaism must be rediscovered. His enthusiasm, like his confidence, gives him a striking resemblance to a Baptist evangelist from Alabama.

He has refused offers of help from the chasidim of Lubavitch and others. Many feel the reason is that he fears others will eventually run the show. He has so far only accepted aid in religious instruction from individuals, not from organizations. He is very critical of the religious establishment in Israel without any real knowledge of the situation.

The critical point is that the observer—himself a ba'al t'shuva—associates charisma and enthusiasm with "a Baptist evangelist" in contrast to knowledge, which he sees as essential to practice and leadership in Judaism. This observer rejects claims to authority based on personal experience or religious feelings. The only authority acceptable to him is that of the Torah, the religious literature that has grown up around it, and implicitly the interpretation of this literature by the Orthodox establishment. Personal salvation and religious experience are not a source of authority.

The emphasis on rationality in teaching and in the experience of ba'alei t'shuva can also be seen in the following discussion with the deans of Yeshiva Ohr Someyach. Commenting on what a student entering the yeshiva is told, one of the deans said: "You tell the guy very simply, you're coming into a rough regimen. It's an all-day program. If you're not inclined to it, this is not the place for you. Our appeal is academic and intellectual, not one of emotion, music, or an extended family relationship."

He was interrupted by another of the deans: "One moment. There is a certain paradox, because although the approach here is intellectually rigorous, TLC [tender loving care] is certainly an important part of this process, as is visiting someone's home. They are not intellectual activities. Both are happening at the same time." In this context the emotional and supportive elements are continually downplayed in the rhetoric, to the point where even the teachers and deans forget their importance. The intellectual and cognitive aspects are thought to be the only basis for religious authority.

THE LACK OF MIRACLES AND DIVINE INTERVENTION

In contrast to converts to Christian groups and born-again Christians, ba'alei t'shuva place little emphasis on miraculous events as having influenced their new commitment. There are no stories of having been persuaded to become Orthodox as a result of some miraculous cure or of

hearing once more from a lost relative or of having a dream about someone dear to them or of having a prayer answered—experiences that are
quite commonly reported by Christian converts and born-again
Christians.[3] Ba'alei t'shuva describe a search for meaning in life, a search
for God, a feeling of having found the truth. But they do not report
miracles.[4]

One does find reports of chance experiences that are interpreted as
evidence of Divine Providence.[5] Most often these stories are presented
with much drama; every detail is considered important and at the same
time not the normal pattern for that person. The out-of-the-ordinary
character of the activity is stressed, making the chance element in the story
stand out. The conclusion that this event implies some Divine Providence
is not stated, as this would indicate a degree of hubris not readily accepted
by the teachers and guides of the ba'al t'shuva. Rather than affirm the
individual's commitment, such stories engender skepticism about his "fit-
ness" to function normally in the Orthodox community, although these
questions are not raised directly to the ba'al t'shuva.

The "evidences" of Divine intervention which brought the ba'al
t'shuva into his religious commitment lose their vigor as the person remains in the Orthodox community. In essence one may say that ba'alei
t'shuva rarely if ever cite Divine Providence when explaining their new
commitment. This is consistent with the rationalistic perspectives of both
the society they leave and the society of the Orthodox, in which miracles
play a limited role. (And, more important, it avoids the grandiose claim
that one was worthy of a miracle.)

Even those living hippie life-styles, those who sought mind expansion,
those who were "into" astrology, tarot, and the like, those who were
Jesus Freaks, even these people are likely to reconstruct their biographies

3. See, for example, Westley 1977 for reports of miracles inducing faith among
Catholic charismatics. This pattern is also widely observed among Protestant Pen-
tacostals. Stories of miracles in Judaism generally emphasize the spiritual powers of
the miracle worker, typically a rebbe.

4. Glanz and Harrison (1978) are not in full agreement with me in this.

5. For example, a ba'al t'shuva at Ohr Someyach reported that he first became
involved with Orthodoxy when on his way to visit a friend in Jerusalem he stopped
at a grocery store to buy a bottle of wine as a gift. Rabbi Nota Schiller of Ohr
Somayach was there and asked if he was buying the wine for Kiddush. They talked,
and he was persuaded to come to Ohr Someyach. He felt that meeting Rabbi Schiller
was a sign of *hashgacha,* of God's concern for each individual, and in this case for
him in particular. Other ba'alei t'shuva gave similar interpretations to their encounters with recruiters.

slowly as they come to understand Judaism better. At the outset of their "conversion" they may tell others that they have experienced special events, more than mere coincidences, which persuaded them to begin learning about Judaism. These people will be eager to learn about Kabbalah and particularly about magical lore associated with this mysticism. (Most of their knowledge of the existence of such a body of magical lore will have been gleaned from non-Jewish sources.) Such inquiry as we have seen will be discouraged by schools for ba'alei t'shuva, for they hold that such holy powers are granted only rarely, perhaps to one in a generation, and are only for the extremely pious, after long years of practice of Judaism. The ba'al t'shuva will be bidden to put off such goals and to start the study and practice of Orthodox Judaism. After he has learned the *Niglah*,[6] the required codes, etc. he may then choose to pursue his studies in Kabbalah.

Thus, although at an early stage in the process of change ba'alei t'shuva may claim that they were motivated to become Orthodox through some Divine sign, as they are socialized into Orthodoxy failure to mute this element in the account of their change leads to the assessment of the conversion as inauthentic or at least incomplete. Slowly, it becomes clear to the ba'al t'shuva that only the extraordinarily pious and learned may exercise holy powers or experience the Divine presence. He therefore reconstructs the biography of his journey in terms of what is acceptable as a motivation.

But Judaism and Christianity share a Bible replete with stories of miracles.[7] How is it, then, that the motivational vocabulary associated with Christian conversion and rebirth emphasizes miracles while Judaism de-emphasizes it?

What distinguishes Judaism from Christianity in this respect is that miracles are interpreted differently. To both Christians and Jews, miracles are signs of Divine intervention in the world, but in Christianity they

6. Niglah literally means the exoteric or public knowledge. This refers to the Bible, the Talmud and the Codes, in contrast to *Nistar*, which literally means the Hidden or esoteric knowledge (Kabbalah).

7. Although the demonology of Christianity finds no parallel in Judaism, miracles are an essential element in Jewish belief as in Christian belief. Moreover, the Jewish tradition of miracles continued beyond the period of the closing of the canon in about 135 C.E. One finds the continuation of this tradition in the Talmud and *aggadic* literature (narrative and homilies of the Oral Law) developed in the first three centuries of the common era and continuing as a minor theme throughout Jewish history to the story of the Golem of Prague, the miracles of the Ba'al Shem Tov, and the miraculous powers of other chasidic rebbes.

are believed to be instrumental in persuading people to follow God, whereas in Judaism they are not, nor is it believed that they ever were. In the last analysis, for Judaism miracles do not make one faithful. The philosophical principle is "All is in the hands of Heaven save fear of God." Miracles did not engender faith even for the generation that Moses led out of Egypt with "the Hand of God." The Pentateuch makes it clear in the account in Exodus and elsewhere that immediately after being saved by miracles or chastised by God's intervention the Jews would turn and sin again. In Judaism's view faith and commitment depend on man's own will. They are not molded, nor should they be, by Divine intervention.[8]

Typical Accounts

In the preceding pages we have tried to show some kinds of accounts for change that are not acceptable in the Orthodox community. We will now describe stories that are acceptable.

THE EMPTINESS OF SUCCESS

Probably no account of religious return has been so widely accepted in the yeshivot for ba'alei t'shuva as that of the "success" who finds his life and success meaningless, or at least finds greater fulfillment in the religious life than in his former "successful" life. Such stories are common among both Americans and Israelis in the ba'al t'shuva yeshivot, although they are more characteristics of the Israelis, for reasons explored later.

Ika Israeli, for example, is a painter of national reputation in Israel and one of the success stories of the t'shuva movement. When I began the study of ba'alei t'shuva at Ohr Someyach, Rabbi Weinbach suggested that I interview Ika. Publicity materials on Ohr Someyach in the 1970s frequently carried his picture. In fact, as Ika had originally attended Yeshivat Hatfutzot-Har Tzion, some of their early publicity also carried pictures of him. Ika's story is paradigmatic, almost identical with that of Mordechai

8. The Talmud recounts that a difference of opinion developed between Rabbi Eliezer and the other sages regarding the ritual purity of a certain oven. Rabbi Eliezer was supported in his claim through a series of miracles and challenged the other rabbis to admit that he was right. In the end, although a heavenly voice proclaimed that the judgment of Rabbi Eliezer was correct, the majority view prevailed, for the rabbis refused to follow his view, claiming that "the Torah is not in heaven" (BT, Baba Metzia 59b). See also BT, Avoda Zarah 54b, 55a for a series of disputations between the rabbis and the philosophers and idol worshipers.

Arnon (Pupik), a well-known Israeli comedian, and Uri Zohar, an Israeli television personality.

Ika was born to parents who were committed socialists and anti-religious. He was raised on a kibbutz and knew very little of Judaism. In his late twenties he spent two years in Paris studying art. By his late thirties he had achieved a measure of artistic success and was well known in avant-garde circles in Israel. Following the Six Day War in 1967, Israel was carried into the hippe and flower children era by the mass media and by visitors from abroad.

Ika opened a discotheque that soon became a success. But he felt that his life was missing something. He left Jerusalem for the mountains of Sefad. After a few weeks of isolation he was persuaded that life must have some deeper meaning and determined to find it. He first joined the Yeshiva Har Tzion, wearing hippie clothing and expressing antiestablishment views, like the other students of Har Tzion at that time. He threw himself completely into this new life, spending his days in study of the Talmud and codes.

He attributed his own change of heart to several factors. First, he saw his religious commitment as a continuation of his parents' pattern of commitment to ideals. In fact, Ika felt it was important that his religious commitment not be seen as a break with his parents; despite their disaffection with religion, he emphasized that they lived a life of ideals.

> "We never pursued money, nor comforts. Father was a party man [a man with strong political commitments]; he taught us Zionism and Chalutziut [the spirit of the *chaluztim,* the pioneers] and socialism. The important motive for a person was the principles for which he lived. Without that, life is not worth living. . . . A person must dedicate his life to *tikun ha'olam* [improving the world], and whatever I do is part of this approach."

A second factor in his change was his experience in the Six Day War. Without mentioning any particular incident, he said simply that seeing hundreds of young people die must shake one up. And although he did not change his life at that time, it left an impression.

Third, he attributed the change to the general questioning of the values of Western civilization by Marcuse (1964) and the hippie and antiwar movements of the late 1960s. These challenges destroyed belief in the legitimacy of establishment values and left room for exploring alternatives. At the same time, drugs, particularly marijuana, hashish, and L.S.D., made people, himself included, realize that there was a deeper reality which could and should be explored.

Finally, alone in his retreat in the mountains of Safad, reading Martin Buber and works on Zen Buddhism, he began to consider the possibility of exploring a religious life. When he returned, determined to give it a try, he sought out the yeshiva of Hatfutzot-Har Tzion, where he heard other hippies were studying Judaism.

No mention was made of mystical experiences, illuminations, voices, or sudden callings. The change was a slow, rational decision based on experience and thought. Ika considered philosophies that justified other life-styles, particularly hedonistic life-styles, to be no more than "rationales." No religious act was really rational; practice of it was critical. He held that "people do things and then find a theory to follow which justifies it."

> They said to me, "Try it and you'll understand. You want to grasp it purely intellectually. You'll never understand." They tell you, "Do this because it is written [in the Torah]. That's the crisis. The minute you get over that obstacle, it doesn't matter what the mitzvah is—except for the intellectual commandments such as not to murder or steal—but all the nonintellectual commandments are equally difficult.

In this last point, Ika is expressing the Jewish perspective on observance of the commandments. His motivation for becoming Orthodox and the stages by which he reached it are thus paradigmatic for those who seek religious answers to the "emptiness of success." Many others in the yeshiva had similar stories, although their early secular successes were more modest. All were looking for something meaningful when they— often by chance—encountered a student or a yeshiva or a recruiter. They were willing and ready to examine another life-style.

WOMEN'S ACCOUNTS

Women in yeshivot do not report that they turned to religion after confronting the emptiness of success.[9] Nor do women report that they were part of the hippie world, although some may have been. Ba'alot t'shuva have been successful in careers as nurses, artists, teachers, and lawyers. At least one is a professional photographer. Perhaps her story demonstrates the difference between the accounts of the successful man and the successful woman.

At age twenty-seven Ruth was a highly successful free-lance photographer. Her photographs had appeared in *Time, National Geograph-*

---

9. Women professionals on the upper west side of Manhattan, however, sometimes describe their return as impelled by a sense of the emptiness of their success.

ic, Life, and a host of less known magazines and newspapers. On a trip to Israel to photograph the holy places she met Chayim, a student at Yeshivat Har Tzion. Chayim, a former hippie, had been at the yeshiva for three years. At age twenty-nine he was one of the older students in the yeshiva. For the past several months he had been pressing Rabbi Goldstein to help him find a wife.

Wandering about Mt. Zion, Ruth chanced to meet Chayim and asked for directions to David's Tomb. He served as her guide for the next few hours. She returned several times during the week to photograph that site and others in the vicinity. By the end of the week, Chayim proposed marriage to Ruth, and she accepted. "When I called home to tell my parents I was to be married they were very happy. My mother asked me how long I had known Chayim. When I told her 'almost a week' she was shocked and insisted I wait until I knew him better. Three weeks later we were married."

When I first met Ruth they had been married for less than a year. She described the events to me and spoke of Chayim in glowing terms. "He's big, handsome with beautiful eyes and a wonderful smile. He's gentle and interested in incredible things." On a return trip seven years later, I visited Ruth and Chayim and met the couple's three children. Chayim still studied at the yeshiva. He, Ruth, and the children lived in a small stone house on Mt. Zion, which would have been picturesque if they had had the money to improve the place. Ruth still did free-lance photography for magazines, and this was an important source of income for the family.

Several features of this story are illustrative of the differences between the accounts of successful men and those of successful women. For men, occupation is the most salient status. A religious commitment produces a sharp devaluation of the importance of occupation in the man's priorities. The occupation or profession is no longer the prime concern and the major criterion for measuring the man's worth; the religious value system is. With it comes a new way of evaluating success and new norms. Some men give up their careers entirely once they have returned, devoting themselves to Torah study. Women, on the other hand, do not generally value their occupational status to the exclusion of other commitments and priorities. Thus a deep and substantial religious commitment will not require the same degree of devaluation of occupational status. A woman may give up her former status, particularly if it is inconsistent with the role of Orthodox women. An actress or a singer might be in such a situation. Women may also give up their occupation even if the two roles are entirely consonant, as in the case of a nurse or teacher. But nothing in the role of Orthodox woman *requires* an exclusive devotion to Torah. On the other hand, there is a norm for men that requires such devotion and thus legitimates a man's giving up a profession to devote himself entirely to study of Torah.

Thus we are left with a paradoxical situation: Men, for whom occupation is a major salient status, find that upon becoming Orthodox they are challenged to consider the possibility of devoting themselves to Torah scholarship exclusively. They must find legitimate reasons for *not* doing so. In contrast, women, for whom occupation is not generally so salient a status that it excludes others, find that Orthodox Judaism does not demand of them an exclusive commitment to Torah. If they had contemplated marriage as well as a career before, they may keep the same expectations after return and feel no pressure to give up a career; at best, they are expected to be helpmates to husbands who are Torah scholars. While their highest duty is to be married, they are usually encouraged to continue to pursue a career. According to their accounts, this provides continuity with their past lives, permits their continued growth, and is consonant with the prevalent value in society that women have the right to develop themselves to the maximum. But an important additional consideration is that her career may put the woman in a position to support her husband for a number of years while he studies Torah. For women, then, return to Orthodoxy does not involve the radical reevaluation of major salient roles. Although rules of modesty, religious observance, and child care limit women and orthodoxy is far from conflict-free, for many women becoming a "religious woman" does not prevent professional growth. In this sense the transition is easier, and this is reflected in the tendency of women's accounts of their return not to include "the emptiness of success."

Although the initial change for men seems more radical and problematic than for women, one might say that the male role of the ba'al t'shuva studying in a yeshiva is more internally consistent than that of Orthodox wife. For women, the initial change is less radical, as occupational and family roles may retain their relative importance. The adjustment may therefore be more difficult as the new demands introduced by her religiosity can produce severe strains in the marriage. And although they are not unique to ba'al t'shuva marriages, the effects of such strains are probably even more strongly felt in such marriages, for the women often expect a life of higher involvements. Having made the decision to become Orthodox, they nevertheless find their lives taken up with washing diapers and other less uplifting activities while their husbands devote themselves to Torah (Wolf 1982). For those brought up expecting to be mothers and housewives, the role is difficult enough. For those who expected something else, it may be a severe disappointment.

RELIGIOUS SEEKERS

Some of the newly Orthodox might be characterized as "drifters." They move from one setting to another without completing the work undertaken anywhere. But they see themselves as rejecting the system, not as failing to measure up.

The account offered by such persons, both Americans and Israelis, indicates that most were attending a university and found the program unsatisfying, not answering the basic questions they had about life. Dissatisfied with school and the establishment, they began traveling, to Europe, perhaps to India. Often they were considering going to India and somehow ended up in Israel.

These are people who have tasted all life's joys—or at least those most valued by Western, youth-oriented societies. They have been free of responsibility, have traveled, have had sex without limits, have experienced drugs, have not been bound by the petty rules and regulations that bind others in society. They have now turned their backs on this freedom and have accepted the encompassing and detailed discipline of Judaism.

The seekers or hippies tend to have some commonalities. Most have started university but have not completed their studies. They have strong attachment to the Jewish people but not to religion. Their parents may have been involved in synagogue but were not Orthodox. They were, however, Zionistically inclined and may have reacted strongly to the Holocaust.

Seekers, more than others, tend to see *hashgacha*, or Divine providence, as affecting their own lives. An unusual event or a happy coincidence brought them in touch with someone who then persuaded them to give Orthodoxy a try.

"Giving it a try" may not be the rhetoric used in other faiths. But this experiential emphasis, so much a part of American culture and hippie perspectives, fits well with the traditional Orthodox perspective of doing first and then evaluating the experience. Although learning to be Orthodox involves enormous intellectual activity, it comes after the actions, not before.

The "hippie-seeker trip" is rarely found among female returnees. Whereas Jewish marital laws and sexual norms frown on promiscuous sex for both men and women, for women promiscuity also introduces several legal liabilities. A woman who has been promiscuous may not marry a *cohen* (a man of the priestly caste). Under certain circumstances promiscuity may introduce difficulties in marrying ordinary Jews as well. Although rabbis and religious courts have often been able to provide relief in these circumstances, the harm accruing to a woman whose account of her return includes a change from drugs and sex to Orthodoxy is clearly greater than it would be for a man. And if men tend to play down the sex and drugs in their past (except when speaking confidentially or when their pasts are too well known to hide), women must be and are even more wary of providing such an account.

Social Ties

THE FIANCÉ FACTOR

Accounts of the "emptiness of success" and "hippie-seeking" are typical of men. Following a husband, a fiancé, or a boyfriend into religion is a typical pattern for women but is not exclusive to women's accounts. I have found one case in which a man became Orthodox because his girlfriend had become Orthodox. (Although in his account he saw himself as motivated solely by religious commitment, the role of the woman was so prominent as to be an unmistakable element in his change even though he eventually carried the change much further.) In another case, a man mentioned his relationship with an Orthodox woman as easing his transition into Orthodoxy.[10]

In five of the seven couples I interviewed in which both were newly Orthodox, the woman began the process of return after the man did,[11] and he took the lead, even though in two of these cases the woman's background and scholastic abilities were, at least at the outset, greater than the man's. The story of Judy and Josh will illustrate.

Judy was born in New York City. Her parents moved to a small town seventy miles from the city when she was seven. She attended a Hebrew school until she was bat mitzvahed at thirteen. (Her father had not been

10. The accounts of religious return of Rabbi Akiva (see chap. 1) and Rabbi Simeon bar Lakish (BT, Baba Metzia 84a) are both described as having been promoted by attachment to a woman.

11. I have interviewed two men whose return to Judaism was clearly a result of their love for women that they had known who became Orthodox, although the men did not describe it in these terms. In one case the man followed her through an Eastern religion and then to Orthodoxy.

bar mitzvahed and wanted this for his daughter.) Although the family was affiliated with a Conservative synagogue, its commitment to religion was weak. Chanukkah was observed sporadically. The family gathered for a Passover seder, "but it was just a family gathering. It could just as well have been Easter." After graduating university as a teacher she had some difficulty getting a job. She spotted an ad in the *New York Times* describing a one-year volunteer program in Israel in social work. Claiming that she felt no particular pull to Israel, she applied for the program.

Josh was of a somewhat more traditional background. He came from a large city in Texas. His grandfather had been Orthodox, and Josh had had close ties to him as a child. His family was affiliated with a Conservative synagogue, but after the death of the grandfather they joined the Reform Temple. After graduating university Josh decided to spend a year abroad. He consulted the local Jewish Agency emissary, and they agreed that the volunteer social work program in Israel was suitable.

Josh and Judy met on the program in July 1973. Neither of them was in synagogue on Yom Kippur, the day the October 1973 war broke out.

In the summer of 1975 they returned to the United States to get married and spent the next year preparing themselves to come back to Israel. They felt no commitment to religion at this point; they were returning simply out of strong feelings of Jewish identification. Josh, however, had decided he wanted to know more about his Jewish heritage. "To be a better Reform Jew I was going back to learn the classics and apply that to Reform Judaism." As for Judy: "I wanted to come back to Israel for Zionistic reasons. I planned to work while Josh was studying."

Here is Judy's account.

> Joshua started school in the beginning of June, and I started working, and within a very short time, I began to notice that there was a gap forming between us. He was coming home with these ideas about things that I'd never heard of—this new type of talk, these new things. I just couldn't relate to them. They didn't have any meaning to me, and the more he learned the wider the gap got until it got to a point where we would argue because he couldn't understand why I didn't feel or understand what he was saying and I couldn't understand why he wouldn't leave me alone, just let me be. And it got pretty bad for a while. This went on for about four months and I had a reaction of anti—. Whereas when I first came to Israel I was neutral or pro-religion, but not participating, now I became hostile. One morning I just woke up and decided that if I was going to save my marriage I'd better do something about it. So I decided I'd go learn, even though I didn't want to. I wasn't interested in it at all. But the alternative was for Joshua to stop learning, and I didn't want

to ask him to stop learning. I shopped around a little bit for a school. At that time, I was planning on working part-time and studying part-time. I eventually decided to go to Hartman's [the name of the school Brovender headed at that time; its name was later changed to Shappel].

I talked to Rabbi Brovender one night after a class I'd sat in on. And he said to me: "Listen, you know I was not going to advise you; I never tell anybody what they should do or what they shouldn't do. But after hearing your story I will advise you. You must quit your job and you must come to study full-time. You just don't have a choice in the matter." I thought about it over the weekend.

We talked about it, and eventually we decided that maybe it would be better if I did quit my job and start studying full-time.

Q. Did you find any of the mitzvot strange or hard to take when you started learning about them?

Judy. I didn't. I don't think I looked at them as being strange. I don't think I passed judgment on them at all.

Q. Did you find some more difficult to accept than others?

Judy. Well, it wasn't a matter of accepting them because I wasn't doing them. It didn't affect me personally because I wasn't prepared to start doing them. I was just watching everybody else doing them. I don't think I even thought about it much really.

Q. And during this time, Josh, were you already practicing?

Josh. Well, not everything, just testing. We were increasing, adding more and more and more; we didn't keep up for probably about three to four months after I was already learning. We went in steps, you know. First, we stopped turning on the lights to see what it felt like and—what did we do? Then we stopped driving on Shabbat, I think.

Judy. Driving? We hadn't driven all year anyway!

Josh. I think we really made the big change when a friend of ours offered us an opportunity to go to the beach on a Shabbat and we thought about should we go, should we not go. We decided not to go just to see if we could turn it down. We would have gone, but we didn't.

Q. That was the first big thing?

Josh. That was the first big thing. I guess from there it all went uphill. Stopped cooking on Shabbat and we stopped—

Q. Did you feel that same way?

Judy. It wasn't for me. It was for Josh, not for me.

Q. What was the turning point for you, then?

Judy. I don't know. I can't say because I had a lot of internal battles, and every step of the way I was fighting something. So I can't say what the turning point was. I can only tell you when the battle started getting easier.

Q. When would that be?
   Judy. About Chanukkah it started getting easier for me.
   Josh. Half a year already.
   Judy. Yeah, well I didn't start studying really full-time till October.

Nothing in Judy's story of her change of heart deals with a personal attachment to Orthodox Judaism. Instead, her change was motivated by her attachment to Josh and her concern to preserve her marriage. The factor producing this change in her was what Kelman (1961) has called the social anchor. And if Josh reverted to his former practice at this stage, Judy probably would not have found it hard to give up her new religious commitment.

A briefer story is told by Shmullie of his and his wife's change. Both Shmullie and his wife had been raised in Orthodox homes. Both had attended yeshiva schools through high school. Both had come from families that were strong in the practice of Orthodoxy. Both had come to Israel for a year of study at the university, and there both had stopped the practice of Orthodoxy, violating Sabbath and kashrut laws. They met at the university in 1969 and began living together. Within a few months they decided to get married and live together in the manner of Orthodox Jews.

> At the end of the year, my wife and I decided we were going to be religious people. We went to get married and to become religious. I had come to Israel when I was seventeen. Just a little while after my nineteenth birthday we were married. My wife is a year older.
>
> I wasn't like one of these kids rebelling against the rabbis. I respect them. But I just couldn't see it. Now I said, "What the heck. There's something in it. What have they got? I've got to check it out." And I did. I remember going to my girlfriend, who later became my wife, and saying to her, "Look, I'm going to go try and be religious." My wife is the one who taught me to read the Rashi in the Chumash. She was a top student. She had studied in Central High School in Manhattan [the girls high school of Yeshiva University]. She always knew the Rashi, and she spoke wonderful Hebrew.

Q. How about your wife? When you started to change, did she immediately agree with you and go along with you?
A. No, not necessarily. But we discussed everything, and by the time we were going to get married we knew what we wanted.
Q. Was she willing to celebrate Shabbos with you?
A. She came to help me out. We spoke about it. But I won't say how fast she decided to do it. She moved at her own pace.

Q. What were the key stages for you, the first thing you did?

A. I put on tzitzit and a kippah.

Q. What were the key stages for her?

A. She agreed not to smoke on Shabbos. . . . For both of us, we stopped touching each other.[12]

   To learn more I spoke to anybody who had a kippah on. Well, most people with kippahs also don't know what they're doing, you know. . . . I'd discuss with my wife everything which she knew, which she remembered. We came to the point where we agreed to keep kosher. By this time we're married, keeping kosher and *niddah* the best we know. Really, you want to see a hysterical picture, my wife coming to university in slacks and with her hair covered.

For Shmullie, covering the hair for religious purposes is utterly incongruous with wearing slacks. Further along in his change when Shmullie decided to devote himself fully to studying Torah, he asked his wife to "back him up on the deal," and she agreed. "And I'll never forget that." In Shmullie's account, then, he led, and his wife followed. The account might be suspected of male chauvinism were it not for the fact that not simply religious practice but expert knowledge is the basis for status in the Orthodox community, and Shmullie was willing to credit his wife with far more knowledge and study skill than he had.

Q. You mentioned that it was about a year before you could read the *Mishnah Berurah* [a widely used authoritative code on Laws of Holidays and prayers, at that time available only in Hebrew] yourself?

A. Oh, it was terrible. By the end of that year I could barely read through things. We had a one-room apartment. And I used to sit all Shabbos long. My wife would be trying to rest a little bit on Shabbos, and I'd be yelling out across the room, "What's this thing, what's that, what's this mean, what's that mean, what you do about that?"

For Marvin and Shannie the prime mover in the change was even clearer. Marvin had already started his transition when he returned to California for a visit. He met Shannie, who had gone to Hebrew school for two years—for a year when she was eight and for another year when she was fourteen, so she could be confirmed. Her parents were affiliated with a Reform temple, had strong feelings of Jewish identity, but observed few practices. They attended the synagogue primarily on the High Holi-

---

12. They began observing the laws of *niddah,* which forbid sexual relations between husband and wife during the period of her menses and for a week following.

days and even then only sporadically. Shannie herself was totally unin-
volved in Judaism, Reform or otherwise, by the time she was twenty.
Marvin reported:

> I talked to her, and we became much closer. We talked constantly. She
> was very interested and wanted to start learning about Yiddishkeit. So I was
> giving her books and she was learning Hebrew, and that's it. . . . I went
> back to Israel in February, eight months later, and I kept writing to her. She
> went back to school and was getting involved in school. I kept writing to
> her, telling her, "Remember what we learned, remember what we learned."
> I got her so she was a little bit involved with some rabbis in the Berkeley
> Chabad [Lubavitcher chasidic organization].

Shannie came to Israel in April. She and Marvin married in May and
moved to the Givat Ada campus of Ohr Someyach, a residential campus
for older students near Haifa. By July 1976, fourteen months later, Shannie wore long-sleeved dresses, covered her hair, was expecting a child in
four months, and was perfectly content to be an Orthodox Jewish wife.
From her account the major factor inducing her to become an Orthodox
Jew was clearly her tie to Marvin. Once the social anchorage to that value
system had developed, reasonable justifications for that choice could be
found.

SIBLINGS, PARENTS, AND CHILDREN

Siblings also persuade each other to become religious. Typically, older
siblings influence younger ones. Usually such siblings have strong bonds
of affection, with the younger one dependent on the older for affection.
When the older one changes to the Orthodox life-style, this tends to
drive a wedge between the two. They cannot share food, leisure, and
other aspects of life easily. Both reach out to close that gap, the older
one trying to teach the younger and the younger willing to examine the
prospect of becoming Orthodox as a means of saving this important
social relationship.

A similar pattern characterizes the few cases in which young parents
decide to accept Orthodoxy. If the children are seven or eight or younger
by the time the parents have completed the transition, they follow along
without much resistance. If they are adolescent before the change in the
parents begins, typically they resist the change. In contrast, if the children
change first, usually their parents do not. In fact, some of the outstanding
personalities in the ba'al t'shuva movement have parents who were and
remain thoroughly resistant to Orthodoxy for themselves, although willing to accommodate their children and even proud of them.

In some cases the parents do change in the direction of their children, becoming Orthodox themselves. Impressionistic data suggest that this occurs most often when the parents were brought up in Orthodox homes and broke away from religion. In this case the return to Orthodoxy connects them not only to their children but to their parents, or to the memory of their parents, as well.

MEMORIES AS SOCIAL TIES: DECEASED PARENTS AND GRANDPARENTS

Religious actions may be performed in response to external pressure. Those who are already tied to religious communities know that attempts to dissociate themselves from the obligations of their religion may result in such social costs as ostracism or even physical punishment. At moments when their inner commitment flags, external social pressures keep them on the straight and narrow. Such behavior is termed "compliance" by Kelman (1961).

At times, the tie to others may be the factor that sustains the religious behavior. Behavior is undertaken not to gain renumerative or other rewards or to avoid sanctions but to gain or preserve the love and approval of others. Kelman calls this "behavior based on social anchors." The cases we have described of siblings or lovers becoming Orthodox are examples of that.

A third type of behavior occurs when a person has developed a normative commitment, when internalization of values leads the person to act without regard for the cost. Here the action occurs because of what Kelman terms a normative commitment.

My data suggests another basis for action—emotional attachment to someone who has died and thus can no longer provide the reward of affection and love except in one's own mind. That attachment to a deceased parent can be an important motive for attaching oneself to Judaism is illustrated by the following account.

Daniel was a young man whose parents were not religious and who had been given no religious education. His father was and continues to be strongly Zionistic. Dan attended a local college and began to date a non-Jewish girl. His mother objected strongly, but Daniel refused to give up his girlfriend.

A. You see, before I got interested in Judaism, I was involved with this Italian girl. My mother was pretty upset about it, to say the least. Every morning, every day, my mother—I would come home from school and she was sick about it, and she'd say, "Why don't you just take a gun and shoot me and get it over with, because you're killing me little by little?" and she was serious; she meant it. . . . I wasn't religious; I didn't care so much. Big deal, why was it so important that I have a Jewish girlfriend? But to her, this was the most important thing.

Q. Was your mother religious?

A. No. Neither my mother nor my father was religious. My mother was orphaned when she was just a little one, and she was bounced around a lot. She didn't get a Jewish education. I didn't want to hurt my mother and make her sick or anything. But the way she carried on, she didn't know what to do. I'd bring the girl home, and she was afraid if she didn't say hello then I'd run off and get married. If she rejected her completely, then I'd rebel, she thought. So she would say hello, and she'd say goodbye, and she didn't have anything else to do with her. With the Jewish girlfriends I used to bring home, oh, my mother would yak with them, and they'd shmooz, and they'd have coffee. Not with this one. She played it pretty good, I think. I didn't go off the deep end out of anger. But finally, one day, she said she read about this Rebbitzin [who] had just started this organization, Hineni, and she was speaking at the Jewish Center nearby, and she said, "I want you to come with me to hear the Rebbitzin." I said, "What's a Rebbitzin?" I didn't know. And once I heard that she was Jewish and religious, I said, "I'm not going. I'm not interested." She carried on! Like, she just nagged. I said finally, "All right, I'll go, but I'm sitting near the back because if I don't like it I'm leaving." So I went with my mother to the Rebbitzin. I see this woman get up, and she spoke about intermarriage. Right away, . . . I felt touched by the whole thing. And that week, I broke off with the girl.

Then I had the good fortune—maybe Hashem was helping out—because I met, I think that week, . . . I met a very nice girl—Jewish and shomer Shabbos [Sabbath observing] and kosher. I didn't start becoming religious or observant, I just had a Jewish girlfriend. But it just worked out nice. We went out, and in no time we were very close and in love. So that's what happened, that reinforced it. She didn't object that I wasn't observant, even though she was. She was from Solomon Schechter Day School, Conservative. That's how I got started becoming religious. Some can do it in a day, but I approached it in stages. I started observing Shabbos and not eating treyf [nonkosher food]. . . . Then I met some friends who were also becoming religious at that time. After a while, I decided to spend a summer in a yeshiva in Israel. The point I reached at the yeshiva was, well, I wish I could live this religious life. I think it would be beautiful; I'm going to do it. I said I was going to do it, but I only did certain things. I didn't really have enough. . . . I was only there three months. I didn't know how to daven, I didn't know what *Shemoneh Esreh* [the core of the prayer service] was. I had to learn. That's what I was concentrating on. Then I came to a higher level, I guess when my mother passed away, several months ago. I think that was like a religious experience for me in a lot of ways. So . . . at that point, I found it easier to do more of the mitzvahs and observances—the tzitzit and things like that.[13]

How They Changed

COMPLEX ACCOUNTS

In most accounts the motives and stages of change are not so clear cut to the returnee. Many people find it difficult to explain why they changed. They find it easier to address the question of how they changed; steps and stages, persons and organizations are the critical elements of their account. Typically, these people describe growing up in a traditional but non-Orthodox home but with a beloved grandparent who practiced Orthodoxy. Sometimes living in a community heavily populated by Jews provided the initial ties. The ties might be to some of the older people in the community or to peers. A boy might describe preparing for his bar mitzvah. A girl might develop an attachment to an Orthodox friend.

Somewhere in early adolescence or childhood these ties were broken. The grandparent died, and the family discontinued its religious celebrations or moved out of the Jewish area. For some years practice lapsed. The earlier styles of life faded. New interests were pursued. After a few years, a sense of isolation from one's earlier self seemed to impel one to begin an intellectual search to find and perhaps reexperience some of the feelings and emotions evoked in childhood.

The road back does not remain a solitary one, however. The intellectual pursuits soon are coupled with an interest in being actively Jewish, which at first often means joining Jewish groups, perhaps Zionist or Jewish cultural groups. This is facilitated by being on a college campus with a large Jewish student body so that heavy involvement in Jewish activities is possible.

A variation on this theme is the account of those who pursued Jewishness less actively in the years between their childhood and college but found that a course in world religion or in Jewish studies provided an opening to the Jewish world. Before the establishment of such programs in the early 1970s learning about Judaism while on campus was only

13. A similarly clear-cut statement of the effect of the death of parents on religious behavior can be found in Paul Cowan's (1981) description of his growing interest in Judaism. Cowan's return to Judaism appears to have started when he learned that his father and mother had died.

possible through the campus chaplain's office. But some students assiduously avoided religious activities. For them, the possibility of having a purely academic experience of Judaism made it acceptable. But having stepped into the Jewish world, they made friends and pursued Jewish political and cultural activities.

The next step in this process is typically meeting an Orthodox person who becomes a source of information about Judaism. The person may be friend, confidant, and teacher for some time. Several of those interviewed mentioned that they had become friendly with a Lubavitcher chasid. Usually the interaction was not confined to religion but encompassed such other pursuits as playing chess, "shooting the breeze," and the like. The Lubavitch might then provide tefillin or wine for Shabbat. Finally, once he had begun to practice in some small area, the returnee might seek to learn more about Judaism in a yeshiva or some formal program.

Ari, a student at Shappel College for Men, told this story:

> My home town is Kansas City. I came to Israel to study at an *ulpan* [an intensive Hebrew language school]. I had just graduated college with a major in Jewish studies, and I wanted to learn Hebrew. A friend invited me to Shappel's for Purim. Because most of the people at the ulpan were in their forties, I jumped at the chance to get out and meet people of my own age. I really had no intention of coming to Shappel's. I came here several times for Shabbat after that and for *Shavuot*. Then, the next thing I knew, I was coming here for a year.
>
> Q. Is your family religious?
> A. My grandparents were Orthodox, and I spent a lot of time with them when I was younger. My parents were traditionally oriented, and we had a kosher home, but we didn't keep Shabbat, except for Kiddush Friday night. It was what you would call a generally traditional Conservative Jewish home. We were affiliated with the Conservative shul and I had the same kind of Hebrew school education as most people. I attended school two nights a week until I was fifteen or sixteen years old.
> Q. Was your own practice traditional when you were on your own in college?
> A. I observed Rosh Ha-Shana and Yom Kippur. I kept kosher. But I didn't do much of anything else.
> Q. You say your grandparents were religious. Did they live with you?
> A. No, they lived by themselves. But from the time I was five until I was 14, I must have spent every Shabbat there. Slept in the same bed with my grandfather every Friday night.
> Q. What about your brother and sister?
> A. My brother is six years younger and is potentially very religious. He's very

much interested in what it has to offer. My older sister is traditional like my parents.

Q. Did she suggest you go to Israel?

A. No, my professor at university suggested that. He thought it would be useful if I went on to do graduate work.

Q. Was the professor religious?

A. Yes. He was head of the Judaic Studies Department, and I was the first graduate of the department. He did have a personal interest in me. I used to visit him in his home frequently.

Q. Was he Orthodox?

A. He was affiliated with the Conservative movement, but as far as individual practice was concerned, he was very Orthodox. My grandfather had been associated with the Orthodox shul, and we were doubly affiliated, with the Conservative and Orthodox shuls. I liked the Orthodox shul better. I used to daven at the amud [pray at the lecturn; that is, lead the prayers]. In that framework, I knew a lot. I learned the last two lines of every prayer so I could read it aloud and lead the prayers.[14]

I was fourteen when my grandfather died, and from that time on my practice began to wane. I was heavily influenced by the youth culture at that time. It was a time of searching out exactly what you were, and a time for reevaluating and introspection. So at that time I heard about Zalman Schechter [Sholomo Carlebach's friend], and I went to Winnipeg and stayed with him for a couple of weeks.

It was a kind of reawakened Jewish consciousness, but it wasn't accompanied by any real observance. My observance began in Israel. At the outset, I was less observant here than in Kansas City. In my last year in the Judaic Studies Program in Kansas City I used to go to the Conservative shul with my mother every Friday night and Saturday (my father worked). I didn't go shopping, I didn't go out, I didn't go running around, I didn't drive. But I didn't find any community there, nor in ulpan. I finally found it when I came to Brovender's yeshiva.

At first I was interested in how Gemara worked, in learning how to learn. That was why Shappel's was so appealing.

The total development of the Jew was not so strongly stressed, that was supposed to come from the learning. For me it did. . . . After I began to learn, I became totally infatuated with learning. It's like nothing that has ever happened to you in your life. It's an accomplishment that is truly Divine. After that I became slowly immersed in Jewish life. And when I looked back, I couldn't identify with the person I was five months before.

14. In Orthodox prayer services the members of the congregation quietly read the prayers. The leader, who is also supposed to read each prayer quietly, reads the last two lines of each prayer aloud, thus signaling the congregation to proceed to the next prayer.

Ari does not use a motive to account for his change. He has not rejected the world. He gains the esteem and the love of no individual by becoming Orthodox. The memory of a loving grandfather does play a role here, but despite this memory Ari slipped away from these practices as a teenager, and by his account, were it not for the dominant values of the late 1960s and early 1970s that urged people to be their authentic selves, he might never have sought out his spiritual roots.

Another complex account is that of a student whose mentor, a professor of world religions who was not Jewish, suggested that he further explore Judaism. Still another attended a Conservative synagogue in a heavily Jewish community in New Jersey. His parents moved to a small town with no Jewish community soon after his bar mitzvah. He renewed his association with Jews and Jewish culture when he attended New York University, joining the Jewish Culture Foundation, becoming an active leader, visiting Israel several times, and finally deciding to study in Israel for a year; in the process he underwent a change and, after attending Pardess Institute, became Orthodox.

Complex accounts are probably characteristic of most ba'alei t'shuva. Their transitions are usually slow, taking place over the space of years rather than months; they come to the yeshiva long after they have developed an active interest in and commitment to Judaism. For the most part these people attempt to maintain their ties to family, although the changes required by Orthodox Judaism invariably place some strains on their relations to family. Most of them live as modernistic Orthodox Jews.

COMMITMENT UNCHANGED

The process of change described below occurred with only one student interviewed. Nevertheless, it so clearly illustrates a major characteristic of Judaism in contrast to Christianity that it is useful to report it in some detail.

Hank's grandparents were born in America. By the standards of the small midwestern community in which they lived, he and his family were observant Jews. They worshipped in a traditional Conservative synagogue. On Friday night they would "light candles and say Kiddush over wine which may or may not have been kosher." In this community, Hank had a reputation as a very involved religious boy.

> On the one hand, this self-image kept me involved with Judaism. On the other hand, it led to great conflicts for me later on, when I realized all of a sudden during my college years and after coming to Israel that perhaps I was

not living the complete Jewish life. I was under the impression that it was almost the way one can choose to be a Democrat or a Republican, one can choose to be or not to be an Orthodox Jew. . . .

My father was active in every temple board, on all the committees. He encouraged me to be active in the synagogue, the B'nai B'rith youth. And when I was on campus I was active in Hillel [Jewish student organization].

Q. What was your religious education?

A. I studied two afternoons a week for an hour and a half starting at about eight until bar mitzvah. It was a class of one. I was the only student. After I graduated from college, I came to Israel and spent five months at an ulpan in Arad, where I learned Hebrew and Judaism. I heard about Arad while working with the U.J.A. [United Jewish Appeal] at the university. After I left Arad I worked for a year in Tel Aviv. I heard about the yeshivot. At this point it was time to change my situation in one way or another, I felt. Going to one of these yeshivot was one way.

While in Tel Aviv I was as observant as I knew how to be. I was shomer [observant of] Shabbat and kashrut, I built my own sukkah, and so on. It's been a long, continuous process. I remember first—I'm not even sure what prompted me—but I decided to start putting on tefillin daily.

Q. How long ago was that?

A. That was the year I graduated college. My Shabbat changed slowly. I was taking halakhah as a guide but not as an authority. In my last year at college I went to weekly Hillel minyan, which happened to be run by halakhic standards. I met people there who were shomer mitzvot [observant of the commandments]; they were the first people I met who were shomer mitzvot. I got to know some. It's one thing to read about what an Orthodox Jew does or to hear about it and another thing to know personally a person who does these things. I went to their homes occasionally. There were two couples and a few single people. I learned a lot from one fellow on the basis of a weekly ping-pong game we had. We played ping-pong, but all the time that we played, I was asking him question after question about Jewish life.

Q. Was there any point at which you felt that you had taken a real step, that some perceptible change had occurred in you? For example, when you put on tefillin?

A. No. There were a lot of little steps, but there was no *one* big step. And it never felt like a commitment. It always felt like an experiment, although a long-term experiment. And this I guess is the issue to this day: Is what I am doing a long-term experiment or a commitment?

Hank's struggle illustrates a point often missed by observers of Judaism. Many assume that those who are most observant of religious rituals, whose lives are most distinct from those of the rest of society, whose clothes mark them off most sharply from others, are also the most deeply committed to Judaism. What is missed is the possibility that this practice may be no more than social custom, a way of life adopted because others in the community approve of it and to abandon it would incur great social costs in love, approval, and esteem. Hank's story illustrates that one may be intensely committed to Judaism without the ritual practice.

At no point did Hank undergo a change in commitment to Judaism. He was intensely committed from the outset. His childhood afternoons spent in solitary classes with the rabbi required a great deal of commitment, but as he got older and left home he realized that other actions were required. And each time he met the challenge, at least in his own view, by fuller participation, moving from Jewish organizational involvement to observance of kashrut and Shabbat and finally coming to Israel. But that was not enough. For in Israel he discovered the Judaism of Meah Shearim. This seemed too much to bear. He could no longer let his feelings dictate how far he must go to prove himself a loyal Jew. He had to find some objective yardstick that could tell him what was authentic Judaism. He sought some authoritative basis for Jewish practice, and at that point he entered Pardess. For him the chasidic Meah Shearim Judaism was unacceptable. And perhaps Orthodox Judaism was also unacceptable. But he needed to find out whether he could draw some authoritative line and, if he could, whether he could live with it.

In other words, a gap existed between Hank's definition of himself as a very committed Jew, one who did whatever was necessary, and what he found in Israel as the life-style of committed Jews. Unaware that the ritual actions might not be so difficult for those who were brought up in that community, he measured himself by their standards and found himself wanting. Perhaps this prompted one of his teachers to refer to him as a "super Jew" who needed to assert his willingness to go as far as anyone.

Hank's story highlights a point embedded in other accounts. It may be seen just below the surface in Ari's account as well, particularly where Ari describes his feelings of isolation in the practice of Shabbat. For those ba'alei t'shuva coming from areas where there are few Orthodox Jews, their religious practice, however incomplete in the view of the Orthodox, may represent an intense level of commitment to Judaism. The commitment of these people does not change as they move to Israel or enter a yeshiva, but rather their practice changes. Of course, this practice has profound impact on their social relations, even with close friends and family. But because theirs is not a changed commitment but a reaffirmation of values taught by the family, the ba'al t'shuva and the family make heroic efforts to bridge the gap created by the new religious practices.

Such ba'alei t'shuva attempt to remain as moderate as possible in their practice so as to minimize the distance from the family. The family often accommodates to the ba'al t'shuva, recognizing that this change represents a continuation of an existing commitment.15

There is no one motive for becoming a ba'al t'shuva and no one pathway to take. But motives for becoming Orthodox fall within a range of the acceptable, and that range tells us something about the nature of Orthodox Judaism.

The accounts avoid miracles in explaining what motivated a return. Returnees seek values, meaning in life, God, truth, and even family and community. Yet some distinctive patterns were found. Americans apparently seek to maintain or deepen ties to their people and seem concerned not to break a link in the chain and cut themselves and their future progeny off from parents and grandparents. Their sense of attachment seems stirred by the threat of loss of attachment, by siblings who intermarry, parents who divorce or die. Israelis are less concerned with ethnic identity and more concerned with finding the meaning of life, turning away from hedonism, and seeking a new personal identity. Women more often express an interest in establishing family ties and seem to be seeking traditional roles. Men seem more often to be seeking adventure and challenge. Expressing these goals affects one's own thinking about how to live and what to become and thus has an impact on the returnee.

15. For example, when Ari's sister married a non-Jew who was willing to convert to Judaism she asked him what sort of conversion he would accept. He told her "Orthodox," and that is the conversion they sought.

Chapter 11

Wrestling with Judaism: Community Boundaries

Entering the world of Orthodox Judaism through the portal of yeshivot is a very different experience from entering it through marriage or through synagogue outreach. In marriage one has a loved one as guide. The experience is softened and transmuted. Synagogues attempt to build bridges to the mainstream of American life so that the first steps into Orthodoxy are often no more than joining a group of friends in a basketball game or at a synagogue dance. As these recruits step into Orthodoxy, the familiar is emphasized. They have the opportunity to develop close ties to friends before being challenged to accept new norms and values.

The yeshiva portal is different. Here the religious challenge is emphasized from the outset and remains the central concern. This is not to say that this transition to Orthodoxy is not eased by the development of social ties. On the contrary, the development of these ties is crucial in determining whether transition has been made successfully. But the religious element holds center stage; social and community ties are incidental.

The new outreach programs developed since the late 1960s by yeshivot for ba'alei t'shuva (and some synagogues) directly challenge the potential recruit to accept these practices even before developing new social relations. With the religious challenge so explicit, what do potential recruits find most difficult or repugnant? What do they find most attractive?

Kashrut

To eat kosher food means to eat only those foods permitted by halakhah (see chap. 2). The complex rules of kashrut impose a discipline on the

Orthodox that in the past was felt primarily in the home. In modern mobile society, keeping a kosher home is the lesser problem. *Where* one may eat is the major difficulty. Travel is restricted by the need for kosher food. Business and professional relationships usually involve socializing and sharing food. The requirements of kashrut thus place a heavy burden on the committed Orthodox in business and in recreational activities. Conservative and less committed Orthodox Jews often follow the practice of maintaining kashrut in the home but abandoning it when eating outside the home.

The sense that one is entering a world where such restrictions apply is captured by one ba'al t'shuva:

> I had been to yeshiva before and knew what eating kosher was. The night before I was supposed to go into yeshiva a group of friends and I went down to MacDonalds to have cheeseburgers and shakes. We really stuffed ourselves on it, really ate like pigs. We all knew this was going to be the last time I would eat it, and I wanted just one more fling. To tell you the truth, I don't have any problems eating kosher here in Israel, but I still would like a nice cheeseburger. I wish it could be kosher.

For this ba'al t'shuva, living in Israel and studying at a yeshiva, the challenge of kashrut is simply appetitive; he'd like to savor the taste of some foods again. But his new commitment means that these delights must be forsworn. Kashrut for this man posed few social problems. He ate with his fellow students at the school, and there he did not need to trouble himself about kashrut. Eating out in Jerusalem also presented few difficulties; kosher food is available virtually everywhere, from kiosks to elegant restaurants. One has to seek out nonkosher restaurants in Jerusalem. The kosher home presented some problems, but none were insurmountable. Two sets of dishes and pots are needed, and meat and dairy dishes and products must be kept separate. This requires additional shelf space and alertness to avoid mixing the two or even washing them together, as well as the exercise of some care in the supermarket because imports and a few locally packed products are questionable. But the practice does not put one in a social bind. On the contrary, when one's fellow students, friends, and neighbors keep kosher, it becomes necessary to keep kosher in order to maintain one's social circle. The yeshivot have overcome the hurdle of kashrut by providing kosher food and their location in Jerusalem eases the problem of eating out.

A very different assessment of the obstacles to keeping kosher emerges when discussing them with students who return home to America after their stay in school or for those who never enter a yeshiva but make the transition while living with their parents. Keeping the laws of kashrut then becomes a major source of tension, particularly with parents but with other siblings as well. "It's very difficult. When I went home I had a shelf in the refrigerator. I keep some pots and dishes at home, and I use them whenever I'm there. I kasher one burner of the stove, and my mother doesn't use it, so I can cook kosher food. But my father eats my stuff sometimes, even though I can't eat theirs, and in general he's annoyed at my keeping kosher."

Another respondent reported: "It's always a fight. They don't like me to keep kosher. You know how it is a Jewish mother likes to feed her son. But it's not really kosher. My mother says it is, but it really isn't. So I don't eat her food, and she is really angry."

Adjustments are sometimes made in the long run. "For a while it was awful. But then we worked it out. My parents kashered the house and keep two sets of dishes. They have become somewhat committed, but not fully. The house is kosher, but they still eat out almost anywhere. They don't eat pork or shellfish, but they don't follow the rules of kashrut."

An almost equally knotty problem is encountered with other relatives.

> I don't have much family, and I've always been very close to my two cousins. We'd go to their house for holidays, or they would come to mine. My mother was partly religious—traditional, really. I became Orthodox as a young man, and over the years we've become stricter about observance. My wife and I are pretty careful about kashrut now. I still want to be close to my cousins, but it's become much harder. They came to my house last year for Thanksgiving, and this year Louise wants to reciprocate and have it at her house. But what should I tell her? If I say I can't go she'll be hurt and never come to us again. She suggested that we could prepare the food at her house, but that's almost impossible. I'd have to bring my own dishes and pots and then kasher her stove. She says she'll do whatever I'd like, but she doesn't realize how difficult it would be and she is sure to resent it. I don't know what to do.

Sometimes, the parents too become returnees, brought to religion by their child's observance. This relieves the strain for the ba'al t'shuva and may strengthen family bonds.

Interestingly, eating at kosher restaurants has unique advantages for the ba'al t'shuva. At least at a kosher restaurant one is not eating from one shelf in the refrigerator on paper plates or eating cold food because the stove has not been kashered. At a kosher restaurant one can eat "like everyone else," have dinner with friends, whether or not they keep kosher, and meet other people who are Orthodox. In a way, the restrictions on eating out provide an advantage for the ba'al t'shuva that are less useful for those who have been Orthodox from birth. They provide an opportunity to socialize with the Orthodox, to enter their intimate world. This advantage seems to mitigate the ba'al t'shuva's feeling of restriction.

KASHRUT AND PARENTS

We have already discussed the rigor with which rabbis may kasher a kitchen in preparation for its use by the newly Orthodox. Interestingly, these same standards are not applied in advising the newly Orthodox about procedures to be followed when returning to their parents' home. Most synagogues and yeshivot advise returnees to use as lenient a standard as possible. Yet even minimal kashrut standards may be too burdensome for some parents, and they may believe that the child is demanding the strictest rules at the behest of an uncompromising rabbi. Sometimes children do use religion as a club in a broader conflict with parents, who are held to strictest standards. And at times strict interpretation of the law *is* demanded by the rabbi or the yeshiva. But in general the normative requirements of kashrut must be weighed against the requirement to love and obey parents. Thus, conflicts involving the strictest interpretation of the laws of kashrut most often develop because of parent-child friction rather than as a result of the teachings of rabbis or yeshivot.

The more traditionalistic and sectarian yeshivot probably hold to more rigorous rules for ba'alei t'shuva to follow in their parents' home and thus engender more conflict with parents. But one should not assume that the more modernistic yeshivot therefore press the ba'al t'shuva to compromise.

At a number of yeshivot I asked how the ba'al t'shuva is advised to deal with kashrut when returning to his parents' home. All the answers were couched in terms of what sorts of compromises the ba'al t'shuva is advised to make: paper plates, precooked kosher meals, cold foods, or advice on how to kasher a part of the kitchen.

Yet Rabbi Morris Besdin, Dean of the James Striar School at Yeshiva University, turned this around.

> You know, he said, I learned how kashrut should be treated when I served as a chaplain in the U.S. Army during World War II. My colleagues were Protestant ministers and Catholic priests. One of the priests, a friend of mine, was particularly adamant that we Jews be able to follow our observances.
>
> You know what I say to that parent? I ask them, if you were to have a Catholic priest to dinner on Friday and he indicated that he did not wish to eat meat for religious reasons, would you insist that he eat meat? You wouldn't, because you would want to show tolerance for the other person's beliefs. You would show respect. It is the American way.
>
> Why shouldn't you treat your son or daughter the same way? Shouldn't

you show them the same respect too? It's the American way. Should Judaism be treated less respectfully than other religions?

This aggressive defense of the ba'al t'shuva's requirement for kashrut by a modernistic yeshiva is based on American values, not on an appeal to Jewish values. Traditionalistic yeshivot have also come to learn the usefulness of this sort of appeal and now apply it widely. Nevertheless, even the aggressive style of argument is tempered by leniency in interpreting the laws of kashrut when dealing with parents.

Shabbat and Holy Days

The Shabbat is the showpiece in the recruitment of ba'alei t'shuva. Neither prayer nor the synagogue nor kosher food is offered as a means of understanding Judaism but the Sabbath. At first, the Shabbat may be no more than an adventure, an experience in going native. As such it can be exciting. In a sense, at the outset it strikes the newcomer as something akin to the holidays, which are also an adventure.

While Shabbat and holidays are a discipline requiring abstention from work, from shopping, and from the bulk of leisure and sports activities, for the Orthodox they are also a journey back to another time and place—to foods familiar since childhood, to songs they may have sung with their siblings, parents, and grandparents, some of whom may be long gone, but recollected in these celebrations.

The foods, the dress, the preparation for a sumptuous and possibly elegant meal give the Sabbath and holidays a special character in the home. Synagogue services are not simply devotional experiences. Friends meet and chat about local news and national and international issues. Young men and women meet. The synagogue is a friendly and social experience in addition to being a place of devotion.

If one lives in an Orthodox community, Sabbath and holidays may be enhanced by visits to friends for a dinner, tea, or for a Kiddush (a light meal of Shabbat specialties following morning prayers). There are also play groups for children, study groups, and informal gatherings.

From inside Orthodoxy, kashrut is often perceived as a discipline, perhaps an ennobling and holy or healthful discipline, but a discipline nonetheless. Sabbath and holidays also have restrictive aspects that make them disciplines in part. But if they are celebrated among a community of Orthodox, they have a unique and exciting character. Without substantial family and community support, Shabbat can come to be felt as a discipline, perhaps more restrictive than kashrut. The very regularity of

Shabbat makes the restrictions oppressive. Shabbat interferes with business activities more seriously than kashrut. Because the Sabbath starts at a
few minutes past 4:00 P.M. in the short winter days, Orthodox Jews must
often leave their jobs an hour or more before 4:00 to allow time for travel
and are often limited in the types of jobs they can hold. In some cases,
unless one has worked out some special arrangement, holding a job becomes difficult.

To a far greater degree than kashrut, Sabbath cuts one off from the
mainstream of American life. Can one give up half of one's weekends for
life to keep the Sabbath? And what does one do on the Sabbath? No ball
playing. No television. No movies. No beach. It can be a repressive,
boring time. The holidays at least have their special celebrations, their
special rituals. But what does one do week after week on the Sabbath?
Little activity beyond praying and eating and sleeping seems possible.
Problems in interaction arise as well; one loses friends and alienates
relatives by this observance of Shabbat. But one also faces a much more
serious internal struggle. In one's own home, in a yeshiva, or in an area
where kosher food is readily available, the discipline of kashrut is not felt
as heavily as the Sabbath. But even in one's own home, where all preparations have been made for the Sabbath, the day can be a stifling, oppressive
yoke if one has not built the relationships and the cultural tastes to enjoy
it.

Those living where there are few other Jews to provide the community
essential for the enjoyment of Shabbat find it difficult to maintain. Just
how difficult can be seen from the number of Jews who attempt to keep
kashrut in the home even while abandoning most aspects of Shabbat
observance.

How does the ba'al t'shuva get past the point where Shabbat is a
restriction to the point where it can be experienced as joy? The answer is
slowly, with slow acceptance of restrictions and simultaneous building of
new pleasures.

One ba'al t'shuva described his ordeal when he was first becoming a
Shabbat observer. "I was at Kfar Chabad that Shabbat. It was some time
after I had decided that I was going to try to be Orthodox. And in the
middle of the afternoon I just had to have a cigarette. I snuck my cigarettes
and matches out of my room, walked into the field behind the bushes and
tall grass, and smoked a cigarette. If anyone had found me there that day
and raised any fuss about it, I would have quit the whole thing right then
and there and never come back."

A teacher described how he got one Russian couple to observe some of
the Shabbat commandments. "The hardest thing for them seemed to be

not to turn on the lights on Shabbat. So at the beginning I suggested that they simply not use one switch at all, although they could turn on any other lights they needed and slowly they got used to the idea of not turning on lights on Shabbat."

Paul Cowan (1981) describes a critical moment in his commitment at the point when on a Saturday afternoon he felt a need to write some notes for a project he was working on but made the decision not to write until after Shabbat. He looked back on that moment as the beginning of his acceptance of Shabbat. Cowan later became a Conservative Jew.

While an act of sacrifice can engender commitment, if the sacrifice becomes too burdensome the entire commitment is jeopardized. A network of social relations must be established. Without it, even after a commitment is made, each Shabbat becomes trying and difficult. Without family to join in the celebration of Shabbat, observance of Shabbat becomes an experience in restriction, isolation, and loneliness that is hard to bear. Furthermore, when one's family is not Orthodox, each Shabbat becomes a struggle to retain some symbols of Shabbat observance in the face of what often appears to be hostile or provocative behavior by other family members. One leaves a light on in the living room so that one can read on the Sabbath, only to find that someone else has forgotten and switched the light off—and halakhah forbids asking anyone to turn it on again. One leaves one's food on a burner so that it will keep warm for Sabbath, only to find that someone else has eaten it, removed it from the stove, or turned off the flame under it. The television set blares in the living room, the phone rings and is answered, and all the while one tries to capture the sense of calm and serenity that is seen in homes where Shabbat is celebrated.

Living alone eliminates some difficulties, but also many of the rewards. With whom shall one sing the Sabbath zemirot, share the challah or the Kiddush wine, discuss the Torah portion of the week, or simply pass the time in pleasant conversation? To enjoy the Shabbat one needs family with whom one can share the day.

One must learn how to enjoy Shabbat, and this takes some experience. One ba'al t'shuva, a young man from a Conservative home, when asked what he liked best about Shabbat replied, "The preparation on Friday afternoon. I love the hustle and bustle, the cooking and smells of Shabbat. But the day itself is often a drag. I don't know what to do with myself. Even if some friends come over, we have trouble learning something new together. We just don't have the skills. So we sit around and it gets boring."

The rabbis in the yeshivot do not see Shabbat as a major problem. Even during the week there are no television sets in the yeshivot, nor any coming and going to the movies or plays or other entertainment. Students are expected to study all day and into the evening hours. Apart from such essentials as eating and sleeping there are no extracurricular activities—no clubs, no organized sports, no political activity. Those who accept this rigorous program all week long may find the Shabbat, with its change of pace, its afternoon nap, its zemirot, and its more elaborate menu, a welcome change.

But probably most important in making this adjustment tolerable is the tendency to view the Shabbat as an experiment that one may decide to abandon. If one does not feel bound to it by external constraints, one may leave the yeshiva, perhaps temporarily, and abandon the practice of Shabbat. Often a student leaves the yeshiva after several months and takes up life again as before, only to return to yeshiva or begin following Orthodox practices again, perhaps more slowly this time.

That yeshivot often arrange for students to take their Shabbat meals with some Orthodox family suggests the powerful connection between the celebration of Shabbat and family life—a connection so powerful that even in yeshivot experiencing the Shabbat fully outside the context of family and community is difficult.

HOLY DAYS AND FAMILY

To a large extent, holidays have the same character as Shabbat. Their celebration, too, is strongly rooted in the family. There are somewhat fewer restrictions on most holidays than on Shabbat. For example, one may cook[1] and one may carry, so that coats or books or food may be taken to another house and baby carriages may be wheeled in the street. But in another sense these holidays may be more restrictive. On Passover one may not eat leavened bread or any product that has the slightest bit of leaven in it or has been prepared in utensils used for leavened food. On Sukkot one must eat in the sukkah unless the weather makes this an impossibility. On Yom Kippur one must abstain for more than twenty-four hours from all eating and drinking, from washing, and from wearing leather shoes. Many ba'alei t'shuva come from homes where some of these holidays are celebrated. The key, of course, is that not all the restrictions are observed. Families continue to celebrate holidays long after they have abandoned their restrictions on work, using electricity, or riding in automobiles. People may still attend a seder and eat matzo, and some refrain from leaven for all eight days of the holiday. In Israel, one

---

1. One may cook on a stove already lit, but one may not ignite a new fire.

often sees a sukkah in a home where Shabbat is not celebrated. Even for people who do not come to the synagogue at any other time of the year, Yom Kippur and Rosh Ha-Shana remain days that are widely observed, days when people attend services even though they may drive their car to the synagogue, in violation of halakhah.

The holidays present some surprising difficulties for ba'alei t'shuva. Understandably, Passover is particularly difficult because of the rigorous food restrictions. The fact that the Passover celebration is typically a family occasion might make it even more difficult. The ba'al t'shuva who has since childhood attended seders with grandparents, aunts, uncles, and cousins may find it difficult to attend or participate, as travel is forbidden on the holiday. Even when arrangements are made to stay with relatives, they may not adhere to the strict standards of Passover observance that the ba'al t'shuva has been taught at yeshiva. The combination of rejection of the family's religious service and rejection of the family itself by refusing to participate makes this a most difficult holiday.

One might expect to find that Rosh Ha-Shana and Yom Kippur are far easier, as they are synagogue related.[2] Surprisingly, in more traditional but non-Orthodox families the problems are reversed. In these families, the ba'al t'shuva back from a year or more in the yeshiva is now considered the resident expert on how to conduct the seder or prepare for the holiday. Passover is a family time, and if the ba'al t'shuva is not using religion as a weapon against his parents, he may use his newly acquired religious expertise to enhance the holiday celebration. In contrast, synagogue-related holidays are often more difficult. The more tradition-minded family is likely to attend a synagogue on the High Holy Days. If they are committed people, they may be officers of the synagogue. Their son or daughter may have worshipped with them for years. Now that he has attended a yeshiva for a year or two, the parents wish to demonstrate proudly the sincere commitment of their child. They hope that he has learned to appreciate their religious commitment and will be equally proud of them. Instead they find that the ba'al t'shuva does not wish to worship in their temple or center but prefers the Orthodox synagogue. And so begins a heartbreaking conflict between parent and child, in which the parents, precisely because they have strong commitments, feel particularly betrayed.[3]

2. Sukkot, also an important holiday, presents a minor problem for those in the suburbs. The ba'al t'shuva can take his meals in the prefabricated sukkah built in the yard. Although strange, this is not disruptive.

3. In a school like the James Striar School of Yeshiva University, this pattern

The struggle involved in becoming a ba'al t'shuva does not always relate to the religious distance traveled. The pain can be greater precisely because the parents are also committed and follow practices of their own out of sincere conviction.

Family Purity

Family purity (*taharat hamishpakhah*) is the third practice that marks off Orthodox from non-Orthodox Jews. It differs from the other two in that its most essential core remains private, known only to husband and wife, not even known to children, parents, or siblings of the married couple.[4] Religious law requires this as a matter of modesty.

The core practice requires that the wife separate herself from her husband during her period of menses and for a week following, a "week of purity." On the evening following that week she proceeds to a mikveh, bathes carefully, and then immerses herself in the mikveh. She is then ritually pure, and husband and wife may have marital relations.

Ba'alei t'shuva relate to the practice of family purity differently from their relation to the other two practices. Most ba'alei t'shuva have some awareness of Shabbat and kashrut before beginning their return, as most have had some Jewish experience or educational background. But ba'alei t'shuva are less likely to have knowledge of family purity practices. Furthermore, these laws are in conflict with society's sexual, recreational, and dress norms.

At the very same time that the sexual mores of society have become

---

comes up more frequently than at other schools. Since the school is more mainstream than other ba'al t'shuva yeshivot, students who come here tend to be less countercultural, to have somewhat less conflict with parents. In fact, Rabbi Morris Besdin, Dean of the James Striar School, alerted me to this pattern. When such situations arise he often suggests that the student join his parents in their synagogue even if the student prays alone first.

The decision as to when to ask the new recruit to compromise and when to ask the parents to be more flexibile and forthcoming is a difficult one, involving a consideration of the personal sensitivities of both and the halakhic implications of the actions.

4. While the laws of modesty make it difficult to be aware of the central practice of family purity, other practices associated with these laws are observable. Modesty of dress is often taken as an indicator of observance of these laws. It is assumed among the Orthodox that women who do not wear slacks or short-sleeved dresses and who wear their hair covered are more likely to observe family purity laws.

more permissive, current practice in Orthodoxy has shifted in a traditionalistic direction, and presently males and females are seated separately at social occasions where in the past seating was mixed.[5] The gap between the norm of the larger society from which the potential recruit comes and the norms of Orthodoxy toward which he or she moves has become a yawning chasm. As bathing suits have become skimpier, films, plays, and songs more sexually explicit, college dorms less restrictive, dating more likely to involve sexual intimacy, Orthodox Jews have moved away from the mixed swimming and social dancing of a generation ago. Many more women wear wigs or cover their hair. Although a large majority of the Orthodox still go "mixed swimming" or dance and attend all sorts of shows and films, the more traditionalistic stance is officially espoused, in the yeshivot in particular. These norms, which restrict social and leisure activities, become a substantial obstacle to involvement with Orthodoxy.

The laws of family purity affect recruiting and retention in Orthodoxy differently in the dating and marriage situations. Teenagers often join a synagogue youth group because they cherish their ties to the Jewish people and they (or more likely, their parents) want to socialize with and marry someone Jewish. Synagogue youth groups facilitate participation in social activities in a Jewish framework and with Jewish peers. In the past, when efforts were made by the Young Israel or others to reach out to the non-Orthodox, the tendency was to be as lenient as possible with regard to the interpretation of these laws. Presently the Orthodox National Council of Synagogue Youth, which is considered a major recruitment program, does not separate boys and girls. Boys and girls intermingle at synagogue-sponsored socials, *kumsitzes,* and at outings to parks and skating rinks. They have songfests at which both boys and girls sing, a practice forbidden in traditionalistic Orthodoxy. Teenagers interested in learning more about Orthodoxy may be referred to a yeshiva in Israel when they have come of age, but not all are sent on. Group leaders are well aware of the attitudes of potential recruits and recognize the risks of sending to a yeshiva someone who might find these norms objectionable.

Yeshivot serve a somewhat older clientele. Their students are college age or older. Sexual standards in the society at large are more permissive

5. The custom of separate seating of the sexes at secular functions has spread from Chasidim to other segments of Orthodoxy in the last generation. Perhaps unable to resist pressure from traditionalists, Carlebach offered his first separate seating concert in 1984, a practice he had not found it necessary to follow in the past.

for this group than for teenagers. And yeshivot follow much stricter norms of separation of the sexes than do youth organizations.

The challenge for ba'alei t'shuva of college age or older is therefore more severe. Some find these norms too restrictive and either avoid the yeshivot or leave them, as the extent of the restrictions and their implications for social life become apparent. Still others may become more traditional after a stay in yeshivot but find the norms too restrictive and join the Conservative movement.

Yet the very restrictiveness of sexual norms is sometimes attractive. Teachers and deans in the school for ba'alei t'shuva report that some students seem to seek out these normative restrictions. The argument goes that some of those who have experienced an unrestricted sexual life wish to find guidelines and rules for behavior. Religion provides the framework and stability for a life that has been chaotic and impulse driven. The ba'al t'shuva seeks to provide order and direction for wild and chaotic sexual urges, to transmute and transform sexual experience and to hallow it.[6]

FAMILY PURITY AND CHOICE OF MATE

In courtship and marriage the laws of family purity have a different impact on ba'alei t'shuva from in dating and socializing. Rabbi Dovid Weinberger of Ohr Someyach described some of the problems relating to family purity that ba'alei t'shuva encounter.

> Often a girl who is ba'alat t'shuva will want a husband for whom learning is an important value, so that the home they build will revolve around Torah study. That kind of a fellow may have a double standard. He's gone to bed with some girls when he was fooling around. He's done t'shuva [repentance] for that so he is okay. But he does not want a ba'alat t'shuva. It is not the laws of niddah that are the problem—at least not any more than the laws of Shabbat. So maybe their *yetzer harah* [evil inclination] got the better of them once, and they made a mistake. But the critical problem for the guy is who else was she in bed with.
>
> Women have problems, too. We have a fellow who was here for a few years, a really good student. His courtship dragged on for a long time. The problem was that she was a sheltered girl from an Orthodox religious family and had to get used to the fact that he had been to bed on several occasions.

6. This is a pattern also encountered in the new radical religions. Among the Hare Krishnas, strict sexual abstinence is practiced. Sexual activity is also limited in the Unification Church and in Protestant Fundamentalist groups.

This wasn't her image of the man she was going to marry. My advice was "forget it," don't try to adjust things. They are married, and I wish them all the best, but I don't eliminate the possibility for trouble later on.

A fellow can more easily deal with the fact that he has had sexual relations with girls that he shouldn't have had, with girls that are niddot [menstrual] or non-Jewish or whatever. He did it. He did an *averah* [he sinned], but to him it's probably no worse than having eaten treyf [nonkosher food]. But from her perspective, she's been violated personally, she's gone through a trauma. I've heard a lot about these problems from people I respect at Neve. They are professional; they are skilled and sensitive. And they try to deal with these problems.

Q. How is it that there are no lectures dealing with this at Neve?
A. It's all done privately. Teachers at Neve spend hours with the girls who feel troubled by these problems.

The difference, then, is that, unlike violation of the laws of Shabbat or kashrut, for a woman, at least, violation of the laws of family purity may leave a permanent mark, may change her status somewhat, so that in regard to a Cohen, for example, the earlier violations continue to have consequences. And even where they don't, the double standard of the larger society gives them unique weight in Judaism.

MARRIAGE AND PURITY

Because the practice of family purity is an intimate matter between husband and wife, the problems that are encountered by ba'alei t'shuva and even by those born Orthodox—are not discussed. Couples may know that husband and wife must abstain from sexual relations for at least twelve days of each menstrual cycle, but they do not discuss the strains they may experience as a result.

The husband or wife who needs reassurance, a hug, an embrace, a kiss of affection, needs some comfort against the strains of the day, finds that the partner tries to maintain distance so as to keep the laws that forbid these actions. At other times these same gestures would be welcomed and reciprocated. Especially at the beginning of a marriage, when the bonds between husband and wife are still new and not yet firm, to refuse to reciprocate causes strains. Perhaps the other simply wanted a little comfort, but perhaps it wouldn't stop there. Even if both are committed to the laws, these people have married because they are attracted to each other. This powerful attraction must now be satisfied or denied depending on an arbitrary time schedule.

Those brought up in Orthodox families are aware that these laws can be managed. How this is achieved is another matter. Observation of whether or not the laws are breached in part or in whole is not easy. This is not discussed among the Orthodox, in contrast to the open and constant discussion of Shabbat observance and which products are or are not kosher.

This matter is rarely discussed in public by ba'alei t'shuva either; the topic is strictly off limits and cannot easily be raised by a researcher, even with men. Ba'alei t'shuva must wrestle with this themselves. Whether transgression of these norms produces immense guilt or can be shrugged off easily is difficult to say.

Yet the periodic separations of men and women are said to give freshness and a sense of renewal to a marriage, providing a "honeymoon" each month for husband and wife. There are reports that couples with troubled marriages who have not been practicing the laws of family purity have been advised to begin this practice as a means of restoring some romance to their sex life, and informants suggest that it seems to work.[7]

Dress

While the first three practices tend to distinguish the Orthodox from other Jews, differences in dress distinguish only some of the Orthodox from the larger community of Jews and Gentiles, but they do distinguish subcommunities within Orthodoxy. Thus dress style indicates one's attitudes regarding secular education, the status of women, and the state of Israel. It also draws community boundaries indicating the group to which one has loyalties and the people to whom one feels the closest sense of social and even ethical obligation.

Distinctions in dress are most sharply evident in regular yeshivot, where dress codes are quite specific although not formally promulgated. Ba'al t'shuva yeshivot cannot easily dictate standards of dress. Hippies, people in sport clothes, shorts, or jeans and sweat shirts, are all accepted into ba'al t'shuva yeshivot as they are. Men will be asked to don a kippah, but no other changes are required for entry. Over time, modifications of dress and hairstyle occur, which bring the student in line with the norms of the yeshiva.

At the modernistic yeshivot, dress codes are not a problem. Even the

7. Clearly these cases represent a select group with the combination of a troubled marriage, the willingness to consult a rabbi or some other Orthodox person for counsel, and sufficient interest in Judaism to follow this advice.

rosh yeshiva may wear slacks with a shirt or sport jacket rather than a dark suit. But traditionalistic yeshivot for ba'alei t'shuva seek to model themselves along the lines of regular traditionalistic yeshivot, which favor a formal style of dress. The roshei yeshiva tend to wear formal clothes— black suits, black homburg-style hats, and coat-length jackets. Yeshivot for ba'alei t'shuva therefore are ambivalent about dress styles.

As yeshivot represent different communities, their dress styles vary somewhat. At the Lubavitcher yeshivot in Israel and in the United States students effect the Lubavitcher style of dark hat, beard, white shirt, and dark slacks. At Brovender's students wear sport shirts and slacks. The only visible difference from the attire of the general public is the kippah seruga. At Ohr Someyach many of the rebbis wear business suits in dark colors, but students tend to dress much more informally. The newest arrivals are still in the clothes of the outside world. Those who have been at the yeshivot longest have made the closest adjustment to the yeshivot.

Even at yeshivot for ba'alei t'shuva, new recruits are under some pressure to change clothing and hairstyle so as to fit into the community with which the school identifies. This affects Americans and Israelis, men and women, differently.

AMERICAN MEN

At modernistic yeshivot the only dress requirement distinguishing students from outsiders may be the kippot worn by the students. At traditionalistic or chasidic ba'al t'shuva schools the students tend to adopt the custom of wearing a black hat indoors and outdoors. A black hat is not ordinarily worn in the larger community and implies a unique commitment.

Hairstyle, too, is sometimes a mark of identification. At traditionalistic yeshivot hippies could simply allow their beards to flourish, but this would not be taken as an indication of commitment. For them, having a regular haircut is considered an indication of commitment.

At the early stages of their involvement in the Orthodox community, hippies were highly visible. Even with regular-length hair and beards, the combination of black hat and jacket with jeans and bright shirts let the world know that these were people who had recently joined a yeshiva. They retained their own identity. They were not fully part of the yeshiva world; they were part of the ba'al t'shuva world, a world of its own with its own past experiences and its own uncertain commitments. This style of dress proclaimed the wearer's ambiguity and gave the ba'alei t'shuva a life space of their own. It suggested that they were simply trying on Orthodoxy.

Interestingly, the rabbis and teachers, while alert to the students' symbols of identity with the hippie community, were not eager for them to move too rapidly to identification with the yeshivishe velt. Rabbi Mendel Weinbach of Ohr Someyach insisted that he would not permit his students to wear long peyot and black hats. "It's unhealthy for them, and it's not the image of the yeshiva we want to project." By implication, the yeshiva is reaching out, and a student body of this sort might scare away potential returnees.

Rabbi Dovid Vichnin of Lubavitch in America mentioned also that such a rapid change was unhealthy for the ba'al t'shuva. "If they turn so fast, they can turn right back again." In addition, he said, "I wouldn't let boys put on a black hat or a jacket too soon. It's a kind of arrogance for someone who has just come in to wear that kind of clothes. If he's been here for some time and I see that he's reached the stage where it's befitting for him, then I'll let him do it."

Status in the community is signaled by dress, and dressing in this manner prematurely signals the wrong status to the members of the community. Besides, should the person dressed as a yeshiva bochur backslide after having become identified with the community, he becomes a reproach to the entire community, a *chillul Ha-Shem* (literally, a desecration of the Holy Name). Even roshei yeshiva of traditionalistic yeshivot seem bent on holding back the ba'al t'shuva from adopting the yeshivishe or chasidishe clothes. Instead, what they look for is a gradual change from hippie style to a relatively straight style as part of the process of transition. Only after a period of some months is the ba'al t'shuva encouraged to don progressively more formal clothes, and his appearance becomes increasingly more yeshivishe.

AMERICAN WOMEN

In addition to signaling identity with a community, for women clothes raise the issue of modesty. A dress may be too décolleté, or its hem or sleeves may be too short. Pants or slacks are considered immodest.

Differences in minimum standards of dress for men and women are indicated by the requirements for visiting the Kotel. Men, even in T-shirts and jeans, may be asked to put on a skullcap. Women in shorts or jeans may be asked to wear a wrap-around skirt provided by the ushers or a shawl if their shoulders are bare or their dress too low cut.

Part of the problem of indicating standards of dress for women is resolved if the women have been picked up at the Kotel, where someone other than the school sets the standard for dress. Those at the Kotel have accepted it, at least temporarily, and may be prepared to do so temporarily again. But for someone like Shlomo Carlebach, recruiting on the campuses of American universities, in hippie communities, or at concerts, the problem is difficult. Little can be done to suggest modification of clothing without alienating some of the potential recruits. Neve Yerushalayim and other schools for women face a similar problem when they recruit at the bus stop or the university in Jerusalem. Teachers therefore attempt to go slowly. Neve is traditionalistic, but one sees girls in a variety of outfits. Almost certainly, those wearing the "wrong kinds of clothes" are newcomers. Teachers do not suggest to these girls that they should dress differently. They are only visitors for a lecture or a meal. Yet potential recruits cannot help but notice the style of dress of the majority of students and teachers.

During the cooler months of the year, the style of dress is not sharply different from that of larger society, except that the girls do not wear jeans or slacks, and even that may not be easily apparent, as a few newcomers may still do so. Differences are more apparent in the summer, when girls at Neve wear long-sleeved blouses and stockings. Female teachers who are married wear wigs, as do married women in the homes where the girls are placed for Shabbat.

Potential recruits soon realize that the wearing of a wig signals an array of restrictions of life. In the community where women wear wigs, they ordinarily do not engage in mixed swimming or social dancing, and the types of entertainment they are permitted are limited. Covering the hair thus symbolizes attachment to a particular Orthodox community and its way of life.

Acceptance of the dress codes was least problematic for hippie women. They already favored long gingham or denim skirts and long-sleeved blouses, which met the standards of modesty. Even covering the hair was a part of hippie culture, although their style of hair covering was distinctive. Hippie women used a kerchief to cover the hair in front of the head entirely while permitting the hair to flow from behind the kerchief down the back. A hippie ba'alat t'shuva might tie her hair in a braid or tuck some of it under her kerchief. But often it was not worn in the style of the Orthodox community. Her clothing might be fully acceptable as *tzniusdik* (modest), but it did not identify her as Orthodox.

Hippie, nonconformist, and sporty styles of dress present teachers with something of a dilemma. Despite the absence of halakhic objections to these styles, students are made to feel that such clothes are inappropriate. This is particularly confusing since the social function of dress as identifying one with a specific community is not clearly articulated. Yet style of hair covering, for example, identifies one with a very specific Orthodox community. Rabbi Revson of Neve discouraged his students from covering their heads with kerchiefs after marriage. "We encourage our girls to wear a *sheitel* [wig]. We don't want them to wear a kerchief. That's another community. That's fine for Meah Shearim." Partially covering the head with a kerchief is insufficiently pious. Covering the head completely seems to be too pious.[8]

Because clothing carries a heavy religious weight for women, it may be the most significant outward sign of a woman's commitment, akin in a sense to the man's willingness to spend hours in the yeshiva.

ISRAELI MEN AND WOMEN

At ba'al t'shuva yeshivot that cater to both Israelis and Americans, language differences occasionally make it necessary to offer separate classes. At such times it becomes apparent that it is primarily the Israelis who dress in the dark clothes now typical of Orthodoxy's yeshivishe *velt*. And at Yeshivat Ohr Hachayim, an Israeli ba'al t'shuva yeshiva attended primarily by Sephardim (Jews from Arab lands), advanced students dress in the dark clothes of the Ashkenazi yeshivishe velt. Why does this clothing style characterize Israeli rather than American ba'alei t'shuva? Why do Sephardic ba'alei t'shuva adopt the dress styles of Ashkenazim?

The difference in the clothing styles calls attention to the different processes that Israeli and American ba'alei t'shuva are undergoing. Whereas for Americans becoming a ba'al t'shuva is at the outset a matter of ethnic identity not of religion, for Israelis it is a matter of religion and social status.

The Israeli already has Jewish ethnic identity. Ordinarily he has a second ethnic identity—that of Ashkenazi or Sephardi. Sephardic ethnic identity in Israel is ranked lower than Ashkenazic, and Sephardim seem to constitute the bulk of Israeli students at ba'al t'shuva yeshivot. For the Israeli school dropout or former drug user, becoming a ba'al t'shuva means leaving a low-ranking status and attaining a higher-ranking status; one is no longer an *avaryan,* a deviant or delinquent. For Sephardim it means association with the style of the higher ranked ethnic group—

8. A practice that was also discouraged was covering the hair with a kerchief in the style of the modern Orthodox so that some hair showed. The preferred hair covering at Neve is a wig.

Ashkenazim. Thus, the Israeli seems bent on losing his earlier identity and putting a new self in place.

Perhaps, therefore, the Israeli ba'al t'shuva, once persuaded to turn to religion, finds that clothing provides a quick means of changing identity. Here again the rabbis occasionally hold the student back rather than press for a change in clothing style, for fear that the backsliders may shame them. But in the Israeli context, teachers encourage change of style for reasons that do not apply to Americans. Rabbi Tucker of D'var Yerushalayim for Girls put it this way:

> The clothes the American girls wear are halakhically all right. But they are not very different from those of secular Israelis. American girls are far from home and are not likely to be pulled back into the secular influences of home and friends. But the Israeli women go back home; sometimes they go home every night, sometimes for weekends. Relatives and friends are always around. Their friends can't see that they have changed, but our girls want to somehow show their friends they have changed. That's why they prefer to wear clothes that set them off from others, and we encourage them to do so.

Rabbi Elbaz of Ohr Hachayim said: "I want the boys to wear the clothes of yeshiva students. I don't want them to go too far too soon, but I don't think it's proper for a yeshiva student to wear sports clothes. He will be no different from anyone else on the street. Even if he wears a kippah, if he wants to go to a movie or do something not proper for a yeshiva student, all he needs to do is slip it off his head. But if he wears the clothes of a yeshiva student, he remembers who he is at all times."

When physical distance separates the student from his former environment, unique clothing to mark him off as a ba'al t'shuva may be unnecessary. He becomes a yeshiva bocher soon enough, and pressing him to change clothing style too soon increases the risk of his backsliding and thus bringing shame to the institution. For the Israeli, in contrast, no physical distance separates the ba'al t'shuva from the old network. Despite the risks of backsliding, therefore, the rosh yeshiva may encourage clothing changes that emphasize the new social distance between the ba'al t'shuva and his former friends as a way of minimizing their influence.

The differences in clothing between Israeli and American ba'alei t'shuva, then, seem to reflect the different goals they seek in becoming ba'alei t'shuva, as well as the different social contexts in which they find themselves. Israeli ba'al t'shuva yeshivot that actively recruit former delinquents (such as the Bratzlaver Yeshiva, Yeshivat Ohr Hachayim Migdal Haemek, and similar schools) seek to reform a "criminal" type,[9] and the ba'alei t'shuva at these institutions seek to shed their old identity. Americans seem more interested in establishing an ethnic identity than in shedding an earlier identity. This explains the unique clothing of the hippie ba'al t'shuva, who continues to show in his dress ties to the hippie community. Similarly, it explains why American ba'alei t'shuva who are not hippies continue to wear "straight" clothes for a substantial period of time after joining a yeshiva. Religious commitment may propel the American along in change of dress style. But the tendency for Americans to first identify ethnically and then religiously makes the rate and even the quality of their change different from that of Israelis.

Exaggerated Conformity

The requirement that rituals be performed sometimes discourages people from becoming Orthodox. Putting on tefillin may seem absurd, and some find this act a hurdle they cannot overcome. The proscriptions of Shabbat—no lights, no travel, no cooking—may seem equally absurd. For others, the discipline, rather than the absurdity of ritual, causes difficulty. Kashrut and the rules regulating sex may fall into this category. Seeing ba'alei t'shuva performing rituals in a manner that goes beyond typical Orthodox practice therefore comes as something of a surprise.

In the ritual washing of hands before eating bread, for example, some ba'alei t'shuva lift their hands above their heads when reciting "Lift up holy hands . . . ," a practice followed primarily by chasidic rebbes and not by ordinary Orthodox Jews. Or again, when reciting the blessing over bread some ba'alei t'shuva lift up the bread in the manner in which it is done only on Shabbat by Orthodox Jews. Some ba'alei t'shuva dip the motzi (the bite of bread eaten after the blessing) into salt that they pour out on the table, in contrast to the widespread practice of Orthodox Jews of pouring a bit of salt on the motzi. In doing this the ba'alei t'shuva are following the practice of Lubavitch, although they may not be associated with Lubavitch.

Similarly exaggerated rituals mark the ways in which some ba'alei t'shuva observe Shabbat, Passover, kashrut, and restrictions of relations

9. Some parallels exist with the experience of Black Muslims in America, who were able to reform convicted criminals and successfully rehabilitate them so that they became middle class in dress, discipline, and work habits (see Cromer 1981 and Lincoln 1961 on these parallels and for analysis of Black Muslims).

between the sexes. Some of this occurs simply because the ba'al t'shuva is not familiar with the halakhah, some because he seeks maximum conformity.[10]

This behavior occurs because of an element of ambiguity in the structure of the Orthodox normative system: the question of just what is halakhah. In Orthodox Judaism the rules regarding behaviors and ritual practices are many and cover all aspects of life. For the most part there is agreement on these rules so that standards for Shabbat (and the holidays), kashrut, and family purity used by Jews anywhere in the world will be accepted by other Jews. The Orthodox laity generally assumes that minor differences exist regarding only the customs characterizing one group or another and that no differences exist in halakhah. In fact, some *halakhot* have been abandoned by the entire Orthodox community, although the basis for this neglect is unclear; customs have developed that seem directly contradictory to halakhah, and still other customs have acquired the force of halakhah. Although halakhah provides a web of rules, a mazeway, most of which is embodied in a legal system, the system itself is based on the Torah, rabbinic decisions, and the practices of the committed community.

Those raised as Orthodox Jews follow the practices of their local community, which sometimes include practices that contradict points of halakhah. But the ba'al t'shuva is not reared in Orthodoxy and lacks a community tradition. He may not appreciate the role of the community in setting standards and may not be aware that a different norm is acceptable. Moreover, in a mobile society where propinquity is no longer the basis for community, differences in practice can be marked. This can be seen especially in Israel, where the ingathering of diaspora communities has made the differences between them apparent.

The ba'al t'shuva's exaggerated observances, therefore, which some regard as an expression of arrogance, may be no more than an effort to follow different community practices by someone whose ties to commu-

10. Rabbi Ralph Pelkowitz, a close observer of the ba'alei t'shuva in New York, has written: "Too many of them . . . are worried about their ability to live up to the requirements of their new found religion and confused about its true standards. As a result emphasis is often placed upon externals—one's garb and manifestation of ritual appearance and apparel— . . . but one wonders to what extent there has been an inner transformation" (1980). Such charges touch a very sensitive nerve, and in the very next issue of the journal that published Pelkowitz' article, Rabbi Pinchas Stolper, executive vice president of the Orthodox Union, expresses regret in some detail that Rabbi Pelkowitz' article was published by the journal of the Orthodox Union (1981, 24–29).

nity are still weak. Yet people whose hospitality and lessons on Judaism were good enough at the outset read into this behavior—at times correctly—a rejection of themselves and their Judaism by the ba'al t'shuva. While ba'alei t'shuva may be welcomed as an indication that Orthodoxy is viable and attractive in the modern world, they also produce hostility for what is perceived as a "holier than thou" attitude, even among the Orthodox. Ba'alei t'shuva are a source of irritation to Conservative and Reform Jews for the same reason.

In sum, the three areas of ritual practice by which the Orthodox community defines itself represent social interactional barriers that promote solidarity among its adherents by limiting or modifying their social contracts with the larger society. They are also barriers that tend to keep out new recruits. From the outside, the Orthodox world seems restricted and rigorously disciplined. The ba'al t'shuva must cross a barrier to enter the Orthodox world and must perceive it as the Orthodox do. He or she does this by accepting restrictions gradually, while at the same time building social ties and learning the pleasures and joys of Orthodox life. The transition is eased by partial involvement or by a process of periodically moving in and out of Orthodox life.

The world the ba'al t'shuva enters is, for a time at least, somewhat different from the world of those raised as Orthodox Jews in the kinds of problems encountered and the solutions developed. Practices that even some Orthodox Jews see as restrictive, such as keeping kashrut in the home, eating in kosher restaurants, and sexual restrictions, may be perceived by ba'alei t'shuva as advantageous: the kosher home becomes an entree into the community, an opportunity to invite guests; the kosher restaurants, an opportunity to once again eat a full meal together with others rather than in isolation. Shabbat and holidays may be redefined several times, from adventure at the outset to crushing boredom as the routine and restrictions take hold to quiet pleasure as the social relations and cultural tastes necessary for its enjoyment develop. Sexual restrictions probably turn many away from involvement with Orthodoxy. But a few are attracted and become involved precisely because the norms regarding relations between the sexes order and organize these relations.

Styles of dress are another matter. They distinguish some of the Orthodox from the non-Orthodox, and they also distinguish subcommunities within Orthodoxy. The clothing styles have no religious significance per se, yet they have taken on a value of their own, particularly in the traditionalistic community. Similarly, what appears to be exaggerated conformity to custom ties one to a specific community.

Chapter 12

Wrestling with Judaism:
Practices and Beliefs

Reform Jews pray in the vernacular—Americans in English, Germans in German—reserving Hebrew for a few phrases or prayers. Conservative Jews pray in Hebrew with a substantial admixture of English. But Orthodox Jews pray in Hebrew, whether or not they understand the words they utter and even though with minor exceptions halakhah permits prayer in any language one understands and prayer, according to halakhah, is considered "a service of the heart" that implies sincerity, commitment, and understanding. This is a custom that is universally accepted among the Orthodox, whether Ashkenazic or Sephardic, chasidic or mitnaggedic.

The practice seems totally dysfunctional, as it obstructs pouring out one's heart in worship and seems to turn worship into a wooden and meaningless ritual. But it also binds the Jewish community together, for no matter where one comes from or what language one speaks, when one steps into a synagogue for prayer, the words are the same. The inflections and pronunciation may be different, but the prayers remain familiar.

For the Orthodox, then, particularly for young children first learning to pray, prayer is ritual that involves speaking words and phrases they do not understand. As they mature and their knowledge of Hebrew expands, the ritual takes on more meaning. This procedure is in line with the Jewish pattern of education of children and with the educational philosophy of Judaism. In fact, prayer is a lesson in that educational philosophy.

Using only the traditional Hebrew limits what can be expressed in prayer. Using a vernacular opens prayer up not only to understanding but also to the possibility that worshippers may add their own thoughts and pleadings. Conservative and particularly Reform rabbis take advantage of the greater latitude provided by English to introduce new prayers, perhaps expressing current concerns of worshippers. Orthodoxy's prayers seem to leave no room for this.

The Hebrew words do not add pomp and ceremony to the worship service. No one is specially designated to utter them; all do so. Nor are the prayers sung or chanted in sonorous dignity; rather, each utters them on his or her own. This seems to offer neither the personal expression of the heart nor the dignified song of the religious community.

But the Orthodox see the original Hebrew prayers as offering a mold into which one can pour one's own thoughts.[1] The words teach supplicants about God's relation to man, expressing lofty ideas in phrases that cannot be surpassed. Does one compose new songs whenever one wants to sing, or does one sing the beautiful tunes that masters have composed?

If one needs to express one's own feelings, then it is best to select a psalm and repeat it, using one's feelings as the guide in selecting the most expressive psalm. If this does not suffice, one may utter one's own words at designated moments in each prayer. There are prayers in Yiddish for women and children who are unfamiliar with the Hebrew prayers, but traditional prayers are offered in their traditional form.

Orthodox Jews at times feel constrained by this pattern. But overwhelmingly they learn to use it, to appreciate it, to inject their own thoughts and feelings into the prayers, to use the Hebrew words to ex-

---

1. An oft told chasidic tale illustrates the Orthodox view of prayer. It is said that one Yom Kippur a poor farmer came to worship at the synagogue of the Berdichiver Rebbe, bringing his son with him. Having grown up in the countryside, the lad had never learned Hebrew. He spent his days tending his flock, using a whistle to call them. On this day, as the men prayed the lad looked on, unable to join them, feeling the prayers well up within him but unable to express them. As the prayers moved toward a climax of intense worship, the lad took out his whistle, feeling a need to express his love and devotion in some manner. His father stopped him, but the boy's urge to pray grew. Finally the boy, unable to contain his prayerful feelings, whipped his whistle from his pocket and blew a shrill and powerful note. All prayer stopped, and the congregation turned to the boy angrily. The Berdichiver intervened. "The lad has saved the day for us all. All day long we stormed heaven with our prayers but could not enter. But this boy's whistle blast, which expressed the deepest feelings of his heart, breached the gates of Heaven and with it, our prayers entered too." This perspective in prayer is an ancient tradition in Judaism and derives from the blowing of the *shofar* (ram's horn) on the New Year (Num. 29:1) and in times of trouble (Num. 10:9). The closing psalm of the Book of Psalms celebrates the wordless worship of God with the sound of musical instruments and the shofar.

press their own thoughts. Or if they don't understand the words fully, they allow the utterances of a religious language to comfort them, for at least the mechanics of prayer are not unfamiliar. They know the words and repeat them daily or weekly; they are familiar with the customs of prayer, knowing when to rise and when to sit, when to join in and when to be silent. But what of the ba'al t'shuva who knows nothing of this and for whom the mechanics can become an overwhelming problem?

In fact, prayer becomes one of the major problems faced by ba'alei t'shuva. While the Orthodox Jew who has been repeating the morning prayer since childhood may take twenty to forty minutes for *shacharit* prayers, the ba'al t'shuva may require an hour and a half or more for shacharit even after two or three months of practice. Afternoon prayers that require five to ten minutes for those who are practiced may require twenty minutes for the ba'al t'shuva, and similarly evening prayers, prayers after meals, on lying down to sleep, before eating, after washing, and so forth. These become matter-of-fact, almost unconscious rituals for the Orthodox from birth (to the dismay of the rabbis, who see in this a loss of sincere "service of the heart"). But for the ba'al t'shuva, they are difficult and tedious rituals and can be a major obstacle.

The difficulty of prayer is evident in part because Shabbat and kashrut are automatically cared for by the yeshiva, and family purity is an abstract concern for the unmarried. Prayer is one of the few areas the students must really confront, and it is the major daily encounter with Judaism. Prayer is also taken more seriously in yeshivot than it is in synagogues. While morning prayers in a synagogue may be hurried as congregants rush to get through and go to work, in the yeshiva they are recited slowly, with great emphasis on *kavvanah* (sincerity) and purity of thought.

The rote and mechanics of prayer may be difficult for the ba'al t'shuva, and the yeshiva attempts to accommodate. New recruits are taught only the most central prayers so as to ease the burden, at least until they have mastered the language. To accommodate beginners the pace of prayer at the ba'al t'shuva yeshiva is even slower than at the standard yeshiva, which itself is slow relative to most synagogues. But at the yeshiva no other accommodations will be made. The page to be read is not announced; for that information, one must turn to one's nearest companion and quietly ask, or one has a friend who leads one along. Some modernistic Orthodox synagogues do announce the prayers, particularly at the High Holy days, when a new text, a *machzor* rather than a siddur, is used and when many congregants even in Orthodox synagogues are not familiar with the prayers. Yeshivot and more traditionalistic synagogues do not do this.[2]

PRAYER AND SYNAGOGUE

Newly Orthodox often voice two complaints about synagogue prayer: that it is taken lightly—people chat with others about the weather, baseball, business, and generally show a lack of respect for the sanctity of the synagogue and of prayer—and that it is unfriendly.

The first complaint is widespread, and the Orthodox themselves are first to make this charge. By consensus, decorum in the synagogue is at an all-time low, talking to one's seatmate occurs at even the most sacred moments of prayer, and the noise level in Orthodox synagogues has made prayer difficult.[3] But decorum is not a problem in yeshivot. Orthodox worship can be intimate, separate, foreign, individualistic, and yet project an aura of sanctity and respect.

But whereas yeshivot seem capable of maintaining this aura through intense commitment and concentration, typical Orthodox synagogue services seem to turn into social events rather than occasions for a prayerful attitude. Ba'alei t'shuva find this hard to take, as it seems to belie the ideals of Orthodox belief. Rabbi Buchwald reports that at the Lincoln Square Synagogue those at the beginners' minyan are reluctant to join the main minyan even after they have acquired the necessary prayer skills because they are unwilling to risk losing the sense of sanctity of prayers.

Ba'alei t'shuva also complain of the unfriendliness of other worshippers toward them. They expect to be welcomed into the synagogue as they have been welcomed into the yeshiva, and at Lubavitch or the Lincoln Square Synagogue, where strong recruitment efforts are made, they may

2. At the Lincoln Square Synagogue the minyan for ba'alei t'shuva does use English at times for some selections and offers translations of others during the course of the prayer service.

3. The problem may be old, as exhortations to cease disruptive talking exist in Jewish literature. More than a half century ago, when the Young Israel movement was initiated, one of its chief concerns was to maintain decorum in the synagogue during worship. In years past, when Conservative or Reform Jews charged that Orthodox synagogues were noisy without decorum or respect, the Orthodox would excuse their behavior with the remark that they were in their Father's house, they were familiar with it, they were there all the time, and they were behaving appropriately. Decorum has been maintained in some of the larger Orthodox synagogues, particularly the German, but one could argue that the large synagogues became decorous after being Westernized.

indeed be inundated with solicitous inquiries and friendliness. But elsewhere they may be ignored.

The two problems represent aspects of the same social fact. Orthodox congregations are *communities*. The community factor is so powerful that one cannot sit down next to another person without passing a few words in friendliness, admiring the other's visiting child or grandchild, inquiring about the family, remarking about politics. In large synagogues or in Reform or Conservative synagogues, where these contacts are less frequent, such neighborly behavior is not so pressing a social obligation. Only where religious norms are defined as clearly overriding, as in yeshivot, is this pattern avoided.

This very pattern of community, which makes the Orthodox feel at home, makes the ba'al t'shuva feel very much an outsider, an intruder at an intimate gathering of friends. The ba'al t'shuva discovers that he or she has entered not simply a place to pray but rather a community.

Study

On entering a yeshiva, a ba'al t'shuva encounters a rigorous regimen of studies and prayer. Students are awakened at 6:30 or 7:00. Morning prayer services (shacharit) start about a half hour afterward and last for an hour to an hour and a half. This is followed by breakfast. Study starts in earnest at about 9:30. Normally, in preparation for the Talmud lecture, or shi'ur, of the rosh yeshiva an hour or two is devoted to reading the page of the Talmud that will be studied that day, as well as the relevant commentaries. The lecture lasts about two hours. A lunch break starts at about 1:00 or 1:30, and the next seder (study program) starts at about 3:00. The lecture may be reviewed in small study groups at this time. Classes are also held in Chumash (Pentateuch), Nach (prophets), or dinim (laws). In addition, students may attend lectures on the Talmud that stress breadth of knowledge (*b'kiut*) while studying a tractate different from the one studied in the morning lecture. At yeshivot for ba'alei t'shuva, they may also attend workshops (*ulpanim*) in the Hebrew language. At 6:00 or 7:00 they break for supper. An hour and a half later the men are back at their studies with additional shi'urim in any of the aforementioned subjects. This last set of lectures is referred to as the third seder. Normally by this time of the day there are few formal lectures; the period is devoted to individual review and study. Although most students end this third seder at about 10:00 P.M., *matmidim* (zealous students) will continue their studies after the late-evening study session, even late into the night.

One might imagine that such a regimen would quickly wear students down. But students do not mention this as problematic. What makes it possible for students to be so intensely involved in study while at a yeshiva?

Yeshivot generally are much more informal than universities. One studies Torah because it is a mitzvah to do so, not in order to acquire a degree. Yeshivot are not seminaries for rabbinical training, although prospective rabbis are trained there. Therefore, the level of achievement required at yeshivot is generally measured by informal means. Although a specific level of competence in certain materials is required for ordination, *b'chinot* (oral exams) are given infrequently, and no grades are given. Students may enter whatever shi'ur they feel fits their abilities and interests and may stay at the yeshiva for an indefinite period. If it is clear that a student does not seem to be benefiting from study, however, he may be advised to leave. Yeshivot for ba'alei t'shuva reflect much less demanding requirements for objective academic achievement than do yeshivot generally. In addition, the intellectually relaxed and open atmosphere makes greater involvement possible.

THE CHAVRUTA

The *chavruta*[4] typically involves two students who study together, teach each other, review and prepare for lectures together, and ordinarily form close bonds of friendship. It is an intellectual "buddy system." Sometimes three or even four students may constitute a chavruta in a yeshiva. But two students are the ideal number. A student may have one chavruta for the first seder, a second for the second seder or for special studies.

But the style of interaction makes the chavruta study process unique. One might imagine that a buddy system of two people studying together would involve quiet, calm discussion. But anyone who enters a bet hamidrash of a yeshiva must be struck by the animated discussions, which often look like serious quarrels, by the level of noise, the shouting, the gesticulation. Rabbi David Gottlieb described the scene: "They appear to be angry at each other; they shout at each other, they pound the tables,

---

4. Samuel Heilman (1983) uses this term to refer to the group of students in a class, all equal in the learning enterprise, who study together under the tutelage of a teacher, who may or may not be considered one of the chavruta. The students are associates (*chaver*); he is the master (*rav*). Such a group is typically called in the yeshiva a *chevra* (an association) with another term indicating the subject studied, such as a chevra shas, an association for the study of a tractate of the Talmud, or a chevra mishnayot, an association for the study of the Mishna. The term chavruta is specifically used to refer only to a study partner or partners.

they seem to hate each other. It is completely different from a university experience where students when studying on their own sit silently in the library in peace and quiet."

The process needn't always be the emotionally charged intellectual argument that Rabbi Gottlieb describes; it is often a simple discussion of people trying to clarify a point together. But the study process can and does involve one emotionally in the study. This involvement or excitement makes the hours pass quickly, gives one a sense of achievement and a measure of satisfaction. It does not simply bind one person to the other, although it does that too. It binds one directly to the learning experience. You have not just passively absorbed; you have created, you have understood a view, argued for it, transmitted it, defended it. It is now you as much as anything else.

The chavruta, then, is a unique feature of the study system of the yeshiva as a system of education. It makes possible a degree of intensive study and commitment that ordinarily can be achieved only by highly dedicated and talented individuals pursuing study on their own. This system gives some of that experience to large numbers who could not do this on their own and enables those with the talent to move forward quickly to intellectual creativity on their own.

HOW MUCH STUDY IS ENOUGH?

Orthodox Jews do not spend their entire day in Torah study. Some attend a class or lecture on Shabbat. A few set aside time for study on a daily basis. The norm they are exhorted to follow is "set aside a regular time for the study of Torah" (Avot 1:15). Yeshivot exhort their students to "Reflect on it [Torah] day and night" (Josh. 1:1). This norm, restated again and again,[5] shows the great weight placed upon Torah study. The roshei yeshivot and rebbis sometimes use this phrase to contain and direct the energies of the men to Torah alone and away from competing interests or loyalties. It is used as an argument against secular education, against the reading of magazines and newspapers, against involvement in popular culture or sports. This norm is used as a justification for cutting oneself off from the outside world, particularly in traditionalistic yeshivot.[6]

---

5. So much emphasis is placed on the constant study of Torah that a number of terms are available as part of the yeshiva vocabulary for admonishing students: *bittul Torah*, wasting [time for the study of] Torah; *bittul z'man*, wasting time; *batalah*, loafing; a *batlan*, someone who does nothing, in contrast to a *matmid*, one who constantly studies; *batling*, loafing (an Americanization of the term).

6. But the conflict still rages even in modernistic yeshivot; see for example Y.

For those ba'alei t'shuva who have rejected the world and wish to retreat from it, this single-minded focus is not distressing. For others, such an open and unlimited demand for the study of Torah produces conflict. On the normative level the returnee feels torn between Torah and other studies, or other forms of culture or art. On the social level the conflict is between study of Torah as an all-consuming activity and socializing outside the study hall, which is often seen as a waste of time in yeshivot. On the psychological level the totalistic claim for the study of Torah may leave the student with feelings of guilt when playing, relaxing, daydreaming, or participating in amusements. For some ba'alei t'shuva especially, these conflicts may cause severe stress.

The open-ended obligation to study Torah is occasionally exploited by the student to avoid the obligation to earn a living, to support his wife and children, or to take on responsibilities to the Jewish community.[7] This conflict manifests itself in the occasionally heard complaints and exhortations to students by Orthodox Jews and even yeshiva administrators that it is the obligation of men to support their wives, that they can't remain students all their lives, although at the same time teachers and deans at yeshivot encourage students to spend several more months or another year and yet another at the yeshiva.

Inquiring about the major problems encountered by ba'alei t'shuva, I received the following response from Rabbi Mendel Weinbach:

> The major problem is how to divide their time between learning and teaching. They want to learn. They feel they are growing. But they know they also have a responsibility to teach. For example, we have a fellow here from Baltimore, Moshe. A new fellow came in and needed a tutor. Moshe calculates, "Who can tutor him? I'll give up my ulpan, but there still won't be enough time." He roped one of the publishers of our magazine into teaching by telling him that everyone here has to teach. That's the major conflict here. How much of themselves do they have to give up for others?

Ghatan's article in *Hamevaser,* the student publication of Yeshiva University (May 1985).

7. This is a problem not only for ba'alei t'shuva but for advanced yeshiva students generally. Many of the complaints raised with regard to the ba'al t'shuva yeshiva students are also raised for kolel students as well and about those joining chavurot. *The Jewish Catalog* (1973) was criticized because it made no mention of affiliation with the larger Jewish community. *The Second Jewish Catalog* (1976) seemed to make matters even worse by providing information on community resources on which ba'alei t'shuva could draw but not suggesting where or how they could contribute. Only with *The Third Jewish Catalog* (1980) did the focus on "creating community" develop.

This tension between personal growth in a holy life and obligations to others, even religious obligations, underlies many other conflicts. It falls to the rebbi to reorient the ba'alei t'shuva, to emphasize responsibility to the collectivity. Teaching Torah is one area in which this is done. It is also an activity that fits both orientations, for in teaching one also learns.

Problems of Belief

Surveys consistently show that American Jews are far less likely than Protestants or Catholics to express a belief in God, heaven and hell, the End of Days, or resurrection (Herberg 1960, 211–31; Greeley 1972; Greeley 1979; Hoge 1974). The first task in recruiting ba'alei t'shuva would therefore seem to be persuading nonbelievers of belief. Without this, nothing else makes sense. With it, one could argue that everything else follows.

Yet neither recruiters nor yeshivot today spend much time on these beliefs. Nor are they simply avoiding them. These beliefs are not generally raised by potential recruits, and when beliefs are presented by recruiters or in yeshivot or synagogues, they seem to be easily and even eagerly accepted. Aish Hatorah does lay emphasis on beliefs. It has fashioned the most innovative program to deal with recruitment, developing a curriculum totally new to yeshivot. Yet in 1976 the confrontational approach it used, the metaphors it drew on, and the opponents it designated—atheism and Communism—seemed more appropriate to a religious movement of the 1950s than to a movement of the 1970s. By 1982 Aish Hatorah had shifted its focus, as it came to learn what interested potential recruits. No longer were the "proofs of God's existence" the key arguments to which students were introduced. Instead the new opening argument was "Do you want to learn to be happy?"

Ohr Someyach and other yeshivot avoid these issues entirely, instead plunging students directly into the study of Talmud. Beliefs may be handled tangentially in the study of prayer or the Pentateuch and perhaps in private conversations, but they are not treated systematically in the yeshivot. In fact, these questions are not generally raised even during recruitment seminars of the Jewish Learning Exchange (a program sponsored by Ohr Someyach and Neve Yerushalayim), not because of reluctance to discuss them, but because these topics seem to evoke little interest from the participants.

Rabbi Buchwald of the Lincoln Square Synagogue reported that in his outreach work he sometimes discusses God and finds little resistance. What surprised him was a pattern he found in his minyan for beginners. "I would translate the prayers and come to the prayer thanking God who revives the dead," he reported, "and someone would say, 'Oh, I didn't know Jews believed in resurrection!' But they wouldn't argue the point or ask for proof. They would just want to know if this was so. And they seemed happy to accept it."

The quick acceptance by ba'alei t'shuva of a number of core beliefs, as indicated by the recruitment and yeshiva programs, seems to suggest that the Jewish reticence to affirm belief in God or in other core religious doctrines may not be deep-seated. Instead it may be a position assumed as a means of distancing oneself from the Gentile world when one is not familiar with one's own group's beliefs. Buchwald said, "Judaism is a great product. It practically sells itself. There is no problem turning kids on. You only have to tell them about it. The problem is keeping them involved." Apparently, the beliefs are no bar to involvement. Rather, the problem seems to be involving the ba'al t'shuva in the plausibility structure, the social relationships that support those beliefs.

These beliefs may be readily accepted because those who come to the synagogues or yeshivot are predisposed to accept them. But this does not entirely explain the lack of interest in the beliefs. At another time or place, possibly, these issues would have been of moment and would have been discussed. But in our time few people are interested in arguing about beliefs; rejection of religion is expressed in other terms. To conclude that intellectual and rational arguments play no part in acceptance of a belief system is probably a mistake. But it is only necessary that the system prove itself persuasive by seeming to be rational, not that specific questions be answered, even though they might seem crucial from an outsider's perspective.

Another point must be considered here. Judaism has few developed doctrines. The lack of discussion of these issues, therefore, in part reflects that there is little the newcomer must accept.

MIRACLES

Judaism deals with miracles in detail, and miracles set the parameters for the basic beliefs about the nature of God, good and evil, and life after death. Although Judaism has no official dogma, the Bible and other sacred literature present accounts of such miraculous events as the Ten Plagues and splitting of the Red Sea, which form a part of Jewish belief. Yet literal belief in miracles contradicts the scientific assumption that the laws of nature are immutable and predictable and that only empirical phenomena affect the workings of nature. The Bible includes many accounts of the Divine power not only establishing the laws of nature but intervening in the order and changing it. Scientific and religious modes of thought seem to be contradictory. How are people recruited to Orthodoxy if its mode of thought apparently contravenes the prevalent thought patterns?

Several answers are relevant. First, those recruited may be people who reject the scientific perspective to a greater or lesser degree.[8] This applies even to people who have received intensive scientific educations. One of the most effective speakers for Ohr Someyach in its recruitment efforts was a reserve officer who had commanded a submarine in the Israeli Navy. He saw the work of a Divine hand in the events of Jewish history. His argument was cast in semiscientific terms. He argued that the ability to predict accurately was the basis of scientific authority; if one predicted that a tower would fall the next day and it did, this would lend credibility to the person who made the prediction. Therefore, if the predictions of the Pentateuch come to pass, this would affirm the validity of Judaism and the Torah. That the Torah is ancient and preceded the destruction of Israel is unarguable, he said. The Greek translation of the Torah (the Septuagint) existed before the destruction of the Second Temple; therefore the Torah must have preceded this destruction. Yet observe how accurately the prediction of the Torah (Deut. 28) describes what took place under the Romans, what took place in exile, and what finally took place under the Nazis. This could not be coincidence.

He referred to other biblical predictions that he saw as fulfilled, all of which in his view supported the truth of the Torah. Pressed by the listeners, a group of army officers, on the alleged predictions of Nostradamus and of astrology, he conceded that he believed that something could be said for astrology, that it had a predictive power.

One gets the sense that his views on the differences between science and religion are not clear. Despite his training as an engineer and sea captain, he confuses empirical and supraempirical generalizations and prediction. The positions he takes are not likely to be adopted by those with a more sophisticated sense of the methodology of science. Yet he is not alone in

8. Superstition and folk religion are widespread in industrialized societies. A study in London found that approximately 23 percent of the respondents strongly believed in astrology, 60 percent believed in premonitions, and 30 percent believed in "ghosts or spirits that can be seen or sensed by people" (Abercrombie et al. 1970, quoted in McGuire 1981, 242).

his views. One of the rebbis at Brovender's Yeshivat Hamivtar (modern-istic) said that he believed in reincarnation and astrology and did not see as problematic Rabbi Nachman's claim to be a great soul reincarnated. Nor are the teachers alone willing to accept the nonscientific perspective. Many students seem to accept assertions of miracles without objection. The critical question seems to be, how deep do their beliefs go? Some of those who accept miracles without question quit Orthodoxy altogether a short time later. One has to consider what the acceptance of miracles means to them.

In the context of the yeshiva, where teachers feel more at home than when they are recruiting, they may be more willing to present arguments for miracles. In recruiting on a college campus, at a Jewish Learning Exchange Seminar, or in some other more skeptical territory, a different set of arguments is used.

A second response may be seen in the following remarks of Rabbi David Gottlieb, a rebbi at Ohr Someyach and former associate professor of philosophy at Johns Hopkins, specializing in logic and epistemology.

Gottlieb, dressed in a wide-brimmed black felt hat, long black bekeshe, and untrimmed beard, seems the image of the parochial chasid. In re-sponse to a question, however, his unaccented and excellent English is matched by the precision and clarity of his thought. At a Jewish Learning Exchange seminar he was asked, "How are we to understand angels?" He answered:

> Angels are not to be understood as literally physical beings. They may be a vision or a dream, as Maimonides suggests. Technological society presumes that we can answer all questions if only we have the tools. The effect on the person is to restrict reality to those things that can be mea-sured. Thus extrasensory perception for which there is some evidence, but which is extremely difficult to measure, is controversial and denied by many. When you or I read about angels, our response is to reduce it to something we have experienced. Alternatively, we can move from that which we have experienced and attempt to expand our reality rather than deny that which we haven't experienced, to attempt to open ourselves to this possibility. Typically we are attracted to technological developments. We hear of heart implants, computer imaging, and space probes because of their technological aspects. We focus on technology rather than on human nature. I respectfully suggest that there may be realities that we have not experienced.

The answer provided here suggests a position sharply different from the approaches described previously, which seek to persuade one of the scientific legitimacy of miracles. Gottlieb's answer rationalizes the miracles. Miracles become metaphor or dream. Discussing creation on another occasion, Rabbi Gottlieb referred to the "big bang theory" of the origin of the universe, implying that scientific reinterpretations of miracles are possible. The implicit argument for the truth or at least for the persuasiveness of Orthodox beliefs is Gottlieb himself. Here is an obviously knowledgeable and sophisticated man ably defending Orthodox beliefs. Moreover, this defense is not just words. His garb indicates a commitment to that part of Orthodoxy that is often labeled "fanatic." And although he appears radically different from the ba'alei t'shuva who are also Israeli military officers and who teach at Ohr Someyach, his strategy for persuasion is essentially the same as theirs. One finds evidence at least of their reasonableness, if not truth, in the person of the recruiter who has accepted these beliefs.

One's beliefs regarding miracles define many other theological concerns, such as the meaning of life, reward and punishment, and the nature of God. The kinds of answers given, even at a single yeshiva like Ohr Someyach, run the gamut from those that are so simplistic that they leave the rebbi open to ridicule to those that are so sophisticated that they imply the rebbi has a better grasp of science than his critics. Traditionalist yeshivot have typically avoided or ignored questions about miracles that derive from a scientific perspective. The assumptions and philosophic underpinnings of science were simply derided and minimized, if not suppressed, in yeshivot. That Yeshiva University chose to incorporate scientific study into its curriculum, making its motto "Torah and Science," raised fears about it in traditionalistic circles. But ba'al t'shuva yeshivot, even those that are traditionalistic, reach out to the wider society to recruit and make their appeal in broad terms. Recruiters also adopt scientific perspectives. Science does not become a part of the curriculum in these yeshivot, but it is part of the outreach effort. The most successful recruiters are those who have a scientific background, and many of these are ba'alei t'shuva. In these yeshivot, then, the scientific knowledge of men like Rabbi Gottlieb provides legitimacy to religion; at the same time, it legitimates the scientific perspective because their position demonstrates that one need not denigrate science to remain religious. This approach also affects the Orthodox from birth, who often attend recruitment seminars and outreach programs as a religious evening out, an opportunity for a fresh experience. Because this yeshiva is traditionalistic and because Rabbi Gottlieb chooses to dress in a traditionalistic chasidic fashion, this approach penetrates even further and faster into the traditionalistic community than does a similar approach when voiced by modernists.

The range of responses offered at Ohr Someyach, from the simplistic to the sophisticated, could produce conflicts over "correct" interpretations. One reason it does not is that common commitment to traditionalism means that those professing a scientific perspective accord full respect to the traditionalists and do not publicly disagree with them.[9] As the arguments are never addressed head-on by the scholars themselves, a good deal of confusion remains, and it appears that recruits may be persuaded not by the content of the answers but by the stature of the people professing them. The plausibility structure rather than the meaning system comes to be persuasive, perhaps for all but a small minority.[10]

This line of analysis also suggests an answer to another question of belief. Even at Pardess, where the staff is modernistic in approach and the school seeks specifically to bridge the gap to Conservatism, questions about the validity of the Bible from the perspective of higher criticism do not arise, possibly because few people are familiar with the Welhausen school of higher biblical criticism whereas many are familiar with evolutionary theory and scientific perspective. Furthermore, many of the specific arguments of higher criticism have been undermined by archaeological finds.[11] In fact archaeological finds often support biblical narrative that had been thought to be metaphor or poetry. And archaeology that supports the Jewish claim to Israel is indeed a national pastime with the sites of digs scattered all over the land and national museums displaying the finds. A system of criticism derived from one paradigm, the liberal scientific approach of nineteenth-century Germany, has been undermined by another paradigm also claiming scientific validity, archaeology. The believer need not examine the details of one or the other paradigm and weigh them; he may simply elect to follow those that promote a perspective compatible with his own, particularly if it also has

9. Another reason is that those who hold their opinions strongly leave to set up their own institutions, so that in any one yeshiva opinions tend to be homogeneous.

10. The importance of this minority, however, for whom the arguments themselves—the meaning system—carry great weight, should not be underestimated. They become the core group promoting the continuation of the effectiveness of the religion.

11. Albright (1957) argued for the historical veracity of the biblical accounts based on growing archaeological evidence. So much support for his position has accumulated that in a recent book review Miller (1987) refers to the approach to the Bible of two schools—the critical and the archaeological and to the scientific validity of the latter position.

legitimacy in the same scientific and secular world. Finally, while the Holocaust undermined scientific prestige among Jews, the potential for what is now called a nuclear holocaust has undermined scientific prestige in the larger society, so that the thought system of science has lost its standing and is now vulnerable to rejection on moral grounds.

SOUL, RESURRECTION, AND TRANSMIGRATION

Judaism's teachings on the nature of the soul and resurrection are not clearly formulated and are at times contradictory, leaving them open to philosophic reformulation. Since the notions of soul and resurrection are also widespread in Western societies through the influence of Christianity and Islam, they seem not to raise serious questions for ba'alei t'shuva.

Mystical circles in Judaism have also taught a doctrine of the transmigration of the soul (*gilgul*). Although these teachings are associated with Chasidism, they also have a place among mitnagdim who are followers of Kabbalah, although there is no reference to it in the Talmud. The notion of transmigration of souls is part of a broader doctrine of the nature of God, the process of creation, and the nature of reward and punishment. There are numerous parallels between this doctrine and Indian religious views. The idea of gilgul has been controversial in Judaism and was rejected by the leading medieval Jewish philosophers as mistaken if not heretical.[12] Nevertheless, it has entered into Jewish folk religion.[13]

Given the folk character of these beliefs, *maskilim* (enlightened ones) and modernists have rejected them. They retain a powerful hold on chasidim, where the major rebbes claim (privately) to be reincarnations of famous Jewish personalities. Thus Rebbe Nachman of Bratzlav claimed to be a reincarnation of Rabbi Shimon Bar Yochai, the reputed founder of Kabbalah, and of the Ari, the great sixteenth-century Safad mystic who reformulated the major kabbalistic doctrines and provided the foundation of later kabbalistic theology. Others have claimed ties to equally renowned personalities including King David and the future messiah.

Through the nineteenth century and into the mid-twentieth century it was assumed that such notions could not appeal to educated and enlightened persons. The t'shuva movement raised questions about this

12. See Saadiah Gaon, *Sefer ha-Emunot ve-ha-De'ot* (Constantinople, 1562), and Joseph Albo, *Sefer ha-Ikkarim* (Soncino, 1485).

13. See the fiction of I. B. Singer in particular for a modern example of the use of these notions in folklore.

assumption. Lubavitch and Bratzlaver chasidut, both of which claim that their leaders (in the latter case their deceased leader) are gilgulim of great souls, have attracted a large number of ba'alei t'shuva. Although this is primarily a result of their outreach efforts, the appeal of the mystical doctrine should not be underestimated. For hippies seeking to escape a rationalized and bureaucratized world, the rumor of angels was compelling. Moreover, because these ideas had parallels in Indian religions that were then entering the counterculture, they quickly achieved the legitimacy of accepted countercultural notions.

In these circumstances interest in Jewish mysticism grew. Buber's work on Chasidism had laid the groundwork a generation earlier. The counterculture provided the mass interest necessary for the spread of mystical ideas. Courses in mystical teachings became popular at universities, and mainline groups began to look at them with renewed respect. The ideas might need to be presented more abstractly, philosophic underpinnings provided, and the folk elements sifted out so that the ideas themselves could be accepted.

In the last analysis, although these ideas were not major factors in the growth of the t'shuva movement, they presented no obstacles to that movement and to some extent even facilitated it, despite, or perhaps because of, their strangeness.

Problems of Jewish Beliefs

Up to this point, the beliefs we have discussed characterize Christianity and Islam as well as Judaism. They seem to present no particular difficulty for those attempting to reach out and recruit. They also do not seem to be questioned often by ba'alei t'shuva. The issues that seem to be of greatest concern to recruits are those that uniquely characterize the Jewish and particularly the Orthodox positions.

HOLOCAUST

The issue cited most often by those who deal with new recruits is the Holocaust. The question is not the broad one of theodicy, "Why do the good suffer?" but rather the specific question of "If Judaism is true, how could there have been a Holocaust? Why would God allow six million Jews, men, women, and children, to be put to death in a most brutal fashion?" This is a question widely discussed by Jews of all stripes, not only the Orthodox. All have difficulty answering it.

The traditional answer—that Jews were punished for breaking the Divine laws of the Torah—does not seem applicable here; for the most traditional Jewish community—that of eastern Europe—was wiped out, while assimilated communities elsewhere fared far better.

A variety of philosophic answers are offered, such as, "We cannot know God's will, as our understanding is limited," or "One suffers in this world but will be rewarded in the world to come" (or "at the coming of the Messiah and resurrection"). The latter answers are more acceptable to the Orthodox; the first, although also traditional, is more acceptable to Reform and Conservative Jews. In reaching out to the uncommitted, the "we cannot know" answer is most often used. As the person moves further along in commitment, as miracles come to be accepted, the latter answers are more often discussed. Those who use this sequence recognize that to appeal broadly one must use broadly acceptable arguments. An unintended consequence is that even in traditionalistic ba'al t'shuva yeshivot rebbis tend to use the broader arguments, introducing students to a more rationalistic Judaism.

It is hard to assess how serious a hurdle to recruitment the Holocaust is. It probably discourages recruitment in the United States and other diaspora communities. Like other catastrophes of Jewish history, the Holocaust is interpreted by some Christians as just punishment of the Jews for not accepting Christianity. Jews may respond by questioning how Christianity could be true and still lay the groundwork for such horrific persecutions in the name of love (see Weisel 1966). But people are still left with the question of how to attach themselves to a religion that leaves the Master of the Universe responsible for the suffering of the people they are being asked to become involved with. Strangely, for some of those who return, the Holocaust is a motivating factor. One older returnee, who had served in the U.S. Army during World War II said, "When I began to hear about the Holocaust, I felt I had to become more Jewish. I couldn't let the chain of tradition be broken. I couldn't let Hitler win."

For others the experience of the Holocaust was so frightening that they joined other religions rather than risk remaining part of a persecuted people. The experience of persecution and fear of the Holocaust is probably related to the disproportionate numbers of American Jews who joined various cults, comprising twice their proportion of the general population in the Unification church and ten times their proportion among Zen Buddhists (Melton and Moore 1982).

In Israel, the Holocaust has a different resonance. That an independent Jewish state exists once again, that control of the ancient city of Jerusalem and the holy sites is again in Jewish hands, plays counterpoint to a more intense experience of the Holocaust. Many Israelis are survivors of concentration camps or some other sort of persecution in Arab lands or in Russia. The overwhelming sense that Jews have been singled out, that they are not like others, is confirmed by their treatment in other lands in the present as well as in the historic past. The rebirth of Israel shows that God is still involved with the fate of the Jews. They are sometimes made to suffer terribly, but the special relationship exists. In fact, the continuous wars against Israel have given an impetus to the ba'al t'shuva movement in Israeli society generally. For Israelis, as we have seen, the movement began in the wake of the Yom Kippur War, which Israelis do not see as a victory but at best as a war not lost. The Holocaust, then, is an issue that surfaces continually. It may discourage some from becoming Orthodox Jews. But it also supports the claim that God is still interested in the fate of the Jews and that Jews are terribly important.

Problems in Orthodox Beliefs

THE PLACE OF WOMEN IN JUDAISM

The question of the role and status of women in Orthodox Judaism recurs most powerfully and persistently in recruitment efforts. It is directed only at Orthodoxy, as Reform and Conservative Judaism long ago agreed that the Orthodox position was demeaning to women and have modified the ritual and liturgy and redefined the position of women. Reform Judaism, with its futuristic perspective, argues that in the past Judaism had primitive notions but has now rid itself of them. Conservative Judaism, which places greater weight on respect for tradition, has had more difficulty with this position but has followed Reform's lead. Orthodoxy's view of the eternal truth of halakhah has forced it to defend a number of practices rejected by the other branches of Judaism: the mechitzah, the exclusion of women from being counted in the minyan, the refusal to permit women the honor of reading from the Torah in public prayer, the refusal to allow women to become rabbis, the recitation of morning blessings by every Orthodox male thanking God for "not having created me a woman," the laws of niddah, which separate husband and wife during a period of each menstrual cycle. None of these is a problem for Conservative or Reform Judaism (with the exception, at the time of this study, of the ordination of women in the Conservative movement).

The place of women is not much studied in yeshivot for men, although the rules that give rise to the problem are studied, the morning blessing is pronounced, and a mechitzah is in place in every sanctuary (except at Pardess). It is, however, very much an issue in women's schools, particularly in outreach efforts such as the Jewish Learning Exchange and the Lincoln Square Synagogue. The following conversation between a woman at Har Tzion Yeshiva and another who had been placed with an Orthodox family for Shabbat was overheard on a Saturday night in 1976:

Woman 1. Judaism puts women up on a pedestal.
Woman 2. Some pedestal. It all sounds fine, Shabbat and family and togetherness. But while he was sitting there at the table like a king, she was running in and out like a good little servant.
Woman 1. Give it another chance. You don't understand it.
Woman 2. I've seen enough. If this is Judaism, it's not for me.

At Lincoln Square Synagogue Rabbi Buchwald reported that in the early 1970s, in response to persistent questions from women, he found it necessary to discuss the meaning and importance of the mechitzah in the synagogue about once a month. By 1980 the issue seemed to have faded—women seemed to be aware of the mechitzah and to take their seats on the women's side without fuss or the need for directions—but the reason for the change was not apparent.

The issue was still a live one at the Jewish Learning Exchange program in December 1982, when Rabbi David Gottlieb of Ohr Someyach was closely questioned by several participants at a three day seminar. The men's morning blessing was particularly troubling. Other teachers responded, but their answers did not seem satisfying, and the seminar participants continued to press the matter. Gottlieb suggested that to follow the change introduced in the Conservative service (instead of thanking God for "not having created me a woman," the new blessing seeks to avoid invidious comparison and thanks God for "having created me a man") would mean putting one's own existence in the forefront. In the context of a talmudic discussion on the meaning of life, the academies of Hillel and Shamai agreed after a two-and-a-half-year debate that "It were better to offer thanks for what existence one has not been made to suffer than to offer thanks for one's existence when one addresses The Cause and Master of All Existence." This is a fine philosophical point that apparently went above the heads of many listeners. One of the most enthusiastic participants, a young women whose statement approving the Jewish Learning Exchange program ("I have learned more in these last three days than in all my years in Hebrew School") was later used in a mailing advertising an upcoming seminar was interviewed a year later and said:

A. I learned a lot at that seminar.

Q. What did you learn?

A. For one thing the meaning of the blessing that men say that I'm glad I'm not a woman or a dog. I mean, women have their own status.[14]

No blessing compares men or women with dogs; nor was the comment intended ironically. The response indicates that she misunderstood the men's blessing and that her satisfaction with the response to questions about the blessing had nothing to do with its content but rather concerned its context—an articulate spokesman said something that appeared to be intelligent.

The most radically countercultural response was offered by Rabbi Krupnick, Dean of Brovender's Shappel for Women, a modernistic school:

> Judaism doesn't believe that all people are the same. Sure, they are all equal in the sense that they are all creatures of God, all made in His image, all having a soul, all descended from the same human line. But women and men are not the same. Men have one role, and women have another. And if you deny that, you might just as well deny that the Torah distinguishes the Cohen and Levi and the Israelite or that the Jews are uniquely God's chosen people.[15] All are born into their roles; they don't compete for them.

Again the key seems to be not so much that the answers are satisfactory as that they were made in an intelligent way by an articulate spokesman with the proper credentials—that is, advanced secular education.

But the place of women involves not only beliefs but also action and rituals. As I have discussed previously, the laws regarding relations between men and women are much more problematic in recruitment than are the beliefs.

THE AUTHORITY OF TORAH SHEH BA'AL PEH

I have pointed out that ba'alei t'shuva have found it especially problematic to accept the authority of Torah sheh ba'al peh—the belief that

14. This woman did not become Orthodox or adopt any Orthodox practices.

15. It has been argued that the three blessings of the morning prayers, which thank God for not having created one a Gentile, a slave, or a woman, were added to the original list of morning blessings specifically to reject Paul's formulation (Gal. 3:28): "There is no difference between Jews and Gentiles, between slaves and free men, between men and women: you are all one in union with Jesus Christ." (Heineman 1977; compare BT, Berachot 20b with BT, Menahot 43b). My thanks to Norman Fredman for calling this to my attention.

along with the written Torah a set of oral interpretations of the law was given to Moses at Sinai and that these oral interpretations are therefore authoritative.

Traditionalistic yeshivot attempt to identify those authorities the student should follow *and those that may be ignored.* This amounts to insisting on one's ties to a community. But the ba'al t'shuva, not grounded in a particular community, has no basis on which to decide which authority to follow. The result is that these yeshivot have difficulty convincing ba'alei t'shuva of their authority.

The problem of belief is resolved not through an academic discussion and clarification but rather through practice and growing attachment to a community. The question for ba'alei t'shuva then becomes, which is the "authentic" community. Interestingly, several of the major problems of belief faced by ba'alei t'shuva—the status of women, the authority of the law, and the status of Jew and Gentile—are matters not simply of belief but of social interaction.

JEWS AND GENTILES

Laws involving Jewish-Gentile relations present a major problem for Orthodoxy. For example, a Jew may not accept interest payments from another Jew, but he may take interest from a Gentile (Exod. 22:24 and Lev. 25:35–37). More difficult still is the law that permits any manner of work to rescue a Jew on Shabbat and in theory forbids work on Shabbat to save the life of a Gentile, although in practice the Gentile must be rescued.

Rabbi Mendel Weinbach of Ohr Someyach feels that these laws are particularly difficult for ba'alei t'shuva to accept. "These are people with a highly developed sense of ethics and morality. These questions really bother them."

They are not problems for Reform Jews, who can simply say that they are the primitive conceptions of morality of an earlier age. Conservatives attempt to explain these laws in terms of the prevailing social and economic conditions at the time they were laid down. But for the Orthodox, to whom the laws are eternal and unchanging, they present a problem. Nor is it satisfying to respond that the laws are no longer applicable, that Orthodox Jewish law today *requires* the violation of Shabbat law to save the life of a Gentile because of *darkei shalom* (to promote peace between Jew and Gentile), for that still leaves unanswered the question of the ethic of the law. Nor is it meaningful to argue that other faiths make distinctions between the faithful and infidels that are far more shocking, that call for the faithful to kill and destroy unbelievers. That position is of little comfort for the Orthodox Jewish believer. It reflects the relativistic position of modern religious and anthropological thought, not the position of one who believes that his or her religion is truly Divinely revealed and without flaw. Nor can one suggest that the rabbis erred in their interpretation of the law. In the framework of rabbinical Judaism, the rabbis of the Talmud do not err in their interpretations of the law. Their interpretation would be true even if contradicted by some Divine sign or miracle. Conceding error once a majority decision has been accepted by the community of committed is theologically impossible and would raise the most weighty questions about the nature of the authority of Jewish law. In fact this concept of authority is the heart of the difference between Orthodoxy and the other wings of Judaism.

Weinbach's answers to the question of taking interest and the question of violating laws of Shabbat to save a life demonstrate how these knotty issues are treated. Regarding interest, Weinbach says: If you were to borrow someone's car or live in his house for a period, you would expect to pay for the use of that commodity. There is nothing unethical about this; we do it all the time. The Torah acknowledges the equity and ethical character of this arrangement by specifically allowing one to rent another's ox or land. By the same token, there is nothing ethically or morally reprehensible about charging a person interest for the use of money. However, the Torah requires that a Jew be especially concerned with his brother the Israelite. To show this brotherhood and concern, he must not take interest from a fellow Jew. This is not a matter of ethics or morality but a matter of showing a particular connection and concern. To all others one must act morally and ethically. But that does not preclude the taking of interest, which is simply equity or fairness.16

The theoretical (not actual) inviolability of Shabbat law, even when following it may endanger the life of a Gentile, is answered by stressing the holiness of Shabbat. Confronted with this issue by a ba'al t'shuva who insistently beseeched him for an answer, Weinbach replied by asking: "How would you feel if you were the one assigned to drop the atomic bomb on Hiroshima? You knew that the war effort and the lives of tens of thousands of your countrymen depended on you. But you also knew that

---

16. It has long been a practice for Jews to charge interest for lending money to other Jews, and this is not considered a breach of halakhah. Rabbeinu Tam, a twelfth-century Tosafist, instituted the *Heter Iska,* a document that makes the lender a partner in the venture and thus eligible for a share of the profit—that is, interest.

tens, maybe hundreds, of thousands of people would be killed and many more times that maimed by the bomb. You would hesitate. Well, violating Shabbat is like dropping that atomic bomb. The Shabbat is so holy, so important, you can't violate it with impunity even if the reasons are terribly important." The answer seemed to satisfy the ba'al t'shuva, who decided to remain at the yeshiva.

Yet the question of why the Sabbath may be violated as a matter of course in order to save a Jew remains. Weinbach's answer suggests the terrible moral dilemma one is in regarding this law. Perhaps all the student wanted was to know that the teacher was also sensitive to this moral problem and made uncomfortable by it.

Modernists, who follow Maimonides' teachings a little more closely, sometimes answer the question by pointing out that these laws referred not to Gentiles generally but to "star worshipers," a precise legal category meaning those who deny the existence of deity, who practice no law and no justice, whose ways are cruel and murderous. Judaism's daughter religions do not fall into this category.[17] The case of the Gentile who is not helped is therefore a legal category, but concretely an empty one. It exists primarily to teach a lesson about religious values rather than about how to conduct oneself in relation to others. Halakhah *does require* that the Gentile be rescued even if this involves the desecration of Shabbat.

The most problematic answers in terms of universalistic values are offered by those whose theory of souls suggests that some have holier souls or are derived from higher Divine sparks than others. But, as already pointed out, discussion of souls is part of the "hidden knowledge" (*nistar*) that is only alluded to. Such a position seems acceptable to those who believe in reincarnation and the progression of souls from lower to higher levels through continued rebirth, a view not inconsistent with the teachings of Far Eastern religions and gnostic and mystical Christianity. This perspective, however, and to a lesser extent the traditionalistic one still leave the community of the most worthy drawn very tightly, with only a few—the critical sparks—as the chosen, and the rest of lesser importance. Furthermore, the more countercultural the stand, the more tightly have the boundaries between "we" and "they" been drawn and the smaller the community of the "we" has been.

17. This position is clearly stated in a much earlier source (see BT, Hulin 13b quoted with approval by Rashi, BT, Kiddushin 68b, and Tosafot; BT, Avodah Zarah 2a) and also by the Me'iri (Bet Ha Behirah on Avodah Zarah). Jacob Katz (1961) discusses this fully. It is puzzling that these sources are not cited in traditionalistic yeshivot.

The positions articulated here are not doctrinal. These questions have begun to be addressed seriously in yeshivot only since the beginnings of the t'shuva movement. The ba'al t'shuva movement is forcing a rethinking of these boundaries, as is apparent in the moral struggle expressed in Weinbach's answer. It demonstrates that a critical definition of the boundaries of moral obligation is under stress and in the process of change, at least in the ba'al t'shuva yeshivot.

Jews have at one and the same time made claims for universalism— God's fatherhood of all creatures, the descent of all mankind from one ancestor, the equality of all before the law—and for their particularistic relationship to God through the Covenant as a chosen people, a light unto the nations, "a people that dwells alone." Reform Judaism has tended to stress the former, Orthodox Judaism the latter. For Reform, Jews are no different from the rest of mankind. If this leaves the Jew with the question, "If this is so, why be Jewish?" so be it.

Orthodox Judaism's emphasis on particularism also has negative consequences in that the moral circle to which one is responsible is drawn smaller. Not simply good people versus evil, nor God-fearing versus idolators, nor Jews versus Gentiles, nor Orthodox versus non-Orthodox. It progresses to "only our type of Orthodox," our small community of followers of this or that leader.

These two values come into conflict when the ba'al t'shuva moves from involvement with the more left-wing movement, which emphasizes universalism, into Orthodoxy. Orthodoxy, even of the traditionalistic type, is now confronted with this problem as it is raised by the ba'alei t'shuva.

I have examined some of the points that ba'alei t'shuva seem to find problematic. For the most part, they involve practices—prayer, study, dress, ritual conformity (and of course kashrut, Shabbat, and family purity).

Beliefs and values seem to present fewer problems than practices, although there are some significant problems related to belief. The ethical perspective and belief system taught by Judaism and spread through its daughter religions is so pervasive that it is not seriously questioned. Belief in God, in revelation, in an afterlife, in reward and punishment, and even in resurrection and transmigration of souls seems to be accepted easily by seemingly skeptical Jews, although they may be abandoned just as easily. These beliefs seem not to be of great consequence, in part because their meaning is related to one's understanding of "miracles." Great latitude exists here. Beliefs seem to be validated not by their logic or scientific validity but by the legitimacy of those who profess them. The uniquely Jewish belief problem is how to make sense of God, the world, and Jews in the aftermath of the Holocaust.

The ethical issues that seem problematic to ba'alei t'shuva relate to Orthodoxy only. The place of women in Orthodoxy raises problems primarily for women, although many ba'alot t'shuva seem ready to accept these norms, possibly because they appear balanced by a close family structure that is attractive. The Orthodox position on role differences between men and women is also consistent with that of many of the new religions. The authority of the Oral Law and of the rabbis presents difficulties because the position professed by some of the yeshivot seems unclear and inconsistent. The issue does not involve a conflict with norms of the larger society but reflects instead conflicts about authority within Judaism and specifically within Orthodoxy. Jewish-Gentile relations present a problem not because of practices of Orthodoxy, which in fact treats Jew and Gentile alike, but rather because of the claim of Orthodoxy that halakhah is unchanging and not subject to adjustment in response to changed social conditions. Although practice has changed with the application of a different halakhic principle (that is, either the argument that it is socially necessary or that this rule was never intended to apply to any other than "star worshipers"), a philosophic defense of the ancient halakhah is necessary in order to engage in outreach.

Chapter 13

Striking Roots

How do the ba'al t'shuva's newly accepted values affect his ties to parents? And how does he develop and establish new family ties? To examine this process more systematically I use the metaphor of "life course" and "life convoy" (Abeles and Riley 1977).[1] The life of the ba'al t'shuva moves in a new direction following his new commitment and the change in life course affects his relationship to each of the members of his convoy in a radical way.

New Values and Old Ties

PARENTS AND THE NEWLY RELIGIOUS

A major problem among such new religions as the Hare Krishna and the Unification Church is the relation of the new convert to his parents. Parents of some of those who have joined these new religions have occasionally attempted to snatch their children away from these groups. Those who succeed often find that the children attempt to rejoin the cult. Some children have taken their parents to court to gain freedom, not from the cult but from the parents. In desperation, some parents have hired deprogrammers to break down the barriers to family and former friends erected through the cult's "brainwashing" techniques. The methods used by deprogrammers involve isolation of the person, abusive language, and

1. The life course is the trajectory that people's lives follow through childhood, adolescence, adulthood, and so forth. Their life convoy are those who accompany them on their course: parents, friends, mate, and then perhaps their own children. Each of these joins the person at an expected time and may leave, perhaps to be replaced by others, before the person has completed his life course.

deprivation. There are even reports of deprogrammers using violence to achieve their ends. So severe is the process that such cases have gone to court, and deprogrammers have been jailed. The court records describe in detail the severity of the deprogramming techniques. The violence and abuse to which a person is sometimes subjected in the course of deprogramming have led sociologists to see a parallel between joining a cult and "possession by demons" in the minds of the parents and deprogrammers. The literature and legal briefs that have grown up around these cases make it clear that the new religions were involved in a problem of major proportions on the American scene (Robbins 1980).

Parents whose children have "converted" to a cult charge that the children are changed personalities, that they are cut off from the friends, amenities, and comforts they formerly enjoyed, and that they have severed their ties to their parents—all this for reasons that the parents and former friends find irrational. Surprisingly, not a single similar case involving those who have returned to Judaism has arisen, although the change in life-style that the ba'al t'shuva undergoes is equally radical.

The child refuses to eat in the parents' home or makes conditions for eating in the parents' home, such as "only if you buy new dishes" or "only kosher foods." One can easily see the laws of kashrut alone cutting children off from parents, siblings, other relatives, and former friends at social, familial, and even religious occasions. Certainly they eliminate the casual family outing to the local Chinese restaurant or to MacDonalds, the hot dog at the beach, and even the occasional ice cream (unless it's kosher). They cut the person off from the home on a daily basis, even when the parents accommodate by providing the ba'al t'shuva with a shelf in the refrigerator and some pots and dishes of his or her own. The separation of food and dishes is a constant reminder of difference and distance, whereas until this "conversion" food and meals were an expression of cohesion. As Max Weber has pointed out, one of the major activities reinforcing social cohesion is commensality. But beyond this and still more disruptive and painful is the ba'al t'shuva's refusal to participate in those holiday and ceremonial celebrations of the family in which *all* have always participated. The ba'al t'shuva may refuse to participate in the family seder, in the family wedding, in the most central family occasions. No matter how slow is the transformation of the ba'al t'shuva from former self to Orthodox Jew, this is seen as a radical change, almost as a betrayal.

All this is only the beginning, for the ba'al t'shuva also marks himself or herself off from others by the observance of Shabbat. Parents may not object if the child wishes to light candles or attend services at the synagogue. But the special arrangements required to warm food on the Sabbath and the refusal to use the phone, electricity, or the automobile create a separation between child and parent, child and sibling, and child and former friends that undermines these relationships. Orthodox Judaism regulates every area of behavior with specific rules and rituals. It creates not only a different set of values but a different life-style. A recording produced by the Jewish Education Program (JEP, an affiliate of Agudat Israel of America) to attract Jewish youngsters to Orthodoxy includes a song ostensibly about a ba'al t'shuva that contains these lines:

> My parents don't want me to daven;
> They say "Do something!" instead.
> But my parents don't see I'm filled with emotion;
> I'm serving Ha-Shem with total devotion.
> (*Kol Yisrael Arevim,* Jewish Educational Program Records)

For the majority of Jews the Lubavitcher are not as strange or as cultlike as the "Moonies" or the Hare Krishna groups. But for some they are indeed a cult. In April of 1977 Rabbi Arthur J. Lelyveld, a past president of the Central Conference of American Rabbis (Reform), president of the American Jewish Congress, and holder of other prominent national positions in the American Jewish community, raised a storm of controversy by suggesting in a sermon widely reported in the press that Chabad-Lubavitch is a cult. Referring to the Moonies, the Children of God, Scientology, Hare Krishna, Jesus Freaks, and Jews for Jesus, Rabbi Lelyveld noted "the corruption of the cults, their venality, their hidden political purposes" and expressed deep concern about "evils that go beyond this," of which he listed four: "(1) surrendering to the authority of a charismatic leader, (2) irrationality, (3) deliberately driving a wedge between parents and their children, and (4) removing 'those who have been captured' from the mainstream of society 'so that they are lost not only to their parents, but to Jewish life in the form which we have come to cherish.'" Rabbi Lelyveld continued, "All the evils I have mentioned are present in contemporary Chabad [Lubavitch]."

In an interview discussing the controversial sermon, Rabbi Lelyveld dwelt at length on the third point, deliberately driving a wedge between parents and children. "Soon you'll be eighteen, they say, and you won't have to listen to your parents any more. Is that *kabed et avicha v'et imecha* [honoring thy father and thy mother]?" he asked. To the remark that at least Lubavitch is Jewish, Rabbi Lelyveld's response was, "So were Shab-betai Tzevi and Jacob Frank."[2]

Rabbi Lelyveld unequivocally identified Lubavitch with cults that are characterized as noxious, evil, and dangerous. His view was echoed by Gerson Cohen, chancellor of Conservative Judaism's Jewish Theological Seminary, who in an address on "the state of world Jewry" (October 1982) condemned the "anti-intellectualism and the seeds of intolerance that are planted in the ba'al t'shuva yeshivot." He accused them of aliena-tion from the Jewish people at large, of hostility to modernism and plu-ralism, of renouncing all Jewish thought and literature.

> They are not appeals to the return of religion, much less the healing of breaches; they are appeals to magic ritual, to rank anti-intellectualism and superstition and above all, to rebbe-worship. The ba'alei t'shuva, those young people who have ostensibly returned to the Jewish fold by enrolling in the diverse yeshivot that have been set up to serve them, in fact find their fulfillment in an anti-intellectual study of the Torah, in a rejection of the world, in a hero-worship and ritualism that we easily recognize—and con-demn—in others. How different are they, after all, from the Moonies, the Hare Krishna, the Ayatolah Khomeini, or the Moral Majority? They are Jews, to be sure, but they are no source of strength for the Jewish people.

These sentiments probably characterize the feelings of substantial por-tions of Reform and Conservative Jews. Yet despite this, one does not find reports of snatchings, deprogrammings, or legal contests between chil-dren who have become Lubavitcher and their parents.[3]

Apparently, although some parents of newly converted Lubavitcher may agree with Gerson Cohen and with three of Rabbi Lelyveld's points, they disagree with him with regard to respect for father and mother, and this seems to be the most critical factor for them. Judaism and Christianity differ with regard to obligations of the newly religious to parents, and these normative differences have implications for social structure and for personality. A clue to distinguishing these two normative systems may be

2. Jacob Frank (1726–1791) was the founder of an antinomian Shabbetean sect that secretly engaged in orgiastic rituals.

3. The Anti-Cult and Missionary Program in New York reports that they have been asked by some parents to help prevent their children from becoming chasidim. Their response has ordinarily been to contact the group and put them in touch with the parents, and this has generally resolved the problem. Similarly, there is an association of parents of ba'alei t'shuva in Israel opposed to the t'shuva movement. But this has not resulted in snatchings or court actions in Israel or the United States.

found in the work of Rosabeth Moss Kanter (1968), who points out that to maintain the loyalty of their members utopian religious communities of the eighteenth and nineteenth centuries often required renunciation of the family. She quotes the following Shaker hymn as illustrative (1968, 508–509):

> Of all the relations that ever I see
> My old fleshly kindred are furthest from me
> So bad and so ugly, so hateful they feel
> To see them and hate them increases my zeal
> O how ugly they look!
> How ugly they look!
> How nasty they feel!

Kanter points out that the purpose of this requirement is to increase in-group cohesiveness, as is indicated later in the same hymn.

> My *gospel relations* are dearer to me
> Than all fleshly kindred that ever I see. . . .
> . . . .
> Oh how pretty they look! . . .

That estrangement from parents and friends is permitted and even encouraged in Christianity may also be seen in the story of Jesus' rejection of his mother and brothers when they come to visit him. Saying "Who is my mother? Who are my brothers?" and pointing to his disciples exclaiming, "Here are my mother and my brothers," Jesus cuts the familial ties and replaces them with ties of faith. This episode, repeated in three of the gospels (Matt. 12:46–48; Mark 3:31–35; Luke 8:19–21), can and apparently does provide legitimation for such commitment mechanisms as cutting oneself off from parents and former friends.

Normative Judaism teaches that respect and love for parents are every child's obligation, even when one suffers severe financial loss, when the parents are not Jewish, or if they return this respect with gross disrespect.[4]

Respect for parents is not simply a normative requirement, it actually impinges on recruitment to Orthodoxy. The following excerpt from an interview conducted in Jerusalem illustrates this.

A. I ran away from home when I was fifteen. I ran away because of *Pesach*. . . . I left my parents a note and all kinds of things, but I didn't tell them where I was.

4. See BT, Kiddushin 31a ff. for the story of Dama bar Nesina.

Q. Did your parents know you went to a religious place for Pesach?
A. Yes. But they didn't know exactly where it was. They had police cars out, but
   that didn't mean much. And then the rebbe said, "You should contact them
   during *chol ha'Mo'ed* [the intermediary days of the festival when use of the
   phone is permitted]. So I called them up and told them that I was all right and
   that I wouldn't tell them where I was unless we agreed on certain things. So
   they agreed. At that time, I wanted to go to a yeshiva in New York. They
   didn't want me to. We made a compromise that I would go to a yeshiva in
   Elizabeth.

   The following summer I went to Gan Yisrael . . . a Lubavitcher camp. In
   the middle of the summer, on Tisha B'Av [a day of fasting and mourning
   commemorating the destruction of the First and Second Temples] I went to
   speak to the [Lubavitcher] rebbe. . . . I told him I lived in Elizabeth and I
   wanted to learn in a more frum [pious] yeshiva. He told me I should do it with
   darkei shalom . . . peaceful ways.

Bearing in mind that this episode refers to Lubavitch, the very group
that Rabbi Lelyveld has characterized as a cult and accused of having no
concern or respect for parents, one might have anticipated that Luvabitch
would emphasize the centrality of true religious commitment and de-
emphasize attachment to parents. Instead this young man was advised to
return home, to continue to treat his parents with respect, and yet to try to
live as an Orthodox Jew in that household.

This is not an isolated case characteristic of Lubavitch alone but reflects the values of normative Judaism. This same story was repeated with
variations in a number of interviews. Tension arises between returnee and
parents over the change, and parents fear losing their children to a strange
cult. But returnees are taught that respect and love for parents are essential values, and they are urged to maintain contact.[5]

This value system places the Jewish returnee in a situation different
from that of other newly religious. The new Moonie or Krishna follower
is urged to sever contact with parents and to live in the religious commune. The normative system thus enables the convert to avoid dealing
with parents and removes any sense of guilt toward parents by providing

5. A taped lecture by Rabbi Dovid Gottlieb distributed by the Jewish Learning
Exchange (affiliated with Ohr Someyach) provides students with advice on how to
remain close to their parents and siblings, urging them to make every effort to
maintain close ties to parents, to avoid any remark that might be construed as
prosletyzing, to renew interest in the parents' everyday activities, and to seek above
all a loving and respectful relationship with parents. The practical point, which is
repeatedly emphasized, is that unless they love you they will not love your religion.

a religious legitimation for rejecting them. It may even encourage the new convert to exploit parents—for example, by manipulating them into turning over large sums of money to the new religion.

The Jewish returnee, in contrast, is not permitted to resolve the problem in this way. He or she must return to the parents, honor them, and yet uphold a religious commitment that puts the ba'al t'shuva at odds with them in many particulars.

If anything, the ba'al t'shuva is likely to develop a strong sense of guilt in this situation. New value commitments do not permit the resolution of conflicts between filial piety and religious piety by role segregation but rather demand that the ba'al t'shuva bear the contradictory demands of these roles and resolve them. Although this may eliminate court litigations or problems of snatching and deprogramming among Jews, it probably also makes it much more difficult for returnees to succeed. Because of the burden it places on them, some will fail and, encouraged by the value of respect for parents, return to their former lives.

A second set of factors mitigating conflict between the ba'al t'shuva and parents is suggested by application of the life-convoy metaphor to the parents of the ba'al t'shuva and their parents. The data suggest that these relatives were committed to providing a Jewish education for their children. Students in ba'al t'shuva yeshivot all report having received some religious training at home.[6] This may have been Sunday school, an after-school program, or lessons for bar mitzvah or bat mitzvah, but in every case the ba'al t'shuva had had some sort of formal training in Judaism (although generally not in Orthodoxy) and some experience with its traditions, either in the nuclear family or with other relatives. In contrast, 37 percent of all Jewish elementary school children in America were enrolled in Jewish schools in 1959, and an even smaller proportion had been enrolled earlier (Fishman 1973, 115). These parents then seem more committed to providing a Jewish education for their children and to maintaining their Jewish identity than the majority of Jews.

Although the parents of the ba'alei t'shuva may not be sympathetic to the style of life their children have chosen and may even be deeply resentful of and bitter about it, they are nonetheless compelled by their *own* commitments to see it in a more favorable light than they would see a

---

6. Danzger (1977), based on interviews with students in ba'al t'shuva yeshivot in Jerusalem, and Kovacs (1977), based on a study of students in the Lubavitcher yeshiva in Morristown, New Jersey, demonstrate this. Aviad's (1983) findings duplicate Danzger's.

change to any of the other cult groups. Contrary to Rabbi Lelyveld, parents may agree that Orthodoxy is better than other cults, for "at least it is Jewish."

Most of the ba'alei t'shuva are no more than two generations removed from Orthodox Judaism. Their parents or grandparents had practiced some Jewish rituals in their homes. When the ba'al t'shuva returns to Judaism, therefore, even if the grandparents who practice the religion are no longer alive, there is probably a cousin, an aunt, or an uncle who is still traditional and who acts as mediator in the conflict between the ba'al t'shuva and parents. These relatives also serve as the haven, the halfway house, the role models, and the contact or point of entry into the Jewish community.

SIBLINGS AND FRIENDS

Ties to siblings and friends frequently prevent a potential recruit from becoming Orthodox. These ties provide social and emotional anchors that keep the person in a given social trajectory. But powerful as they are, in modern mobile society they are also fragile and subject to disruption when a person changes location.

Parents can be loved and respected or hated and despised, but they cannot easily be ignored. If parents object to what a child is doing, even if the child is adult, as long as he or she is dependent on the parents, as many college-age ba'alei t'shuva are, conflict is possible. Siblings or friends, in contrast, wield no effective remunerative sanctions and can be ignored.

The attitude in some yeshivot toward the friends of new recruits presents an interesting contrast to the attitude toward parents. Some yeshivot encourage students to break with former friends, feeling that they will be a negative influence, that as long as old relationships are maintained the new recruit may easily slip back into his former pattern. As I have already pointed out, for an American being in Israel or in a relatively isolated American community assists in the process of breaking former relationships and tends to support the transition.

In Israel, which in many areas is still very much a society of villages (shtetlakh), the Israeli ba'al t'shuva may be encouraged to move out of his or her former neighborhood into a religious neighborhood.[7] If physical

---

7. In Israel, neighborhoods are identified not only by whether occupants are Arab or Jewish but also by whether they are religious or secular. This is an even sharper distinction than that between Sephardi and Ashkenazi or between wealthy and poor neighborhoods.

distance cannot be maintained, traditionalist yeshivot encourage the Israeli student to dress in a distinctive manner, to set him off from former friends.

Ties to girlfriends illustrate a variation on this theme. Usually the ba'al t'shuva abandons his former girlfriends as he returns. At times, however, as the ba'al t'shuva enters the new world and seeks a mate he may turn again to former girlfriends. These young women were sometimes surprisingly willing to be persuaded by a ba'al t'shuva to undertake a religious life.[8]

Ties to girlfriends thus tend to become quickly resolved: in most cases the relationship dissolves; sometimes the relationship produces a change in the girl's (less often in the boy's) position, and she becomes Orthodox; or elements of the former relationship are incorporated into the new role (for example, he is a partial ba'al t'shuva observing Shabbat and kashrut but not family purity, and she remains his girlfriend, adjusting to his kashrut requirements and Shabbat observances, yet remaining uncommitted to Orthodoxy). The last seems to occur infrequently, possibly because there is no community support for this position.

Friendships with those of the same sex seem to follow a similar pattern. Sometimes the ba'al t'shuva will recruit his friends to Orthodoxy; more often the relationship is terminated. Occasionally people remain friends although one has returned and the other has not, but this seems to be the exception. Siblings fall between friends and parents. They are similar to parents in that the relationship is lasting, even when there is hostility. Yet like friends they can be and often are ignored. The most enduring and troublesome tie is between parents and ba'al t'shuva.

Matching and Mating

Possibly the most important social relationship in either preventing someone from becoming Orthodox or cementing ties to the Orthodox community is the marital bond. As all aspects of Orthodox Jewish religious life are located in the home, an attempt by either mate to become religious alone is likely to cause severe strain in the family. Married couples ordinarily undertake such a change jointly or not at all. Cooperation of the spouse, even if reluctant, must be won, and the woman's role here, as I

8. Five such couples were interviewed in this study. This pattern appears to occur quite frequently.

have noted, is more critical than the man's. For a single person, commitment to Orthodoxy remains tenuous and uncertain until marriage. Marrying someone who is Orthodox, whether from birth or by choice, also makes it difficult to leave Orthodoxy, for to do that often also means breaking with one's spouse.

Because marriage is a powerful stabilizer of religious commitment and the commitment of the newly Orthodox person is untested, there is some wariness among the Orthodox about marrying a ba'al t'shuva. Rabbi Mendel Weinbach, Dean of Ohr Someyach Yeshiva, writes:

> The *shidduch* [matchmaking] situation is probably where the most mistakes are made by the people with the best intentions. The tendency has been to fault the Orthodox community for discriminating against the *baal teshuva*, accusing many of its members of refusing to accept a *baal teshuva* even if they first discover his status five minutes before the *chuppah* [wedding ceremony]. One could honestly say that too many Torah Jews are guilty of practicing "but-don't-move-on-my-block" liberalism in regard to *baalei teshuva* by encouraging them to join the ranks but not to intermarry with those of *yichus* [honorable lineage]. (*Jewish Observer*, June 1980)

There are some clues that one who has been a ba'al t'shuva is stigmatized and therefore must settle for a less desirable mate. During an interview, for example, the dean of a girls' school in Jerusalem received a phone call from someone interested in arranging a match for a widower with several children. The dean treated the caller curtly and then remarked that people sometimes call with such suggestions on the assumption that a ba'alat t'shuva is somehow flawed. Some believe, the dean added, that a ba'alat t'shuva may not marry a cohen, as she is probably not a virgin. Ba'alei t'shuva also are considered less trustworthy, having had the opportunity to play the field before settling down. Those who become ba'alei t'shuva earlier in life, who have therefore had less opportunity for sexual experience and in addition have been a part of the ba'al t'shuva yeshiva world for several years, may overcome this stigma. Otherwise, such men may find that their opportunities for meeting a match are restricted to the ba'al t'shuva community.

Sydelle Levy (1973) finds a pattern of marriage in the Lubavitch community that again suggests nonacceptance of ba'alei t'shuva as marriage partners. She writes:

> Lubavitchers speak of total acceptance of each other, rich and poor, educated or uneducated . . . but some are more equal than others. Much covert conflict is generated within the Lubavitch community by members'

overt insistence on equality between categories, and the strong desires of members of categories I [descendants of Lubavitcher chasidim] and III [ba'alei teshuva] to marry others in their category. However, no Lubavitch male is ever publicly regarded as "ineligible" for any Lubavitch female. On one occasion I heard a woman speak about a group of ba'alei teshuva (category III) young men. She said, "Oh, they find nice ba'al teshuva girls." The community repercussions of this public comment were severe. There was much negative comment about this woman who, in effect, voiced what everyone practices; that is, she indicated that members do not seek spouses outside their own category. Over ninety percent of all marriages recorded in my geneologies were either marriages to members of the same category, or the one deviant form that is accepted, hypergamy. (52–53)

Hypergamy, Levy explains, is the marriage of a male Lubavitcher to a female non-Lubavitcher, with the understanding that she will accept the Lubavitcher practices.

In an impassioned statement of the difficulties faced by a ba'al t'shuva in the courtship process, Ira Axelrod (1976) warned that unless the Orthodox community changed its attitudes and permitted their own daughters to marry ba'alei t'shuva they would effectively shut the door against any substantial influx of ba'alei t'shuva to the Orthodox community. Apparently, acceptance into the Orthodox community receives final approval only when the ba'al t'shuva has married. As Rabbi Wienbach, describing the stages of entry into Judaism, put it with a laugh, "Getting married, that's the final nail in the coffin."

YICHUS: HALAKHIC ELIGIBILITY

For a couple to be married by a rabbi in Israel, both partners must be Jewish. The prospective couple's parents must be Jewish by birth or conversion and no other problems of lineage can remain. If one of the mothers is a convert, for example, she must have been properly converted to Judaism.[9] (For those seeking to become Orthodox, an improper conversion includes conversion by anyone other than an Orthodox rabbi.) This requirement presents few halakhic difficulties, but it may present

---

9. Improperly converted fathers present no problem, for it is descent from a Jewish mother that makes one Jewish. Even if a Gentile father never converted, the child is Jewish if the mother was born Jewish. Reform Judaism has recently adopted patrilineal descent as determining Jewishness, but this has not been accepted by Conservative or Orthodox Judaism.

substantial personal or psychological obstacles. The halakhic solution is simply to convert the halakhically non-Jewish partner to Judaism.[10]

Improperly divorced parents or grandparents present a much more serious problem. Halakhically, if a woman is divorced but has not received a proper *get* (religious bill of divorcement), a child from any subsequent husband will be considered a *mamzer* (bastard).[11] Such a person is excluded from the congregation of Israel—that is, may not marry a Jew. With the increase in divorce and in marriages performed by rabbis who are not concerned about halakhah this becomes a more serious problem for the Orthodox. Ba'alei t'shuva who think that their acceptability as a marriage partner requires only being committed and observant may find that serious obstacles remain.

Both men and women may find that their personal status reflects a situation over which they have never had control and which yet may seriously handicap their prospects for marriage despite their sincere interest in being Orthodox. Halakhically invalid marriage and divorce may have serious consequences for the future of the t'shuva movement. Given the difference in rules for determining personal status in the various wings of Judaism, the problem of mamzerim may become so significant that it completely closes off the possibility of marriage between Orthodox Jews and other Jews. If this occurs, the t'shuva movement may fade substantially in the diaspora, able to draw only on the Orthodox who have left their practices for a while. Joining the Orthodox may become so difficult for other Jews that even those who are eligible may be discouraged from attempting it. In Israel, where the Orthodox rabbinate is the authority over marriage and personal status, this will occur infrequently.

The eligibility of men as marriage partners is unaffected by previous divorce or by having had forbidden relations with other women. But a

10. For a woman this simply requires going to a mikveh to immerse herself and accept Judaism. For the man, circumcision may also be required. The ba'al t'shuva in a yeshiva who believes he is Jewish undoubtedly is already circumcised so that in most cases only his ritual immersion would be required. Some individuals might, however, respond negatively to the disclosure that they are halakhically not considered Jewish unless such a conversion ceremony occurs. Ethiopian Jews who had fled to Israel reacted in this way when told they had to go through immersion in order to be regarded as Jewish.

11. The problem of mamzerim is not new; a substantial literature exists on this topic in responsa. Some solution to this halakhic problem may be found, but careful rabbinic review of each case is required. If halakhic relief is found, it is most often because some technical flaw occurred in the first marriage that nullifies it.

woman who has been divorced, even if she received a get, or who has been married to a non-Jew can not marry a Cohen, as these unions could not be halakhically acceptable.[12]

YICHUS: FAMILY HONOR

A second type of yichus refers to status or honor in the community. A prospective mate whose family is learned or pious provides such yichus. At the beginning of the t'shuva movement, lack of yichus (or more accurately in this case, social location) may have been a bar to marriage for a ba'al t'shuva. But interviews with ba'alei t'shuva and observation of their courtship patterns suggest that it is no longer a major problem. Yichus is most likely a major consideration for elite yichus groups, but for masses of Orthodox it is not very important.

A more important factor seems to derive from the difficulty for the newly Orthodox Jew of learning about the rituals that identify members of this group to each other simply from attending synagogue services. The ba'al t'shuva must familiarize himself with daily practices that are not open to public observation through formal study at a yeshiva. Furthermore, in contrast, to the new Christian who may quickly assimilate public worship, the ba'al t'shuva may find it difficult to master even public prayer.

As a result, a ba'al t'shuva may continue to be identified as someone new to Orthodox Jewish practice for two to three years. Throughout this period, the ba'al t'shuva may be encouraged and welcomed, but the Orthodox may feel that he or she is still not fully "one of us." The seriousness of the commitment is in question. Those who have recently joined may easily leave. But here is the dilemma: one cannot marry until one is accepted, but one is not fully accepted until one marries.

Whereas for men this testing or waiting period may be several years, for women it is about a year, perhaps because the religious status of a family is determined in large part by the man's ability to carry out rituals, such as reciting the Kiddush, saying grace after meals, participating in or leading worship in the synagogue, "learning" or knowing halakhah. Many newly Orthodox women have been raised in traditional homes and know the rules of the home, which are central to Orthodoxy. But the family's religious standing is determined in larger measure by the man's

12. Here too a halakhic solution may be possible, such as finding that the prospective husband is in fact not a cohen. But again, this requires evaluation on a case by case basis.

ability to show off his knowledge through public practice of ritual or through his learning. Women have less opportunity for this.

The prime reason for hesitancy in accepting the ba'al t'shuva as a possible mate may be neither concern for elite yichus nor prejudice against ba'alei t'shuva. Although Axelrod (1976) and Weinbach (1980) believe that such prejudice is rampant, no ba'al t'shuva interviewed mentioned it. Rather, members of the Orthodox community believe that a man needs to practice Orthodoxy for some time before he can be trusted to remain Orthodox, if he lacks social ties that support Orthodox commitments. There seems to be less fear that women will leave Orthodoxy. The ba'al t'shuva yeshiva then is not simply a place to study, but a place where a man's commitment to Orthodoxy is tested by time.

Marriage is problematic for the ba'al t'shuva because at a time when many of their peers have already married he must wait two to three years before taking this step. The wait is made all the more difficult by the rules separating men and women, which make customary dating practices simply impossible.

Ba'alei t'shuva are not the only newly religious to experience this difficulty. Bromley and Shupe (1979) describe the problems encountered by those entering the Unification Church as follows:

> Total celibacy to the point of abstaining from even the most "innocent" of romantic attachments was normatively, and in reality fairly strictly, followed prior to marriage. Moon required each member to remain celibate for a minimum of three years and often longer after joining the U.M. Members openly spoke of problems experienced in coping with sexual desires and quenching them through a combination of frequent prayer and cold showers. Yet despite the enormous theological significance of the sin of fornication, such self denial appears to have been beyond the abilities of some members in both centers as well as out in the field. (184)

The ba'al t'shuva finds himself in a more restrictive environment still, for norms in the ba'al t'shuva yeshivot regulate the courtship situation in a manner not paralleled in other religions on the American scene.

Further, while the norms are restrictive, no specific waiting period is prescribed, nor does any one authority determine how long the ba'al t'shuva must wait before marriage. Thus the waiting period varies. For example, after perhaps a year in a yeshiva a rosh yeshiva will probably suggest to the older ba'al t'shuva that "it is time." He will be encouraged to consider marriage and to meet young women for this purpose. But a prospective bride in the Orthodox community, or her family, may find that the religious behavior and attitudes of the ba'al t'shuva reflect a lack of knowledge of Yiddishkeit (meaning here the intimate nuances of parochial Judaism) or, more critically, suggest an awareness of worldly things that often is seen in those on their way out of the Orthodox community. Such a young man is likely to find a match more easily among the ba'alot t'shuva, women of similar background.

Ba'alei t'shuva may also prefer each other in marriage because of their mutual familiarity with the world of nonreligious relatives, college, and living in a Jewish community outside New York City and a sense that they will not throw their past lives up to each other, as those in the Orthodox community might. They often share values and interest in religion—for example, a tendency to take religion seriously or an interest in macrobiotics or in meditation.

The experience of those who became ba'alei t'shuva at age seventeen or eighteen demonstrates that hesitancy in the Orthodox community may not be prejudice but rather uncertainty. Five or six years later, by age twenty-three or twenty-four, these ba'alei t'shuva will find acceptance even in elite families, where there is normally a concern for yichus. One case in point is that of a long-time student at Ohr Someyach who married the daughter of one of the roshei yeshiva. This acceptance is widespread and perhaps explains why single males, who outnumber females in the ba'al t'shuva yeshivot by at least three to one (Danzger 1977),[13] are not noticeably numerous in the Orthodox community. In all probability, they have married into the Orthodox community.

Women appear to have greater difficulty meeting formal halakhic criteria of marital eligibility. But if they have met the halakhic standards and have learned to keep an Orthodox home, acceptance comes quickly. Men, in contrast, find formal halakhic eligibility easier but are suspected of less stability of commitment, perhaps because their role requires more public participation in ritual so that the newness of their commitment is more visible.

In any case, the "trial" period before women are encouraged to marry is substantially shorter than for men. Coupled with the greater propensity of women than men to enter Orthodoxy through marriage, this may help explain why fewer women are in the schools for ba'alei t'shuva.

13. In 1975–1976 in Israel the ratio was about four to one. Although this ratio had narrowed by 1982, it had still not gone much beyond three to one, giving women a substantial advantage over men in choosing a mate.

Old Values and New Ties

By and large, returnees meet their mates, develop new friendships, and maintain and create family ties, much as do others in society at large. But some patterns, while not characteristic of the majority of returnees, are unique to this group.

COURTSHIP AND MARRIAGE

The relationships the ba'al t'shuva enters are radically affected by the normative pattern of courtship in Orthodox Judaism. A number of practices set these relationships off from those of the non-Orthodox community; the two most prominent are *yihud* and *negiyah*.

The laws of yihud forbid a man to be alone with a woman prohibited to him. In some Orthodox circles these laws are interpreted so strictly that whether one may get on an elevator alone with a woman even if the ride lasts for less than a minute is a matter of discussion. Sitting in a parked car alone with a woman may be forbidden unless the window is rolled down or the car is on a well-traveled street. In an office, when a man and woman meet alone the door must be kept open.

In some circles the laws of negiyah ("touching") are interpreted to mean that a man may not touch or even shake the hand of any woman other than his mother, sister, daughter, or wife at any time, lest she be menstrual. (It is assumed that these relatives will somehow indicate to him their status so he may know how to behave toward them.) Laws forbidding a man to look at women with lewd intent are interpreted to forbid swimming, attendance at theater, films, concerts, and even some museum exhibits. A man may not listen to a woman sing or enjoy her perfume. The norms in these circles so radically redefine relations between men and women that courtship in the pattern common in contemporary society is not possible. Yeshivot present these norms as halakhah, the standard for Orthodox behavior.

How, then, is a new recruit to meet an eligible man or woman? What can courtship be? For returnees outside yeshivot this is not often a problem. These laws are so often breached and so infrequently preached that they are not known even to the large majority of observant Orthodox as anything other than the practices of a few "extremists." The woman returnee who has entered the Orthodox community through marriage or the man who has entered through a synagogue may be fully accepted in the Orthodox community and unaware of the existence of such rules. For these persons, the major problem may be finding someone to date, as they have not established the network of relations in the new community that give rise to contacts. They don't have friends to invite them to parties or relatives to suggest a "nice girl" or boy. But if they do meet an eligible person, dating and courtship may follow a pattern similar to that in the larger society, although circumscribed by well-known religious prohibitions against premarital sex.

The yeshivot teach the rules of negiyah and yihud and emphasize them not only by separating men and women in different schools but also by insisting on separate social functions and often on separate seating for men and women at weddings and other shared social occasions. The yeshiva then becomes obliged to assist the returnee in the courtship process, particularly as marriage is so highly valued in Judaism.

Yeshivot facilitate courtship by acting as *shadkhanim* (matchmakers). Traditionalist and modernist ba'al t'shuva yeshivot follow somewhat different patterns. Both types of yeshivot take seriously the obligation to help a man or woman meet someone who might be a suitable mate. Modernist yeshivot take a stance that could perhaps be described as avuncular—helpful, involved, but to a large degree leaving matters in the hands of the returnee. Traditionalist yeshivot take a position closer to that of the parents in traditionalist families.

The patterns for Ohr Someyach, Aish Hatorah, D'var Yerushalayim for Men, and Neve Yerushalayim for Women tend toward this traditionalistic model. In the traditionalist yeshiva, a staff member or the wife of one of the staff may have the informal role of matchmaker. This person (sometimes more than one acts in this capacity) is someone who knows the returnee well, believes his commitment to be stable, and is aware that he is now interested in marriage. The returnee may specifically mention to the shadkhan that he is interested in marriage, of if he has been at the school for a sufficiently long time and has proved himself the shadkhan may suggest the possibility of marriage. They may discuss several prospects, so that the young man or woman has an opportunity to inquire about background, education, religiosity, family, looks, and other concerns in advance of agreeing to meet the prospective mate. If both parties agree to a meeting, the man will then phone the woman to set up a meeting in a public place, so as to avoid the problems of yihud.

The conversation may be witty or dull, humorous or serious, but the point of the meeting is clear. They are not there simply for a good time. The *tachlit* (purpose) is marriage, and the discussion is aimed at determining whether they might be suitable for each other or, at the very least, whether it is worth continuing to meet so as to explore that possibility. No touching or handholding occurs, even if the relationship proceeds for several meetings. The most traditionalistic will probably not attend a show, film, concert, or other cultural event, as this would simply get in the way of serious discussion and furthermore may be forbidden.

After each date both man and woman report back to the shadkhan (sometimes to respective shadkhanim) on the progress of the matter. This happens for the first two or three dates in particular, when each wants to know the other's reaction without having to be embarrassed by directly raising the matter or testing it through flirting. If after the first several dates the relationship develops, the couple will continue to meet, as well as talk by phone. After four to six weeks the couple will be expected to be considering marriage, and the shadkhan may again be consulted, perhaps for still more information on the other person or perhaps for advice on the wedding plans. The man and woman may be in touch with their parents, and the shadkhan or rosh yeshiva may then be called upon to ease problems with parents. The prospect that their son or daughter is about to marry someone who is Orthodox may frighten some parents, for they know this step implies that the commitment, which up to this point could be taken as simply an "experiment" with an Orthodox style of life, is likely to become permanent. The parents of the woman may need to be assured that the man will be able somehow to support a wife. Such an assurance is also important to the boy's parents, who may be concerned at the prospect of having to support their son's family as well as their son.

At a traditionalist yeshiva, designated members of the staff will meet with the couple after a few dates to advise on whether they believe they are suitable partners and the relationship should proceed further. The meeting may be at the school but is more likely to be at the home of the staff member involved in the matchmaking. There the girl may meet the boy's rosh yeshiva over coffee, and the boy will meet the girl's teachers. The staff members will raise the direct questions that traditionalist parents raise with little embarrassment, for these staff members feel that they are acting in loco parentis. How serious the man and woman are about Orthodoxy, the kind of religious life they desire, where they expect to live, what they expect to do to support themselves, their family backgrounds, are all fair game at this interview. Some of these issues, such as family background, may be pursued further after the meeting through the staff's own channels.

A similar process takes place at modernist yeshivot, but the style is somewhat different. The advisors attempt to distance themselves from the developing relationship and to convey the idea that the matter is entirely in the couple's hands. If their advice is sought, it will be offered, but only reluctantly; the staff is not there in loco parentis, and the couple is undertaking this relationship on their own. Modernist yeshivot are even reluctant to give the impression that they are involved in matchmaking. Dating in modernistic yeshivot may involve going to a concert, a museum, or even a film. Tachlit is important here too, but it is more muted a theme. The entire process is more informal and less obtrusive, but it is carried on in much the same way.

Engaged couples at the yeshivot are invited to *chasan* (groom) and *kallah* (bride) classes, where the laws of family purity, including yihud, negiyah, and niddah (laws of a menstrual woman) are taught. These classes are held separately for men and women, with men taught by men and women by women. (This is always the rule with regard to these classes.) The classes are small and informal, sometimes held for one student alone. Here the returnees, who are likely to be almost totally unfamiliar with the rules governing marriage, are taught the details of these rules. In recent years, similar classes have been held for the Orthodox by birth.

In sum, the courtship process is highly organized, with the more traditionalistic yeshivot generally exercising tighter control than the modernistic yeshivot. The period of courtship is compressed, it involves little "play," and the settings are limited, all of which facilitate conforming to the halakhic rules that guide relations between the sexes during courtship.

Outside of the yeshiva aegis these rules are much more difficult to follow. Because the entire matter involves two consenting adults in an intimate relationship, knowing the degree to which these laws are followed is difficult. Also, the practice of teaching details of halakhot after the announcement of the engagement leaves the couple with some latitude at the early stages of dating.

FAMILY PURITY AND FAMILY LIFE

After marriage, the laws of family purity make cross-sex social contacts much more difficult and may be seen as a factor preserving marriage. One woman expressed it this way: "We have several friends we see regularly. There is never any touching or grabbing. I don't have to worry about that kind of thing. It's really been pleasant."

The partners may miss some of the ego gratification that comes from flirting with other men or women, but they also avoid the jealousies, the need to calculate how far one can go without overstepping the bounds, the conflict over whether flirting and touching are part of the game that one must play. The rules of family purity make flirtatious play almost impossible. They also permit one to avoid unwanted attentions and some of the tensions and conflicts between husband and wife that might result from flirting.

New families everywhere face a difficult period of adjustment. In addition, the ba'alei t'shuva face the problem of religious adjustments with their mates. This includes such problems as husband or wife becoming more (or less) religious than the other spouse, the woman's expectation that her religious role will be synagogue- or study-related rather than domestic, and financial problems faced when the husband continues to study in yeshiva with the burden of support on the wife, even after she has had several children. And because the rituals of Judaism are practiced at home, differences in religious conviction may cause greater friction for Orthodox Jews than for Christians. Ba'alei t'shuva, who have risked ties with friends and family because of their newfound convictions, may be willing to sacrifice ties to a spouse over similar issues.

The interviews suggest two potential sources of conflict. One is the possible differences between husband and wife concerning the pace of change. In several cases, the husband had spent more time at a yeshiva than the wife had. His practices became more intense than hers. The wife began to feel that his life was restricting her, that she was being stifled by convictions she did not feel. In one case, a wife who did not object to the restrictions nevertheless felt that she no longer understood or was part of his world, that he was drifting away from her.

Alternatively, the husband or wife may swing back, abandoning the companion of his or her religious journey. In one case, a husband and wife moved from middle-class nonreligious to hippie Orthodox together and then became traditionalist Orthodox. Some time later he became persuaded that his traditionalism was not genuine and became modernist, but she clung to the traditionalist position, and they divorced. Impressionistic data seem to indicate that the man usually leads in moving from one level of conviction to another, leaving his wife to follow if she chooses. Only rarely does she seem to be the one initiating a new conviction. The conflict instead seems to occur when she no longer wishes to move along with him.

Another problem occurs when a couple in the first flush of their marriage decide that the husband will devote his life to the study of Torah and the wife will support him. The problem is described by Shimon Naftalis, a former ba'al t'shuva who now dresses in the long kapote and wide-brimmed beaver hat of the chasid. For a number of years Naftalis ran the Lubavitch Chabad house in the Old City of Jerusalem and taught at Yeshiva D'var Yerushalayim. He commented:

When ba'alei t'shuva marry they may have several problems: the problems of being frum [religious], of being newly married, and very often financial problems. Many of the men are convinced they should study in a kolel, but they can't make it financially. Some of them have a profession but feel that now that they are frum they can't go into a profession, that they have to stay in the yeshiva. By the time they realize that yeshiva may not be the place for them, they find they can't easily get back into their professions.

CHILDREN

Children of ba'alei t'shuva are an important source of rootedness in a community. But when parents change their religious commitment over a period of several years, relations with children become strained. Preschoolers and children up to the age of six or seven rarely present problems. If parents change their convictions the children change along with them. Beyond this age children become progressively more resistant to changes in convictions, sometimes rejecting the changes altogether and cleaving to former patterns. The rebellion against parents' newfound religious convictions may not manifest itself immediately but may instead appear in late adolescence.

Attending an *aufruf* (calling of the bridegroom to the Torah on the Shabbat before his wedding) at the Kotel of the son of someone who had been a hippie ba'al t'shuva early in this movement, I observed three generations in conflict. The grandfather, a man of about seventy was clean-shaven and dressed in ordinary street clothes; his son, father of the groom, about forty-five, wore a long black bekeshe and fur striemel, a white shirt without a tie, and an untrimmed beard. One would not guess from his appearance that he was a widely respected physician. The groom, a clean-shaven young man of about twenty, was also in bekeshe and striemel but seemed uncomfortable in this outfit and not well acquainted with the prayers. The grandfather had been raised in a traditional Jewish home, abandoned Jewish religious practices as a young man, and had now come to accept some practices of Orthodox Judaism. The father had rejected his father's nonreligious life-style and become chasidic while retaining his early hippie connections and commitments. The son had for several years rejected his father's religious commitments but now was somewhat reluctantly following his father into hippie chasidus.

OCCUPATIONS

Solomon Poll (1962) has suggested that the cohesion of the chasidic community of Satmar is facilitated by its economic clustering in a relatively few occupations. This provides an insulation against the wider community, paralleling the physical isolation that provides cohesion for the Amish and similar groups. This tendency to cluster in a few occupations seems to characterize the Orthodox community to a larger extent than the Jewish community at large. Within the Orthodox community, modernists tend to have more secular education and enter a wider variety of occupations and professions, including many that place them under cross-pressure from the conflicting demands of religion and the wider culture. Traditionalists, with less secular education, enter the professions less frequently and tend to cluster more tightly in occupations owned and run by Orthodox Jews, such as the diamond trade. More recently this has included computer sales and programming, which do not require a college degree and provide the worker with latitude in organizing his own life space. Thus conflicts between religion and work may be avoided. The tight occupational clusters provide a network of relations in which religious beliefs are accommodated and even supported.

Yeshivot for ba'alei t'shuva, particularly the more traditionalistic ones, have adopted a strategy of attempting to channel students into occupations that will support their continued involvement in Orthodoxy. The most direct of these efforts provides support for the married student in the kollel of the yeshiva, where the student continues to study and receives a stipend from the yeshiva to help keep him in a religious environment. But the stipends provided are small. The wife's earnings and parental support are needed to supplement it, and after several children these may no longer be sufficient. In addition, keeping students in the kollel is expensive for yeshivot. Yeshivot have therefore developed a variety of occupations for ba'alei t'shuva.

In 1976 Yeshivat Har Tzion had programs to train students as *sofer* (religious scribe), *mohel* (performer of circumcision), or *schochet* (one who slaughters animals in conformity with religious requirements). This permitted students to integrate with the larger Jewish community while remaining in a religious occupation. Similarly, Ohr Someyach had a shop to train students to make the leather boxes for tefillin and a program for training and certifying teachers in Jewish subjects. It also developed computer classes, both to train students for work and as a means of attracting new people. Ohr Someyach had many students who had professional training and could enter other occupations, but it attempted to place students who had no chosen profession in a religiously protected occupational environment. In contrast, Brovender's and Yeshiva University's programs are directed at educating students to hold a variety of occupations outside of a support structure. For those students who want it, rabbinical and teacher training is offered.

Singles

The Orthodox community is organized around the family, and singles, even those raised in the community, feel excluded from the social and synagogue life.[14] Most returnees are young single people. As long as they are in yeshiva, being single is not a problem. The yeshiva connection ties them to the Orthodox community. But many, perhaps most, of those who attend a yeshiva have spent some years attempting to live Orthodox Jewish lives before enrolling, and most do not marry before leaving the yeshiva. Others become Orthodox without ever entering a yeshiva. What social connections do these people have in the Orthodox community?

RELATIVES

Because returnees are no more than two or three generations from grandparents who practiced Orthodox Judaism, they may have cousins or uncles and aunts who are Orthodox. These relatives may perform a variety of functions that facilitate the entry of the newly religious into the Orthodox community. They may mediate between returnee and parents, provide a home in which the returnee may spend Shabbat or a holiday, teach the returnee rituals and religious practices, and when the returnee wishes to marry provide the family connection that attests that the returnee derives from legitimate Jewish stock.

The relatives serve as a reminder that the returnee's new commitment is neither new nor strange, that grandparents or great-grandparents lived this way. They provide a living link to the picture of the bearded grandfather and bewigged grandmother that once hung on the wall.

But the importance of relatives seems to go beyond the very real contribution they make to the integration of the returnee in the Orthodox community. People in the Orthodox community, and indeed in the Jewish community at large, pride themselves on connection to mishpokheh (extended family). One needs cousins, uncles, and aunts, and, most important, grandparents.

So important are grandparents that returnees sometimes seek out

14. Unmarried and divorced people have become more vocal in their protests over their exclusion from the Orthodox community. In recent years articles have appeared in Jewish journals describing this problem, and some synagogues have begun developing programs addressing this group.

grandparent surrogates, old Jewish men or women, and adopt them by visiting them, doing errands for them, and otherwise befriending them.

The pattern of visiting old people seemed to have developed into a movement in the 1970s as part of a general trend to make personal efforts to improve the world, to do good.[15] It also had the effect of connecting the ba'al t'shuva directly to his or her people, enhancing the sense of identity through action. Personal contacts with elderly Orthodox Jews helped many ba'alei t'shuva learn how to live as Orthodox Jews. Some of them became the surrogate zaydeh or bubeh, the grandfather or grandmother they never had, who could transmit the traditions and the personal experiences of living an Orthodox life in the "old days." Such a person might be "adopted"—for example, invited to the wedding of the ba'al t'shuva as an honored guest. It sometimes becomes difficult to determine who adopted whom. The surrogate zaydeh was also reaching out, finding a new grandchild, one who will carry on the old ways, which his own children may have abandoned. It provided these "grandparents" with the opportunity to teach someone the meanings life had for them. For them the outreach was both a mitzvah and an affirmation of their own life.

15. Helping the Jewish poor is predominantly in the hands of Jewish philanthropic organizations (see Elazar 1976). In the 1970s, however, a movement to help various Jewish causes developed parallel to broader social movements in the larger society. Soon after the war on poverty began, yeshiva and day schools began to sponsor visits to old age homes, packages for the poor, and more direct person-to-person assistance for the needy; for example, the Tomchie Shabbos organization was founded to provide food packages for the needy on Shabbat, and the Hatzolah ambulance service involved Orthodox Jews directly in getting the sick or injured to hospitals, even on Shabbat and holidays. These were basically attempts to humanize assistance to the needy, to take it out of the hands of the bureaucrats, to allow people to contribute in ways other than by giving money. This change in philanthropic emphasis was characteristic of the broader community in the late 1960s and 1970s—a rebellion against the "establishment philanthropies"—and it reached the Jewish community in the mid- and late 1970s.

Probably because Jewish philanthropy was bureaucratized and professionalized, it was avoided by the ba'alei t'shuva at first. The first two editions of the *Jewish Catalog* make no mention of the Jewish poor or contributing to the Jewish community. Only in the third edition, and after criticism for this omission, was this included. In joining the Orthodox, the ba'alei t'shuva took on the stance of Orthodoxy regarding philanthropy; the Orthodox, particularly traditionalistic Orthodox, were suspicious of the philanthropic establishment, which they saw—for the most part correctly—as hostile or at least indifferent to Orthodox Judaism. With the development of a personal and humanistic philanthropy, this, too, became part of the ba'al t'shuva experience.

BA'AL T'SHUVA NODES AND NETWORKS

Ba'alei t'shuva generally tend to be swallowed up and unnoticed in the Orthodox community. Few ba'al t'shuva communities remain visible. Rabbis Gedaliah Fleers, Dovid Cohen, and Meir Fund have each developed the reputation of being knowledgeable and open in the ba'al t'shuva community. They have built small synagogues attended primarily by ba'alei t'shuva. Congregants live within walking distance, so they need not ride on Shabbat to attend the synagogue. Thus each rabbi has a nucleus of community in his immediate vicinity that enables him to lodge and feed a number of guests for Shabbat or holidays. Particularly at Passover, ba'alei t'shuva may be guests in one of these communities.

Ba'alei t'shuva also join together in social circles of their own, celebrating Shabbat or holidays in one another's homes. The circles vary; some consist of men alone, some of only women, and some of both men and women. The participants may take turns preparing for a holiday or a Shabbat, or they may make it a cooperative effort. Men as well as women help with the domestic chores, cleaning, and cooking. This is obviously necessary in single-sex circles, but it also occurs in mixed groups, as distinguished from other new religious and commune groups in America, where women seem to do all the domestic chores. But this seems to have more to do with the tradition that men help with preparation for holidays and Shabbat than with egalitarian values.

The social network of singles, then, seems to consist of nodes and circles that attempt to fill the gap left by the lack of ties to Orthodox family. The nodes are the yeshivot or recruiting programs and synagogues where ba'alei t'shuva meet one another and members of the Orthodox community. Some attachments are developed with members of the Orthodox community through these nodes, and these attachments may become ties for the ba'alei t'shuva. Attachments to other ba'alei t'shuva often lead to the development of their own social groups, in which the Sabbath and holidays may be celebrated.

COMMUNITIES AND BA'ALEI T'SHUVA

In several communities the number of newly Orthodox are substantial enough to be visible, and these communities develop reputations as places especially open to the newly Orthodox. A few of these, such as Tzefat, in Israel, and Crown Heights, Brooklyn, are highly traditionalistic, but most such communities in the United States are modernistic.

As might be expected, newly Orthodox tend to live near the recruitment centers—in Jerusalem, in Crown Heights, Brooklyn, in Brookline, Massachusetts, on the west side of Manhattan, in Riverdale, in Forest Hills, Queens, in Monsey, New York, and in other areas with recruitment facilities. Entirely apart from centers of recruitment one also finds clusters of ba'alei t'shuva in Israel around Bar Ilan University, in the Negev community of Tifrach, in the ancient Galilean city of Tzefat, as well as in Atlanta, Georgia; Venice, California; Edison, New Jersey; Vancouver, British Columbia; Hillcrest, Queens; New Hyde Park, Long Island; Borough Park and Flatbush, Brooklyn.

Some of these, such as the Lincoln Square Synagogue and the Jewish Center of Riverdale, are located in areas where many singles live and cater to this group. They serve primarily as recruiting grounds and during the transitional phase from ba'al t'shuva to Orthodox. For the most part the newly Orthodox integrate into existing Orthodox communities.

There have, however, been some indications of problems in the relations between these communities and the larger Orthodox community. Pelkowitz (1980) claims that rejection of ba'alei t'shuva by the Orthodox community results in their remaining ba'alei t'shuva even after they are no different from other observant Jews. But others (Margolis 1987) claim that charismatic leaders at times cut off their followers from the rest of the Orthodox community. This has not become a major problem in America but has the potential to become troubling in Israel, where such communities may emulate other sectarian religious communities.

Becoming newly Orthodox while still living with parents is a stressful social experience; for those living on their own the conflict with parents is not as keenly felt. Those who enter yeshivot learn an Orthodoxy that places greater restrictions on social relations between men and women than do those who become Orthodox through marriage or synagogue. Nevertheless, many of those outside of yeshivot probably experience these pressures to some degree. For newly Orthodox, the process of transition involves an implosion of social relations to a greater or lesser degree. Building a new set of satisfying relationships takes time, and the transition process can be difficult. Once inside, the new set of relationships can be more satisfying than the old, and often some of the old relationships can be restructured on a new basis.

In a sense, becoming Orthodox is like getting married. One moves out and away from parents and ties oneself to a new relationship. In the process, old relationships are changed, if not broken. And, as with love and marriage, the motives impelling this change are complex and not fully articulated.

IV
Conclusions

Conclusions

A profound change is occurring in American Judaism, a change that mirrors developments in American religion at large. In the past, one was socialized into Orthodox Judaism and accepted it as a given without questioning its truth or its worth. Today Orthodoxy is becoming a matter of choice.

The emergence of the scientific perspective in the seventeenth century began to have an intellectual impact on Judaism in the late eighteenth and early nineteenth centuries. But Jewish identity was not substantially weakened until political emancipation began. In America, ethnic and religious identity were bound together for all Americans, Gentiles as well as Jews. For a while, ethnic identity was maintained through religious identity. But over the years the churches and synagogues underwent a slow process of Americanization, a process by which ethnicity was muted and religion became the dominant theme.

Mainstream Judaism—which is to say Reform and Conservative Judaism—had become so Americanized by the 1960s that when the counter-cultural movements of that period rejected the "establishment" and attacked its soft underbelly, education and organized religion, Reform and Conservative Judaism came to be rejected as well.[1] A new ethnic consciousness paved the way for a renewed interest in Orthodox Judaism. Jewish identity bifurcated: While many Jews simply lost interest in Judaism, some became more involved in religion as the twin realities of the Holocaust and the State of Israel began to penetrate their consciousness. The middle did not hold.

Orthodox Judaism was not prepared for this. The very mechanisms

---

1. Despite the growth of Reform Judaism, there is evidence that this trend is part of a process of disaffiliation (Cohen 1983, 51).

that enabled it to maintain its identity—the erection of social barriers to the larger society—made entry difficult. But the apparently sincere interest of ba'alei t'shuva in Judaism required a response. That response was ba'al t'shuva yeshivot and outreach programs. While outreach programs were not new, having been developed by synagogues and yeshivot a generation and more earlier, the countercultural and antiestablishment attitudes that prevailed in the late 1960s and 1970s fit in well with similar attitudes prevailing in traditionalistic yeshivot and enabled traditionalists to engage in outreach in terms of their own values, which were antiestablishment and countercultural. For the first time, the traditionalistic core of Orthodoxy, which had maintained its continuity by taken-for-granted socialization processes, attempted to present itself as a reasonable choice.

Returnees

I started with the question, Who are the returnees and why do they return? Cohen and Ritterband's (1981) study of Jews in the metropolitan New York area suggest that as many as a quarter of Orthodox Jews (highly observant) are newly Orthodox. Even if the more stringent measure of nonobservance of kashrut is taken to indicate nonobservance, at least 10 percent are newly Orthodox. Based on this study we estimate that probably more than one hundred thousand of the Orthodox are new to Orthodoxy and almost half of them have made radical changes in their religious lives to become Orthodox. At present their numbers do not appear to balance the outflow from Orthodoxy. Yet by making Orthodoxy a commitment of choice as well as birth, they change the net direction of the flow to and from Orthodoxy.

Most of the newly Orthodox have become Orthodox through marriage, involvement in synagogue programs or in Talmud Torah programs. Probably 85 percent of the newly Orthodox did not attend ba'al t'shuva yeshivot, although some attended regular yeshivot perhaps starting as teenagers. These people are most often simply referred to as "lacking background." I have focused primarily on those in ba'al t'shuva yeshivot because they were easily identified, their experience was more intensive, and the institutional responses to their needs made it easier to understand the processes and problems of transition to Orthodoxy.

In many respects this group appears similar to those "lacking background." Yet there are some differences. Yeshiva students are disproportionately men; those who become Orthodox through synagogue programs or marriage are more often women. The former are more often labeled ba'alei t'shuva, particularly at traditionalistic yeshivot; the latter, both men and women, are thought of by synagogue leaders as lacking background. Although a number of those lacking background seemed to be actively interested in Judaism prior to marriage or involvement in synagogue programs, most were not "seekers" in the sense of searching through different religions, nor were they likely to have been hippies in the 1960s. They were mainstream rather than countercultural and, one guesses, less likely to be involved in conflict with family prior to becoming Orthodox.

No careful records are kept at ba'al t'shuva yeshivot of the numbers of students that have entered. Many of the present students come from Orthodox or traditional families, and I cannot estimate whether these enrollments represent growth or new recruitment for Orthodoxy. Nor are data available on the backsliding of those who have attended the yeshivot. I have, however, found that a surprising number of those interviewed in 1976 were still part of the community in 1982, and I see no reason to question the stability of their commitment. Given the numbers attending the yeshivot, it is likely that more than ten thousand returnees have attended these yeshivot and that the great majority remain practicing Orthodox Jews.

The newly Orthodox tend more often to be women, to have had a good Jewish education, and to be children of immigrants than the general Jewish population. In terms of general education, social class, and even age, they are not significantly different from the general Jewish population.

Returnees at yeshivot for ba'alei t'shuva tend typically to be young adults, in their late teens or early twenties, unmarried, from middle- and upper-middle-class families, with a high level of education, most often including college and occasionally graduate or professional school as well. Typically, they recollect one or more Orthodox grandparents, have some memories of Jewish holidays, and have attended some after-school Hebrew school for a year or two. Among them are some whose parents had a synagogue affiliation for a period of time and others whose parents were infrequently affiliated with religious organizations but were associated with Jewish social organizations. We found none without prior experience with Judaism, either in the family or at some school. For some, the initial interest in Orthodoxy was triggered by an event perceived as traumatic: parents' divorce, intermarriage of a sibling, death of a parent or sibling, and occasionally their own divorce. More often, the trigger was a visit to Israel that resulted in a chance encounter with a recruiter, perhaps at the Western Wall, or meeting a friend who had become Orthodox. One also found seekers among the returnees, but this was more typical of the late 1960s and early 1970's.

As for why they return, I have argued that the reasons offered reflect the acceptable vocabularies of the recruiting agencies or the culture of the times. Although there is a "fit" between recruiters' vocabularies and recruits' needs, more is learned about these institutions and cultures by examining recruits' "motives" than about what impelled the recruits to act.

My analysis suggests five factors that affect the returnees and their paths of return: whether they have entered Orthodoxy through synagogues and marriage or through yeshivot, whether returnees are men or women, whether they are Israelis or American Jews, whether they are considered to be lacking background or are termed ba'alei t'shuva, and whether they have been introduced to modernistic or traditionalistic Orthodoxy. Differences in motivation, in experience, and in the process of change can be distinguished for these different types. Comparisons between them suggest some uniquely Jewish considerations that affect the path of the returnee.

COMMUNITY

Analyses of conversion to new religions have often provided detailed descriptions of the beliefs themselves or of the characteristics of the group the convert joins. The group is described in terms of leadership and followership and occasionally also in terms of social-economic characteristics. In this book, the importance of community, not just the synagogue one joins or the leader one follows, becomes clear. One enters the world of Orthodoxy or, more specifically, one of the two worlds of Orthodoxy that we have described. (Less frequently one enters the third world of Chasidism.) The returnee becomes anchored in this community, which is narrower than Orthodoxy yet more than a local congregation. The belief or meaning system does not seem to hold him so much as the "plausibility structure," the network of persons sharing the meaning-belief system. For Orthodox Judaism, family is the almost irreducible unit of this plausibility system—almost but not quite, for some individuals who are part of the system are not part of an Orthodox family, although this situation is typically temporary. The community plays a far more important role in Orthodox Judaism than in Christianity. The important issue is which Orthodoxy one is a part of—not the beliefs or meaning but the identification with the community through style of dress, place of residence, level of education, and style of life, particularly with regard to relations between men and women. These outward signs define the boundaries of community. Because community plays such an important role in anchoring returnees (and Orthodox Jews generally), boundary-defining mechanisms have themselves become central among Orthodox Jews, as they have among the Amish.

Different approaches to recruitment derive from the nature of each community's relation to the larger society. Modernistic Orthodox tend to structure their outreach programs to reach those lacking background, whereas traditionalistic Orthodox attempt to recruit ba'alei t'shuva. Modernists seek to build bridges, to emphasize the familiar while introducing the new recruit to Orthodoxy. Traditionalists seek to confront the potential recruit so as to emphasize the break with his or her former life.

But the differences should not be exaggerated. For just as these communities overlap and converge in some respects even as they grow apart in others, so the various recruitment techniques and the curricula of the yeshivot themselves also tend to converge in some respects. The traditionalistic ba'alei t'shuva yeshivot also seek to build bridges, as is evident from their unwillingness to allow clothing style to go too far in differentiating their students from other young people and in their toleration of sports, reluctant though it may be. Similarly, the modernistic schools move in the direction of beginning to recruit ba'alei t'shuva, to introduce the study of mysticism, and to be more traditionalistic in other ways. Despite the tendency of these two communities and types of yeshivot to drift apart, they seem bound together by inextricable ties of commitment.

Hypotheses Reviewed

At the beginning of this book I hypothesized that return to Judaism might be radically different from rebirth in Christianity and posited some reasons for this. I have in fact addressed the differences in some detail and summarize their implications here.

1. Judaism emphasizes acts over beliefs as an indication of commitment. Furthermore, despite the survey evidence that Jews do not profess religious beliefs, Jews become believers without much discussion of belief. New recruits seem to accept the religious beliefs easily. The actions, in contrast, are problematic.

2. Christian rebirth requires a single step of great weight whereas Judaism involves the performance of many commandments. The new recruit to Judaism is not "filled with the spirit," is not "saved," does not "witness" nor by any other act demonstrate charismatic power. Entry, therefore, remains a slow process. Of those who become Orthodox it is likely that a smaller percentage backslide than in some other religions, as what is considered entry is much further along the road to integration into the community.

3. The home-centeredness of Judaism in contrast to the church-centeredness of Christianity means that one cannot enter the inner sanctum of the Jewish community as readily as one may enter into Christianity. Another level of acceptance is required: one must be accepted into a Jewish family or establish one's own family. Whereas strains exist in the Christian family if one member is a born-again Christian and the others are not, the major practices of Orthodox Judaism—kashrut, Shabbat, and family purity—make it almost impossible to remain Orthodox while living in a family that is not. Conversely, once one becomes part of an Orthodox family, family pressures operate to keep one Orthodox.

Because the sanctum of Judaism is the family, spending Shabbat with an Orthodox family is a major recruiting mechanism. Outreach efforts expose the family in its most sacred and intimate moments to potential returnees who may well be skeptics. Outreach therefore becomes a challenge to Judaism in a quite different and potentially riskier way than it is for other religions. Synagogue and yeshiva outreach provide a buffer for the family and act as screening devices. In Israel, however, the openness of recruitment at the Western Wall brings potential recruits to families even before they enter yeshiva or synagogue. Only the recruiters stand between the family and the potential recruit, and given the numbers placed in homes every Shabbat, the recruiters cannot know much about the visitors they place. The hosts thus run the danger of being affected by the new recruit's attitudes and questions. Broad appeals through the mass media and public campaigns to become more religious (revivalism) without the assistance of yeshivot or families ready to accept and teach the returnee work best in Israel among people whose families are Orthodox or tradition-minded (*mesorati*).

4. Study of sacred literature is essential to Judaism and leads to the adaptation of yeshivot—institutions for study—as appropriate institutions for recruitment. Yeshivot are apparently most compatible with the value system of Orthodox Judaism than are chavurot, communes, or missions. Because of the emphasis on study, entry into the Orthodox

community becomes a process that for some is located in the yeshiva. It may be half a year or more before the person is considered sufficiently versed in Orthodoxy to be assisted by the teachers into the Orthodox community through marriage, housing, jobs, and the like. Although the majority become Orthodox on their own, if one enters through a yeshiva one gains not only the required knowledge but also a credential for acceptance by the Orthodox community.

Recruits who enter through a yeshiva are acquainted with the Judaism of the yeshiva, which is a more intense and separatist experience than that of the wider Orthodox community. The rebbis and roshei yeshiva provide the guidance. In other religions, in contrast, the minister or priest may be instrumental in conversion or rebirth, but once a decision has been made the individual typically becomes involved in the community, not in a seminary.

5. Judaism is both an ethnic and a religious identity. Involvement in Judaism in the United States seems to entail involvement in Jewish identity or ethnicity. As identity develops it comes to involve a religious connection as well. In Israel, where the ethnic element can be taken for granted, return to Judaism seems to be a more personal and spiritual religious experience, focused on the otherworldly and the mystical, and may occur much more rapidly than in the United States; ethnic elements of Judaism are already known or may easily be learned, as Hebrew is spoken and Judaism is the dominant religion.

For diaspora Jews, return is a two-step process: identifying first as a Jew and then as a religious Jew. Living in Israel substantially facilitates this process. Commitment to Israel in its secular as well as religious character is an important factor at the early stages of return. (Yeshivot play this down, sometimes causing friction with potential returnees.) Furthermore, in Israel the problem of the paradoxical juxtaposition of Universal God and Chosen People fades, since the majority of the population are also "chosen." The question becomes not Why be a Jew if most others are not? but Why not be a Jew, since most others are? The philosophic problem of universal God and chosen people may remain unresolved, but the psychological and social difficulties of that position fade.

6. For a Jew to become an Orthodox Jew in the United States is different from a Christian joining a fundamentalistic sect. The latter involves hyperconformity to the dominant American religious values. The former involves choosing religious values and rituals that are outside the mainstream, that are nonconformist and to that extent deviant.

In the United States, particularly prior to the 1960s, Orthodox Judaism was considered strange, alien, almost cultlike. In Israel, on the other hand, Judaism is the dominant religion, and Orthodoxy represents hyperconformity to the religious values of the society. The traditionalistic Orthodox are sectarian in their attitudes, rejecting the state and the nonreligious because they are not committed to Judaism.

Recruitment to Orthodoxy in Israel thus has a substantially different character from that in the United States. It is more open, more assertive, willing to dare the noncommitted to try religion and to allow them into the bosom of the family on Shabbat. American Jews in Israel are thus exposed to an open recruiting drive more typical of Christian efforts in the United States. This social environment and these new tactics become powerful instruments in the effort to gain new recruits to Orthodoxy, even to traditionalistic Orthodoxy.

7. Recruitment to the religion of the persecuted has occurred historically. (Conversion to the early Christian church is an example.) The widely accepted view is that such conversions occur primarily among the dispossessed, who have nothing to lose by converting and feel rejected by the prevalent religion of their society. The occasional conversion of middle- or upper-class people to the religion of the persecuted is explained in terms of personal deviance, unique motivation and circumstance, or a particularly effective theodicy.

But the Holocaust and a history of persecution have led some Jews to believe that even in an open society they cannot escape from their Jewishness. Continued anti-Semitism and attacks on Israel (and on Zionism) seem to support this view. Some attempt to escape these persecutions by loosening their ties to Jews and Judaism. But at times, as in the period preceding the Six Day War in 1967, the threat to Jews seems real and escape unlikely. The upsurge in Jewish identity that occurred then seems to have been a factor in the initiation of a new wave of return.

8. Earliest Christianity's doctrines were explicitly countercultural, permitting and encouraging the recruit to reject his or her parents as well as the establishment. Religious revivalism today calls upon that tradition. Judaism, too, has countercultural elements as we have seen, but rejection of parents is to be avoided. This suggests that the countercultural character of many of the new religions involves (1) rejection of the establishment and its values and (2) rejection of parents, two elements that require separate consideration.

Rejection of parents by those who join the new religion may cause it to be considered cultlike. The rejected family members may lead society in defining the new religion as a "cult"—which is to say, an illegitimate religion (Danzger 1987). Other factors might, of course, contribute to the definition of a religion as a cult. But relation to family, particularly parents, is an important factor that might lead to such a definition. That the movement of return to Orthodoxy has substantially avoided charges of being cultlike is probably partially attributable to its attempts to encourage newly Orthodox to maintain their ties to parents.

Conflict with parents, however, cannot be entirely avoided. The change in religious commitment introduces conflict. In addition, a substantial number of the ba'alei t'shuva could have a prior history of problem-ridden relationships with their parents. The new religious commitment often exacerbates the conflict.

The difference between Jewish and Christian doctrine with regard to parents—the former insisting on respect and love for parents, the latter permitting their rejection if they are not true Christians—spills over into recruitment. Missionizing is limited in Judaism not because there are any religious limitations on it (certainly not if the potential recruit is Jewish) and not only because Jews are in a minority in the diaspora. It is limited because religious doctrines require respect and love for parents. Neither recruits nor recruiters can get around this directly. One could undermine these doctrines through behavior that implies a lack of respect or through redefinition of the doctrines so that they seem not to apply, but this does not eliminate the effect of the norm to honor parents. If the family is non-Orthodox the potential new recruit is placed under heavy cross pressure, which has the effect of slowing recruitment. Yet the obligation to honor parents also mitigates conflict between recruits and parents.

This pattern in Judaism illustrates the complexity of countercultural value systems. Although returnees may have conflicts with parents and may be encouraged to reject their old friends now that they have returned to their religion, they may not reject their parents. Entry into Orthodox Judaism is, to a far greater extent than for some other religions, a family matter.

The Future of the American T'shuva Movement

The movement of return began in the United States in the late 1940s and became a yeshiva-oriented t'shuva movement in the early 1970s. Presently, it appears that the locus of the movement in America has shifted to synagogues. The emergence in 1987 of a national coordinating agency for synagogue outreach programs indicates this tendency. As for yeshivot for ba'alei t'shuva in the United States, by the early 1980s those in the movement reported that the movement had slowed. Hippies had faded from the scene. In Israel, however, yeshivot continue to grow. The reasons for this divergent experience are twofold: first, the type of person entering ba'al t'shuva yeshivot for Americans, both in Israel and in America, changed; second, the Israeli and American ba'al t'shuva movements represent substantially different phenomena.

The new non-Israeli returnees in Israel are no longer hippies and dropouts but are mainstream. They include South Africans and Australians from tradition-observing homes who have not had the opportunity to study in a yeshiva. A decade earlier they might have gone to Yeshiva University, but the students and their parents feel strong ties to Israel, and now that ba'al t'shuva yeshivot exist, they provide a viable alternative.

More significant, the ba'al t'shuva yeshivot now include substantial numbers of students who have been Orthodox all their lives but still have questions and doubts. Perhaps they lack the enthusiasm for Orthodoxy that they see in members of their own family. Perhaps their study skills are poor despite their years of training, and they feel inadequate in circles where Talmud is discussed. The ba'al t'shuva yeshivot provide a second chance for these students, an opportunity to learn things that they or their schools had ignored in the course of their education. The outreach programs of synagogues and yeshivot also serve these purposes.

The yeshivot and outreach programs serve another function as well. These portals of entry to Judaism have also become portals of exit. Basic questions are explored; values are articulated and examined. The atmosphere is open and accepting. This takes place in a supportive environment; potential recruits are interested in coming in, and the setting is organized and directed to show Orthodoxy in the best light. But the programs are still liberating experiences. If they are not a portal to the outside world, they are at least a window through which that world can be examined. This has an impact on the Orthodox themselves.

This phenomenon differs from the outreach efforts of the modernistic Orthodox that attempted to bridge the gap to the secular world. In that process a subtle sense of direction was transmitted so that while it facilitated the transition to Orthodoxy, the focus on social activities gave sanction to them. Traditionalists tended to reject these outreach initiatives and protected themselves by remaining insulated from society.

Currently, the emphasis has shifted from demonstrating that one can be Orthodox while also participating in the larger society to demonstrating that Orthodox religious life offers much that is valued even in secular terms, such as family, stability, a sense of direction in life. This new outreach focus has new risks. Letting down the barriers lets people out as well as in. Moreover, as this outreach approach is acceptable to traditionalists, it reaches into their community and results in closer contact with the secular world. Judaism comes to be felt to be a matter of choice rather than an immutable fact of birth.

The ba'alei t'shuva themselves have for some time been integrating into the Orthodox community without much difficulty and providing to that community a leavening of people who are sincerely committed to Judaism and at the same time carry some valuable experience of the larger world. This, of course, has been happening since "those lacking background" started entering Orthodoxy, in the 1940s. But the self-consciousness of the ba'al t'shuva movement in the last decade has made for an identity and an assertiveness that did not exist previously. Some ba'alei t'shuva seem to choose this status as an identity rather than a transitional status. The membership of some synagogues remains ba'alei t'shuva no matter how long ago the members became Orthodox. This occurs to some extent in the hippie ba'al t'shuva group, but it goes beyond this as well. There has been some discussion among traditionalistic ba'alei t'shuva of setting up an organization that will speak for the interests of ba'alei t'shuva. Thus far nothing has come of it. But it is significant, for it suggests that some ba'alei t'shuva may wish to retain their identity and remain outside of the Orthodox mainstream.

Returnees have been sufficiently concentrated to establish small synagogues for ba'alei t'shuva in a number of areas: Venice, California; Borough Park, Brooklyn; the upper west side of Manhattan; Far Rockaway, New York; Edison, New Jersey; and Brookline, Massachusetts. These communities have an indirect impact on the Orthodox community in America far beyond what their simple numbers might suggest. The excitement they generate as visible signs that Orthodoxy is attractive in the modern world gives their innovations and emphasis unique influence. They may be a bellwether of American Orthodoxy.

Since the early 1980s stories in the mass media about the return to Orthodoxy in America have stimulated sufficient interest to make it less necessary for synagogues to advertise their outreach programs. Some young urban Jewish men and women seek out these programs, and stories about their interest in Orthodoxy have helped make Orthodoxy an accepted religious option in these circles. The Lincoln Square Synagogue no longer dispatches a Mitzvah van to appeal to people on the streets. And synagogues need not rely on social activities to attract the non-Orthodox.

Newcomers now appear to be interested in the religious experience itself. The Orthodox religious experience, at least in the context of the synagogue, is no longer considered strange and foreign, but much more a legitimate American denomination.

The Future of the Israeli T'shuva Movement

Unlike the American t'shuva movement, the Israeli movement is not propelled by a search for ethnic identity, nor is it primarily a countercultural movement. Its roots can be traced to the aftermath of the Six Day War in 1967, when peace and acceptance by the Arabs were not forthcoming, despite Israel's victory. This was followed by the near disastrous Yom Kippur War of October 1973, which undermined faith in Israel's military might. The 1975 United Nations resolution equating Zionism with racism dashed hopes that secular Zionism might provide an answer to the problem of anti-Semitism. The Israeli t'shuva movement is part of a national search for purpose and direction, an expression of despair of finding some rational solution to the problems confronting Israel, an escape from an intolerable reality.

The changes in Israeli ba'alei t'shuva appear to be changes in personal rather than ethnic identity. Some of those who changed in the earliest period of the Israeli movement were probably influenced by the American countercultural movements of the 1960s. Changes from a hedonistic hippie style to a religious hippie style were probably of this sort. But the Israeli army veterans who joined the t'shuva movement probably reflected uniquely Israeli factors, particularly those that created a sense of despair about the political situation in Israel. Still a third group were the deviant or criminals (avaryanim). The media popularized the story of American ba'alei t'shuva and the changes occurring among pop culture heroes who returned. These returnees became models to be emulated. With the reported success of religious revival programs in the rehabilitation of drug addicts, petty criminals, and the like, more and more joined the bandwagon. The government, seeing an opportunity to both rehabilitate criminals and gain political credit for support of religion in Israel, provided funds for a variety of rehabilitation attempts.[2]

2. Some of the programs—for example, Migadal Ha'emek and the Yeshiva Ohr Hachayim—were highly successful and attracted much attention. By 1982 many mainline yeshivot had opened programs for ba'alei t'shuva. They were programs for all sorts of people basically designed for radical reorientation of personality.

As regular yeshivot joined in this movement, the impetus shifted from one in which people sought the change to one in which the people were offered an opportunity under government auspices to undergo rehabilitation, including religious indoctrination. In Israel the t'shuva movement had in part become establishment.

In supporting the American ba'al t'shuva yeshivot, the Israeli government sought to encourage immigration (aliyah) from the diaspora. It also saw these programs as an opportunity to bolster a fading Zionist ideology by adding a religious appeal to it. Israeli ba'al t'shuva yeshivot attracted interest as innovative social welfare programs helping to rehabilitate and remotivate people peripheral to society—social failures, delinquents, and addicts. Financial support for ba'al t'shuva programs induced regular Israeli yeshivot to offer them. Between 1978 and 1982 the number of regular yeshivot that claimed to have ba'al t'shuva programs in Israel jumped from four to forty, according to figures offered by the Department of Yeshivot. In a few years, t'shuva institutions are likely to be a part of the religious institutional structure in Israel, a new adjustment to modernity. But whereas in the United States yeshivot help returnees maintain an identity separate from the dominant society, in Israel they are likely to play a role somewhat similar to missionizing pentacostal groups in the United States. However, Orthodox Judaism's emphasis on laws and rules, its charismatic-legal authority structure, and its strong community ties are likely to enable it to retain a countercultural quality for some time to come.

THE IMPACT OF OUTREACH ON ORTHODOX JUDAISM

Since emancipation from the ghetto, Judaism has struggled to hold on to its adherents. Some strategies involved the building of increasingly high walls of religious separation between Orthodox Jews and others, a path followed by such groups as the Satmar Chasidim. Others have attempted to synthesize Torah study and Western scholarship. The first group has held that Orthodoxy can survive only if it isolates itself from the world. The second group has held that Orthodoxy can survive only if it learns to participate in the modern world.

Representatives of both traditionalistic and modernistic perspectives have engaged in outreach in the past. Traditionalists have focused on children and young teenagers. Modernists have been able to reach out to those of college-age and beyond. But the beginning of the hippie movement for the first time provided the opportunity for the traditionalists also to reach out to the college-age group and beyond. This group, educated and more mature, enabled the traditionalists to demonstrate the attractiveness of their position, for they could now point to their ability to persuade not only children but also adults who have tasted the outside world. Nonetheless, the newly Orthodox also represent a serious challenge to the traditionalists. Traditionalists' answers to questions must reflect familiarity with the culture to which the potential recruits have been exposed. The contacts must be consistent, long-term, and between relative equals. The danger that the recruiters will themselves go astray is real, for in the attempt to frame answers to the questions raised by mature potential recruits the recruiters must look at the world from the perspective of the doubter. In the process the traditionalists open themselves to the broader world in their innermost recesses—Shabbat and family life. Even if they are successful, their own beliefs are transformed from unarticulated, taken-for-granted practices to reasoned choices. The nature of their beliefs is changed. It may be strengthened—but not necessarily.

Finally, Israel is critically important in this entire phenomenon. Traditionalists cannot recruit outside of Israel, except among children. Traditionalist yeshivot in the United States, with the exception of Lubavitch, offer no program for adults. Israel offers the possibility for traditionalists to recruit among Jewish adults, non-Israelis as well as Israelis. Diaspora Jews visit Israel out of religious feelings. There, Jewish life is visible as it is nowhere else, not only because the Orthodox are heavily concentrated but because Jewish religious life is public: it is presented in the media; it determines the public calendar and the national character of the country. Orthodox Judaism in Israel is not a tiny religious minority but a substantial portion of the population.[3]

Since before the inception of the state, Orthodox and secularists have been engaged in a *Kulturekampf,* a struggle for the soul of Israel, with two models of the ideal society—the kibbutz and the religious community—vying for supremacy (Etzioni 1959). For a long time the religious community seemed to be in retreat. Since the mid-1960s, particularly the beginning of the t'shuva movement, the religious model has gained. But the Kulturekampf is more likely to result in the transformation of the adversaries themselves than in a victory for either side. For the moment traditionalist Orthodoxy still represents a countercultural group rejecting so-

3. In the United States there are approximately six hundred thousand Orthodox Jews—about 10 percent of all Jews and two tenths of a percent of the total population. In Israel the Orthodox are estimated at about six hundred thousand or 25–30 percent of the Jewish population and almost 20 percent of the total population—proportionately about a hundred times more than in America.

ciety and the state to some extent. It is now in position to become the equivalent of Protestant Fundamentalist groups in the United States. At the same time efforts at revivalism and recruitment are likely to sustain ba'alei t'shuva as an Orthodox phenomenon. The t'shuva movement is thus likely to remain viable for the foreseeable future. In the process, being Orthodox is likely to become more clearly a matter of choice rather than birth, and this is likely to have a major impact on the belief system and organizational structure of Orthodox Judaism.

Appendix

Tables on the Newly Orthodox in the Greater New York Metropolitan Area

The following tables are based on data gathered in the 1981 Greater New York Population Survey, directed by Paul Ritterband and Steven Cohen under the auspices of the Federation of Jewish Philanthropies of New York. A random sample of 4,505 Jewish subjects was interviewed by telephone in the largest random sample population study of American Jews to date. Figures in the table are weighted to facilitate the analysis. The weighting affects the numbers shown responding to questions, with some tables showing as many as 6,913 responses. (For a discussion of the methodology used see Ritterband and Cohen 1984a). Respondents provided data on their own ritual observances and those of their parents, permitting the identification of a newly Orthodox population. Steven Cohen did the special computer runs that generated the tables. Categories in the tables are as follows:

High observance—does not handle money on Sabbath;

Moderate observance—lights Sabbath candles and has two sets of dishes, as required by the laws of kashrut;

Low observance—fasts on Yom Kippur and lights Hanukkah candles;

Non-observance—reports no observance of rituals, or only ritual is the seder on Passover.

These categories are scalar; those reporting that they do not handle money on the Sabbath also observe the other rituals. Similarly, each category observes the rituals of the lower ones.

Table A-1
Observance of Jews in the Greater New York Area and Their Parents' Observance

Respondent's observance		Parents' Observance				Total	
		Non-Observant	Low Observant	Moderate Observant	High Observant	N	%
Nonobservant	N	341	330	287	52	1,011	17.0
	row %	33.7	32.7	28.4	5.2		
	col. %	46.2	25.1	11.8	3.6		
Low observant	N	255	809	1,112	382	2,559	43.0
	row %	10.0	31.6	43.5	14.9		
	col. %	34.6	61.5	45.6	26.1		
Moderate observant	N	95	155	946	517	1,714	28.8
	row %	5.6	9.0	55.2	30.2		
	col. %	12.9	11.8	38.8	35.3		
High observant	N	46	22	91	511	669	11.2
	row %	6.8	3.2	13.6	76.4		
	col. %	6.2	1.6	13.6	34.9		
Total	N	737	1,316	2,437	1,463	5,952	
	%	12.4	22.1	40.9	24.6		100.0

Note: Observance is defined on the bases of respondents' reports of their own and their parents' ritual observance. Of those in the high-observance category, 10.0 percent have parents in the low-observance or nonobservance category. Another 13.6 percent have parents in the moderate-observance category. But although these people light candles on the Sabbath, if they handle money they probably travel, shop, and engage in other activities that eliminate them from the category of Sabbath-observing Orthodox. Thus, according to this survey, almost 24 percent of the highly observant population of the New York metropolitan area are new to this level of observance.

Because of rounding, percentages may not add up to 100.

Table A–2

The Jewish Population of New York and the Newly Orthodox
(High Observance) Compared for Age

Age	Newly Orthodox N (%)		Others N (%)		Total N (%)	
18–34	42	(28.8)	1,607	(24.8)	1,649	(24.9)
35–49	42	(28.8)	1,632	(25.2)	1,674	(25.3)
50–64	31	(21.1)	1,891	(29.2)	1,922	(29.0)
65+	31	(21.1)	1,347	(20.1)	1,378	(20.8)
Total	146		6,477		6,623	

Note: Degrees of freedom (DF) = 3; X^2 = 4.75 (not significant at 0.05 level). Because of rounding, percentages may not add to 100.

Table A–3

The Jewish Population of New York and the Newly Orthodox
(High Observance) Compared for Education

	Newly Orthodox N (%)		Others N (%)		Total N (%)	
High-school graduate	43	(28.1)	1,929	(28.9)	1,972	(28.9)
Some college	20	(13.1)	1,214	(18.2)	1,234	(18.1)
B.A.	60	(39.2)	2,134	(32.0)	2,194	(32.2)
Beyond B.A.	30	(19.6)	1,391	(20.8)	1,421	(20.8)
Total	153		6,668		6,821	

Note: DF = 3; X^2 = 4.746 (not significant at 0.05 level). Because of rounding, percentages may not add to 100.

Table A–4

The Jewish Population of New York and the Newly Orthodox
(High Observance) Compared for Jewish Education

	Newly Orthodox N (%)		Others N (%)		Total N (%)	
None or Sunday school	40	(27.7)	2,533	(37.4)	2,573	(37.2)
Hebrew school	71	(49.3)	3,491	(51.6)	3,562	(51.5)
Yeshiva or day school	33	(22.9)	745	(11.0)	778	(11.2)
Total	144		6,769		6,913	

Note: DF = 2; X^2 = 21.43 (significant at 0.01 level). Because of rounding, percentages may not add to 100.

Table A–5
The Jewish Population of New York and the Newly Orthodox
(High Observance) Compared for Generations in America

	Newly Orthodox		Others		Total	
	N	(%)	N	(%)	N	(%)
Foreign-born	48	(31.3)	1,117	(16.8)	1,165	(17.1)
American-born of foreign-born parents	72	(47.0)	3,269	(49.1)	3,341	(49.1)
American-born of American parents	33	(21.6)	2,270	(34.1)	2,303	(33.8)
Total	153		6,656		6,809	

Note: DF = 2; X^2 = 25.68 (significant at 0.01 level). Because of rounding, percentages may not add to 100.

Table A–6
The Jewish Population of New York and the Newly Orthodox
(High Observance) Compared for Sex

	Men		Women		Total
	N	(%)	N	(%)	N
Newly Orthodox	35	(25.0)	105	(75.0)	140
Others	2,632	(40.7)	3,834	(59.3)	6,466

Note: DF = 1; X^2 = 14.04 (significant at 0.01 level). Because of rounding, percentages may not add to 100.

Table A–7
The Jewish Population of New York and the Newly Orthodox
(High Observance) Compared for Visits to Israel

	Orthodox		Newly Orthodox		Others		Total	
	N	(%)	N	(%)	N	(%)	N	(%)
None	127	(25.7)	62	(38.7)	4,179	(66.7)	4,368	(63.2)
One	125	(25.4)	39	(25.1)	1,334	(21.3)	1,498	(21.7)
More than one	242	(48.9)	58	(36.2)	748	(11.9)	1,048	(15.2)
Total	494		159		6,261		6,914	

Note: DF = 5; X^2 = 14.3 (significant at 0.01 level). Because of rounding, percentages may not add to 100.

Glossary

An asterisk following a word indicates that it is the name of a person, organization, or religious tract.

*Agudat Israel.** (Heb., also *Agudas Israel;* "Union" or "Association" of Israel) World Jewish movement and political party seeking to preserve Orthodoxy by adherence to halakhah as the principle governing Jewish life and society.

*Aish Hatorah.** (Heb. "fire of Torah") A yeshiva in Israel.

Am ha-aretz. (Heb. "the people of the land") An uneducated person.

Am Yisrael. (Heb. "the people of Israel) The Jewish people.

Amud. (Heb. "pillar" or "stand") The lectern in the synagogue at which the prayer leader stands.

Arba kanfos. (Yid., from the Hebrew; literally "four corners") An undergarment with *tzitzit* (Heb. "fringes") worn by men.

Ashkenazi. (Heb., pl. *Ashkenazim*) Jew from European lands.

Atarah. (Heb. "headband" or "crown") A decorative band, often of silver, attached to the *tallit* (prayer shawl) and draped over the head.

Atchalta d'geulah. (Aram.) The beginning of the period of messianic redemption.

Aufruf. (Yid. "calling up") Calling of the bridegroom to the Torah on the Sabbath before his wedding.

Avaryan. (Heb., pl. *avaryanim*; "sinner," "transgressor") A delinquent or criminal.

Averah. (Heb. "sin," "transgression").

Ba'al mofsim. (Yid. "master of wonders") A performer of miracles.

Ba'al t'shuva. Also *Ba'al teshuva.* (Heb. masc. "master of return") A penitent. As used in this book, someone who has chosen to become Orthodox.

Ba'alat t'shuva. (Heb. fem. of *ba'al t'shuva*).

Ba'alei tosafot. (Heb.) Twelfth- to fourteenth-century commentators on the Talmud.

Ba'alei t'shuva. (Heb., pl. masc. of *ba'al t'shuva*).

Ba'alot t'shuva. (Heb., pl. fem. of *ba'al t'shuva*).

Balebatesheh minyanim. (Yid.) Prayer quorums of ordinary people.

Bar mitzvah. (Heb. "son of commandments") An adult with adult religious responsibilities. The ceremony in which a boy is inducted into adulthood.

Batim. (Heb., sing. *bayit*) Houses.

Bat mitzvah. (Heb. "daughter of commandments") As in Bar Mitzvah, for a girl.

B'china. (Heb., pl. *b'chinot*; "exams") Oral exams in yeshivot.

Bekeshe. (Yid.) A long satin jacket, ordinarily black, worn by chasidim at religious occasions. Sometimes called a caftan, kapote, or *chalat*.

Beki'im. (Heb.) Those with encyclopedic knowledge of the Talmud.

Bet midrash. (Heb. "house of study") Study hall.

Bimot. (Heb., sing. *bimah*; "raised place") Large lecterns for the reading of the Torah scroll.

Bittul z'mahn. (Heb. "waste of time") Wasting time.

B'kiut. (Heb. "breadth of knowledge").

B'nai B'rith. (Heb. "sons of the covenant") A Jewish fraternal organization.

Bobeh. (Yid.) Grandmother.

Bund. (German) An association.

Chabad. (Heb.) An acronym for Lubavitch, representing *ch*ochmah (wisdom), binah (understanding), and *da*'at (knowledge).

Chag hasmikhah. Also *Hag hasmikhah.* (Heb. "ordination celebration") A rabbinical commencement celebration occurring every third year at Yeshiva University.

*Chaim Berlin.** A yeshiva in Brooklyn.

Challah. Also *Hallah.* (Heb., pl. *challot*; "loaf of bread") Twisted Sabbath breads.

Chanukkah. Also *Hanukkah.* (Heb. "dedication") Festival of lights, occurring in December. Celebrating the rededication of the Temple after the victory of the Maccabees over the Selucid Greeks (165 B.C.E.).

Chasan. Also *Hatan.* (Heb.) Bridegroom.

Chasid. Also *Hasid.* (Heb., pl. *chasidim*; "pious") Follower of the chasidic movement.

Chasidishe velt. (Yid. "the chasidic world") The chasidic community.

Chasidism. Also *Hasidism.* A religious movement founded by Israel Ba'al Shem Tov in the seventeenth century. Directed at the poor and less educated classes, it emphasized piety, mysticism, good deeds, and loyalty to the leader or rebbe.

Chasidut. (Heb., Yid. *chassidus*) The lore and seminal writings of chasidim.

Chalutziut. Also *Halutziut.* (Heb.) The spirit of the Israeli *chalutz* or pioneer.

Chaver. Also *Haver.* (Heb., pl. *chaverim*; "associate") Friend.

Chavruta. Also *Havruta.* (Aram.) A study partner.

Chavurah. Also *Havurah.* (Heb., pl. *chavurot*) A fellowship.

Chazzan. Also *Hazzan.* (Heb.) Cantor.

Cheder. Also *Heder.* (Heb., Yid. *cheyder;* a room) A one room schoolhouse.

Chiddush. Also *Hiddush.* (Heb., pl. *chiddushim*) Novel Talmudic interpretation.

Chillul Ha-Shem. Also *Hillul Ha-Shem.* (Heb. "Desecration of the Name," i.e., of God).

Chizuk kirovim. (Heb. "strengthening of those who are near") Revitalization of the religiously committed.

Cholent. (Yid., from the Old French "to cook slowly") A hot dish made with meat, beans, barley, potatoes, or rice and placed in the oven before Sabbath.

Chol ha-mo'ed. Also *Hol ha-mo'ed.* (Heb. "weekdays of the festival") The intermediary days of the festival, when work is permitted.

Chozer b't'shuva. (Heb., pl. *chozrei b't'shuva*) Returnee in repentance. Used in Israel as a synonym for *ba'al t'shuva.*

Chumash. Also *Humash.* (Heb.) The five books of Moses, i.e., the Pentateuch.

Cohen. (Heb., pl. *Cohanim,* "chief") A member of the priestly caste.

Da'at Torah. (Heb., Yid. *da'as Torah;* "knowledge of Torah") Torah perspective.

Dat Yisrael. (Heb.) Jewish custom, a halakhic term.

Darkei shalom. (Heb. "peaceful ways") Peacefully.

Daven. (Yid.) Pray.

Dinim. (Heb. "laws") Religious laws.

Dreidel. (Yid.) A top used in games played on Chanukkah.

Emunat chachamim. (Heb., Yid. *Emunas chachamim*) Belief in the sages.

Eretz Yisrael. (Heb.) The land of Israel.

Etrog. (Heb.) Citron fruit used in connection with the rituals of the Sukkot or harvest holiday.

Farbrengen. (Yid.) A festive gathering of chasidim.

Frum. (Yid. "pious") Religious, careful in observance.

Gabbai. (Heb., pl. *gabbaim*) Sexton, an officer of the synagogue.

Gartel. (Yid. "belt") A sash or cummerbund worn by some of the pious during prayers, often with the kapote.

Gedolim. (Heb., sing. *gadol;* "the great") Great talmudic sages.

Gemara. (Aram., sometimes *Gemora*) The record of discussions and explanations of the Mishnah of the third to sixth centuries. Together with the Mishnah it comprises the Talmud.

Get. (Heb.) Religious bill of divorcement.

G'milat chassadim. Also *Gemilat hassadim.* (Heb.) Acts of kindness.

Golem. (Heb.) A mythical manlike creature made of clay.

Greener. (Yid.) New immigrants to America.

Gush Emunim. (Heb.) Faith block. A political party primarily of religious Zionists intent on settlement of the territories captured in the Six Day War.

Guteh kasheh. (Yid.) A good question.

Guteh teretz. (Yid.) A good answer.

Gut Shabbos. (Yid. "Good Sabbath") A Sabbath greeting.

Halakhah. (Heb., pl. halakhot; "the way") The body of Jewish religious law.

Hallel. (Heb.) A prayer of thanksgiving that is part of the holiday liturgy.

Hamantasch. (Yid., pl. *hamantaschen*) A traditional three-cornered tart stuffed with poppy seed, eaten on Purim.

Harbatzat Torah. (Heb.) The spreading or teaching of Torah.

Ha-Shem. (Heb. "The Name") A reference to the ineffable name of God, or to God Himself.

Hashgacha. (Heb. "supervision") Divine Providence.

Hashkafa. (Heb.) Perspective or weltanshauung.

Haskala. (Heb.) The Enlightenment.

Havdalah. (Heb. "separation") The ceremony marking the end of the Sabbath.

Hesder yeshivot. (Heb. "yeshivot in the arrangement") Yeshivot in which military service is combined with yeshiva study.

Heychal Hatorah. (Heb. "The Hall of Torah") A yeshiva for students lacking background in Orthodoxy.

Hillel. (Heb.) A campus youth organization supporting Jewish values.

Kabbalah. (Heb. "that which is received") The esoteric and mystical teachings of Judaism.

Kaddish. (Heb.) A prayer proclaiming the glory of God said by mourners.

Kallah. (Heb.) A bride.

Kasha. (Yid.) A question.

Kasher. (Heb., vb.; also *kosher,* adj.) Ritually pure. To kasher something, such as a pot or a stove, is to make it ritually pure.

Kashrut. (Heb.) Compliance with rules for things kosher; that is, the religious laws that forbid the consumption of certain animals and their products and that require the separation of meat and milk foods and dishes.

Kavvanah. (Heb. "intention") Sincerity and purity of thought in prayer.

Kehillah. (Heb. "community") Community as a governing body.

Kiddush. (Heb. "sanctification") A benediction over a cup of wine at the commencement of Sabbath and holiday meals. A light meal of Sabbath specialties following Sabbath morning prayers.

Kinot. (Heb., sing. *kinah;* "elegies") Recited on Tisha b'Av.

Kippah. (Heb.) A small skullcap worn by males.

Kippah seruga. (Heb. "a knitted skullcap") A style of skullcap worn by Zionistically inclined Orthodox.

Kiruv r'chokim. (Heb. "drawing close of those who are afar") Outreach to non-Orthodox Jews.

Kolel. (Heb.) An advanced school for the study of Talmud open to married men and providing them with a stipend.

Kol isha. (Heb. "a woman's voice") A woman singing is considered sexually arousing and halakhah forbids a man to hear a forbidden woman (a woman other than one's wife or blood relative) sing.

Kotel. (Heb. "The Wall") The Holy Western Wall, a remnant of the wall surrounding the Temple compound in ancient Jerusalem. Sometimes referred to by non-Jews as the "Wailing Wall," a term that Jews feel is pejorative.

Kugel. (Yid.) A pudding, often made of potatoes or noodles and typically eaten on the Sabbath.

Kumsitz. (Yid. "come sit") A party or gathering of teenagers.

Latkes. (Yid. "potato pancakes") A traditional dish for Chanukkah.

*Likutei Maharan.** (Heb.) Excerpts of the sermons of Rabbi Nachman of Bratzlav, a great chasidic rebbe (1772–1811) as recollected by one of his disciples.

*Lubavitch.** (Yid.) The name of the Russian town associated with the first of the Lubavitcher rebbes, Schneur Zalman. The movement is often referred to by this name.

L'Chaim. Also *Le Hayyim.* (Heb. "To Life") A traditional toast.

Lulav. (Heb.) A palm frond, used in the holiday rituals of the Sukkot festival together with the etrog.

Ma'ariv. (Heb.) The evening prayer.

Machzor. Also *Mahzor.* (Heb.) Prayer book for the High Holy Days.

Maharsha. An acronym for *Moreinu* (our teacher) *Harav* (the rabbi) Samuel Eliezer ben Yehuda Halevi Adels (1555–1631), a commentator on the Talmud.

Mamzer (Heb., pl. *mamzerim*) A child born of an illegitimate relationship.

Masorah (Heb.) Tradition.

Matmid (Heb., pl. *matmidim;* "those who are constant") Zealous students.

Mechitzah. Also *Mehizah.* (Heb. "partition") A partition separating men and women in public prayer.

Medinat Yisrael. (Heb.) The State of Israel.

Melavveh malkah. (Heb. "the accompanier of the queen") A festive gathering following the Sabbath.

Meshulachim. (Heb. "those who are sent") Fund raisers for religious institutions.

Mesorati. (Heb.) Tradition-minded Jews.

Midot. (Heb., also *midos*) Virtuous behavior, character.

Midrash. (Heb.) Study. The compilation of broadly philosophical interpretation of books of the Bible, originating in Mishnaic times.

Mikveh. (Heb.) A pool of water for the purpose of ritual purification, constructed in accordance with halakhic requirements.

Minchah. Also *Minhah.* (Heb.) Late afternoon prayers.

Minyan. (Heb., pl. *minyanim*) A prayer quorum.

Mishnah. (Heb.) The collection of rulings of the Oral Law that is the basis for the Talmud.

Mishpakhah. (Heb., Yid. *mishpokheh*) Family.

Mitnagdut. (Heb.) The movement of those opposed to Chasidism.

Mitnagged. (Heb., pl. *mitnaggedim,* adj. *mitnagdic,* Yid. *misnagged;* "an opposer") Those who opposed Chasidism.

Mitzvah. (Heb., pl. *mitzvot;* "commandment") Good deed.

Motzi. (Heb.) The blessing over bread. The bite of bread one eats after reciting the blessing.

Musar. (Heb. "moral instruction") Ethical teaching introduced into the curriculum of yeshivot by Rabbi Israel Salanter (1810–1883).

Nach. (Heb.) An acronym for the Bible excluding the Pentateuch.

Negiyah. (Heb. "touching") Laws forbidding a man to touch a woman.

Niddah. (Heb. "a menstrual woman") Laws forbidding a man to have sexual relations with his wife and reducing contacts between them during a portion of her menstrual cycle.

Niggun. (Heb., pl. *niggunim;* "tunes") Religious songs and hymns.

Niglah. (Heb. "that which is revealed") The exoteric or publicly taught part of Jewish teachings.

Nistar. (Heb. "that which is hidden") The esoteric teachings. Kabbalah.

Ohr Someyach. (Heb. "joyous light") The name of a yeshiva in Israel.

Oker Harim. (Heb. "An uprooter of mountains") A sharp and logical thinker.

Orchim. (Heb.) Guests.

Pasuk. (Heb.) A sentence.

Pesak. (Heb.) Halakhic decision.

Peyot. (Heb.) Side locks.

Pilpul. (Heb. "peppery") Complex talmudic discussion.

Po'el yeshu'ot. (Heb. "activator of salvations") One who can call upon heaven to provide help.

Purim. (Heb. lottery) A carnival-like, early spring holiday celebrating the victory of the beautiful Queen Esther and her Uncle Mordechai over the wicked Haman who plotted to kill the Jews and "cast lots" to determine the date of destruction.

Rabban Gamliel.* Rabban Galiel of Jabneh (first and second centuries C.E.).

Rashi.* (Solomon ben Isaac, 1040–1105) A leading commentator on the Bible and the Talmud.

Rebbe. (Yid.) A chasidic leader.

Rebbi. (Yid.) Teacher in a yeshiva.

Rebbitzin. (Yid.) Wife of a rabbi. An honorific title.

Responsa. (Lat.) Responses to questions that have been asked of halakhic authorities.

Rosh Ha-Shanah. (Heb.) The new year holiday. A day of prayer on which the shofar (ram's horn) is blown, and the kingdom of God is proclaimed.

Rosh yeshiva. (Heb., pl. *roshei yeshivot;* "head of yeshiva") The leading authority in a yeshiva.

Sanhedrin. (Gk., Heb.) The highest halakhic judicial and legislative body. Active in the period of the Second Temple.

Seder. (Heb. "order") A ceremonial meal celebrated on the first nights of Passover, enjoyed at home with family and friends. Study program in a yeshiva.

Sephard. (Heb. "Spain") The customs of the Jews of Mediterranean and Arab lands. Customs of Jews who follow chasidic rituals and liturgy.

Sephardi. (Heb., pl. *sephardim*) A Jew from Mediterranean or Arab lands.

Se'udah shelishit. (Heb. "the third meal") Meal eaten on the Sabbath between late afternoon and evening prayers.

Sevarah. (Heb.) Reasoning or logic.

Shabbat. (Heb., pl. *Shabbatot,* Yid. *Shabbos*) The Sabbath.

Shabbatone. (Heb.) A weekend Sabbath celebration for adolescents or young adults in which members of one community host people from other communities.

Shabbetai Tzevi.* (1626–76) A self-proclaimed messiah who stirred wide interest and gathered a large following before converting to Islam.

Shabbeteanism.* The movement of the followers of Shabbetai Tzevi.

Shacharit. Also *Shaharit.* (Heb. "morning") The name of the morning prayer service.

Shadkhan (Heb., pl. *shadkhanim*) Matchmaker.

Shalakhmonot. (Heb., Yid. *Shalach Mones;* "sending presents") Gifts of cakes and goodies traditionally sent to friends on Purim.

Shavuot. (Heb. "weeks") A spring holiday celebrated seven weeks after Passover, celebrating the receiving of the Torah on Mount Sinai and the offering of the first fruits.

Sheitel. (Yid. "wig") Worn for religious reasons by married women to cover their hair.

Shikool ha da'at. (Heb. "weighing of knowledge") Consideration of argument.

Shi'ur. (Heb., pl. *shi'urim*) A lecture.

Sh'ma. Also *Shema* or *Shema Yisrael.* (Heb.) The profession of faith, "Hear O Israel . . ."

Sh'moneh esrai. Also *Shemoneh esrai.* (Heb. "eighteen") The eighteen benedictions that are the central core of the prayer service.

Shmooz. (Yid.) Chat, talk.

Shomer mitzvot. (Heb., pl. *shomrei mitzvot*) Observant of the commandments.

Shomer Shabbat. (Heb., pl. *shomrei Shabbat*) Sabbath-observing.

Shtetl. (Yid., pl. *shtetlakh*) Little town or village.

Shtieble. (Yid., pl. *shtiblakh*) Little house, small synagogue. Associated with Chasidism.

Shul. (Yid.) A synagogue.

Siddur. (Heb., pl. *siddurim*) Prayer book.

Simchat Torah. Also *Simhat Torah.* (Heb. "The joy of the Torah") Celebrated after the Sukkot holiday in the fall. The Torahs are taken from the ark, and the congregation dances with them and rejoices in the Torah.

Soud. (Heb.) Secret. A reference to mystical knowledge.

Streimel. (Yid.) A fur-trimmed hat worn by chasidim on festive occasions.

Sukkah. (Heb., pl. *sukkot;* "a booth or hut") A small dwelling roofed with boughs or twigs in which meals are eaten and the Sukkot holiday is celebrated.

Sukkot. (Heb.) The fall holiday during which Jews celebrate by dwelling in sukkot.

Tachlit. (Heb.) Purpose, goal.

Taharat hamishpakhah. (Heb. "family purity") Referring to observance of the laws of niddah.

Talmid. (Heb.) Student or disciple.

Talmid chacham. (Heb., pl. *talmidei chachamim;* "disciple of the wise") A talmudic scholar.

Talmud. (Heb.) The compendium of the Mishnah and Gemara, which together constitute the Talmud.

Talmud torah. (Heb. "study of Torah") Afternoon religious school that supplemented public schools.

*Targum.** The authoritative first-century translation of the Bible in Aramaic.

Tefillin. (Heb.) Phylacteries. Small, black leather boxes containing portions of Scripture. They are worn on the bicep and above the forehead during weekday morning prayers.

Tichel. (Yid.) Kerchief.

Tikun ha'olam. (Heb. "repairing or improving the world") A mystical concept.

Tisha b'Av. (Heb.) The ninth day of the Hebrew month of Av, a day of mourning marking the destruction of the first and second Temples, the fall of Betar, as well as other national disasters.

Tiyul. (Heb.) Tour or camping trip.

Toda'ah Yehudit. (Heb.) Knowledge of things Jewish. Also a program conducted by the Government of Israel to educate soldiers.

*Tomchei Temimim.** (Heb. "supporters of the simple or pure") The Lubavitch yeshiva for ba'alei t'shuva.

Torah. (Heb. "The Teaching") The five books of Moses. The entire Bible. All of the tradition, both scripture and oral.

Torah sheh ba'al peh. (Heb. "The Oral Teachings") The oral tradition.

*Torah Vodaath.** (Heb. "Torah and knowledge") A yeshiva in Brooklyn.

Tosafists. Twelfth- to fourteenth-century commentators on the Talmud and particularly on Rashi's interpretation.

Tosafot. (Heb.) Additions. The collections of comments on the Talmud and in particular on earlier talmudic authorities. Begun by Rashi's pupils and descendants.

Treyf. (Yid.) Nonkosher, forbidden food.

T'shuva. Also *Teshuva.* (Heb.) Repentance, return.

Tumah. (Heb.) Defilement.

Tzadik. (Heb.) A righteous person, a great soul.

Tzitzit. (Heb. "fringes") A fringed garment worn by Jewish males in conformity with the command of the Torah.

Tzniusdik. (Yid.) Behavior reflecting the value of tzniut.

Tzniut. (Heb. "modesty") Referring to clothes and behavior with members of the opposite sex.

Ulpan. (Heb.) Intensive Hebrew language study course. Sometimes a school and dormitory facility where Hebrew is learned.

Viduy. (Heb.) A confession of sins. Also a last rite performed when death is imminent.

Yarmulke. (Yid.) A skullcap worn for religious reasons so that the head is always covered.

Yeshiva. (Heb., pl. *yeshivot,* poss. *yeshivat*) School for religious study. Originally a school for advanced talmudic study, sometimes used in this narrower sense.

Yeshiva bochur. (Yid., pl. *yeshiva bochrim*) Yeshiva boy or student.

Yeshiva gedolah. (Heb.) Higher yeshiva. A school for the advanced study of Talmud.

Yeshivishe. (Yid.) Having the characteristics of yeshiva.

Yeshivishe velt. (Yid.) The world of yeshivot. The yeshiva community.

Yetzer horah. (Heb.) The evil inclination, temptation.

Yichus. Also *Yihus.* (Heb.) Status or honor. Often based on lineage.

Yiddishists Those seeing the survival of the Jewish people as dependent on their use of the Yiddish language.

Yiddishkeit. (Yid.) Judaism. Jewish culture, particularly religious customs. The intimate nuances of parochial Judaism.

Yichud. Also *Yihud.* (Heb.) Rules that forbid a man to be alone with any woman prohibited to him (i.e., married women other than his wife).

Yiush. (Heb.) Despair.

Yiras shamayim. (Heb. "fear of heaven") Respect or awe.

Yom Kippur. (Heb. "the day of forgiveness") Following Rosh Ha-Shana by ten days. A day of fasting and prayer.

Zaydeh. (Yid.) Grandfather.

Zemirot. (Heb. "songs") Sabbath hymns sung at the table.

References

Abeles, Ronald P., and Matilda White Riley. 1977. "A Life Course Perspective on the Later Years of Life: Some Implications for Research." In *Social Science Research Council Annual Report, 1976–77, 1–16*. New York: Social Science Research Council.

Abercrombie, Nicholas et al. 1970. "Superstition and Religion: The God of Gaps." In *Sociological Yearbook of Religion in Britain,* ed. D. Martin and M. Hill, vol. 3, 93–129. London: SCM.

Alba, Richard R., and Mitchel B. Chamlin. 1983. "A Preliminary Examination of Ethnic Identification among Whites." *American Sociological Review* 48, no. 2:240–47.

Albright, William Foxwell. 1957. *From the Stone Age to Christianity,* 2d ed. Garden City, N.Y.: Doubleday, Anchor.

Alexander, C. Norman, Jr., and Mary Glenn Wiley. 1981. "Situated Activity and Identity Formation." In *Social Psychology: Sociological Perspectives,* ed. Morris Rosenberg and Ralph H. Turner. New York: Basic Books.

Argyle, Michael. 1959. *Religious Behavior.* Glencoe, Ill.: Free Press.

Asch, Solomon E. 1958. "Effects of Group Pressure on the Modification and Distortion of Judgments." In *Readings in Social Psychology,* 3d ed., ed. Eleanor E. Macoby, Theodore M. Newcomb, and Eugene L. Hartely. New York: Holt, Rinehart, and Winston.

Aviad, Janet. 1983. *Return to Judaism: Religious Renewal in Israel.* Chicago: University of Chicago Press.

Axelrod, Ira. 1976. "A Baal T'shuvah Strikes Back." *Perspective* (Rabbinical Alliance of America) 3, no. 1:38–50.

Balch, Robert W., and David Taylor. 1977. "Seekers and Saucers: The Role of the Cultic Milieu." *American Behavioral Scientist* 20, no. 6:839–60.

Beck, Mordechai. 1977. *Learning to Learn: A Guide to the New Yeshivot in Israel.* 2d ed. Jerusalem: World Union of Jewish Students.

———. 1984. "Ba'alei Teshuva Yeshivot in Israel: The Last Ten Years."

Beckford, James A. 1985. *Cult Controversies: The Societal Response to the New Religious Movements.* New York: Tavistock.

Begun, Dov. 1979–80. "The Sweet Waters of Torah." *Jewish Life* 3, 4:29–36.

Bellah, Robert N. 1967. "Civil Religion in America." *Daedalus* 96:1–21.

Berger, Peter. 1967. *The Sacred Canopy.* Garden City, N.Y.: Doubleday.

Berkowitz, Eliezer. 1984. *Not in Heaven.* New York: Ktav.

Berman, Lewis. 1982. *Vegetarianism and the Jewish Tradition.* New York: Ktav.

Bromley, David, and Anson D. Shupe. 1979. *"Moonies" in America: Cult, Church and Crusade.* Beverly Hills, Calif.: Sage Publications.

Brown, Roger. 1965. *Social Psychology.* New York: Free Press.

Buber, Martin. 1947,1948. *Tales of the Hasidim.* New York: Schocken.

Cantril, Hadley. 1941. *The Psychology of Social Movements.* New York: Wiley.

Carlebach, Shlomo. 1970. "The Heart of Tomorrow (Communications)." *Midstream* 16 (May):66–67.

Carlin, Jerome E., and Saul Mendlowitz. 1958. "The American Rabbi: A Religious Specialist Responds to Loss of Authority." In *The Jews: Social Patterns of an American Group,* ed. Marshal Sklare, 377–414. New York: Free Press.

Cohen, Gerson. 1982. "The State of the Jews 1983: Reflection on Jewish Normality, Agony, and Glory." *Moment* 8 (December):17–20.

Cohen, Steven M. 1983. *American Modernity and Jewish Identity.* New York: Tavistock.

Conover, Patrick W. 1975. "An Analysis of Communes and Intentional Communities with Particular Attention to Sexual and Gender Relations." *Family Coordinator,* October, 453–64.

Cowan, Paul. 1981. *An Orphan in History.* New York: Doubleday.

Cromer, G. 1981. "Repentent Delinquents." *Jewish Journal of Sociology* 23:113–22.

Danzger, M. Herbert. 1976. "Signposts Along the Road Home: An Analysis of the Rhetoric of Return to Judaism." Paper presented at the annual meeting of the Israel Sociological Society, Tel Aviv, Israel.

———. 1977. "Portals of Religious Return: The New Yeshivot in Israel." Paper presented at the annual conference of the Association for Jewish Studies, Boston.

———. 1980. "The Ba'al T'shuva in the American Community: New Values and Old Ties." Paper presented at the annual conference of the Association for Jewish Studies, Boston.

———. 1986a. "Recruitment to Orthodox Judaism: Jerusalem and New York Compared." Paper presented at the annual meeting of the Association for the Sociology of Religion, New York.

———. 1986b. "Religious Revival in Comparative Perspective: Toward a Redefinition of Sect and Cult." Paper presented at the annual meeting of the International Society for the Comparative Study of Civilizations, Santa Fe, New Mexico.

———. 1987. "Action and Study: Ritual and Religious Grounding in Orthodox Judaism." Paper presented at the annual meeting of the Association for the Sociology of Religion, Chicago.

———. 1987. "Towards a Redefinition of 'Sect' and 'Cult': Orthodox Judaism in Comparative Perspective." *Comparative Social Research* 10:113–23.

Deshen, Sholomo. 1978. "Two Trends in Israeli Orthodoxy." *Judaism* 27:397–409.

Dexter, Louis. 1970. *Elite and Specialized Interviewing*. Evanston, Ill.: Northwestern University Press.

Dostoyevski, Fyodor. [1880] 1955. *The Brothers Karamazov*. New York: Random House.

Druckman, Chaim. 1979–80. "Chaim Druckman, M. K., A Poet of Teshuva: An Interview." *Jewish Life* 3, no. 4: 25–28.

Durkheim, Emile. [1915] 1955. *The Elementary Forms of Religious Life*. Trans. J. W. Swain. New York: Free Press.

Elazar, Daniel. 1976. *Community and Polity: The Organizational Dynamics of American Jewry*. Philadelphia: Jewish Publication Society.

Etzioni, Amitai. 1959. "Alternative Ways to Democracy: The Example of Israel." *Political Science Quarterly* 74:196–214.

———. 1961. *A Comparative Analysis of Complex Organizations: On Power, Involvement and Their Correlates*. New York: Free Press.

Festinger, Leon. 1957. *A Theory of Cognitive Dissonance*. Stanford, Calif.: Stanford University Press.

———. 1962. "Cognitive Dissonance." *Scientific American* 207, no. 27:93–98.

Festinger, Leon, Henry W. Riecken, and Stanley Schachter. 1956. *When Prophecy Fails*. Minneapolis: University of Minnesota Press.

Fishman, Priscilla, ed. 1973. *The Jews of the United States*. New York: Quadrangle, New York Times Book.

Forster, Arnold. 1950. *A Measure of Freedom*. New York: Doubleday.

Frank, Blanche. 1975. "The American Orthodox Jewish Housewife: A Generational Study in Ethnic Survival." Sherrow Prize Essay.

Fromm, Eric. 1941. *Escape From Freedom*. New York: Farrar and Rinehart.

Garrison, Winfred E. 1948. "Characteristics of American Organized Religion." *Annals of the American Academy of Political and Social Science* 256:14–24.

Gartner, Lloyd. 1973. "Young Israel: Its Early Days and Some of Its Early Personalities." Hebrew University, Jerusalem. Mimeo.

Gevirtz, Eliezer. 1980. "Reaching the Kids—The JEP Connection." *Jewish Observer* 14, no. 9:31–35.

Glanz, David, and Michael Harrison. 1978. "Varieties of Identity Transformation: The Case of Newly Orthodox Jews." *Jewish Journal of Sociology* 20, no. 2:129–41.

Glaser, Hollis. 1980. "Rebbe With a Cause." *Subject to Change: The Washington University Quarterly* 6, no. 3. Reprint. Yeshiva Aish Hatorah.

Glazer, Nathan. 1957. *American Judaism.* Chicago: University of Chicago Press.

———. 1970–71. "On Being Deradicalized." *Commentary* 50 (October):74–80; 51 (January):22–23.

———. 1979. "American Jews: Three Conflicts of Loyalties." In *The Third Century: America as a Post-Industrial Society,* ed. Seymour Martin Lipset, 224–41. Stanford: Hoover Institution Press.

Glock, Charles Y., and Audrey Stark. 1966. *Christian Beliefs and Anti-Semitism.* New York: Harper and Row.

Goffman, Erving. 1963. *Stigma: Notes on the Management of Spoiled Identity.* Englewood Cliffs, N.J.: Prentice Hall.

Goldberg, Hillel. 1980. "Review of Israeli Intellectual Life." *Tradition* 18:212–23.

———. 1980. "The Teshuva Solicitors." *Jewish Observer* 14, no. 9: 10–12.

Goldman v. Weinberger. 1986. No. 84–1097, Slip B. U.S. Supreme Court No. 106, S. CT. 1310.

Goldscheider, Calvin, and Dov Friedlander. 1983. "Religiosity in Israel." In *American Jewish Yearbook* 83:3–39.

Goldstein, David. 1978. "My Bag: The Yeshiva." *Jewish Observer,* March, 9–10.

Goldstein, Sidney, and Calvin Goldscheider. 1974. "Jewish Religiosity: Ideological and Ritualistic Dimensions." In *The Jew in American Society,* ed. Marshall Sklare, 203–21. New York: Berman House.

Greeley, Andrew M. 1972. *The Denominational Society.* Glenview, Ill.: Scott, Foresman.

———. 1979. "Ethnic Variations in Religious Commitment." In *The Religious Dimension: New Directions in Quantitative Research,* ed. Robert Wuthrow. New York: Academic Press.

Grossman, Lawrence. 1986. "The Politics of Aggadic Interpretation." *Midstream,* Aug./Sept., 28–30.

Hanan, Ben. 1977. "Headlines Over-Stated Lelyveld's Criticism of Chabad as Cult?" *Jewish Week,* 14 Sept.

Handelman, Susan. 1984. "The Honeymoon is Over: Ba'alei Tshuva after Ten Years." *Melton Journal,* Summer, 6ff.

Harrison, Paul M. 1959. *Authority and Power in the Free Church Tradition.* Princeton: Princeton University Press.

Heilman, Samuel. 1976. *Synagogue Life.* Chicago: University of Chicago Press.

———. 1977. "Inner and Outer Identities: Sociological Ambivalence among Orthodox Jews." *Jewish Social Studies* 39, no. 3:227–40.

———. 1983. *The People of the Book*. Chicago: University of Chicago Press.

Heineman, Joseph. 1977. *Prayer in the Talmud*. New York: Walter DeGruyter.

Heirich, Max. 1977. "Change of Heart: A Test of Some Widely Held Theories of Conversion." *American Journal of Sociology* 83:653–80.

Heller, Celia Stopnicka. 1977. *On the Edge of Destruction: Jews of Poland between the Two World Wars*. New York: Columbia University Press.

Helmreich, William G. 1981. *Study of Yeshiva Graduates: A Survey*. Mimeo.

———. 1982. *The World of the Yeshiva: An Intimate Portrait of Orthodox Jewry*. New York: Free Press.

Herberg, Will. 1960. *Protestant, Catholic, Jew*. New York: Doubleday.

Herman, Simon N. 1970. *Israelis and Jews: The Continuity of an Identity*. New York: Random House.

———. 1977. *Jewish Identity: A Social Psychological Perspective*. Beverly Hills, Calif.: Sage Publications.

Himmelfarb, Harold S. 1975. "Measuring Religious Involvement." *Social Forces* 53, no. 4:606–18.

Hoffer, Eric. 1951. *The True Believer*. New York: Harper and Brothers.

Hofstadter, Richard. 1955. *Social Darwinism in American Thought*. Rev. ed. Boston: Beacon Press.

Hoge, Dean R. 1974. *Commitment on Campus*. Philadelphia: Westminster.

Janis, Irving L., and Bert T. King. 1954. "The Influence of Role Playing on Opinion Change." *Journal of Abnormal and Social Psychology* 49:211–18.

Johnson, Benton. 1961. "Do Holiness Sects Socialize in Dominant Values?" *Social Forces* 39:309–16.

———. 1963. "On Church and Sect." *American Sociological Review* 28:539–49.

———. 1971. "Church and Sect Revisited." *Journal for the Scientific Study of Religion* 10:124–37.

Jungreis, Esther. 1977. "Rebbetzin's Viewpoint." *Jewish Press* 18 Nov., 22ff.

Kanter, Rosabeth Moss. 1968. "Commitment and Social Organization." *American Sociological Review* 33:499–517.

Kaplan, Mordechai M. 1934. *Judaism as a Civilization: Toward a Reconstruction of American-Jewish Life*. New York: Macmillan.

Katz, Jacob. 1961. *Exclusiveness and Tolerance*. New York: Schocken.

———. [1958] 1971. *Tradition and Crisis*. New York: Schocken.

———. 1973. *Out of the Ghetto*. Cambridge: Harvard University Press.

Kaufman, Debra Renee. 1985. "Women Who Return to Orthodox Judaism: A Feminist Analysis." *Journal of Marriage and the Family* 47:543–51.

Kelman, Herbert. 1961. "Process of Opinion Change." *Public Opinion Quarterly* 25:57–78.

Kennedy, Ruby Jo Reeves. 1944. "Single or Triple Melting Pot? Intermarriage Trends in New Haven, 1870–1940." *American Journal of Sociology* 49, no. 4.

Kiser, Clyde V. [1949] 1958. "The Diversity of American Society." In *American Minorities*, ed. Milton Barron. Reprint. New York: Alfred Knopf.

Klaperman, Gilbert. 1969. *The Story of Yeshiva University: The First Jewish University in America.* Toronto: Macmillan.

Kol Yisrael Arevim. 1976. Jewish Educational Program Records [Division of Agudat Israel of America].

Kovacs, Malcolm. 1977. *Dynamics of Commitment: The Process of Resocialization of Baale Teshuvah.* Ann Arbor, Mich.: University Microfilm.

Kramer, Mordechai. 1972. "The Yiddies: A Report on Hippies Turned Orthodox Jews in Israel." Paper presented at seminar on the Student Revolt. Hebrew University, Jerusalem.

Laster, Paul. 1979–80. "A Young Man from Virginia Teaches 'Jewish Identity' To Israel's Defense Forces: An Interview." *Jewish Life* 3, no. 4: 45–54.

Latane, Bibb, and Jean A. Rodin. 1969. "A Lady in Distress: Inhibiting Effects of Friends and Strangers on Bystander Intervention." *Journal of Experimental Social Psychology* 5:189–202.

Lazerwitz, Bernard. 1979. "Past and Future Trends in the Size of American Jewish Denominations." *Journal of Reform Judaism* 26, no. 3:77–82.

Lazerwitz, Bernard, and Michael Harrison. 1979. "American Jewish Denominations: A Social and Religious Profile. *American Sociological Review* 44:656–66.

Lemert, Edwin M. 1974. "Beyond Mead: The Societal Reaction to Deviance." *Social Problems* 21:457–68.

Levine, Saul V. 1980. "Alienated Jewish Youth and Religious Seminaries—An Alternative to Cults?" Hebrew University, Jerusalem. Mimeo.

Levy, Sydelle Brooks. 1973. *Ethnic Boundedness and the Reinstitutionalization of Charisma: A Study of Lubavitcher Hassidim.* Ph.D. diss. City University of New York.

Liebman, Charles S. 1965. "Orthodoxy in American Jewish Life." In *American Jewish Yearbook* 66:21–97.

———. 1973. *The Ambivalent American Jew.* Philadelphia: Jewish Publication Society of America.

———. 1979. "Orthodox Judaism Today." *Midstream* 20:19–26.

Liebman, Charles S., and Eliezer Don-Yehiya. 1983. *Civil Religion in Israel.* Berkeley: University of California Press.

Lincoln, C. Eric. 1961. *Black Muslims in America*. Boston: Beacon Press.

Lofland, John. 1966. *Doomsday Cult*. Englewood Cliffs, N.J.: Prentice-Hall.

———. 1977. "Becoming a World Saver Revisited." *American Behavioral Scientist*, ed. James T. Richardson, vol. 20, no. 6:805–18.

Lofland, John, and Rodney Stark. 1965. "Becoming a World Saver: A Theory of Conversion to a Deviant Perspective." *American Sociological Review* 30:862–74.

McGuire, Meredith B. 1981. *Religion: The Social Context*. Belmont, Calif.: Wadsworth.

Malinovich, Myriam M. 1983. "A Haven Among the Hasidim." *Present Tense* 2:41–43.

Marcuse. Herbert. 1964. *One Dimensional Man*. Boston: Beacon Press.

Margolis, David. 1987. "The Flawed Miracle on Venice Beach." *Baltimore Jewish Times*, 23 Oct., 76ff.

Mayer, Egon. 1985. *Love and Tradition: Marriage between Jews and Christians*. New York: Plenum.

Melton, J. Gordon, and Robert L. Moore. 1982. *The Cult Experience*. New York: Pilgrim.

Milgram, Stanley. 1964. "Behavioral Study of Obedience." *Journal of Abnormal and Social Psychology* 67:371–78.

Miller, Norman. 1987. Review of *Ancient Judaism: Biblical Criticism from Max Weber to the Present*, by Irving M. Zeitlin. *Contemporary Sociology* 16, no. 5:727–28.

Mills, C. Wright. 1940. "Situated Actions and Vocabularies of Motives." *American Journal of Sociology* 5:904–13.

Mishnah Berurah. Hebrew-English Edition. 1984. Ed. and trans. Rabbi Aharon Feldman. Jerusalem: Feldheim.

Niebuhr, H. Richard. 1929. *The Social Sources of Denominationalism*. New York: Meridian.

Novack, William. 1970. "The Making of a Jewish Counterculture." *Response* 7 (Spring–Summer).

Novak, David. 1984. "Women in the Rabbinate?" *Judaism* 33, no. 1:39–49.

Ofshe, Richard. 1980. "The Social Development of the Synanon Cult." *Sociological Analysis* 41:109–27.

Omer-Man, Jonathan. 1984. "The Needs and Expectations of the Religiously Alienated Jew." *Melton Journal*, Summer, 14–15.

Pelkowitz, Ralph. 1980. "The Teshuva Phenomenon: The Other Side of the Coin." *Jewish Life* 4, no. 3:16ff.

Piazza, Thomas. 1976. "Jewish Identity and the Counterculture." In *The New*

Religious Consciousness, ed. Charles Y. Glock, and Robert N. Bellah. Berkeley: University of California Press.

Pilch, Judah, ed. 1969. *A History of Jewish Education in the U.S.A.* New York: National Curriculum Research Institute of the American Association for Jewish Education.

Poll, Solomon. [1962] 1969. *The Hassidic Community of Williamsburg.* New York: Schocken.

Polsky, Howard W. 1958. "A Study of Orthodoxy in Milwaukee: Social Characteristics, Beliefs and Observances." In *The Jews: Social Patterns of An American Group,* ed. Marshal Sklare, 325–35. New York: Free Press.

Pope, Harrison, Jr. 1974. *The Road East: America's New Discovery of Eastern Wisdom.* Boston: Beacon.

Potok, Chaim. 1967. *The Chosen.* New York: Simon and Schuster.

Raphael, Marc Lee. 1984. *Profiles in American Judaism: The Reform Conservative, Orthodox and Reconstructionist Tradition in Historical Perspective.* San Francisco: Harper and Row.

Reich, Charles. 1970. *The Greening of America.* New York: Random House.

Reisman, Bernard. 1977. *The Chavurah: A Contemporary Jewish Experience.* New York: Union of American Hebrew Congregations.

Ritterband, Paul, and Steven M. Cohen. 1984a. "Sample Design and Population Estimation: The Experience of the New York Jewish Population Study, 1981–1984. In *Perspectives in Jewish Population Research,* ed. Steven M. Cohen, Jonathan Woocher, and Bruce Philips. Boulder, Colo. and London: Westview.

———. 1984b. "The Social Characteristics of the New York Area Jewish Community, 1981." *American Jewish Yearbook,* 128–61.

Robbins, Thomas. 1979–1980. "Religious Movements, the State and the Law: Reconceptualizing 'The Cult Problem.'" *Review of Law and Social Change 9,* no. 1:33–49.

Robbins, Thomas, and Dick Anthony. 1972. "Getting Straight with Meher Baba." *Journal for the Scientific Study of Religion* 11:122–40.

Robertson, Ian. 1987. *Sociology.* 3d ed. New York: Worth.

Robertson, Roland. 1978. *The Sociological Interpretation of Religion.* New York: Schocken.

Rosenberg, Stuart E. [1964] 1965. *The Search for Jewish Identity in America.* New York: Doubleday, Anchor.

Rosenzweig, Franz. [1921] 1971. *The Star of Redemption,* trans. W. W. Halo. New York: Holt, Rinehart, and Winston.

Roszak, Theodore. 1968. *The Making of a Counter Culture.* Garden City, N.Y.: Doubleday.

Roth, Philip. 1959. *Goodbye, Columbus and Five Short Stories.* Boston: Houghton Mifflin.

Rubin, Israel. 1972. *Satmar: An Island in the City.* Chicago: Quadrangle.

Sarna, Jonathan D. 1982. "The Great American Jewish Awakening." *Midstream,* October, 30–34.

Schiller, Mayer. 1978. *The Road Back.* New York: Feldheim.

Schiller, Nota. 1980. "Studying Talmud—The Means and the End." *The Jewish Observer,* June, 13–15.

Scholem, Gerschon. 1972. "Kabbalah." *Encyclopedia Judaica.* Jerusalem: Keter.

Scott, M. D., and S. M. Lyman. 1968. "Accounts." *American Sociological Review* 33:43–62.

Selengut, Charles. 1985. "Cults and Jewish Identity." *Midstream,* January, 12–15.

Shaffir, William. 1983. "The Recruitment of Baalei Tshuva in a Jerusalem Yeshiva." *The Jewish Journal of Sociology* 25, no. 1:33–46.

Shupe, Anson D., Jr., Roger Spielman, and Sam Stigall. 1977. "Deprogramming: The New Exorcism." In *American Behavioral Scientist,* ed. James T. Richardson, vol. 20:941–71.

Siegel, Richard, Michael Strassfeld, and Sharon Strassfeld. 1973. *The First Jewish Catalog.* Philadelphia: Jewish Publication Society.

Silver, Marc. 1978. "Giving Up the Assimilated Life." *Baltimore Jewish Times,* 20 January, 32–43.

Singer, David. 1974. "Voices of Orthodoxy." *Commentary,* July.

———. 1976. "The Yeshiva World." *Commentary,* October, 70–73.

Sklare, Marshal. [1955] 1972. *Conservative Judaism.* New York: Schocken.

———. 1974. "The Greening of Judaism." *Commentary* 58, no. 6:51–57.

Sklare, Marshal, with Marc Vosk, and Mark Zborowski. 1955. "Forms and Expressions of Jewish Identification." *The Jewish Journal of Social Studies* 17:205–18.

Soloveitchik, Joseph Dov. 1944. "Ish haHalakhah." *Talpioth* 1:651–735.

Stark, Rodney, and William Sims Bainbridge. 1985. *The Future of Religion.* Berkeley: University of California Press.

Steinsaltz, Adin. 1984. "The Ba'al Teshuva: Entering a New World of Difficult Social Relations." *Melton Journal,* Summer, 9–10.

Stolper, Pinchas. 1981. "The Teshuva Phenomenon: Responses from our Readers." *Jewish Life* 4, no. 4:24–29.

Strassfeld, Sharon, and Michael Strassfeld. 1976. *The Second Jewish Catalog.* Philadelphia: Jewish Publication Society.

———. 1980. *The Third Jewish Catalog.* Philadelphia: Jewish Publication Society.

Sturm, Ephraim. 1984. Address by Executive Vice President of Young Israel National Council at Young Israel National Convention.

Tabory, Ephraim. 1984. "Rights and Rites: Women's Roles in Liberal Religious Movements in Israel." *Sex Roles* 11, nos. 1,2:155–66.

Takooshian, Harold, and Herzel Bodinger. 1979. "Street Crime in Eighteen American Cities: A National Field Experiment." Paper read at the annual meeting of the American Sociological Association, Boston.

Teller, Hanoch. 1980. "How Do You Handle a Hungry Heart?" *The Jewish Observer,* June, 16–19.

Tobin, Gary A. 1986. *A Population Study of the Jewish Community of Greater Baltimore.* Waltham, Mass.: Center for Modern Jewish Studies.

Tobin, Gary A., and Alvin Chenkin. 1985. "Recent Jewish Community Population Studies: A Roundup." *American Jewish Studies* 85: 154–78.

Troeltsch, Ernst. [1931] 1960. *The Social Teachings of the Christian Churches.* Trans. O. Wyon. 2 vols. New York: Harper and Row.

Trow, Martin. 1966. "The Second Transformation of American Secondary Education." In *Class, Status and Power: Social Stratification in Comparative Perspective.* 2d ed., ed. Reinhard Bendix and Seymour Martin Lipset, 437–48. New York: Free Press.

Turner, Ralph H., and Killian, Lewis M. 1957. *Collective Behavior.* Englewood Cliffs, N.J.: Prentice-Hall.

Waxman, Chaim I. 1976. "The Centrality of Israel in American Jewish Life: A Sociological Analysis." *Judaism* 25, no. 2:175–87.

———. 1981. "The Fourth Generation Grows Up: The Contemporary American Jewish Community." *Annals American Academy of Political and Social Science,* 454:70–85.

———. 1983. *America's Jews In Transition.* Philadelphia: Temple University Press.

Weber, Max. 1958. "Class, Status, and Party." *From Max Weber: Essays.* Ed. Hans Gerth and C. Wright Mills. New York: Oxford University Press.

———. 1958. "Politics as a Vocation." *From Max Weber: Essays.* Ed. Hans Gerth and C. Wright Mills. New York: Oxford University Press.

———. [1904] 1958. The Protestant Ethic and the Spirit of Capitalism. Trans. Talcott Parsons. New York: Scribner.

———. [1922] 1960. *The Sociology of Religion.* Trans. E. Fischoff. Boston: Beacon.

Weinbach, Mendel. 1967. *The Religion of India.* New York: Free Press.

———. 1980. "The Baal Teshuva in the United States." *Jewish Observer* 14, no. 9:25–26.

Westley Frances R. 1977. "Searching For Surrender: A Catholic Charismatic Renewal Group's Attempt to Become Glossalalic." *American Behavioral Scientist* 20, no. 6:925–40.

Wiesel, Elie. 1972. *Souls on Fire*. New York: Random House.

———. 1966. *The Gates of the Forest*. New York: Holt, Rinehart and Winston.

Wirth, Louis. 1928. *The Ghetto*. Chicago: University of Chicago Press.

———. 1938. "Urbanism as a Way of Life." *American Journal of Sociology* 44, no. 1:3–24.

Wolf, Janet. 1982. " 'Baruch Ha'Shem, Not So Good' Some Concerns of Jewish Women." *Jewish Life* 6, no. 1:47–53.

Yearbook Religious Zionism, 1983–1984. Jerusalem: Mesilot.

Yerushalmi, Yosef Hayim. 1980. *The Re-education of Marranos in the Seventeenth Century*. The Third Annual Rabbi Louis Feinberg Memorial Lecture in Judaic Studies. Judaic Studies Program, University of Cincinnati.

Yinger, J. Milton. 1982. *Countercultures: The Promise and Peril of a World Turned Upside Down*. New York: Free Press.

Zborowski, Mark, and Elizabeth Herzog. [1952] 1962. *Life is with People*. New York: Schocken.

Index

Accounts, 224, 232–33, 235
Action (vs. belief), 128–32, 242, 331
Agudat Israel, 146n, 148
Aish Hatorah, 124–25, 127, 129, 205, 281
Akiva, Rabbi, 14, 16
Alba, R. R., 74n
Anti-Semitism, 18, 22, 23. See also Holocaust
Assimilation, 14–15, 16–18, 23
Attitudes, 222n–24n
Authority. See Charismatic authority; Religious authority
Axelrod, Ira, 311

Ba'alei t'shuva: courtship and, 306–13; demographic characteristics of, 193–95, 329–30; differences among, 7; identity of, 337; vs. Jews "lacking background," 328–29; Judaism and, 8, 197; as label, 79–81, 94; marriage between, 307–08, 312; nodes and networks of, 322; phenomenon of, 1–2; relations with parents and, 162, 298–305. See also Returnees; Women
Ba'al t'shuva yeshivot: for Americans, 2, 113–15; beginnings in Israel, 66–70; commitment to Orthodoxy and, 311, 329; courtship and, 311–12, 314–16; cults and, 301; dress style and, 265–70; as entry into Orthodoxy, 55–58; intimacy of, 105–06; in Israel, 339; for Israelis, 113–15; men's curriculum in, 117–28; percentage of newly Orthodox attending, 328; prayer at, 275–76; vs. regular yeshivot, 103–11; in

U.S., 1, 55–66, 115–16, 218–19, 220, 335–36; in U.S. vs. Israel, 220; values of Israeli society and, 159–61; for women, 111–13; women's curriculum in, 133–41
Bar mitzvah, 31, 32
Beliefs: vs. actions, 331; Jewish, 289–90; Judeo-Christian, 281–88, 296–97; Orthodox, 290–97; plausibility structure and, 286
Besdin, Morris, 65, 108, 254, 260n
Biblical criticism, 173–75, 286–87
Black Muslims, 72–73
Bostoner Rebbe. See Horowitz, Levi Yitzhak
Brandeis Institute, 51
Bratzlaver chasidim, 183, 288
Bromley, David, 311
Brovender, Chaim, 68, 69, 70, 90–92, 156–57, 188–89
Brovender's, 68–69, 127–28, 319–20. See also Hamivtar; Shappel College
Brown, Roger, 129n
B'ruria College, 70, 138–39, 140
Buchwald, Ephraim, 36–38, 39, 41, 107–08, 281–82

Carlebach, Shlomo, 1–2, 59, 85–86, 89, 93, 94, 123
Celibacy, 311
Central Europe, religious identity in, 17–18
Chamlin, M. B., 74n
Charismatic authority, 165, 227; antinomianism and, 182; halakhah and, 184–85; modernistic yeshiva and, 181; Orthodox community and, 323; outreach and, 85–89; tradi-

Charismatic authority (*continued*)
  tionalistic view of, 177–81. *See also*
  Religious authority
Chasidim, 1; Bratzlaver, 183, 201;
  countercultural view of, 81–82;
  gilgul and, 287–88; as models of
  revival, 15–16; Sabbath guests and,
  110–11. *See also* Lubavitch
Chasidishe velt, 53. See also *Chasidim*
Chavruta, 132, 278–79
Chavurah, 52–53, 99–103
Chavurat Shalom, 99–100
Cheder, 44–45, 46, 48
Children of *ba'alei t'shuva*, 163, 241,
  318. *See also* Family; Parents;
  Relatives
Chizuk kirovim vs. *kiruv r'chokim*, 16
Christianity. *See* Religious revival, in
  Christianity vs. Judaism
Civil rights movement, 71–74
Class, and sects vs. cults, 114*n*
Cognitive dissonance, 129–30, 224*n*
Cohen, Gerson, 301
Cohen, Steven, 328, 342
Columbus Platform of *1937*, 25–26
Commitment: development of, 129–
  30; study and, 133; symbolic-
  interactionist approach and, 165–
  66; waiting period and, 310–12;
  without ritual practice, 247–50
Community. *See* Orthodox community
Compliance, 242
Congregational schools, 47–48
Conservative Judaism: authority in,
  101, 166; chavurah in, 99–100;
  countercultural values and, 86; Eastern European immigrants and, 23–
  24; origins of, 23–24; prayer at the
  Kotel and, 202, 204; study of Talmud in, 100, 102; view of women
  in, 290
Counterculture, 79*n*, 86, 93; dress
  style and, 265–66, 267–68; drugs,
  114*n*; *1960s* emergence of, 74–77,
  79*n*; Orthodox Judaism and, 81–83,
  142; religion and, 76, 77, 81–83;
  traditionalist vs. modernist values
  and, 185–88

Courtship: difficulties of, 306–13;
  laws of family purity and, 262–63;
  yeshivot and, 311–12, 313–16
Cowan, Paul, 105, 257
Cults: American Jews and, 289;
  Orthodoxy and, 198, 199, 300–03,
  333–34; parents of converts and,
  298–99; recruitment and, 198, 199;
  vs. sects, 114*n*, 116

Darchei Noam-Shappel College, 70*n*
Dating situations, 261–62, 315–16
Da'at Torah, 167, 180
Day schools, 49
Dead rebbe. *See* Chasidim, Bratzlaver
Divine intervention, 227–30
Divorce, 309
Domesticity in women's curriculum,
  136–37
Dress style: adjustment of, 264–70;
  American female ba'al t'shuva and,
  266–68; American male ba'al
  t'shuva and, 265–66; of black hat
  vs. modern Orthodox, 143–46;
  community and, 266, 272; Israeli
  ba'al t'shuva and, 268–70; laws of
  family purity and, 260*n*
Durkheim, Émile, 3
D'var Yerushalayim: for men, 70;
  women's institute at, 112, 113, 138

Eastern European Jews: Conservative
  Judaism and, 23–24; Orthodox Judaism and, 24–25; postwar immigration of, 25–26; Reform Judaism
  and, 23; religious identity and, 17–
  18; in U.S., 21–22
Eastern religions, 76–77
Education. *See* Jewish education; Secular education
Elefant, Mordechai, 68, 156, 157
Eliezer ben Hyrcanus, 181–82
Ethnic identity: civil rights movement
  and, 71–74; Israeli ba'alei t'shuva
  and, 268–69, 338; religious identity
  and, 17–18, 23, 327–28, 333; Six
  Day War and, 78, 79

Family: children of ba'alei t'shuva, 163, 241, 318; in Christianity vs. Judaism, 301–03; grandparents, 242, 320–21; holy days and, 258–60; integration into Orthodoxy and, 42–43, 332; laws of kashrut and, 253; motivation for return and, 241–42; observance of Shabbat and, 257; plausibility system and, 330; siblings, 241, 305–06. *See also* Parents; Relatives
Family purity, laws of, 260–64, 316–17
Festinger, Leon, 129
Friends, 305–06

Gadol, 177, 181
Gedolim, 54
Gemara, 117–19, 127, 134, 138–39, 140, 170–71. *See also* Talmud
Gender roles. *See* Women, role of
Gentiles. *See* Jewish-Gentile relations
Gesher organization, 219
Gilgul, 287
Glazer, Nathan, 24–25, 26, 131
Goffman, Erving, 144n
Goldstein, Mordechai, 67–68, 69, 86–89, 92, 93, 94, 124
Gottlieb, David, 278–79, 284–85, 291–92
Grandparents, 320–21

Hairstyle, 137, 265. *See also* Wigs
Halakhah, 119; authority of, 166–67, 175–77, 181–82; charisma and, 184–85; community tradition and, 271–72; marriage eligibility and, 308–10; Orthodox Jews and, 102; Orthodoxy's view of women and, 290; role of women and, 153–54; traditionalistic vs. modernistic yeshivot and, 166–67; Young Israel and, 34–35
Hamivtar, 171–72, 174–75, 181. *See also* Brovender's; Shappel College
Hartman School. *See* Brovender's; Hamivtar; Shappel College
Hasidim. See Chasidim

Hatfutzot-Har Tzion, 68, 69, 87–89, 93, 94; charismatic authority at, 177–81; countercultural values and, 185–86; curriculum at, 123–34, 127; occupational training at, 319; role of women and, 139–40
Heilman, S., 278n
Helmreich, W. G., 150, 151
Heychal Hatorah, 62–63
Himmelfarb, H. S., 130n
Hippie, 79n, 186–88, 204, 265; disappearance of, 336; and women's dress, 267. *See also* Counterculture
Holiday celebrations. *See* Holy days
Holocaust, 26, 288–90, 334
Holy days, 102, 255–66, 299
Holy sites in Jerusalem, 198, 201–02, 203. *See also* Kotel; Western Wall
Home, and social relations, 27–28
Horowitz, Levi Yitzhak, 66, 81
Humanist-rationalist philosophy, 17

Igud Harabonim, 146
Integration, process of, 40–42, 337
Interest payments, 293, 294
Introduction to Seder Zeraim (Maimonides), 182
Israel: army of, 158–61; ba'al t'shuva yeshivot in, 66–70, 115–16; clusters of ba'alei t'shuva in, 322, 323; future of t'shuva movement in, 338–41; government support in, 333, 338–39; Holocaust and, 289–90; kashrut in, 108–09, 252; modernistic Orthodoxy in, 90–92; outreach to Israelis in, 113–15, 219, 269–70, 338; recruitment in, 198–215, 332, 334, 340; relations to friends in, 305–06; as religious symbol, 78–79; Sabbath guests in, 110–11; traditionalistic vs. modernistic view of, 147–49, 157–63, 187; visits to, by New York returnees, 345
Israel Ba'al Shem Tov, 16
Israel Torah Research Institutes (ITRI), 68, 70

James Striar School (JSS), 1, 65, 116, 259n

Jerusalem, recruitment sites in, 198–205

Jewish-Gentile relations, 293–97

Jewish Catalog, 52–53

Jewish Center of Riverdale, 323

Jewish education: in America, 45–50; chavruta and, 279; community schools and, 44–45; newly Orthodox and, 194, 195, 344; parents of ba'al t'shuva and, 304–05. *See also* Secular education; Women, schools for; *Yeshivot*

Jewish Education Program, 218

Jewish identity. *See* Ethnic identity; Religious identity

Jewish Learning Exchange, 281, 291–92

Jewish Theological Seminary, 24, 34

Joseph Shapiro Institute, 38

Joshua ben Hanania, 181–82

JSS. *See* James Striar School

Kabbalah, 82, 85, 229; in men's curriculum, 119–23, 124, 126–27

Kaddish, 31, 32–33. *See also* Prayer

Kanter, Rosabeth Moss, 302

Kashering, 38, 39, 254

Kashrut: adjustment to, 251–55; ba'al t'shuva yeshivot and, 107–08; countercultural values and, 82; family relationships and, 299; social impact of, 27–28, 39, 251–52; women and, 29–30

Katz, Jacob, 44, 53

Kehillah, 53–54

Kelman, Herbert, 223n, 239, 242

Kinot, 174

Kippah seruga, 143

Kolel, 68, 139, 151

Kosher. See *Kashrut*

Kosher restaurants, 253–54

Kotel, 199–205, 266–67

Kotler, Aaron, 150–51

Kulturekampf, 340

Laster, Paul, 159

Laws. *See* Family purity; Jewish-Gentile relations; *Kashrut; Negiyah; Shabbat; Yihud*

Lelyveld, Arthur J., 300–03

Levine, Baruch, 110, 124, 206–10

Levy, Sydelle, 307–08

Life convoy, 298n, 304–05

Life course, 196–97, 298n

Likutei Maharan, 181

Lincoln Square Synagogue, 36–42, 64, 276; beliefs and, 281–82; clusters of ba'alei t'shuva in, 323; kashrut and, 107–08; place of women as issue at, 291; recruitment and, 218; Sabbath guests and, 109–10; Shapiro Institute at, 38, 112

Liturgical poetry, 173–75

Lubavitch: countercultural values and, 86; as cult, 300–03; and courtship, 307–08; in Israel vs. U.S., 217n; men's curriculum of, 121, 126–27; recruitment by, 58–62, 125–26, 217; respect for parents and, 303; state of Israel and, 162–63; yeshivot for ba'alei t'shuva and, 66, 115–16. See also *Chasidim*

Machon Meir, 112, 113–15

Magen Avraham, B'nei Brak, Israel, 66–67

Maimonides, 182

Marriage: between ba'alei t'shuva, 307–08, 312; to ba'al t'shuva, 306–13; family honor and, 310–13; halakhic eligibility and, 308–10; integration into Orthodox community and, 40–42; laws of family purity and, 263–64; motivation for return and, 236–41; period of adjustment in, 316–18; as portal to Orthodoxy, 29–30; strains from religiosity in, 234–35; waiting period and, 310–12; women's curriculum and, 137. *See also* Courtship; Family purity; Matchmaking

Matchmaking, 314–16

Meah Shearim, 206–11

Mechitzah, 34, 103–04, 152, 154n

Melavveh malkah, 89

Messiah and messianism, 147–48

Military service, in Israel, 148–49, 158–63

Minyan: beginners', 36–38, 40, 276; for children, 34–35; of women (prayer group), 136

Miracles, 228–30, 282–87

Mishnah Torah, 169–70, 182

Mitnagdut, 173, 176

Mizrachi. See Zionism

Modernistic Orthodox: in Israel, 90–92; Jewish-Gentile relations and, 295; vs. other Orthodox, 53; outreach and, 85, 90, 336. *See also* Traditionalistic vs. modernistic Orthodox

Moral dilemmas, 295–96. *See also* Values

Motivation, 330; complex accounts of, 244–47; social psychological view of, 222*n*–24*n*; social ties as, 236–44; typical accounts of, 230–50; unacceptable accounts of, 224–30

Musar, 16

Nachman of Bratzlav, Rav, 124*n*, 181

Naftalis, Shimon, 317–18

National Council of Synagogue Youth, 8, 216–17, 261

Negiyah, laws of, 313

Neve Yerushalayim, 112, 115, 136–37, 139, 267

Newly Orthodox. See *Ba'alei t'shuva*; Returnees

Nodes, 322

Normative commitment, 242

Observance, and parents' observance, 343

Occupation, and Orthodoxy, 318–20

Ohr Hachayim, 114

Ohr Someyach, 9, 68; beliefs and, 281; emotional attachments at, 173–74; halakhic decisions and, 176; occupational training at, 319; role of yeshivot in Israeli society and, 160–61, 163; study of Talmud at, 170; views of miracles at, 283–85; women's institute at, 112, 113

On the Origin of Species (Darwin), 20

Oral tradition, 168–69, 177–81, 292–93. *See also* Religious authority; *Torah sheh ba'al peh*

Orthodox community: anchoring of returnees and, 330–31; ba'al t'shuva in synagogue and, 277; definition of, 28*n*; enjoyment of Shabbat and, 255, 256; impact of outreach on, 339–41; integration into, 40–42, 337; Jewish hippies and, 83–92; marriage and acceptance into, 306–12; in 1950s U.S., 24–25; openness to ba'alei t'shuva in, 322–23; proportion of returnees in, 328; singles in, 320–23

Orthodox National Council of Synagogue Youth, 261

Outreach programs: ba'al t'shuva in Israel and, 160–61, 162–63; charismatic, 85–89; on college campuses, 58–61; grandparent surrogates and, 321; impact of, on Orthodox Judaism, 339–41; for Israelis, 113–15, 219; label of ba'al t'shuva and, 81; Orthodox circles and, 188–89; outcomes of, 92–95; science and, 285; in synagogues, 335, 336, 337–38; in synagogue vs. yeshiva, 116; in U.S., 38–39. *See also* Recruitment

Pardess Institute, 103

Parents: of ba'al t'shuva, 162, 241–42, 298–305, 323; Jewish vs. Christian doctrine regarding, 334–35; kashrut and, 254–55; marriage of ba'al t'shuva and, 315; motivation for return and, 241–42; obligation to, 301–03; rejection of, in cults, 334–35; with religious commitments, 259–60. *See also* Children of *ba'alei t'shuva*; Family; Relatives

Particularism, 296

Passover. *See* Holy days

Pelkowitz, Ralph, 271*n*, 323

Philanthropy, 321*n*

Pittsburgh Platform of 1885, 24

Plausibility structure, 45, 286, 330–31

Political rights, 13, 14–15, 17

Poll, Solomon, 318

Prayer: at ba'al t'shuva yeshivot, 275–76; entry into Orthodoxy and, 31–33; Kaddish, 31, 32–33; at Kotel

Prayer (*continued*)
    plaza, 200–02; Lincoln Square Syn-
    agogue and, 36–38; Orthodox view
    of, 273–76; synagogue and, 276–
    77; women's curriculum and, 135–
    36
Promiscuity, 236

Rabbinical Council of America (RCA),
    146
Rabin, Yitzhak, 78, 162
Racism, 71–74
RCA. *See* Rabbinical Council of
    America
Rebbi, 57
Recruitment: approaches to, 219–21,
    331; belief in miracles and, 283–86;
    centers of, 322–23; devices of, 198–
    99, 204–06; Holocaust as hurdle to,
    288–90; in Israel, 219–21; in Israel
    vs. U.S., 219–21, 334; Jewish per-
    secution and, 334; Meah Shearim
    and, 206–11; opportunities for, in
    Israel, 198–215; in U.S., 215–21,
    and women, 207–11; *See also*
    Outreach programs
Reform Judaism: antinomianism and,
    182–83; authority in, 101, 166;
    chavurah in, 99–100; counter-
    cultural values and, 86; in early
    American, 19–21; Eastern Europe
    and, 18, 23; prayer at the Kotel and,
    202, 204; rejection of, 327; study of
    Talmud in, 102; view of women in,
    290
Rehabilitation, Israeli t'shuva move-
    ment and, 114, 269–70, 338
Reincarnation, 287–88, 295
Relatives: deceased, 242–44; moti-
    vation for return and, 241–42; in
    Orthodox community, 320–21. *See
    also* Family; Parents
Religious authority: in branches of Ju-
    daism, 100–01, 103, 166–67; cha-
    risma vs. knowledge and, 227; da'at
    Torah and, 167, 187; in Europe, 54;
    historical positions on, 181–83;
    Jewish-Gentile relations and, 294; of

oral tradition, 101, 168–69, 177–
    81, 292–93; potential returnees and,
    168–69; in sociology, 165–66;
    study and, 53–54, 132. *See also*
    Charismatic authority
Religious identity, 17–18, 23, 327–28,
    333, 334
Religious practice, in branches of Juda-
    ism, 100–03
Religious revival: in Christianity vs.
    Judaism, 4–6, 197, 227–30, 331–
    35; countercultural tradition in,
    334; within Orthodoxy, 15–16; in
    secular society, 3–4; sociological
    problem of, 3–8
Research methodology, 8–10
Resurrection, 287
Returnees: as challenge to tradi-
    tionalists, 340; characteristics of,
    194–96, 328–30, 344, 345; factors
    in paths of return of, 330; Israeli vs.
    American, 7; newly Orthodox vs.
    ba'alei t'shuva, 328–31; in New
    York City, 342–45; organizational
    perceptions of, 7–8; those "lacking
    background" among, 328–29. See
    also *Ba'alei t'shuva*; Women
Returnees, rhetoric of: acceptable ac-
    counts and, 230–36; inauthentic vs.
    authentic, 224–27; miraculous
    events and, 227–30
Revson, David, 69–70, 139
Riskin, Steven, 36, 41
Ritterband, Paul, 328, 342
Ritual: commitment without, 247–50;
    in curriculum, 130; difficulty of
    learning, 310; exaggeration of, 270–
    72; home-based, 29–30; in Judaism
    vs. Christianity, 4; meaning and,
    130–32; of prayer, 273–75; of Sab-
    bath meal, 211–15; in synagogue
    service, 31–32
Rosenzweig, Franz, 15
Rosh Ha-Shana. *See* Holy days
Rosh yeshiva, 9, 177–81

Sacrifice, and commitment, 257
Schachter, Zalman, 58–59, 60–61, 94

Schechter, Solomon, 24
School dormitories, 56, 57, 106–08
Schools. See *Ba'al t'shuva yeshivot*;
  Religious education; Secular education; *Yeshivot*
Science, and beliefs, 282–87
Sects, 5, 114*n*, 116, 333–34
Secular education, 149–51, 157, 158,
  344. *See also* Jewish education;
  Women, schools for; *Yeshivot*
Secularization, 16–18
Seekers, 235–36
Sefer Hakhinukh (Halevi), 128
Seidel, Jeff, 206–07
Sephardic Jews in America, 18–19
Sex differences: in data sources, 196;
  in motives for return, 233–34
Sex segregation: adjustment to, 260–
  62; in ba'al t'shuva yeshivot, 103–
  05; countercultural values and, 188;
  social impact of, 261. *See also*
  Women
Sexual mores, 260–61. *See also* Family
  purity
Shabbat (Sabbath): adjustment to restrictions of, 255–58; as drama,
  206–11; family relationships and,
  299–300; hosts, 108–09; meal,
  109–11, 204–15, 332; saving a life
  and, 293, 294–95; social impact of,
  27–28; symbolic meaning and, 211–
  15
Shabbetai Tzevi, 15, 16, 120*n*, 147, 182
Shabbeteanism, 184
Shadkhanim, 314–16
Shapiro Institute, 38, 112
Shappel College: outreach at, 90–92;
  for women, 69, 70, 136, 154–57.
  See also Brovender's; Darchei
  Noam-Shappel College; Hamivtar
Sh'or Yoshuv, 1, 65–66
Shupe, Anson D., 311
Shuster, Meir, 124, 199, 205
Sibling relationships, 305–06
"Singing chasid." *See* Carlebach,
  Shlomo
Singles, in Orthodox community, 38*n*,
  320–23

Six Day War, 77–79, 86–87
Social anchors, 239, 242
Social Darwinism, 22, 23
Social networks, 322
Social relationships, motivation for return and, 236–44
Soul, 287, 295
Star of Redemption, The (Rosenzweig),
  15
Steinzaltz, Adin, 114
Striar School (JSS), 1, 65, 116, 259*n*
Study, 277–81; as action, 130–32;
  amount of, 279–81; role of yeshivot
  for returnees and, 332–33; teaching
  and, 280–81. See also *Ba'al t'shuva
  yeshivot*; *Talmud*; *Torah*; *Yeshivot*
Success, emptiness of, and return,
  230–32, 233–34
Sukkot. See Holy days
Summer camps, 50–51, 216, 217
Symbols, 211–15. *See also* Ritual
Synagogue: decorum in, 276; outreach
  programs and, 33–42, 335, 336,
  337–38; as portal to Orthodoxy,
  30–42; prayer and, 276–77; recruitment and, 28–29

Talmud: informal study groups and,
  131–32; levels of students of, 54–
  55; religious authority and, 168–72;
  study of, 101–03, 130–32, 169–72;
  in women's curriculum, 135
Talmud torah: Orthodox education
  and, 46–48; Young Israel and, 35–
  36
Tanya, 119–20, 127
Tefillin, 60, 126
Tisha B'av, 174*n*
Torah, study of, 279–81
Torah Institutes, 51
Torah Leadership Seminars, 51, 64–65
Torah sheh ba'al peh, 101, 168, 292–
  93
Torah Vodaath, 9, 56–59
Traditionalistic vs. modernistic
  Orthodox: approaches to Talmud
  study and, 170, 171–72; convergences among yeshivot and, 157–

Traditionalistic vs. modernistic
  Orthodox (*continued*)
  63; differences between, 9*n*, 143–
  54; emotional attachments and,
  173–75; halakhic decisions and,
  175–77; matchmaking and, 314–
  16; outreach and, 339–41; religious
  authority and, 164–89; study of
  Talmud and, 170–72
Transmigration of souls. *See*
  Reincarnation
Troeltsch, Ernst, 53
T'shuva movement, 1–2, 10; beginnings of, 18, 338; future of, in
  America, 335–38; future of, in Israel, 338–41

Universalism, 72, 295, 296

Values: Jewish vs. American, 142; recruitment strategy and, 220–21; traditionalistic vs. modernistic yeshivot
  and, 146–54
Vichnin, Dovid, 266
Virginia Act of Toleration of *1786*, 15*n*

War of Redemption, 77–79
Weber, Max, 165, 223*n*, 299
Weinbach, Mendel, 9, 160–61, 170,
  280, 307, 311; Jewish-Gentile relations and, 293, 294–95
Weinberg, Noach, 66–67, 68, 124–25
Weinberger, Dovid, 262–63
Western Wall, in Jerusalem, 198, 199–
  205
Wigs, 267–68
Women: accounts of return by, 232–
  35; countercultural values and, 187–
  88; curriculum for, 133–41; fiancé
  factor for, 236–41; laws of family
  purity and, 263; marital eligibility
  and, 309–10, 312; marriage as portal to return and, 29–30; proportion
  of, among returnees, 194–95; recruitment in Meah Shearim and,
  207–09, 210–11; religious law and,

104*n*; as religious seekers, 235–36;
  role of, 137–40, 140–41, 151–54,
  290–92; schools for, 69, 70, 111–
  13, 291–92; standards of dress for,
  266–68; waiting period for, 310–
  11, 312. See also *Ba'alei t'shuva*;
  Sex segregation

Yeshiva University: beginnings of
  t'shuva movement and, 1, 63–66;
  dormitory facilities and, 56; hippie
  religious movement and, 84–85;
  James Striar School at, 65, 116,
  259*n*; kashrut and, 108, 109; men's
  curriculum at, 127; occupational
  training at, 319–20; recruitment
  and, 216–17; scientific study at,
  285; Torah Leadership Seminars
  and, 51, 64–65
Yeshivishe velt, 53–55. See also *Ba'al
  t'shuva yeshivot; Yeshivot*
Yeshivot: in America, 1, 48–50;
  chavruta and, 278–79; distinctions
  in dress in, 264–65; elementary
  school and, 48–50; entry into
  Orthodoxy and, 94–95; in Europe,
  44, 45; hesder, 148–49; Israeli
  t'shuva movement and, 339; Kabbalah and, 119–22; process of return and, 332–33; ratio of men to
  women at, 111; recruitment at Kotel
  and, 204–05; sex segregation and,
  261–62; study and, 277–78; for
  those "lacking background," 56–57,
  61–62, 65; traditionalist vs. modernist, 143–54. See also *Ba'al
  t'shuva yeshivot*
Yichus: family honor and, 310–12;
  halakhic eligibility and, 308–10, 312
Yihud, laws of, 313
Yom Kippur. *See* Holy days
Young Israel movement, 33–36, 216

Zionism, 122*n*, 147–49, 157–58
Zohar, 119–20, 123
Zohar, Uri, 129, 130